# Always-On Enterprise Information Systems for Business Continuance:
## Technologies for Reliable and Scalable Operations

Nijaz Bajgoric
*University of Sarajevo, Bosnia and Herzegovina*

**BUSINESS SCIENCE REFERENCE**
Hershey · New York

Director of Editorial Content:     Kristin Klinger
Senior Managing Editor:            Jamie Snavely
Assistant Managing Editor:         Michael Brehm
Publishing Assistant:              Sean Woznicki
Typesetter:                        Michael Brehm
Cover Design:                      Lisa Tosheff
Printed at:                        Yurchak Printing Inc.

Published in the United States of America by
     Business Science Reference (an imprint of IGI Global)
     701 E. Chocolate Avenue
     Hershey PA 17033
     Tel: 717-533-8845
     Fax:  717-533-8661
     E-mail: cust@igi-global.com
     Web site: http://www.igi-global.com/reference

Library of Congress Cataloging-in-Publication Data

Always-on enterprise information systems for business continuance :
technologies for reliable and scalable operations / Nijaz Bajgoric, editor.
     p. cm.
  Includes bibliographical references and index.
  Summary: "This book provides chapters describing in more detail the
structure of information systems pertaining to enabling technologies, aspects
of their implementations, IT/IS governing, risk management, disaster
management, interrelated manufacturing and supply chain strategies, and new IT
paradigms"--Provided by publisher.
  ISBN 978-1-60566-723-2 (hbk.) -- ISBN 978-1-60566-724-9 (ebook)  1.
Information technology--Management. 2. Management information systems. 3.
Electronic commerce. 4.  Client/server computing. 5.  Business enterprises--
Computer networks. I. Bajgoric, Nijaz. II. Title.

  HD30.2.A398 2010
  658.4'038011--dc22

                                                      2009006923

British Cataloguing in Publication Data
A Cataloguing in Publication record for this book is available from the British Library.

All work contributed to this book is new, previously-unpublished material. The views expressed in this book are those of the authors, but not necessarily of the publisher.

# Editorial Advisory Board

# Table of Contents

# Detailed Table of Contents

**Chapter 1**

*Mario Spremic, University of Zagreb, Croatia*

Most organizations in all sectors of industry, commerce, and government are fundamentally dependent on their information systems (IS) and would quickly cease to function should the technology (preferably information technology–IT) that underpins their activities ever come to halt. The development and governance of proper IT infrastructure may have enormous implications for the operation, structure, and strategy of organizations. IT and IS may contribute towards efficiency, productivity, and competitiveness improvements of both interorganizational and intraorganizational systems. On the other hand, successful organizations manage IT function in much the same way that they manage their other strategic functions and processes. This, in particular, means that they understand and manage risks associated with growing IT opportunities, as well as critical dependence of many business processes on IT and vice-versa. IT risk management issues are not only marginal or 'technical' problems but become more and more a 'business problem.' Therefore, in this chapter, a corporate IT risk management model is proposed and contemporary frameworks of IT governance and IT audit explained. Also, it is depicted how to model information systems and supporting IT procedures to meet 'always-on' requirements that comes from the business. In fact, a number of IT metrics proposed in the chapter support the alignment of IT Governance activities with business requirements towards IT.

**Chapter 2**

*Andrea Kő, Corvinus University of Budapest, Hungary*

Many organizations are struggling with a vast amount of data in order to gain valuable insights and get support in their decision-making process. Decision-making quality depends increasingly on information and the systems that deliver this information. These services are vulnerable and risky from security aspects, and they have to satisfy several requirements, like transparency, availability, accessibility, convenience, and compliance. IT environments are more and more complex and fragmented, which means additional security risks. Business intelligence solutions provide assistance in these complex business situations. Their main goal is to assist organizations to make better decisions. Better decisions means that these solutions support the management of risks, and they have a key role in raising revenue and in reducing cost. The objectives of this chapter are to give an overview of the business intelligence field and its future trends, to demonstrate the most important business intelligence solutions, meanwhile highlighting their risks, business continuity challenges, and IT audit issues. In spite of the fact that this chapter focuses on the business intelligence solutions and their specialities, risk management and the related IT audit approach can be applied for other categories of information systems. IT audit guidelines, best practices, and standards are presented as well, because they give effective tools in controlling process of business intelligence systems.

# Chapter 3

Real time collaboration solutions are critical during a large scale emergency situation and necessitate the coordination of multiple disparate groups. Collaborative technologies may be valuable in the planning and execution of disaster preparedness and response. Yet, research suggests that specific collaborative technologies, such as group decision support systems, are not often leveraged for decision-making during real time emergency situations in the United States. In this chapter, we propose a theoretical model of the impact of disaster immediacy and collaboration systems on group processes and outcomes. Using a 3D model of the dimensions of space, time, and situation, we explore media richness and group polarization within the context of collaboration technologies and disaster situations. We also present the next generation of collaboration technology extensions in order to address the need for more contemporary decisional settings. This set of principles and theories suggest how collaborative technologies may be positioned to better manage future disasters.

# Chapter 4

The data requirements of e-business applications have been increased over the years. These applications present an environment for acquiring, processing, and sharing data among interested parties. To manage information in such data-intensive application domain, independent enterprise e-business applications have developed their own solutions to information services. However, these solutions are not interoperable with each other, target vastly different systems, and address diverse sets of requirements. They require greater interoperability to enable communication between different systems, so that they can share and utilize each other's resources. To address these challenges, we discuss principles and experiences for designing and building of a novel enterprise information system. We introduce a novel architecture for a hybrid information service, which provides unification, federation, and interoperability of major Web-based information services. The hybrid information service is designed as an add-on information system, which interacts with the local information services and assembles their metadata instances under one hybrid architecture. It integrates different information services using unification and federation concepts. In this chapter, we summarize the principles and experiences gained in designing and building the semantics, architecture, and implementation for the hybrid information service.

**Chapter 5**

*Sumita Dave, Shri Shankaracharya Institute of Management & Technology, India*
*Monica Shrivastava, Shri Shankaracharya Institute of Management & Technology, India*

Enterprise resource planning (ERP) today is being adopted by business organizations worldwide with a view to maximize their capabilities. But more often than not the expected outcomes are not delivered due to inaccurate calculations with respect to the organization's ability to adapt to the change. Although the benefits of enterprise information systems in streamlining the functions of the organization cannot be questioned, preparing the organization to adopt the new system needs more focused efforts. In order to ensure that the existing capabilities of the organizations are an enabler and not an inhibitor in the adoption process, they need to be learning organizations. A study was conducted in Bhilai Steel Plant (BSP), one of the leading steel manufacturing public companies in India, where ERP is to be adopted. In spite of the fact that it has a strong backbone of resources in terms of information technology (IT) infrastructure, the implementation process is virtually on a standstill. In this chapter, an evaluation of the psychological capabilities of the organization is done. This can be evaluated through the mindset of the workforce and the willingness with which they are ready to adopt change.

**Chapter 6**

*Serdal Bayram, Siemens, Turkey*
*Melih Kırlıdoğ, Marmara University, Turkey*
*Özalp Vayvay, Marmara University, Turkey*

In today's world, it is essential for a business to provide a seamless and continuous service to its customers. Such an always-on service is required, not only for the strong competitive environment but also because of the fact that most the customers also have to offer seamless and continuous service to their own customers. In this chain, failure of one of the systems even for a short time can result in a disaster in the entire service chain. A wise approach to provide a continuous service should consider all possible failure areas in a computer-based information system. Since hardware and software are vulnerable to a myriad of problems that can halt the normal operation of a system, an ideal solution should not only consider both of these two components, but also should seek to find ways for them to work in support of each other against a malfunction. This chapter is an attempt to develop a model that provides this functionality. Service oriented architecture (SOA) is implemented in the model due to its tenets that are suitable for such functionality.

# Chapter 7

Data management in always-on enterprise information systems is an important function that must be governed, that is, planned, supervised, and controlled. According to Data Management Association, data management is the development, execution, and supervision of plans, policies, programs, and practices that control, protect, deliver, and enhance the value of data and information assets. The challenges of successful data management are numerous and vary from technological to conceptual and managerial. The purpose of this chapter is to consider some of the most challenging aspects of data management, whether they are classified as data continuity aspects (e.g., data availability, data protection, data integrity, data security), data improvement aspects (e.g., coping with data overload and data degradation, data integration, data quality, data ownership/stewardship, data privacy, data visualization) or data management aspect (e.g., data governance), and to consider the means of taking care of them.

# Chapter 8

In today's business environment, it is usual that data relevant to business is stored on different hardware, inside different databases, different data warehouses, inside as well as outside of the organization. Accuracy, quality, timeliness, and especially availability of such distributed data make crucial role in the process of business managing. Now, one of the biggest challenges is to ensure continuous availability of that data, even in critical and disaster situations. This chapter gives a short overview of the most used solutions for database availability that have become industry standards and gives examples of implementation of these standards by, in this moment, three main database vendors: Oracle (Oracle 11g), IBM (DB2 Version 9.5) and Microsoft (SQL Server 2008).

The growing competition in the banking sector, resulting in growing demands of the customers, requires from the banks a 24 hour availability of services. The technological development is accompanied by the increase in technologically sophisticated forms of fraud. The answer to these challenges is a more efficient use of information technology. The use of new technologies, besides the defense from unauthorized access into the bank's information system, abuse of information technology, and damage that can be caused, represents the basis for the new service offer which has an important role in market positioning of the banks. An empirical research was conducted in order to determine the level of influence of the information technology to the payment transactions. The results suggest that the level of influence is important due to the enlargement of product range and communication channels with clients, expense reduction for the costumers and the bank, as well as the increase of the business security.

Sumeet Gupta, Shri Shankaracharya College of Engineering and Technology, India
Miti Garg, The Logistics Institute – Asia Pacific, Singapore
Mark Goh, The Logistics Institute – Asia Pacific, Singapore
Maya Kumar, The Logistics Institute – Asia Pacific, Singapore

A combination of lean and agile concepts, leagility has gained ground in recent years. While it has found widespread applications in the domain of manufacturing, other domains such as procurement can also benefit from the principles of leagility. We study the application of concepts of leagility in PC manufacturing through the case of Dell and based on our experience with a worldwide retailer, we develop a conceptual framework in this paper which can be used as the basis for applying the principles of leagility in the domain of procurement. The framework would be of particular significance to academics as it extends the field of leagility to procurement. At the same time, manufacturing and retail firms can derive benefits by downsizing their inventory using the principles and conceptual framework discussed in this chapter.

Müjgan Şan, The State Planning Organization, Turkey

As every technological development, information and communication technology also offers new life patterns to human beings. One of them is related to business and its environment. In this context, the main problem is how to manage knowledge and information and assets related to knowledge and information in business. Therefore, we have constructed the business knowledge and information policy model by using triangulation methodology. The business knowledge and information policy model includes the informative business theory, knowledge and information management (KIM) tools and projects. The first one has six characteristics. KIM tools include nine profiles which are common language, strategy, data-information-concepts, personal and social informatics, ICT infrastructure, measurement, cultural informatics and governance. KIM projects could be designed depending on business conditions and goals.

Hina Arora, Arizona State University, USA
T. S. Raghu, Arizona State University, USA
Ajay Vinze, Arizona State University, USA

Information supply chains (ISCs) take an information-centric view of supply chains, where information is not only used to support supply chain operations, but also to create value for customers and enable business partners to collectively sense and respond to opportunities in a networked ecosystem. Creating value in the ISC involves gathering, organizing, selecting, synthesizing, and distributing information. In so doing, ISCs should provide secure, confidential, reliable, and real time access to heterogeneous information, while ensuring that the right information is delivered to the intended recipients at the right time. In other words, security, information quality, and information lead-time delays are critical performance determinants in ISCs. Recent disaster events such as Hurricane Katrina have highlighted the need for and value of ISCs by exposing the vulnerability of supply chains to demand surges and supply disruptions. Mitigating supply chain vulnerabilities requires a mechanism that allows for continuously sensing the environment, detecting existing or anticipated vulnerabilities, and responding to these vulnerabilities in real time through information sharing and collaboration. This chapter describes how the autonomic computing paradigm can be used to build resilient information supply chains by restructuring the associated relationships, chains, and networks.

## Chapter 13

*Miti Garg, The Logistics Institute – Asia Pacific, Singapore*
*Sumeet Gupta, Shri Shankaracharya College of Engineering and Technology, India*
*Mark Goh, The Logistics Institute – Asia Pacific, Singapore*
*Robert Desouza, The Logistics Institute – Asia Pacific, Singapore*
*Balan Sundarkarni, The Logistics Institute – Asia Pacific, Singapore*
*Ridwan Kuswoyo Bong, The Logistics Institute – Asia Pacific, Singapore*

Green computing paradigm is a term used to describe a movement in the field of information technology whereby users and information technology professionals are adopting 'less environmentally destructive' practices to mitigate the detrimental effects of excessive computing to the environment. Environment friendly practices such as virtualization, cloud computing, greening of data centres, recycling, telecommuting, and teleworking are discussed in this chapter. A summary of the initiatives undertaken by government agencies in various countries is also provided.

## Chapter 14

*Stephane Ngo Mai, University of Nice Sophia Antipolis, France*
*Alain Raybaut, University of Nice Sophia Antipolis, France*

Numerous communities of experts supported by firms tend nowadays to form an important part of corporate social capital. Composed of free will agents, those communities aim at creating knowledge through cognitive interactions and heavily rely on ICTs to free themselves from many constraints. Previous studies of such virtual groupings pointed out that their organization features were not similar to market nor hierarchy. Consequently, neither price nor contract or authority are used in such communities which rather seem to self-organize. Instead of traditional economic concepts, notions such as trust and leadership are advanced to explain the functioning of these virtual assemblies. This contribution proposed a tentative model which attempts to grasp some of the empirical aspects of these communities. More precisely, we were interested in the relation between trust, performance, and organizational feature within a given virtual group. Simulations of the model with different functions of swift trust display various organizational structures similar to those described by stylized facts. The organizational attributes range from pure collaborative communities to pure competitive ones. Intermediate cases also emerge with the appearance of leader(s).

# Chapter 15

The concept of power is inherent in human organizations of any type. As power relations have important consequences for organizational viability and productivity, they should be explicitly represented in enterprise information systems (EISs). Although organization theory provides a rich and very diverse theoretical basis on organizational power, still most of the definitions for power-related concepts are too abstract, often vague and ambiguous to be directly implemented in EISs. To create a bridge between informal organization theories and automated EISs, this article proposes a formal logic-based specification language for representing power (in particular authority) relations. The use of the language is illustrated by considering authority structures of organizations of different types. Moreover, the article demonstrates how the formalized authority relations can be integrated into an EIS.

# Chapter 16

Enterprise systems are being transferred into a service-oriented architecture. In this article we present a procedure for the integration of enterprise systems. The procedure model starts with decomposition into Web services. This is followed by mapping redundant functions and assigning of the original source code to the Web services, which are orchestrated in the final step. Finally an example is given how to integrate an Enterprise Resource Planning System and an Enterprise Content Management System using the proposed procedure model.

# Chapter 17

This article contributes to the design of a generic framework for providing a new way to exchange information between enterprises. This concept is a well addressed in the context of B2B standards. Many organizations are increasingly searching for adopting these standards to automate data exchange. But the limit of such models resides in the fact that the content of exchange is defined in several formats which make their use difficult. To overcome this difficulty, we have explored the possibility to integrate new models for describing content involved in B2B transaction which represent a key issue. Our finding establishes the feasibility of integrating product models described by ontology with e-commerce standards especially at the business process level. This article presents a descriptive model allowing partners to exchange information with other organisations without modifying their Information System. The case study also indicates that our system is developed as a Service Oriented Architecture.

# Foreword

It took more than 60 years until 75 percent of households in the USA adopted a new communication technology called the "telephone." The adoption rates have been accelerated for later technologies. For example, it took only about 25 years for "personal computers" to reach three quarters of U.S. households and about 20 years for "cell phones." The "Internet" did not need even 15 years to achieve the landmark. While these statistics were based on a limited population, that is, the consumer market in the U.S., such trends are universal throughout the world, as well as in corporations.

Modern society cannot function any longer without the infrastructure initiated and maintained by the computing and the Internet technologies. As people use more and depend more on these technologies than ever, they start operating with the assumption (at least not conscientiously) that these infrastructures are available all the time like air or water. While everyone may acknowledge that this assumption is not true, in practice, it is not easy to make users constantly guard against any disastrous disruptions. Ironically, this difficulty is worsening as the computing and the Internet technologies are advancing, and more people are embracing these technologies.

Thus, the notion of "always-on" information systems became so critical for today's corporations, as well as the society in general. Despite its importance, the research efforts have been scattered and carried out by a limited number of forward-looking researchers. I am very excited that this new book is finally coming out by collecting many important research findings on "always-on" enterprise information systems for business continuance. I have no doubt that the book will be not only an invaluable contribution to the field, but also an important source of information to educate others on this important subject.

I would like to thank all of the authors of the chapters in the book for their pioneering research works and willingness to share with others. Particularly, I applaud Professor Bajgoric's vision on this topic, insight to select appropriate topics, and efforts to bring together the leading researchers.

*Young B. Moon*
*Syracuse University, USA*
*February 2009*

*Young B. Moon has been on the faculty of the Department of Mechanical and Aerospace Engineering at Syracuse University since 1988. Moon serves as the Director of the Institute for Manufacturing Enterprises and the faculty coordinator for the SAP University Alliance program. Moon holds a Bachelor of Science degree in Industrial Engineering from Seoul National University, Seoul Korea, a Master of Science degree in Industrial Engineering and Engineering Management from Stanford University, and a Ph.D. degree in Industrial Engineering from Purdue University. His doctoral research was carried out in the Engineering Research Center (ERC) for Intelligent Manufacturing Systems.*

# Preface

In modern business, information technologies are implemented in several forms of enterprise information systems (EIS) such as enterprise resource planning (ERP), customer relationships management (CRM), supply chain management (SCM), business intelligence (BI), integrated messaging systems, and other forms of business computing. These systems are designed and implemented by using several approaches and methodologies. No matter which EIS design and implementation methodology is used, each enterprise information system is consisted of several information technologies, such as servers, desktop computers, portable/mobile computing devices, systems software, application software, data communication technologies, and computer networks. In addition, enterprise information systems employ several profiles of IT specialists such as application developers, programmers, system and network administrators, and business analysts.

EIS platforms cover business processes and make them possible in today's e-economy; therefore, there is a high level of correlation between reliability, availability, and scalability of business processes/business operations and IT platforms that enable them. However, several types of IT-related problems such as hardware components' glitches and failures, operating system or application defects and crashes, disastrous events, IT-specialists' errors, such as accidental or intentional file deletion, unskilled operations, intentional hazardous activities including sabotage and strikes, can bring the system down for some time and consequently make data unavailable.

Modern enterprise information systems are expected to be **resilient (continuous)** and operational on an **always-on** basis, in other words, 24 hours a day, 7 days a week, 365 days a year. This is particularly important for multinational companies as their customers, suppliers, partners, and employees are located in many different time zones. Business critical applications, such as e-commerce applications, financial applications and services, call centers, Web servers, and e-mail servers, must be up at all times. The leading multinational companies and most e-business oriented organizations seek for highly available, reliable, and scalable operating environments in order to achieve always-on, reliable, and scalable operations.

In order to stay competitive, today's business has to be resilient or continuous with an emphasis on continuous, always-on, and uninterruptible computing support and data availability. The main prerequisite for such a kind of business is an information system or an integrated IT platform which operates on an always-on basis with a 100% system uptime and zero downtime, or which is characterized by a high availability ratio measured in number of nines, for example, four nines–99.99%, five nines–99.999%, and so forth. The term "business continuance" or "business continuity" (BC) emphasizes the ability of a business to continue with its operations even if some sort of failure or disaster on its computing platform occurs. In short, the concept of continuous computing is all about "having IT-systems up and running," being "always-on" and consequently keeping "business in business."

The book, *Always-On Enterprise Information Systems for Business Continuance: Technologies for Reliable and Scalable Operations,* aims at providing a number of high quality chapters describing in more detail the structure of such information systems, enabling technologies, aspects of their implementations, IT/IS governing, risk management, disaster management, interrelated manufacturing and supply chain strategies, and new IT paradigms.

Chapter 1, *IT Governance and IT Risk Management Principles and Methods for Supporting 'Always-On' Enterprise Information Systems*, by Spremic, argues that the development and governance of proper IT infrastructure may have enormous implications for the operation, structure, and strategy of organizations. IT and IS may contribute towards efficiency, productivity, and competitiveness improvements of both interorganizational and intraorganizational systems. Organizations manage risks associated with growing IT opportunities, as well as critical dependence of many business processes on IT and vice-versa. IT risk management issues are not marginal or 'technical' problems and become more and more a 'business problem'. This chapter proposes a corporate IT risk management model and a framework of IT governance and IT audit. In addition, the chapter explains how to model information systems and supporting IT procedures to meet 'always-on' requirements that comes from the business.

Chapter 2, *Risks Evaluation and IT Audit Aspects of Business Intelligence Solutions*, by Ko, emphasizes the tact that today's IT environments are more and more complex and fragmented, which brings additional security risks. The author focuses on business intelligence solutions that can provide assistance in these complex business situations. Their main goal is to assist organizations to make better decisions. Better decisions means that these solutions support the management of risks and that they have a key role in raising revenue and in reducing cost. This chapter provides an overview on business intelligence solutions and its future trends, and demonstrates the most important business intelligence solutions, by highlighting their risks, business continuity challenges, and IT audit issues.

Chapter 3, *Collaborative Systems for Decision Making for Disaster Preparedness and Response*, by Hahn, Block, Keith, and Vinze, points out that collaborative technologies (CT) have an excellent track record for supporting the important processes of preparing and planning before a disaster situation. These technologies can be the right choice for support of strategic approach and training groups before an emergency situation arises. Using CT before a disaster may allow groups to create emergency procedure manuals, which will be invaluable to first responders during a real-time disaster. Finally, collaborative technologies are equally as beneficial for use after an emergency situation. The next generation of collaborative technologies is media rich—expanding into database driven visualization, simulation, semantic analysis, and communication tools to create comprehensive interoperable collaboration systems. Authors present an example of this next generation of collaborative technologies called the "Decision Theater" at Arizona State University.

Chapter 4, *Principles and Experiences: Designing and Building Enterprise Information Systems*, by Aktas, *discusses principles and experiences for designing and building of a "novel enterprise information system." Author introduces a novel architecture for a hybrid information service, which provides unification, federation, and interoperability of major Web-based information services. The hybrid information service is designed as an add-on information system, which interacts with the local information services and assembles their metadata instances under one hybrid architecture.* The proposed system differs from "local-as-view" approaches, as its query transformation happens between a unified schema and local schemas. It utilizes and leverages previous work on "global-as-view" approach for integrating heterogeneous local data services. The proposed system addresses the limitations of previous work by introducing an "add-on architecture," which runs one layer above the implementations of UDDI and its extensions. It leverages previous work on UDDI and improves the quality of UDDI-based metadata-systems in terms of fault-tolerance and high-performance.

Chapter 5, *Optimization of Enterprise Information System through a 'User Involvement Framework in Learning Organizations'*, by Dave and Shrivastava, is an attempt to evaluate the psychological capabilities of the organization which can largely be evaluated through the mindset of the workforce and the willingness with which they are ready to adopt change. The authors argue that the implementation of any IT enabled operations systems requires a systematic approach which includes the evaluation of the organization's learning capabilities. They present the results of the study conducted in Bhilai Steel Plant, one of the leading steel manufacturing public companies in India, where ERP is to be adopted.

Chapter 6, *Always-On Enterprise Information Systems with Service Oriented Architecture and Load Balancing*, by Bayram, Kirlidog, and Vayvay, proposes a model that aims at achieving continuous EIS operations in terms of hardware and software components where these components work "in tandem." The proposed model is based on service oriented architecture (SOA). SOA, which is implemented as the main software component of the model is described, as well as the quality of service (QoS) and enterprise service bus (ESB) concepts of SOA. Hardware component of the model and the load balancer are described separately and within the tandem working system of SOA and load balancer. Unlike the traditional software where components are tightly coupled in a point-to-point architecture, SOA is based on distributed and heterogeneous architecture and offers loose coupling. A case study which employs Oracle SOA Suite has been developed and presented. Distributed computing allows services to be distributed to different resources, thereby enhancing the backup logic, and loose coupling minimizes the impact of modifications and failures on the whole system when there is a problem in one component.

Chapter 7, *Challenges of Data Management in Always-On Enterprise Information Systems*, by Varga, considers some of the most challenging aspects of data management, whether they are classified as data continuity, data improvement or data management. The chapter explores in more details the most challenging aspects of data management classified into three classes. The first combines data availability, data integrity, and data security, which serve as data continuity aspects that are important for the continuous provision of data in business processes and for decision-making purposes. The aspects in the second class enable innovative, more efficient, and more effective data usage. The problems of data overload, data integration, data quality, data degradation, data ownership or stewardship, data privacy, and data visualization are described. Data governance is also important dimension for planning, supervising, and controlling of all management activities exercised to improve organizational data and information. Consequently, data governance will constantly need to discover novel and innovative ways to deal with data management problems.

Chapter 8, *Continuous Database Availability*, by Tomic and Markic, gives an overview of the most widely used solutions for continuous database availability. It provides a set of examples of these standards and their implementations by three main database vendors: Oracle (Oracle 11g), IBM (DB2 Version 9.5), and Microsoft (SQL Server 2008). It identifies the main threats of continuous database availability grouped into four categories: network, hardware, software, and DBMS, having in mind the distinction between planned and unplanned threats (downtime). Solutions from major DBMS vendors such as backup and recovery, clustering, log shipping, stand-by, replication, mirroring, automated software applications, replication, and virtualization are briefly explained. This chapter focuses on the database aspect of continuous data availability. The presented overview of solutions shows that different approaches and techniques can be used for enabling database continuous availability. Main classification of these solutions is based on the differentiation between two approaches: narrow and broad approach. While narrow approach is focused on IT solutions (backup and recovery, clustering, replication, mirroring), a broad approach considers IT solution only as a part of broader context that includes business processes, management of data and information lifecycle, additional education and training of users and IT staff, disaster recovery strategies, and action plans.

Chapter 9, *Some Aspects of Implementing Always-On IT-solutions and Standards in Banking Sector: The Case of Croatia*, by Pejic-Bach, Draganic, and Jakovic, presents the results of an empirical research that was conducted in order to determine the level of influence of information technologies to the system of payment transactions in Croatia. The results suggest that the level of influence is important due to the enlargement of product range and communication channels with clients, expense reduction for the costumers and the bank, as well as the increase of the business security. The study showed that information technology can help in reducing risks through data access control and risk management (data collection and statistical analysis), but can also be a risk source: the risk of an unskilled use of information technology and the reputation risk (in case of technical failure or employees' abuse if the controls are not implemented). As the results of the study suggest, the level of acceptance of the new distribution channels by the clients depends on the simplicity of the created service and on the stimulation of the clients by lower transaction costs in these channels.

Chapter 10, *Leagility in Manufacturing and Procurement: A Conceptual Framework*, by Gupta, Garg, Goh, and Kumar, describes the concept of "leagility" as a combination of well known concepts in manufacturing: lean and agile manufacturing. The authors argue that the leagility concept can be used not only in manufacturing, but in procurement as well. Based on their experiences with a world-wide retailer, they propose a conceptual framework that can be used in applying the principles of leagility in procurement. In addition, a case study of Dell with regard to this concept is presented. Making the retail firm's procurement leagile can benefit the firm by maximizing gross margin return on investment (GMROI) and the supply chain more efficient and responsive. In identifying the strategies, a retailer must consider the product's GMROI as well as total volume traded, the seasonality of the product and the supply lead time to procure the products. This chapter discusses the framework for identifying the strategies a retail firm can employ to make its procurement leagile.

Chapter 11, *"The Business Knowledge and Information Policy Model*, by San, proposes the business knowledge and information policy model (BKIP). According to this author, the BKIP is a key for the resilient, continuous, flexible, and operational business and provides greater opportunity for businesses to create new design models in order to manage knowledge and information (KI) and assets related to KI (AKI). The BKIP is a kind of lens for business, which obtains the alternative ways for absorbing, processing, using, servicing, and diffusing KI in the frame of the IBT. It organizes to harmonizingly operate all of KIAKI in the frame of equality principles. The BKIP makes easier the process of preparing and integrating enterprise architectures or business models.

Chapter 12, *Information Supply Chains: Restructuring Relationships, Chains, and Networks*, by Arora, Raghu, and Vinze, discusses the importance of information supply chains (ISCs) that take an information-centric view of supply chains, where information is not only used to support supply chain operations, but also to create value for customers and enable business partners to collectively sense and respond to opportunities in a networked ecosystem. Creating value in the ISC involves gathering, organizing, selecting, synthesizing, and distributing information. Authors argue that mitigating supply chain vulnerabilities requires a mechanism that allows for continuously sensing the environment, detecting existing or anticipated vulnerabilities, and responding to these vulnerabilities in real time through information sharing and collaboration. This chapter describes how the autonomic computing paradigm can be used to build resilient information supply chains by restructuring the associated relationships, chains and networks.

Chapter 13, *Sustaining the Green Information Technology Movement*, by Miti, Gupta, Goh, and DeSouza, explores the green computing paradigm, the paradigm that is used to describe a movement in the field of information technology whereby users and information technology professionals are adopting 'less environmentally destructive' practices to mitigate the detrimental effects of excessive computing to the environment. Environment-friendly practices, such as virtualization, cloud computing, greening of data centres, recycling, telecommuting, and teleworking are discussed in this chapter. Several measures can be adopted to provide a sustainable and green computing environment by adopting and implementing old and new ideas. While virtualization and cloud computing are cutting edge technologies, telecommuting, teleworking, and recycling have been accepted by organizations all over the world. The authors argue that governments must work with organizations to chart the right course of action to decrease the carbon footprint. New ideas such as carbon credits traded by companies in international markets can be used to control and regulate the market. Through successful implementation of the green computing paradigm, firms can successfully decrease their carbon footprint and contribute to decreasing the harm wrought to the environment.

Chapter 14, *Swift Trust and Self-Organizing Virtual Communities*, by Ngo-Mai and Raybaut, define the term "swift trust" and propose a research model with different functions of swift trust, which tried to capture both the average preexistent stereotypes in a given opening community and the fragile and cyclical movement of influences depending on relative action during the group lifespan. Contrary to the traditional 'trust need touch' concepts based on small steps learning and long history, swift trust basically relies on preexistent stereotypes at the beginning of collaboration and afterward on current action of others agents. It is then well suited to virtual communities characterized by (i) no common history in bilateral relationships and scarce face to face, (ii) uncertainty about viability, and (iii) possible weak involvement. Swift trust demonstrates to be very fragile and on occasion cyclical. The performance or profit index both at individual and community level has been built in such a way as to encapsulate the idea of knowledge creation as a function of bilateral interaction within a network and of the cognitive distance between individuals. A cost function with a learning effect has also been introduced. Finally, the organizational feature of the community has been seized by two indexes which measure the relative number of positive reciprocal influences between individuals and the relative number of positive influence. Simulations of the model with our different swift trust functions using a replicator equation for the dynamics of the community display various organizational structures similar to those described by stylized facts.

I would like to thank to all the authors whose manuscripts made this book possible.

A further special note of thanks goes to Ms. Julia Mosemann, Development Editor, for her continuous help during the process of working on the book and to the managerial, acquisition, editorial, publishing, and marketing teams at IGI Global.

I am grateful to my wife, Ermina, and son, Adnan, for their understanding during this book project.

*Nijaz Bajgoric*
*Editor*

# Chapter 1

# IT Governance and IT Risk Management Principles and Methods for Supporting 'Always–On' Enterprise Information Systems

**Mario Spremic**
*University of Zagreb, Croatia*

## ABSTRACT

*Most organizations in all sectors of industry, commerce, and government are fundamentally dependent on their information systems (IS) and would quickly cease to function should the technology (preferably information technology–IT) that underpins their activities ever come to halt. The development and governance of proper IT infrastructure may have enormous implications for the operation, structure, and strategy of organizations. IT and IS may contribute towards efficiency, productivity, and competitiveness improvements of both interorganizational and intraorganizational systems. On the other hand, successful organizations manage IT function in much the same way that they manage their other strategic functions and processes. This, in particular, means that they understand and manage risks associated with growing IT opportunities, as well as critical dependence of many business processes on IT and vice-versa. IT risk management issues are not only marginal or 'technical' problems but become more and more a 'business problem.' Therefore, in this chapter, a corporate IT risk management model is proposed and contemporary frameworks of IT governance and IT audit explained. Also, it is depicted how to model information systems and supporting IT procedures to meet 'always-on' requirements that comes from the business. In fact, a number of IT metrics proposed in the chapter support the alignment of IT Governance activities with business requirements towards IT.*

DOI: 10.4018/978-1-60566-723-2.ch001

## INTRODUCTION: MANAGING IT RISKS IS A BUSINESS NOT A 'TECHNICAL' PROBLEM

In the early days of implementing IT in the business, it was often seen as a technical support function and was typically managed by finance departments. When evolving from technology providers into strategic partners, IT organizations typically follow a three-stage approach. Each evolutionary stage builds upon the others beginning with *IT infrastructure management* (ITIM). During this stage, the IT's role in the organizations focus on improving the management of the enterprise (technological) infrastructure. Effective infrastructure management mainly is associated with maximizing return on computing assets and taking control of the infrastructure, the devices it contains and the data it generates (ITGI, 2003). The next stage, *IT service management* (ITSM), sees the IT organizations actively identifying the services its customers need and focusing on planning and delivering those services to meet availability, performance, and security requirements. In addition, IT contributes to the businesses by managing service-level agreements, both internally and externally, as well as by meeting agreed-upon quality and cost targets. Ultimately, when IT organizations evolve to *IT business value management* (*IT Governance*), they are transformed into true business partners enabling new business opportunities (Hunton, Bryant, & Bagranoff, 2004). In that stage, IT processes are fully integrated with the complete lifecycle of business processes improving service quality and business agility. (see Figure 1)

While early IT implementations were clearly focused on automation of clerical and repetitive tasks, in today's highly competitive business environment, effective and innovative use of information technology (IT) has the potential to transform businesses and drive stakeholder value (Weill & Ross, 2004; Peppard & Ward, 2004). According to the recent ITGI-PricewaterhouseCoopers study

results, IT is quite to very important to delivery of the corporate strategy and vision (ITGI, 2007). On the other hand, poorly managed IT investment or badly implemented IT projects will lead to value erosion and competitive disadvantage (COSO, 2004; ITGI & PricewaterhouseCoopers, 2006; Weill & Ross, 2004). A number of or company-level studies and analyses show that IT contributes substantially to company's productivity growth. This contribution is by all means strong where IT strategy is linked with business strategy, thus IT can initiate major changes in organization structure, business processes and overall activities. In one study, Brynjolfsson and Hitt (1993) concluded 'that while computers make a positive contribution to productivity growth at the firm level, the greatest benefit of computers appears to be realized when computer investment is coupled with other complementary investments; new strategies, new business processes, and new organizations all appear to be important.' Central message from the research literature, and one that is universally accepted, is that technology itself has no inherent value and that IT is unlikely to be source of sustainable competitive advantage (Peppard & Ward, 2004). The business value derived from IT investments only emerges through business changes and innovations, whether they are product/service innovation, new business models, or process change.

Therefore, successful organizations that manage to derive business value out of IT investments also understand the importance of IT control environment and manage the associated risks, such as increasing regulatory compliance and critical dependence of many business processes on IT (Spremić, Žmirak, & Kraljević, 2008; Spremić & Strugar, 2002). This in particular means that they manage the risks associated with growing IT opportunities. The risks associated with business processes conducted through IT support are not only any more marginal or 'technical' problems and become more and more a key 'business problem'.

*Figure 1. Evolvement of IT as corporate function*

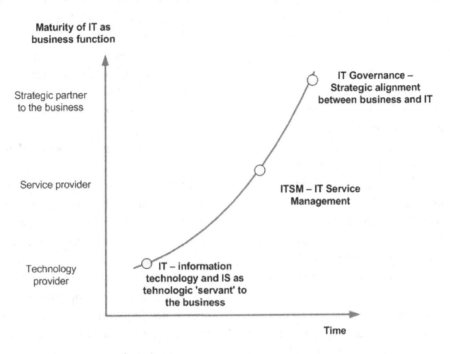

## CORNERSTONES OF IT GOVERNANCE CONCEPT

IT risks are risks associated with intensive use of IT to support and improve business processes and business as a whole. They are related to threats and dangers that the intensive use of IT may cause undesired or unexpected damages, misuses and losses in whole business model and its environment. Conscience about the systematic IT risk management should be present at all managerial level in organizations whose business is in any way related to the functioning of modern information systems (IS), no matter if they are used only for the purpose of business automation, or some vital business process are performed electronically. Since the efficiency, effectiveness and in a great deal the successfulness of all business activities depend on the functioning of the IT and IS, a sound risk management process should not only include technical or operational issues but also executive management' frameworks such as IT Governance and IT Audit.

According to Brynjolfsson (Brynjolfson & Hitt, 1993) the productivity paradox of information technology has had several reasons (mis-measurement of outputs and inputs, lags due to learning and adjustment, redistribution and dissipation of profits, mismanagement of IT). After reviewing and assessing the research to date, it appears that the shortfall of IT productivity is due rather to deficiencies in the measurement and methodological tool kit as to mismanagement by developers and users of IT (Brynjolfson & Hitt, 1993; Groznik, Kovačič & Spremić, 2003; Tam, 1998). Recent research results on IT investments productivity in emerging markets (Groznik, Kovačič & Spremić, 2003) are in line with other studies (Brynjolfson & Hitt, 1993; Tam, 1998), indicating that IT has increased productivity but only when IT initiatives are aligned with business strategy (Spremić & Strugar, 2002).

A number of associations and regulatory institution stressed the importance of growing IT opportunities and IT-risks. In their study on the importance of IT controls in governance and regulatory compliance (Sarbanes –Oxley act, Basel II), ITGI (ITGI & PricewaterhouseCoopers, 2006) reported that information risk and IT have become decisive factors in shaping modern business and many financial services organizations have undergone a fundamental transformation in terms of IT infrastructures, applications and IT-related internal controls (ITGI & PricewaterhouseCoopers, 2006). Operational and information risk management are now seen as essentials in good corporate governance (COSO, 2004; ITGI & PricewaterhouseCoopers, 2006; Symons, 2005; Weill & Ross, 2004).

IT governance concerns relate to IT practices of boards and senior managers. The question is whether IT structures, processes, relational mechanisms and IT decisions are made in the interest of shareholders and other stakeholders, or primarily in the executives' interests. IT governance closely relates to corporate governance, the structure of the IT organization and its objectives and alignment to the business objectives.

IT Governance is the process for controlling an organization's IT resources, including information and communication systems and technology (Hunton, Bryant, & Bagranoff, 2004). According to the IT Governance Institute (2003), IT governance is the responsibility of executives and board of directors, and consists of leadership, organizational structures and processes that ensure that enterprise's IT sustain and extends the organization's strategies and objectives. It is an integral part of enterprise governance and consists of the leadership and organizational structures and processes that ensure that the organization's IT sustains and extends the organization's strategies and objectives. Van Grembergen (Van Grembergen & De Haes, 2005) stands on that point and defined IT Governance as the organizational capacity exercised by the Board, executive management

and IT management to control the formulation and implementation of IT strategy and in this way ensure the fusion of business and IT. The primary focus of IT governance is on the responsibility of the board and executive management to control formulation and the implementation of IT strategy, to ensure the alignment of IT and business, to identify metrics for measuring business value of IT and to manage IT risks in an effective way. Nolan and McFarlan (2005) recently pointed out that 'a lack of board oversight for IT activities is dangerous; it puts the firm at risk in the same way that failing to audit its books would'.

Figure 2 shows a clear difference between IT governance and IT management. While IT management is mainly focused on the daily effective and efficient supply of IT services and IT operations, IT governance is much broader concept which focuses on performing and transforming IT to meet present and future demands of business and the business' customers. This in particular means that executive management members and corporate governance organizations bodies need to take responsibility for governing IT, which makes IT Governance a key executive function.

IT governance focuses areas are (ITGI, 2003):

- Business/IT strategic alignment
- IT value creation and delivery
- Risk management (value preservation)
- IT resource management
- Performance measurement.

In this chapter we particularly stress the importance of IT risk management process and performance metrics that support 'always-on' information systems. Managing risks is a cornerstone of IT governance, ensuring that an enterprise's strategic objectives are not jeopardized by IT failures. On the other hand, performance measurement phase include audit and assessment activities which can create the opportunity to take time corrective measures, if needed.

*Figure 2. Differences between IT governance and IT management concepts*

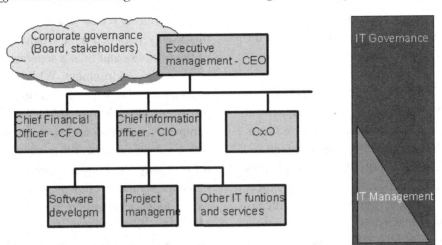

A good, or rather, inevitable approach for managing IT risks include thorough audit and quality assessment of all aspects of IS and IT, including hardware, software, data, networks, organization and key business processes. The primary goal of the information system audit (IT audit) is to identify the key business processes that depend on IT, to systematically and carefully examine their IT controls efficiency, to identify key risk areas and constantly measure the risk level, to warn about possible failures, as well as to offer suggestions to the executive management how to improve current IT risk management practices (Spremić, Žmirak, & Kraljević, 2008).

## CORPORATE IT RISK MANAGEMENT MODEL (CITRM): NEW PERSPECTIVES ON IT RISKS MANAGEMENT

### IT Risk Management

IT Risks represent the likelihood that in certain circumstances a given threat-source can exercise a particular potential vulnerability and negatively impacts the IT assets (data, software, hardware),

IT services, key business processes or the whole organization (Spremić, Žmirak, & Kraljević, 2008).

IT Risks = F (asset, threat, vulnerability)

There are quantitative and qualitative methods of assessing IT risks. Quantitative risk assessment draws upon methodologies used by financial institutions and insurance companies. By assigning values to information, systems, business processes, recovery costs, etc., impact, and therefore risk, can be measured in terms of direct and indirect costs. Mathematically, quantitative risk can be expressed as Annualized Loss Expectancy (ALE). ALE is the expected monetary loss that can be expected for an asset due to a risk being realized over a one-year period.

ALE = SLE * ARO

where:

- SLE (Single Loss Expectancy) is the value of a single loss of the asset. This may or may not be the entire asset. This is the impact of the loss.

- ARO (Annualized Rate of Occurrence) is how often the loss occurs. This is the likelihood or the number of occurrences of the undesired event.

Therefore, if a company faces a 10.000€ loss due to the web site downtime, and if it happens in average 5 times a year, than the Annualized Loss Expectancy (ALE) is 50.000€. This is a rough approximation of the ALE, but if the company insists on measuring the IT performances we may expect the proliferation of the numbers. It also means that the company may spend up to, for example 40.000€ at the minimum for implementation of solid control systems. Constant monitoring of the web site performance is crucial, while it may happen that the web sales grows significantly as well as that the SLE and ALE.

From IT Governance, IT Audit and IT Security perspective, IT risk management is the process of understanding and responding to factors that may lead to a failure in the authenticity, non-repudiation, confidentiality, integrity or availability of an information system. For example, information security program helps organization to measure the IT risk level and provides the management processes, technology and assurance to:

- allow businesses' management to ensure business transactions and information exchanges between enterprises, customers, suppliers, partners and regulators can be trusted (*authenticity and non-repudiation*),
- ensure IT services are available and usable and can appropriately resist and recover from failures due to errors, deliberate attacks or disaster (*availability*),
- ensure information is protected against unauthorized modification or error so that accuracy, completeness and validity is maintained (*integrity*),
- ensure critical confidential information is withheld from those who should not have access to it (*confidentiality*).

Although, IT risks characteristics dramatically change in recent decades, IT is still often mistakenly regarded as a separate organization of the business and thus a separate risk, control and security environment. While since 10 or 15 years ago an IT risk could cause minor 'technical' problems, today it may affect the corporation's competitive position and strategic goals. An attack on Amazon.com, for example, would cost the company $600.000 an hour in revenue and if Cisco's systems were down for a day, the company would loose $70 million in revenues (Nolan & McFarlan, 2005), not to mention indirect costs and reputation risk. It is estimated[1] that IS downtime put direct losses on brokerage operations at $4.5 million per hour, banking industry $2.1 million per hour, e-commerce operations $113.000, etc. Also, Fortune 500 companies would have average losses of about $96.000 per hour due to the IS downtime[2].

## Corporate IT Risk Management Model

Corporate IT Risk Management Model (CITRM) should be a holistic and structured approach that aligns governance policies, business strategy, management procedures, business processes and operational activities with the purpose of evaluating and managing risk and uncertainties the organization faces. The main objective of CITRM model is to align IT resources, IT infrastructure, key resources (data, people, assets, etc.) and business processes with governance policies and management procedures in order to effectively manage IT risk exposure. This in particular means that executive management and Board members become responsible for managing risk associated with using IT in conducting business operations and transactions. Such initiatives are well known 'heritage' of certain regulatory framework (for example, Sarbanes-Oxley act or Basel II framework) and represent the core of IT Governance concept.

The fundamentals of the Corporate IT Risk Management Model are (Spremić, Žmirak, & Kraljević, 2008):

1. **Corporate governance policies for managing IT risks:** Policies that are mandatory at all corporate levels and approved by the highest corporate bodies (Board, executive management). They should be used to define corporate internal standards for governing specific area of IT. Highest corporate bodies should monitor its implementation and improve or update it if necessary. Typical examples are:
   ○ defining the 'risk appetite' which commonly represent the corporate rules and policies for IT risk response strategies (key metrics, Key Risk Indicators - KRIs, Key Performance Indicators - KPIs)
   ○ corporate policies for analyzing the impact IT risks may have on the business (quantitative or qualitative measures for conducting a business impact analysis – BIA, metrics for IT risk validation, IT risk portfolio)
   ○ accountability for IT control activities and framework for the IT risk reports (the dynamics of IT risk reports, who and to whom IT risk reports should be presented),
   ○ establishing committees and other corporate 'bodies' responsible for managing IT risks (Audit Committee, IT Governance Committee)

2. **Procedures for managing IT risks on business units level or functional level:** They represent the standards, guidelines and activities which help in implementation of corporate IT Governance policies (for example, IT security policy, business continuity plan, password policy, access rights procedures, change management procedures, etc). According to the regulatory requirements and specific area of interest, this usually means the adoption of world-wide standards or frameworks (CobiT, ISO 27001, Sarbanes-Oxley, Basel II, ITIL, SANS, SAS 70, …). Periodic internal or external IT audits are needed to detect the level of compliance with standards and regulatory frameworks. Performing IT audits are necessary in order to detect the priority risk areas, to identify specific IT controls needed, to constantly measure the level of their efficiency and to calculate IT risk level on regular basis.

3. **Operational (technical) activities:** 'Driven' by governance policies and management procedures represent the counter-measures, which aim to raise the level of 'immunity' on threats or attacks to IT assets. Typical examples of operational IT controls include access controls, application controls, system controls, change controls, data accuracy controls, integrity controls, business continuity controls, etc.

## IT Risk Management Plan

In order to provide a successful protection against possible misuses, an organization should develop methods and techniques for the control of the IT incidents and for identification of possible risk evaluation methods. An IT Risk Management plan should have following important steps:

1. IT risk identification and classification,
2. IT risk assessment (Business Impact Analysis) and priority determination,
3. IT risk responses strategies – identification of IT controls,
4. implementation and documentation of selected counter-measures (IT controls),
5. portfolio approach to IT risks and alignment with business strategy,
6. constant monitoring of IT risks level and auditing.

## IT Risks Identification and Classification

Perhaps the most difficult aspect of process of managing risks is their identification and classification. IT risk identification process represent not only a listing of expected negative outcomes, but also their classification according to a proposed corporate framework and preparation for their assessment by evaluation of their possible impact on business, categorization of causes and triggers to the risk event, the probability of occurrence and the allocation of the responsibility for the risks (ITGI, 2007). Generally, risks are identified in terms of their relevance to the specific business objectives or impact on business processes.

Some common frameworks or industry standards can help organizations to identify and classify IT risks. Apart from industry or country specific risk and regulatory frameworks (for example, Basel II, Sarbanes-Oxley), in understanding where IT risks exist within the organization, a classic *hierarchical risk approach* should help:

1. **Corporate or company-level IT risks:** these risks are vital part of corporation's overall risk management policies and associated with corporate and executive management activities. Typical corporate or company-level IT risks include various risks associated with setting up and implementing strategies, policies, procedures, governance models, etc. Examples may be: strategic risk (IT strategy planning risks), IT/business misalignment risks, risks associated with deficient IT policies and procedures, reputation risk, loss of business, financial risks (IT project failure[3], IT investments risk[4]), audit risks (risk that financial statements are incorrect, poor internal IT audit practices), acquisition risks, legal and regulatory risks (non-compliance), etc.

2. **Process-level IT risks (IT General Risks):** in the contemporary environment business processes are highly automated and integrated with efficient IS and IT. Therefore, it is obvious that important IT risks are associated with execution of company's business processes[5]. Typical areas of process-level IT risks are: software development or acquisition risks, change management procedures and associated risks, access to program and data risks, physical and logical security risks, business continuity and disaster recovery risks, security administration risks, various security risks, system risks, information management risks.

3. **Specific IT risks (IT Applications and IT Services Risks):** IT managers need to establish sound policies and procedures for controlling key risks with running various IT operations. IT application risks are commonly associated with software applications that directly support specific business processes. IT services risks are mainly affected by their availability (BC and DR) and levels of functionality (Service Level Agreements - SLAs). These IT risks mainly refer to business transaction's completeness, data accuracy, integrity, existence, authorization, segregation of duties and disclosure. IT service risks commonly include risks associated with following operations or activities: network management, database management, operating system management, storage management, facilities management, security administration, capacities, configuration management, etc.

## IT Risks Assessment and Priority Determination

The objective of this step is to assess the important characteristics of IT risks such as 'gravity' and frequency. IT risks gravity is the measure of the damage or potential loss that certain undesired or unexpected activity may cause and commonly it can be expressed in financial terms. According the corporate governance polices, for all identified risks, *IT risk assessment plan* includes following activities:

- identification of the threats to IT resources and the exposure of IT infrastructure to various malicious or accidental acts,
- evaluation of the vulnerabilities to identified IT risks,
- determination of the IT risks probability of occurrence (frequency),
- evaluation of the business impact of IT risks occurrence (severity),
- analysis of the IT risks frequency and IT risks ranking (an example is given in Table 1.),
- calculation of the IT risks 'gravity' and expected value of IT risks (an example is given in Table 2.), and
- preparation for the response strategies and for the control of IT risks level.

This in particular means that risk analysts have performed a business impact analysis (BIA). Business impact analysis is an essential component of an organization's business continuity (BC) plan[6]. It is the management level process to prioritize business functions by assessing the potential quantitative (financial) and qualitative (non-financial) impact that might result if an organization was to experience a business continuity event[7]. BIA is a systematic process aimed to identify: key business processes performed by an organization, the resources required to support each process performed, the impact of failing of performing a process, the criticality of each process, a recovery time objective (RTO) for each process, recovery point objective (RPO) and availability rate for each process.

Classification of IT risks priorities are based on the probability of occurrence of each IT risks and their potential severity (the results of business impact analysis). According to the IT Governance policies and procedures one of most appropriate method for calculating IT risk level has to be defined and Board members and the executive managers need to approve it. Transparent and agreed risk management framework and clear rules and responsibilities for implementing it represent key cornerstones of effective IT risk management process. As mentioned previously, metrics for measuring IT risk level may be quantitative and qualitative. Quantitative metrics may be based on specific, even complex algorithms which executive managers use to quantify the risk level (for example: probability of occurrence multiply by risk severity). The simple algorithms may be improved according to the specific needs (the risk environment, business environment, regula-

*Table 1. Example of analysis of IT risk drivers frequency and severity*

| IT risk scenario | Risk drivers for frequency | Risk drivers for severity |
|---|---|---|
| Authorized users perform illegal activities (confidentiality) | • Users with access to sensitive application functions<br>• Lack of supervisory control<br>• Improper definitions of access permissions<br>• Excessive use of supervisory activities | • Inadequate monitoring of system exception reports<br>• Lack of management control<br>• Lack of audit review<br>• Inappropriate security policies |
| System and services disruption (availability) | • Number of potential damaging incidents that could cause a disruption of service<br>• Susceptibility of hardware and software to damage | • Inability to correctly identify the impact of conditions that can result in disruption<br>• Failure to develop and implement incident detection and escalation procedures<br>• Failure to monitor for events that can result in a disruption of service |
| IT Project implementation failure (financial risk) | • Number of projects<br>• Quality of defined program and project management approach | • Amount of project budget<br>• Number of critical projects<br>• Methods for evaluating project feasibility (ROI) |

*Table 2. Example of the IT risk assessment and priority determination activities*

| IT risk scenario | Potential damage | Potential loss (BIA) | Risk ranking |
|---|---|---|---|
| Authorized users perform illegal activities (confidentiality) | Users have unauthorized access to data, they can view and change them, they can manipulate with the system | 100.000 € | Medium |
| System and services disruption (availability) | Disruption of key business processes and potential loss of important data | 500.000 € | High |
| Incomplete transaction processing (integrity) | Financial reports may be incorrect, decision making process questionable | 250.000 € | High |
| IT Project implementation failure (financial risk) | IT project not finished on time, costs to high, quality poor (Service Level, low functionality) | 300.000 € | High |

tory requirements, etc.). The results of the IT risk quantification are shown in Table 3.

IT Risk may be ranked according to the specific IT Governance policies and rules. For example, an IT Governance policy approved by the Board may be that all the IT risks above the certain risk level are categorized as critical and requires urgent action. Table 4 shows an example of IT Governance policy on classifying IT risks. IT risks identified in previous table (Table 3) may be ranked according to this or any other similar policy. No matter of the algorithm used for calculating the risk level, as well as for method used for classifying it into meaningful levels, the main objective of IT risk management remains to identify, measure and manage the risk level. Inappropriate classifying method (policy) and/or ineffective risk calculating algorithm may cause the situation that organization omit some key IT risks or use the ineffective response strategy.

Periodically conducted information system audits (internal or external) should result in improving IT risk management practices.

If the IT risk management framework propose a qualitative assessment techniques the results may be similar as well as the management activities in reducing the risk level.

## Strategies for IT Risks Responses

Once the organization has identified, classified and assessed IT risks, risk owners and 'affected' process owners are to be identified, appropriate responses should be developed and specific cost-effective controls over those risks should be designed. Responses to IT risk may include following strategies:

- **Acceptance:** the organization chooses to live with the risk and to constantly monitor

*Table 3. Example of IT risk quantification*

| IT Risk scenario | Risk severity based on the BIA (b) | Probability of occurence (c) | Risk level (d) d = b x c | IT Risk ranking (e) |
|---|---|---|---|---|
| Incident A | 5 | 2 | 10 | 2 |
| Incident B | 2 | 4 | 8 | 3 |
| Incident C | 3 | 5 | 15 | 1 |
| Incident D | 1 | 3 | 3 | 5 |
| Incident E | 4 | 1 | 4 | 4 |
| Incident F | 2 | 4 | 8 | 3 |

*Table 4. IT risk classification based on quantification*

| Risk level | Risk category | Management and Board's actions according to the agreed IT Governance procedures and policies |
|---|---|---|
| 21 – 25 | Very high risk | Totally unacceptable, requires urgent executive management and Board's intervention |
| 15 – 20 | High risk | Not acceptable, requires urgent activities towards decreasing its level – implementation speficic controls |
| 10 – 14 | Medium risk | Acceptable risk, monitoring and assessing |
| 4 – 9 | Small risk | No need for any action, just further assessment of IT risks according to the policies |
| 1 – 3 | Very low risk | No need for any action |

its level (gravity and impact on the business and business processes),

- **Reduction:** the organization takes steps to reduce the impact (gravity) or the probability of the risk occurrence,
- **Avoidance:** the organization chooses to fully or partially avoid the risk,
- **Sharing:** the organization transfers the risk by, for example, purchasing insurance, outsourcing risk management services, or engaging in partnership(s) regarding the risk management process to fully or partly

cover risk exposure (especially in business continuity and disaster recovery plans).

Strategies for IT risks responses usually means that specific IT controls need to be implemented and their efficiency constantly monitored. *Control activities* are the policies, procedures and practices that are put into place so that business objectives are achieved and risk mitigation strategies are carried out. Control activities are developed to specifically address each control objective to mitigate the risks identified. An *IT control objective*

*Table 5. Example of qualitative IT risk management assessment and response strategies (IT Risk matrix – threats and probability of occurrence)*

| Impact – risk severity | Probability of occurrence (system vulnerability) | | | | |
|---|---|---|---|---|---|
| | A: very possible | B: possible | C: occasionally | D: rare | E: almost never |
| I (very high) | Risk 1 | Risk 1 | Risk 1 | Risk 2 | Risk 3 |
| II | Risk 1 | Risk 1 | Risk 2 | Risk 2 | Risk 3 |
| III | Risk 1 | Risk 2 | Risk 2 | Risk 3 | Risk 3 |
| IV (low) | Risk 3 | Risk 3 | Risk 4 | Risk 4 | Risk 4 |

| | |
|---|---|
| | **Risk 1:** unacceptable, critical, current control activities not successful in preventing it, requires urgent executives' and Board's response (activities for urgent reducing the risk level) |
| | **Risk 2:** unacceptable, not tolerable, current control activities just partially successful in preventing it, requires corrective activities under the higher and executive management responsibility |
| | **Risk 3:** tolerable, needs to be monitored and assessed according to the IT Governance policies (for example twice a year), with proper reporting mechanisms to the higher executive levels |
| | **Risk 4:** tolerable, no need for any activities, just risk monitoring |

is a statement of the desired result or purpose to be achieved by implementing control procedures in a particular IT activity (ITGI, 2003). IT Audit activities usually include the examination of the IT control efficiency. When doing so, IT Auditors commonly perform test of IT controls using specific metrics (for example, RTO, RPO for business continuity process), maturity models and audit tools (CAATs, ACL software, etc.). Common metrics for testing the efficiency of business continuity plan may be:

- **MTBF** (Mean Time Between Failures) represents an important system characteristic which help to quantify the suitability of a system for a potential application. MTBF is the measure of the systems' functionality and service level. MTBF is often connected to the Mean Time to Repair (MTTR). ITPI (2006) reported that high IT performers know that 80% of all outages are due to the change, and that 80% of mean time to repair (MTTR) is spent to figure out what changed. Analyzing the MTTR of the high, medium and low performers revealed some interesting insights. For small incidents, all performers experienced similar MTTR rates (up to 15 minutes, one to three people to fix). High performers are almost always able to resolve medium severity outages in minutes, while medium performers' resolution times begin creeping into hours. But, in large outages, differences are significant: high performers again resolve issues in minutes, medium performers in a low number of hours, but low performers even in days.
- **Availability** represents the percentage of time when system is operational (for example, 99% availability means that the

system downtime is 3,65 days per year, while 99,99% availability rate means that the downtime is 52 minutes per year).

- **First Fix Rate** measures the percentage of incidents that successfully restored on the first fox attempt. It is leading indicator of system availability and MTTR; that is, how well an IT organization manages First Fix Rate will also result in radically improved MTTR and MTBF. First Fix Rate is commonly used in connotation of the service desk, where it measures how often the incident is resolved at the first point of contact between a customer and the service provider.
- **RTO (Recovery Time Objective)** is the period of time within which systems, services, applications or functions must be recovered after an outage. It is maximum tolerable length of time that a IT infrastructure can be down after a failure or disaster occurs. The RTO is a function of the extent to which the interruption disrupts normal operations and the amount of revenue lost per unit time as a result of the disaster.
- **RPO (Recovery Point Objective)** is the maximum amount of data loss an organization can sustain during an event. It is also the point in time (prior to outage) in which systems and data must be restored to. There is a growing in certain businesses (especially information intensive industries such as financial services) for RTO and RPO to be close to zero. The convergence of RTOs and RPOs to zero will result in exponential cost increase, thus corporate managers together with CIOs (Chief Information Officers) and CTOs (Chief Technology Officers) need to carefully balance these numbers and their costs.

## IT GOVERNANCE METHODOLOGIES AND FRAMEWORKS THAT SUPPORTS 'ALWAYS ON' INFORMATION SYSTEMS

Implementing IT Governance and IT Audit frameworks may help organizations manage IT risk level. In recent years various groups have developed world-wide known IT Governance guidelines to assist management and auditors in developing optimal performance and controls systems for always-on enterprise information systems. Contemporary frameworks are:

- *CobiT* (Control Objectives of Information and related Technology),
- *ISO 27000 'family'* (ISO 27001:2005, ISO 27002:2005) and new ISO 38500, and
- *ITIL* (IT Infrastructure Library).

Developed by ISACA (Information System Audit and Control Association, www.isaca.org) and ITGI (IT Governance Institute, www.itgi.org), CobiT is the widely accepted IT governance framework organized by key IT control objectives, which are broken into detailed IT controls. Current version 4.1 of CobiT divides IT into four domains (Plan and Organise, Acquire and Implement, Deliver and Support, and Monitor and Evaluate), which are broken into 34 key IT processes, and then further divided into more than 300 detailed IT control objectives. For each of the 34 IT processes CobiT defines:

- performance goals and metrics (for example, RPO, RTO, availability time),
- KRI (Key Risk Indicator), KPI (Key Performance Indicator)
- maturity models (0-5 scale) to assist in benchmarking and decision-making for process improvements,
- a RACI chart identifying who is Responsible, Accountable, Consulted, and/or Informed for specific IT process.

CobiT processes of particular interest for modelling always-on enterprise information systems may be DS 4 (Ensure Continuous Service), DS 8 – 13 (Manage Service Desk, Manage Problems, Data and Operations) and wide range of Application Controls (AC 1- 18) which may be useful for modelling data control infrastructure. CobiT represent an 'umbrella' framework for implementing IT Governance policies and procedures. It is a broad and comprehensive de-facto standard which comprises all activities, processes and services an IT organization need to manage (or rather govern). Therefore, when engaging in IT Governance activities it is inevitable to use CobiT framework to in details analyse the alignment of current IS and supporting IT infrastructure and business requirements towards it.

If CobiT-based information system audit or any further 'due diligence' come up with the conclusion that an IT organization underperforms in a specific area, an additional project may be opened to assure the compliance and alignment with business requirements. For example:

- ITIL framework may be used to assure better service delivery and service management,
- Val IT framework may be used to assure efficient management of IT investments which may result with additional business value,
- ISO 27001 norm may be used to manage the level of IT security risks,
- Prince 2 and/or PMBOK may be used to bridge the gap in IT project management activities, etc.

ITIL (Information Technology Infrastructure Library) developed and published in late 1980s by Central Computer and Telecommunication Agency, now the British Office of Government Commerce, becomes widely embraced in private and public sectors as a reference framework for IT Service Management. ITIL is a series of books

*Table 6. The results of corporate IT risk management model implementation*

| Key business process | Sales orders (e-orders) |
|---|---|
| IT risk | System disruption |
| IT risk level | High – critical, loss of data, corporate risk |
| Potential loss (BIA) (per day) | 500.000 € |
| IT Risk Response Strategy | Immediate action, risk level reduction |
| IT (governance) goal | Number of hours lost per user per month due to unplanned outages |
| IT Control | CobiT 4.1. (*DS4, DS5)*<br>ITIL *BCM*<br>ISO 27001 (10, 11, 4) |
| Key Metrics – IT Control Efficiency | Availability >= 99,96%<br>RTO < 3h<br>RPO < 3h<br>First Fix Rate > 90%<br>MTTR < 30 minutes<br>MTBF < 20 minutes |
| Detailed IT metrics | • Percent of availability service level agreements (SLAs) met<br>• Number of business-critical processes relying on IT that are not covered by IT continuity plan<br>• Percent of tests that achieve recovery objectives<br>• Frequency of service interruption of critical systems |
| Responsible person (process owner) | XY |

representing a repository of best practices in IT service management and related processes, promoting business driven approach to the management of IT and a performance driven approach in achieving business effectiveness and efficiency in the use of IS and IT. Basic ITIL process' objectives are:

- to define service processes in IT organization,
- to define and improve the quality of IT services,
- to understand and improve IT service provision, as an integral part of an overall business requirement for high quality IS management,
- to determine what service the business requires of the provider in order to provide adequate support to the business users, and
- to ensure that the customer has access to the appropriate services to support the business functions.

Since the 1980s there were 3 major revisions of ITIL best practices. Version 2 described 11 major IT service areas within two broad categories of:

- **Service Support:** (operational processes, consisted of Service Desk, Incident Management, Problem Management, Configuration Management, Change Management, Release Management) and
- **Service Delivery:** (tactical processes comprising Service Level Management, IT Financial Management, Capacity Management, IT Service Continuity, Availability Management).

New version 3 of ITIL brings evolutionary improvements to the IT Service Management concept, consisting of 5 key categories (Service Strategy, Service Design, Service Transition, Service Operation, Continual Service Improvement), but the supported processes remains the same in its core as in ITIL v2.

The possible results of executive management activities in managing IT risk are presented in table 6. IT Governance and IT Audit activities there give a clear guideline to executive management in managing IT risk.

## CONCLUDING REMARKS

Although, traditionally, only the IT departments were responsible for managing IT risks, their importance affects the fact that the number of companies starting to systematically deal with such problems is ever increasing. As the organizations are becoming increasingly dependent upon IT in order to achieve their corporate objectives and meet their business needs, the necessity for implementing widely applicable IT best practices standards and methodologies, offering high quality services is evident. Always on enterprise information systems represent one of the typical requirements that the businesses expect from IT. The issue of managing the IT risks becomes less and less a technical problem, and more and more the problem of the whole organization i.e. a 'business problem' and many companies nowadays formally nominate executive directors for such activities.

On the other hand, IT profession has been in search for solid standards and performance measurement frameworks for decades, but it seems that by the 1990's such efforts had dramatically improved. One of the reasons for such tendencies may be in changing role of IT performance metrics over years. While in 1980's the focus of IT performance metrics was solely on technical efficiency, in 1990's process efficiency was attached, these efforts nowadays converge to comprehensive concept of value added IT-related business benefits. IT Governance issues are not only any more marginal or 'technical' problems and become more and more a 'corporate problem'. Therefore, we find the proposed corporate IT risk management model incorporating contemporary

IT governance and IT audit issues suitable and inevitable framework for managing 'always on' enterprise information systems.

## REFERENCES

Brynjolfson, E., & Hitt, L. M. (1993). Is information systems spending productive? New evidence and new results. In *Proceedings of the International Conference on Information Systems*, Orlando, FL (pp. 47-64).

COSO. (2004, September). *Enterprise risk management integrated framework*. Retrieved in January 2008, from www.coso.org7publications.htm

Groznik, A., Kovačič, A., & Spremić, M. (2003). Do IT investments have a real business value? *Applied Informatics*, *4*, 180–189.

Hunton, J. E., Bryant, S. M., & Bagranoff, N. A. (2004). *Core concepts of information technology auditing*. John Wiley &Sons Inc., SAD.

ITGI. (2003). *Board briefing on IT governance*, 2nd ed. Rolling Meadows, IL: IT Governance Institute, SAD.

ITGI. (2007). *IT control objectives for Basel II– the importance of governance and risk management for compliance*. Rolling Meadows, IL: IT Governance Institute, SAD.

ITGI & PricewaterhouseCoopers. (2006). *IT governance global status report*. Rolling Meadows, IL: IT Governance Institute, SAD.

ITPI. (2006). IT process institute: Reframing IT audit and control resources decisions. Retrieved in April 2008, from www.itpi.org

Nolan, R., & McFarlan, F. W. (2005, October). Information technology and board of directors. *Harvard Business Review*.

Peppard, J., & Ward, J. (2004). Beyond strategic information systems: Towards an IS capability. *The Journal of Strategic Information Systems, 13*, 167–194. doi:10.1016/j.jsis.2004.02.002

Spremić, M., & Strugar, I. (2002). Strategic information system planning in Croatia: Organizational and managerial challenges. *International Journal of Accounting Information Systems, 3*(3), 183–200. doi:10.1016/S1467-0895(02)00033-7

Spremić, M., Žmirak, Z., & Kraljević, K. (2008). Evolving IT governance model–research study on Croatian large companies. *WSEAS Transactions on Business and Economics, 5*(5), 244–253.

Symons, C. (2005). *IT governance framework: Structures, processes, and framework*. Forrester Research, Inc.

Tam, K. Y. (1998). The impact of information technology investments on firm performance and evaluation: Evidence form newly industrialized economies. *Information Systems Research, 9*(1), 85–98. doi:10.1287/isre.9.1.85

Van Grembergen, W., & De Haes, S. (2005). Measuring and improving IT governance through the balanced scorecard. *Information System Control Journal, 2*.

Weill, P., & Ross, J. W. (2004): IT Governance: How Top Performers Manage IT Decision Rights for Superior Results, Harvard Business School Press, 2004.

## ENDNOTES

[1] Hiles, A. (2004): Business Continuity: Best Practices - World-Class Business Continuity Management 2nd ed., Disaster Center Bookstore, USA.

[2] Ibidem.

[3] Standish Group in their 2004 The Chaos Report, claimed that only 29 percent of all IT projects succeeded while the remainder were either challenged or failed, source: (ITGI, 2006).

[4] A 2002 Gartner publication reported that 20 percent of all expenditure on IT is wasted, representing, on a global basis, annual value destruction of US $600 billion. Source (Gartner, 2002).

[5] For example, Nike reportedly lost more than US $200 million through difficulties experienced in implementing its supply chain software. Failures in IT-enabled logistics systems at MFI and Sainsbury in the UK led to multimillion-pound write-offs, profit warnings and erosion of share price. Source (ITGI, 2006).

[6] Business continuity plan (BCP) is a clearly defined and documented plan for use at the time of a Business Continuity Emergency, Event, Incident and/or Crisis (E/I/C). Typically a plan will cover all the key personnel, resources, services and actions required to manage the business continuity management (BCM) process, The Business Continuity Institute (2002): Glossary of terms, www.thebci.org, accessed 12/2008

[7] The Business Continuity Institute (2002): Glossary of terms, www.thebci.org, accessed 07/2007.

# Chapter 2
# Risks Evaluation and IT Audit Aspects of Business Intelligence Solutions

**Andrea Kő**
*Corvinus University of Budapest, Hungary*

## ABSTRACT

*Many organizations are struggling with a vast amount of data in order to gain valuable insights and get support in their decision-making process. Decision-making quality depends increasingly on information and the systems that deliver this information. These services are vulnerable and risky from security aspects, and they have to satisfy several requirements, like transparency, availability, accessibility, convenience, and compliance. IT environments are more and more complex and fragmented, which means additional security risks. Business intelligence solutions provide assistance in these complex business situations. Their main goal is to assist organizations to make better decisions. Better decisions means that these solutions support the management of risks, and they have a key role in raising revenue and in reducing cost. The objectives of this chapter are to give an overview of the business intelligence field and its future trends, to demonstrate the most important business intelligence solutions, meanwhile highlighting their risks, business continuity challenges, and IT audit issues. In spite of the fact that this chapter focuses on the business intelligence solutions and their specialities, risk management and the related IT audit approach can be applied for other categories of information systems. IT audit guidelines, best practices, and standards are presented as well, because they give effective tools in controlling process of business intelligence systems.*

## INTRODUCTION

Organizations are overloaded by huge amount of data continuously, about their customers, their operation and business, environment and partners. We live in a fast changing environment, where we use several online services, like e-banking, e-learning, online travel services, e-grocers. All these transactions generate lots of data. Companies get too much data too fast and there is a strong need to manage it, to reveal insight from it and to make it more useful,

DOI: 10.4018/978-1-60566-723-2.ch002

actionable. Business intelligence can facilitate this process through several services.

The objectives of this chapter are to give an overview about the most important business intelligence solutions, to display their development and implementation, to demonstrate their risks and audit issues, meanwhile emphasizing their business continuity challenges and monitoring. This chapter provide answers for the following research questions:

- What are the main roles of business intelligence at organizational and personal level?
- What kind of risks and challenges have to be managed at the field of business intelligence, especially regarding its business continuity?
- What are the critical challenges in business intelligence success?
- What are the future trends of business intelligence?

First part of this chapter presents business intelligence overview, with special attention to data warehouses. Business intelligence solutions provide rapid results from various data sources in order to support critical processes. Data warehouse development has special characteristics, which are highlighted and compared with other more traditional development methods in this chapter. Business intelligence solutions are generally organization-wide, so number of users interacts with them; apply them as a key supporting tool in their decision making. They are inseparable from organization's operation, so their business continuity is a critical issue. Most of them, especially data warehouses are large-scale, expensive projects, with several, interrelated risks. These risks can threaten the success of the projects, so they have to be assessed and managed in the

business intelligence projects to avoid further difficulties. Most of the risks can be found in other IT projects too, but they can cause more trouble here, because business intelligence projects affect the whole organization and they are costly. Risks and business continuity challenges of business intelligence solutions are discussed in the second part of this chapter. Most important features of business continuity planning are demonstrated as well. IT audit has a special role in this situation, because it can support the risks identification and mitigation. One key question is, what areas should be audited and how. The third part of this chapter summarizes the risk-based audit approach and demonstrates what areas are important from auditing aspects. IT audit of information system's business continuity is presented too. IT audit guidelines, best practices and standards give effective tools in controlling process of business intelligence systems. Management needs to get business intelligence solutions under control, which can be guaranteed by a control framework. Standards for IT management and security are crystallized by consensus or compromise from best practices discussed by a large group of individuals from various organisations. Fourth part of this chapter deals with IT audit guidelines, best practices and standards. In many cases these standards overlap each other; therefore their relations are presented with special attention to IT governance-related issues. Risks evaluation and management of business intelligence solutions based on IT audit guidelines is the subject of the fifth part of this chapter. Finally, in conclusion part of this chapter; future trends of business intelligence solutions, like BI 2.0 are presented. Business intelligence market has been transformed recently, which has interesting consequences for the next generation of business intelligence solutions. Conclusion summarizes critical challenges for success of business intelligence projects.

## BUSINESS INTELLIGENCE OVERVIEW

Organizations accumulate huge amounts of data nowadays, which is a valuable source for decision makers in a business situation. Hardware, storage capacities are cheaper, than previously, which makes easier for companies to record detailed information about their operation. However data is scattered through the organization and analysts have to cope with data collection and quality challenges too. Vast amount of data doesn't guarantee right business decisions, in many cases it makes more difficult to gain knowledge from it.

One of the key questions in enterprises daily life is how they can capitalize their data in order to gain competitive advantage. Some organizations do it well, but others are not effective enough. At the same time decisions based on the aggregated data have more importance, because right business decisions are vital for enterprises to survive. In order to gain knowledge from data, companies need proper methodologies, analytic tools and appropriate organizational culture. This process is time and resource consuming and in many cases affects the whole organization. Decision support systems use data, information and/or knowledge. These terms are sometimes applied interchangeably in the literature and they have several definitions. One widely accepted determination for these concepts are the following (Turban, 2005):

- **Data** is item about things, events, activities and transactions are recorded, classified and stored, but are not organized to convey any specific meaning.
- **Information** is data that have been organized in a manner that gives them meaning for the recipient.
- **Knowledge** consists of data items and/ or information organized and processed to convey understanding, experience, accumulated learning, and expertise that are applicable to a current problem or activity.

Knowledge can be the application of data and information in making a decision.

Not only managers and executives, but more and more employees need information in their daily activities. At marketing department, e.g. analysts need to know sales information in order to plan customer relationship activities. Financial department has to know debt information and it has to forecast financial figures. IT department need feedback about their services (customer satisfaction) and information about security risks. Compliance to these challenges requires well organised information management. This process is supported and enhanced by business intelligence solutions. *Business intelligence (BI)* solutions were evolved in early 1990s (Power, 2007). As it is common in IT there are several definitions available in the literature for BI. The term was introduced by Hans Peter Luhn in 1958 (Luhn, 1958). In his view "business is a collection of activities carried on for whatever purpose, be it science, technology, commerce, industry, law, government, defence, et cetera. The communication facility serving the conduct of a business (in the broad sense) may be referred to as an intelligence system." Intelligence is also defined by Luhn (1958), as "the ability to apprehend the interrelationships of presented facts in such a way as to guide action towards a desired goal." Business intelligence concept was popularized by Howard Dresner, a Gartner group analyst, in 1989. He determined business intelligence as a set of concepts and methodologies to improve decision making in business through use of facts and fact based systems. He emphasized facts in his approach compared with the business intuition. Facts come from the vast amount of data. Evolution of IT in that time made the necessary technological background available and companies produced more data than before. Data warehouses and data marts started to operate and provided input to business intelligence solutions.

*Figure 1. Role of business intelligence in information cycle of an organization*

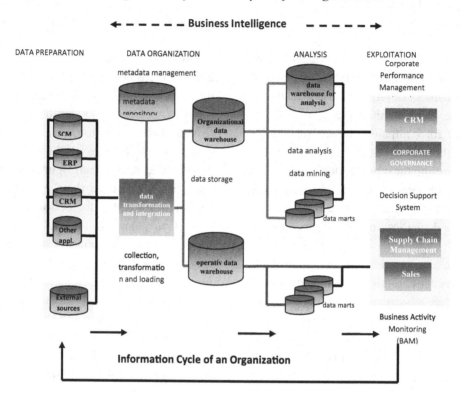

Business intelligence sometimes is described as a decision support system, because it supports better decision making (Power, 2007).Business intelligence covers the whole process from data and information (even knowledge in some cases) acquisition from a wide variety of sources and utilization them in decision making, as it can be seen in figure 1. Based on the definitions above, business intelligence involves technologies and applications, which aimed the assuring access to the necessary data and information, their storage. They have a capability for complex analysis of data and information in order to support organizational decision making. Business intelligence solutions involve data storage, reporting, analytics, forecasting and data mining processes.

Business intelligence includes data warehousing, online analytical processing, visualisation and data mining. Decision makers need data, information and knowledge in order to understand a business context of their problem. These input

must be organised a manner that makes them useful for the users. Data can be raw or summarized and come from internal and external sources. Internal data are about organizational products, people, services and processes. External data has several sources: data about competitors, government and research reports, and economic indicators. During data collection *data quality* has a key role. The situation can be summarized by "Garbage in, garbage out" expression. *Data warehousing* provides the tool which helps to cleanse and organise data in a manner consistent with organizations need. The term data warehouse was introduced by Bill Inmon in 1990, which he defined in the following way: "A warehouse is a subject-oriented, integrated, time-variant and non-volatile collection of data in support of management's decision making process" (Inmon, 1995). Subject-oriented means, that data are organized by subject, e.g. by customer, by product, by services, so it gives more comprehensive way to manage data. Integration offers a corporate view of data, which is one of the essences of the data warehouse environment. This feature is connected to data quality requirements; inconsistencies have to be eliminated and uniform terminology is a must. Time-variant means, that data warehouse has to support time dimension, which provide possibilities for further time-related data analysis, like time series, trend analysis and forecasting. Non-volatile ensures that data are read-only after entered to the data warehouse. Data warehouse and *data mart* are discussed together in the literature (Han, 2004). Based on Inmon view, data mart is a departmentalized structure of data feeding from the data warehouse, where data is denormalized, based on the department's need for information (Inmon, 2002). Data is summarized, and shaped by the operating requirements of a single department. Another decisive author of the data warehousing is Ralph Kimball. He defined data warehouse as follows: "the conglomeration of an organization's data warehouse staging and presentation areas, here operational data is specifically structured for query and analysis performance and ease-of-use" (Kimball, 2002). He states, that "data mart is defined as a flexible set of data, ideally based on the most atomic (granular) data possible to extract from an operational source, and presented in a symmetric (dimensional) model that is most resilient when faced with unexpected user queries" (Kimball, 2002, pp 396). Kimball's approach is different from Inmon's view, because in Inmon's view data in the data mart is very compact and summarized.

In Kimball's view information is always stored in the dimensional model. According Bill Inmon's approach, data warehouse is one part of the whole business intelligence system. One organizational data warehouse exists, and data marts are fed from the data warehouse. Data marts are built on departments need and data is denormalized in them. These two approaches represent different data warehousing philosophies. Data warehouse in many enterprises are closer to Ralph Kimball's idea, because generally development of data warehouses starts as a departmental effort, they originates as a data mart. When more data marts are built, later they can evolve into a data warehouse. In spite of these differences, both agree that data warehouse must consider the needs of the business. (see Figure 2)

Generally data warehouses have additional

*Figure 2. Elements of a data warehouse in Kimball's approach*

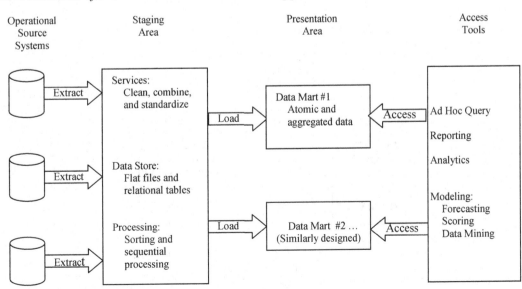

characteristics, which are not detailed in the definitions above, like data are summarized, which means that based on the decision-makers need, data are aggregated (e.g. analysts don't need detailed list of customer's calls, daily sum of calls are enough for them to perform analysis). Metadata (data about data, e.g. format of data) are included. Data warehouse's structure is optimized for reporting. Decision makers, managers usually are under time pressure, they have to work with huge amount of stored data, and they have to produce complex reports. Data warehouses can support them in report preparation, with suitable data input. Based on their need data are generally redundant and not normalized.

## Data Warehouse Development

Data warehouse development has special features compared with other information systems development. It doesn't follow the traditional SDLC model, which starts with requirements analysis. It requires iterative, data-driven approach, with high emphases to the risks analysis. The best candidate for satisfying these requirements is the spiral model (Boehm, 1988). Sometimes the development process is called CLDS (reverse SDLC) (Inmon, 2004), emphasizing that the process starts with

data collection and exploration. One key question is how to capture the relevant data and what kind of quality problems occur, during the data integration. The main steps of data warehouse SDLC are the following (Inmon, 2002):

• Implement warehouse
• Integrate data
• Test for bias
• Program against data
• Design DSS system
• Analyze results
• Understand requirements.

Compared with the traditional approach one interesting difference is that analysts frequently understood their requirements, and the data available to them, only after they had the opportunity to perform various kinds of analysis on that data, so the requirements understanding phase is pushed to the end of the cycle. There is a consensus between researchers in the main steps of the development, which is presented by figure 3.

The above mentioned data-driven, iterative development approach is quite common and widely used by the software companies too. SAS[1] in his white paper offer similar methodology (SAS, 1998), namely SAS Rapid Warehouse

*Figure 3. Data warehouse's development cycle*

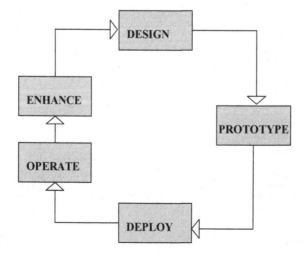

Methodology. The iterative approach has several advantages:

- It allows organizations to reduce the risks in the data warehouse project and achieve a more rapid return on investment
- Organizations can deal with a single data mart or multiple components of a warehouse environment
- Project teams can deliver success faster, regardless of the size of the project or the business area addressed.

Data warehouse design is based on dimensional modelling, which supports high volume querying. This model is implemented by star schemas (figure 4). Star schemas contain central fact table in order to record attributes, which are needed to perform analysis. Other parts of the star schema are dimension tables, linked to the fact table by foreign keys. Dimension tables contain attributes that describe data contained within the fact table. Dimension tables are addressed how the data will be analysed, and fact table shows what data is analysed.

One of the key issues of data warehouse design is the *granularity*. Granularity refers to the level of detail or summarization of the units of data in the data warehouse. The more detail there is, the lower the level of granularity. Granularity determines the type of queries that can be answered in the data warehouse environment and it deeply affects the volume of data that resides in the data warehouse.

In spite of the growing interest in dimensional modelling, entity relationship models can be used to support a data warehousing too (Ballard, 1998). Data warehouse development can be managed several ways. Eckerson distinguished four ways to develop a data warehouse (Eckerson, 2003), which include: top-down, bottom-up, hybrid and federated approach.

The *top-down approach* views the data warehouse as the glue of the entire analytic environment. The data warehouse holds atomic or transaction data that is extracted from one or more source systems and integrated within a normalized, enterprise data model. This approach is advocated by Bill Inmon. A *bottom-up approach*, aims to deliver business value by deploying dimensional

*Figure 4. Star schema*

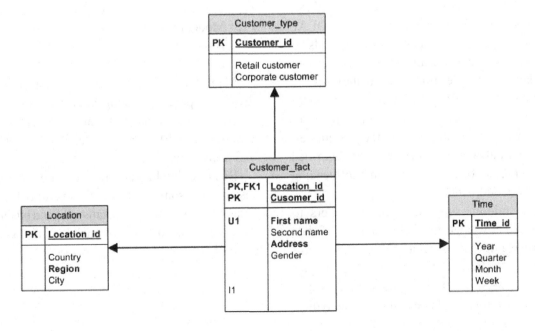

data marts as fast as possible. Data model follows a star schema design for satisfying usability and query performance. Bottom-up approach is represented by Ralph Kimball.

The most important advantages of bottom-up approach are the flexible data structures, customization, no need to drill through from data mart to another structure to obtain detailed data (data marts contain both summary and atomic data) and fast value delivery (no need to build a complex environment).

Difficulties with bottom-up approach are that they designed to optimize queries, so in many cases they don't support batch or transaction processing. Organizations using bottom-up approach needs additional data sources if they need data mining and operational reporting.

The *hybrid approach* tries to combine the best of both "top-down" and "bottom-up" approaches. *Federated approach* is the less known one, from the above discussed ways. It is a complement of the traditional ETL process[2] by creating a single logical view of a single warehouse. Data remains in separate systems in this approach. Semantic web offers another way for data integration, because it can be used to wrap data into repositories.

Organizational assets in data warehouse are utilized by several business intelligence solutions, like reporting, OLAP and data mining. OLAP (online analytical processing) provide methods for managers to conduct analysis on data, slice and dice data, meanwhile visualisation of the steps and the results is supported. Databases customized for OLAP employ a multidimensional data model, allowing for complex analytical and ad-hoc queries. Concepts and characteristics of OLAP described by several authors, one of the most influencing is Codd (Codd, 1993).

Data mining supports decision-makers to discover knowledge in a huge amount of data e.g. revealing hidden relationships, rules, correlations, predictions. It uses several techniques from the fields of statistics, artificial intelligence, machine learning, and mathematics. The typical classes of problems which fit well to data mining are the following:

- **Association:** determines relationship between events, which occur at one time; e.g. market basket analysis
- **Classification:** define characteristics of a certain group (set of classes are known); decision trees and neural networks are useful techniques for it
- **Clustering:** identifies items, which share certain characteristics; e.g. classes of customers
- **Forecasting:** estimates future values
- **Regression:** maps data to a prediction value
- **Sequencing:** determines relationship between events, which occur over a period of time; e.g. repeat visitors of a shop.

Data mining process can be described by the SAS methodology, namely "SEMMA" approach. SEMMA covers the following steps:

- Sampling
- Exploring (revealing data quality related problems)
- Manipulating (data quality improvement)
- Modeling
- Assessment.

Many authors have written about data mining theory and practice, amongst other Berry (2002), Linoff and Berry (1997), Han and Kamber (2004), Edelstein (1999), Adriaans and Zantige (2002) and Kantardzic (2002).

Business intelligence projects are time and resource consuming ones with several risks and challenges. Next session details risks and business continuity related issues of business intelligence solutions.

## RISKS AND BUSINESS CONTINUITY CHALLENGES IN BUSINESS INTELLIGENCE SOLUTIONS

Risks management have a central role in business continuity of business intelligence systems. This chapter presents main risks categories of business intelligence systems. I give a short overview about business continuity planning and its relation to business intelligence systems. During the discussion I rely on mainly materials of ISACA,[3] because they have a solid base of security and audit expertise. Its IS auditing and IS control standards are followed by practitioners worldwide.

Business intelligence systems, similarly other business-related areas cannot avoid risks. Several risks can occur during the development and the operation of business intelligence solutions. Most of them can occur in other IT projects too, but they are more serious here, because business intelligence projects are large-scale, costly projects. Generally these projects affect the whole organization, IT environment, processes, organizational culture and employees too. Business intelligence solutions require right organizational culture, which is characterised by transparency, openness for information sharing and acceptance of fact-based analysis. These requirements are against of human nature as it is examined in several knowledge management books and studies too (Davenport, 2000). As it was stated by Sir Francis Bacon, "knowledge is power" and employees try to preserve their knowledge monopoly, if they have a possibility for it. Contrarily organizations interest to codify their knowledge assets in order to avoid the reinvention the wheel and make profit from it. Therefore besides the technical risks categories, we have to pay attention to the human-related risks too. Organizations are coping with a wide variety of internal and external threats, like (ISACA, 2008):

- **Intentional non-physical threats:** malicious code, identity theft, social engineering, fraud
- **Intentional physical threats:** fire, bomb, theft
- **Unintentional threats:** equipment failure, building damage, fire, water
- **Natural threats:** flood, fire, earthquake, rain.

## Risks Categories of Business Intelligence Systems

Risk is defined by ISACA as a potential that a given threat will exploit vulnerabilities of an asset or a group of assets to cause loss of/or damage to assets (ISACA, 2008). Risks categories are discussed by several authors and by many project management approaches, like PRINCE2, PMBOK (Bentley, 2003), (PMI, 2003). The following risks categories can be used as a starting point at identification of risks related business intelligence projects (OGC, 2002):

- Strategic risks
  - No mission or objective
  - Weak or loss of the sponsor
  - Management is under-perform against expectations
  - Insufficient or inadequate budget
  - Partnership failing
- Data-related risks
  - Quality of source data is not known
  - Source data has no documentation
  - Source data are not understood
  - Data quality is not sufficient
- IT environment-related risks
  - Lack of supporting software
  - Multiple platform (e.g. source data management is done by multiple platform)
  - Geographically distributed environment
  - Contaminated Database
  - Computer processing disruption
  - Loss of key components
  - Loss of key intellectual property

- ○ New technology platform/invention
- BI solution-related risks
  - ○ Metadata is not properly defined
  - ○ BI models don't fit to the problem
  - ○ Outcome of the analysis is not understood
- BI system development-related risks
  - ○ Scope creep
  - ○ Users requirement are not understood
  - ○ Architectural risks
  - ○ Design risks
- Information security risks
  - ○ Unauthorized disclosure or modification of information
  - ○ Computer Virus
  - ○ Facility access control
  - ○ Fire wall breach - external access
  - ○ Intellectual property espionage
  - ○ Inappropriate use of information
  - ○ Information security depends on other risk-creating management functions (marketing, documentation, strategy, etc.)
  - ○ No information safety procedure in the organization
  - ○ No information safety training programme
- Organizational/human risks
  - ○ Key people may leave the project
  - ○ Skills are not in place
  - ○ Users are not familiar with IT environment
  - ○ Culture inadequacies
    - ▪ Culture of non-communication
    - ▪ Culture of navel-gazing
    - ▪ Culture of infallibility
    - ▪ Culture of simples
  - ○ No crisis situation planning
  - ○ Cutting down responsibilities
  - ○ No feedback system
  - ○ No problem and change management
  - ○ Poor leadership
  - ○ Terminological inconsistencies
- Regulatory risks

- ○ Antitrust
- ○ Changes in Leasing Law
- ○ Civil Action
- ○ Contractual Liability
- ○ Currency Exchange Rates
- ○ Changes in Data Protection Law
- ○ Financial Transactions
- ○ Internet Liability
- ○ Lack of Information
- ○ Licensing Failure
- ○ Market Change
- ○ Political Risk/Taxation
- ○ Privacy Law
- ○ Regulatory Ambiguity.

Additionally general risks categories have to be counted e.g.:

- Natural risks
  - ○ Biological contamination
  - ○ Drought
  - ○ Dust Storm/ Sand Storm
  - ○ Earthquake
  - ○ Epidemics/Pandemic
  - ○ Extreme temperature - heat/cold
  - ○ Fire
  - ○ Flood
  - ○ Hail
  - ○ Hurricane
  - ○ Ice Storm
  - ○ Infestation
  - ○ Landslide
  - ○ Lightning
  - ○ Rain Storms
  - ○ Sinkhole
  - ○ Snowstorm
  - ○ Subsidence/Landslide
  - ○ Tsunami
  - ○ Tornado
  - ○ Volcanic/Ash fallout/Lava
  - ○ Wind Storm
  - ○ Wild fire/Smoke
- Manmade risks:
  - ○ Bomb Threat

- ○ Common carrier strike/failure
- ○ Hacking
- ○ Human Error - Non-Employee or Contractor
- ○ Vendor failure
- ○ Intruder
- ○ Theft
- ○ Computer Crime
- ○ Disgruntled Employee
- Environmental risks
  - ○ Fire
  - ○ Liquid Damage (Burst Pipes)
  - ○ Power Outage/Failure
  - ○ Water supply break

From the discussed risks categories, culture inadequacies need additional explanation (Martinet & Marti, 1996). Culture of non-communication means, that there is a resistance against change, especially against technical change. Additionally there is no dialogue between the various departments, which can cause really difficult situation in a BI projects, where several departments have to cooperate. Culture of navel-gazing describes the situation when an organizational unit certain about that their competitors are lagging behind in business and competitive intelligence. Culture of infallibility demonstrates the situation when an organization is sure about its success; they think that they cannot have any failings. Culture of simples means that organization think, that information protection is simple, so few actions are enough to take, e.g. to install cameras.

In spite of the fact, that no model provides a complete picture, risks categories facilitate focusing on key risks management strategies and activities. During his best practice analysis for a typical BI project, namely a data warehouse development, Weir and his colleagues found that more influencing factors are the following (Wier, 2002):

- Data quality

- Training requirements
- Management buy-in and

Less influential factors are the next:

- Project must fit with corporate strategy and business objectives
- End user buy-in
- Manage expectations
- Make time to review progress.

Based on Weir and his colleagues view, one of the most important risk categories are data-related risks. Data quality has a key role in BI projects success; it determines the data usefulness and the quality of decisions too. Data integration and loading can't be automated fully; they require human experts to assist the process, which makes them more risky.

Another speciality of spreading business intelligence solutions, that additional privacy – related risks can appear. Data managers handle personal data, which can be associated with additional information about customers, e.g. their buying habits, their interest's fields, favourite internet applications, telecommunication and media appetites. This information can threaten customer's privacy. Regulation has a key role from these aspects, and IT can offer additional support for protection, like PET (Privacy Enhanced Technology).

Management buy-in factor's importance is obvious, no hit without management commitment; they can provide the necessary resources for a project. A bit surprising, that end user buy-in is less important, because they have also a decisive role in BI projects. Another interesting outcome of their examination is that training requirements are more stressful than the project must fit with corporate strategy and business objectives. Contrary to their opinion, project management methods, like PRINCE2, emphasize a business case – guided approach, so business objectives are stressed more, than training.

ISACA conducted a survey recently amongst ISACA members about top business/technology issues (ISACA, 2007) in which they appointed, that challenges of managing IT risks belongs to the top seven business issues. Responders emphasized most the lack of senior management commitment to IT risk management. Other emphasized issues were the following:

- IT risk illiteracy and lack of awareness
- Poor funding and staffing for risk management purposes
- Risk management processes, if any, don't follow generally accepted principles, practices and standards.

These results draw an attention again to the importance of human resource management related issues in risks management. One of the key field in risks reducing is business continuity planning. Next session gives an overview about it.

## Overview of Business Continuity Planning

Information systems business continuity planning (IS BCP) is a process, which aims to reduce, manage the risks threatening IS processing. The IS BCP has to be consistent with corporate business continuity plan and it should be based on the organizational strategy. Generally BCP process has the following life cycle phases (ISACA, 2008):

- Creation of business continuity policy
- Business impact analysis
- Classification of operation and criticality analysis
- Identification of IS processes that support critical organizational functions
- Development of business continuity plan and IS disaster recovery procedures
- Development of resumption procedures
- Training and awareness program
- Testing and implementation of the plan
- Monitoring.

Business continuity plan is one of the most important corrective control in an organization, which depends on other controls, like incident management. Control is defined by ISACA as follows: policies, procedures, practices and organizational structures implemented to reduce risks are referred to as internal controls (ISACA, 2008, pp. 23).

Business impact analysis covers the identification of events, which can impact the continuity of operation and their financial, human, legal, reputational effect on the organization. To accomplish this task, organization has to be known well, which means that key business processes and their supporting IS resources have to be known. At least three areas are investigated during business impact analysis. First one is about business processes. Important business processes and their criticality have to be determined. Criticality of a business processes depends on characteristics such as time and mode of operation. One example for a critical business processes are paying employees and production. Second area of investigation is the collection of critical information resources related critical business processes. The third area is the critical recovery time period for information resources in which business processes have to be restored before significant or unacceptable losses are suffered. Next step of BCP process is classification of operation and criticality analysis. This step incorporates risks management; risks determination based on critical recovery time and likelihood calculation that a harmful disruption will occur. Risks management related issues are discussed in the following chapters more detailed. Risks-based analysis supports critical systems prioritization. Classification can have four types, critical, vital, sensitive and nonsensitive classes of systems can be distinguished, based on several factors, like the manual replacement possibilities, tolerance to interruption and cost of interruption. This prioritization is used for developing recovery strategies. Two fundamental metrics support recovery strategies determination, the recovery point objective and recovery time objective. Recovery point objective is the earliest point in time in which it is acceptable to recover data. Recovery time objective is the earliest point in time in which the business operation must recover after a disaster. The lower the recovery time objective, the lower the disaster tolerance. Recovery strategies and alternatives are discussed by several authors (ISACA, 2008), (Toigo, 2003), (Zawada & Schwartz, 2003) and standards (ITIL). Based on the business impact analysis, criticality analysis and recovery strategy selected by management, a detailed business continuity and disaster recovery plan is developed. Several factors should be considered during the development (ISACA, 2008), like procedures for declaring a disaster, clear identification of the responsibilities in the plan, explanation of the recovery plan, resources required for recovery. Without proper tests of business continuity plan, it is useless. Test determines how well the plan works, what kind of improvements are needed. Plan, its tests and business continuity strategy has to be reviewed and updated regularly. Business continuity plan should be based on long-range IT plan and it should comply with the business continuity strategy. Regular monitoring of business continuity process is crucial for reliable recovery strategies. Best practices, regulations, standards can provide support to accomplish these complex tasks, like COBIT and ITIL. Following chapter is about audit and monitoring issues of business intelligence systems, especially their business continuity audit.

## IT AUDIT RELATED ISSUES OF BUSINESS INTELLIGENCE SOLUTIONS AND MONITORING OF BUSINESS INTELLIGENCE SYSTEM'S BUSINESS CONTINUITY

Several IT audit challenges have to be managed in business intelligence field. First of all, BI services depend increasingly on data and the systems that deliver this data. These services are vulnerable and risky from security aspects, and they have to satisfy many requirements, like transparency, availability, accessibility, convenience, and compliance. IT environments are more and more complex and fragmented, which means additional security risks. Another difficulty is the communication gap between users and IT managers. They have different terminology, different background, which makes the cooperation demanding in a business intelligence projects. Business intelligence projects are complex, with several interrelated risks, as I demonstrated in the previous sections; therefore costs are often out of control. Users are frustrated, and this situation can lead to ad hoc solutions. Vulnerabilities and a wide spectrum of threats, such as cyber threats and information warfare are spreading. Compliance to the regulatory environment is another challenge. Because of the challenges mentioned above, IT audit has key role in business intelligence. Main objectives of IT auditing are to provide management with reasonable assurance that control objectives are being met; where the significant control weaknesses are, substantiate the resulting risk and advise management on corrective actions. Main steps of risk-based audit approach are the following:

- Obtaining an understanding of business requirements-related risks, and relevant control measures

- Evaluating the appropriateness of stated controls
- Assessing compliance by testing whether the stated controls are working as prescribed, consistently and continuously
- Substantiating the risk of the control objectives not being met by using analytical techniques and/or consulting alternative sources.

One of the most important issues which have to be emphasized during the monitoring of business intelligence projects and solutions are application controls. Application controls refer to the transactions and data relating applications. Their objectives are to ensure the completeness and accuracy of the records and the validity of entries. Data have a special role in BI services, so their proper quality is a must. Only complete, accurate and valid data are entered and updated to the BI system. Because of the risky nature of the development of business intelligence systems, auditing system development, acquisition and maintenance have to be stressed. According to the importance of business continuity and disaster recovery from business intelligence aspects, they are key audit areas as well. Management needs to get IT under control, which can be guaranteed by an IT control framework. One good candidate for IT control framework is COBIT, which is the most spreading and accepted standard by IT community. COBIT has several advantages. It incorporates major international standards, has become de facto standard for overall control over IT, starts from business requirements and it is process-oriented. COBIT supports almost the whole organization in audit-related activities, like executives (to ensure management follows and implements the strategic direction for IT management), management (to make IT investment decisions), users (to obtain assurance on security and control of products and services they acquire internally or externally) and auditors (to substantiate opinions to management on internal controls and to advise on what minimum controls are necessary).

ISACA founded in its survey about top business/technology issues (ISACA, 2007), that disaster recovery and business continuity belongs to the top seven business issues amongst ISACA members. The most important area of this domain (based on the responder's feedback) was business managers' lack of awareness of their responsibility to be able to maintain critical functions in the event of a disaster, which leads to business continuity management (BCM) not being a business-owned and business-driven process. Additional factors which were mentioned by the responders are the following:

- BCM approached as a "one-time" initiative and not as a process
- BCM regarded as a costly planning process and not as one that adds value to the enterprise
- Organizations seldom formalizing and enforcing a BCM policy.

During the audit of information system's business continuity, several tasks have to be performed, amongst other the following:

- Evaluation of business continuity strategy and its connection to business objectives
- Evaluation of business continuity plans
  ○ adequacy and currency
  ○ compliance to the relevant standards and regulations
  ○ effectiveness (evaluation of tests outcome)
  ○ maintenance
- Assessment of off-site storage
- Evaluation of personnel preparation (employee training, emergency procedures)
- Evaluation of business continuity manual (availability, intelligibility).

Audit of business continuity is challenging, but best practices and standards can help the audit process (Von Roessing, 2002). Regarding regulatory environment laws about data privacy and accuracy, non-disclosure of information of partners and confidentiality of data in transit are the most important issues. Next chapter demonstrates standards and best practices, which can be applied in monitoring of business intelligence solutions.

## IT AUDIT STANDARDS AND BEST PRACTICES

Discussion about IT standards can't be complete without IT governance. Key issues of IT governance (Van Grembergen, De Haes & Guldentops, 2003) are the following:

- Strategic alignment between IT and Business.
- Delivery of value to business through IT.
- Risk management.
- Performance management.

IT governance covers two main issues: that IT delivers value to the business and IT risks are managed. It is the responsibility of executive management and the board of directors. Ryan Peterson stresses that IT management deals with internal business orientation and short-term operational problems, whilst IT governance also focuses on external business orientation and has a longer-term perspective.

Based on ITGI's IT Governance Implementation Guide, there is a need for standards when implementing IT governance. Standards for IT audit and IT governance are crystallized by consensus or compromise from best practices discussed by a large group of individuals from various organizations. Standards or methodologies for managing IT services (e.g. COBIT and ITIL), security standards (e.g. Common Criteria, ISO 15408, ISO 17799/BS 7799-2), system acquisition (Bootstrap, ISO 12207), implementation

standards (PMBOK, PRINCE2), quality management (ISO 9001, EFQM), and risk management (COSO) and function point analysis are based on best practices. Most governance regulations (such as the Sarbanes-Oxley Act in the US) require the implementation of these best practices. Spreading of IT best practices has been driven by a requirement for the IT industry to better manage the quality and reliability of IT in business and respond to a growing number of regulatory requirements. Best practices, standards should be applied within the business context. Business management, auditors, and IT managers should cooperate to make sure IT best practices lead to cost-effective and well-controlled IT delivery. IT best practices are important because (ITGI, OGC, itSMF 2005):

- Management of IT is critical to the success of enterprise strategy
- They help enable effective governance of IT activities
- A management framework is needed so everyone knows what to do (policy, internal controls and defined practices)
- They provide many benefits, including efficiency gains, less reliance on experts, fewer errors, and increased trust from business partners and respect from regulators.

Organizations usually choose a de facto standard to be compliant (i.e., the risks of using an internally developed standard with omissions or errors are reduced by using de facto standards), and larger organizations have learned that drafting their own policies for security is often much more costly and less successful than basing their polices on a standard, e.g. on ISO 17799 (Oud, 2005). The challenge is that several standards exist, they overlap each other, and they progress in time; so it is difficult to find out which one is the best candidate in a complex situation. This section presents frameworks, which can be useful in revealing their relationship.

*Figure 5. Key issues of IT governance*

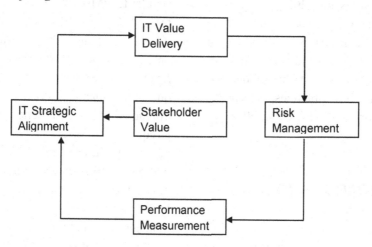

Some of the standards mentioned previously are part of a family of standards. For instance, BS 15000, the British Standard for IT Service Management, consists of two parts. Part one is the specification for service management, and part 2, the Code of Practice for Service Management, is one step lower in the hierarchy. Further down the hierarchy, ITIL gives best practice for the processes described in BS 15000, and the organisation's in-house procedures are found below that. Mapping of standards to each other cannot always be one-on-one, as it was done by the IT Governance Institute during its elaborate mapping of COBIT and ISO 17799, because the COBIT control objectives operate at a higher level and the detail of ISO/IEC 17799:2000 is much closer to the level of detail of the COBIT control practices.

Decisive standards can be mapped to the focus areas of the IT governance framework (figure 5) as follows:

- **IT strategic alignment:** COBIT, ITIL
- **IT value delivery:** PRINCE2, PMBOK
- **Risk management:** ISO 17799, ISO 13335
- **Performance management:** BS 15000, BS 7799
- **Stakeholder Value:** COSO.

Peterson's IT governance model can be applied as a framework, for mapping management and security standards (Peterson, 2003). Mapping a number of the aforementioned standards on Peterson's model is presented on figure 6.

The use of standards enhances the value of IT, but no standard covers every subject in detail. COBIT covers a large subset of all possible aspects but in some cases. It may need to be complemented. To decide where extra standards are required, the recent publication of the ITGI mapping project can be beneficial (ITGI, OGC, itSMF 2005).

Some researchers go beyond IT governance they suggest to introduce business intelligence governance (Fernández-González, 2008; Gutierrez, 2006; Leonard, 2008). IT governance often fails when applied to business intelligence. They can't manage to overcome the gap between IT and business, because of several reasons. One is the too IT-focused feature, which means to deal with information technologies, instead of information systems. Decision-makers need right information and they don't deal with the background technology, which was used to produce information. Another problem is the structured-focus character of IT department. Offering structured information won't fit to the decision support systems needs, because they are semi-structured. Various IT governance tools are structured around hypotheses

*Figure 6. Mapping of standards on Peterson's model*

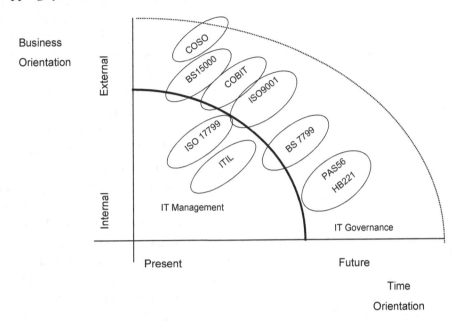

which decision-makers never consider, e.g. users of information systems are not taken into account enough, their needs are ignored, because the "IT knows better their wants". In many cases only CIO is emphasized, but they don't deal with other levels at which decisions are made. In order to see the whole business intelligence domain, to emphasize more the management and human-related side of the field, BI governance is defined recently. One of the most common determinations was given by Larson and Matney (Larson & Matney, 2008):

"It's the process of defining and implementing an infrastructure that will support enterprise goals. Jointly owned by IT and its business partners, the process evolves the direction and the value of BI as a strategy."

BI governance is based on agility, versatility, and human relations which are specifically designed to support decision makers. BI governance tries to manage the whole business intelligence landscape - strategic initiatives, business processes, data, and technology, so it can be a way to govern business intelligence projects.

## RISKS EVALUATION OF BUSINESS INTELLIGENCE SOLUTIONS BASED ON IT AUDIT STANDARDS AND GUIDELINES

Business intelligence solutions have strategic and therefore long term value for an organization, so risk management has a key role in business intelligence projects and it have to be supported by a common operational framework. Managers need current information about all forms risks, which require smooth cooperation and collaboration between the partners. Typical processes of risk management, considering IT audit recommendations are the following (ISACA 2008), (figure 7):

- Determination the scope of investigation
- Risks identification
- Risks analysis and evaluation
- Risks communication and treatment
- Risks monitoring.

Scope of investigation is the first step, in which necessary parameters are defined, so it determines

*Figure 7. Risk management framework*

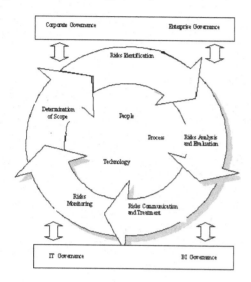

the domain of analysis. During risk identification a comprehensive list of risks is produced, which can have impact for the investigated domain. Risks are characterized by several factors, like its origin, event or accident, its consequences, its protecting mechanism and controls, its time and place of occurrence. Risks categories discussed in previous chapters can be applied as an input in risks identification. Level of risks is assessed during risk analysis phase. Sources of risks, the likelihood that the risks consequences may occur are investigated through this process, together with the assessment of existing controls. Risks analysis techniques are various, interviews with domain experts, using simulation, questionnaires. Risks evaluation is the phase where decision regarding which risks need treatment is defined. This decision is based on impacts (and cumulative impact) of the risks, likelihood of events.

Risks communication is the phase where the information about risks is shared between decision makers and stakeholders. Risks treatment is the process where measures to modify risks are selected and implemented. Risks monitoring is an iterative task for the enterprises, which guarantees that the risks treatment, actions are relevant, updated and complies with the stake-

holders need. Risks management process affected by several additional components, like people, process, technology and governance (figure 7). Risks management activities can't be separated by people, who are sources of risks and they need proper authorities, and competencies to accomplish their tasks. Business processes are influenced by risks management in many cases. They have to be updated and rearranged depending on the outcome of the risks management. Technology, risk management software helps to automate the risks management process, enhance the quality, and makes better and controllable the communication and cooperation activities. Governance (enterprise governance, corporate governance, IT governance and BI governance) has a key role in risk management process, because it determines how key decisions that affect the entire enterprise are prepared.

Organizations have at least four strategies to follow, during risk management:

- Accept the risk
- Treat the risks with proper control mechanism
- Transfer the risks for another party
- Terminate their activity.

The above described general risks management process can be customized for business intelligence projects as follows.

First step of the risk management according to the previously described general risk management process is risks identification. Risk identification is a list of risks, which we can determine in our business intelligence project. During risks identification a previously discussed risks categories can help, so the main categories can be the following: strategic risks, data-related risks, BI solution-related risks, human risks and regulatory risks. Next step is risks analysis and evaluation, where impacts of findings are revealed (table 1). A numeric value is assigned to each risk dimension with a range of 1 (commendable) through 5

*Table 1. Risk evaluation*

| Finding | Risk categories | Weighted Audit Rate | Significance level | Likelihood | Risk level |
|---|---|---|---|---|---|
| Description of finding. | Strategic risks | 3 | Low | High | Medium |
| | Data-related risks | 3 | | | |
| | BI solution-related risks | 1 | | | |
| | Human risks | 5 | | | |
| | Regulatory risks | 2 | | | |
| | Weighted audit rate | 2,8 | | | |

(unsatisfactory) (table 2). A weighted audit rate is the average calculated from the subjectively assigned value to each of the risk dimensions (in our example it is 2,8). Risk categories are the risks groups, which I described in the previous sections. If the weighted audit rate is below 3, the significance level is low, if it is 3, the significance level is medium, if it is above 3, and the significance level is high. Likelihood is a subjectively assigned value (it can be low, medium and high). The assigned level of likelihood is a reasonable reflection of a chance, that the weakness may be capitalized. Significance level and the likelihood determine risk level according to the risk rank matrix (table 3).

If a risk level is high, there are substantial deficiencies in our business intelligence project. If a risk level is medium, there are weaknesses, but not from the all aspects. If a risk level is low, the project activity was well managed.

After the analysis and evaluation next steps of

risks management framework should be followed. During the risks analysis audit rating scale was used. Rating can be a result of a compliance test using COBIT control objectives. One alternative for risks identification, analysis and evaluation is the application of COBIT (ITGI, 2005).

## CONCLUSION

Business intelligence has a key position in organization's life. They affect key areas like, corporate and IT strategy, business processes, performance management. Business intelligence solutions have to operate in a volatile environment, meanwhile their usage is high and growing. Besides the close competition between traditional business intelligence solutions, new technologies and solutions appeared recently. Open source systems endanger them from technological side, like e.g. BIRT (an open source Eclipse-based reporting system) with

*Table 2. Audit Rating Scale*

| Rating | Description |
|---|---|
| 5: Unsatisfactory | The auditable dimension/activity was not in compliance with policies, systems and procedures. |
| 4: Improvement is needed | The auditable dimension/activity was not always in compliance with policies, systems and procedures. |
| 3: Average | The auditable dimension/activity was generally in compliance with policies, systems and procedures. |
| 2: Good | The auditable dimension/activity was in compliance with policies, systems and procedures. Some control deficiencies were identified, but these are not expected to lead to major risk. |
| 1: Commendable | The auditable dimension/activity has achieved its goals and objectives. The auditable dimension/activity was in compliance with policies, systems and procedures. No significant control deficiencies were identified. |

*Table 3. Risk Rank Matrix*

| Significance level | Likelihood | Risk level |
|---|---|---|
| High | High | High |
| High | Medium | High |
| Medium | High | High |
| High | Low | Medium |
| Low | High | Medium |
| Medium | Medium | Medium |
| Low | Medium | Low |
| Medium | Low | Low |
| Low | Low | Low |

interactive OLAP applications, Pentaho BI Suite with metadata-based reporting and Jaspersoft. At the same time, data warehousing has to face with the new generation platforms, which provide higher performance and cheaper price. New innovative technologies are available now for data warehouses, which offer better figures for speed, capacity and price/performance. DW Appliance is the new term for data warehousing referring the "easy" deployment and operation. Unfortunately this is only the part of the truth. Typical problems, like loading of source data and training of users remain still. Because of special needs of data warehousing, programming improved a lot recently. One method for increasing speed is omission of indexing, which save storage capacity too.

Business intelligence role is more important in company's life nowadays, than it was in the past. The business intelligence market has been essentially transformed during the previous two years. Mega – vendors, like SAP, Oracle, IBM and Microsoft are the decisive actors. Acquisition influenced several independent players, like Cognos, Business Objects, Hyperion. According the new alliances, new integrated business intelligence services appeared. Consolidation process doesn't mean the BI market has reached its maturity, they have a huge potential to improve (Dresner, 2008).

Because of business intelligence solutions importance, their risks and business continuity issues have to be stressed. Risks have to be managed during their business continuity planning, and when risk-based audit is applied. Monitoring and IT audit of business intelligence solutions can offer a strong control for management. There are some critical challenges for business intelligence success, based on the literature and developers feedback. Data quality has to be emphasized; poor data quality has a bad impact on business profitability. Metadata definition and maintenance has a central role in business intelligence solutions, they has to be business driven. Some BI solutions offer central metadata management, which makes metadata handling more comfortable, because metadata repositories can offer additional functions beyond the querying, like classification and advanced searching capability. Web services can make available BI metadata for other applications. Metadata determines at the same time the types and scope of the outcome of business intelligence solutions.

Business intelligence project is a cross-organizational business initiative, so it requires different project management approach than a stand-alone project. Some project management areas, like project management organization, communication, risks management, problem and incident management have to be more stressed. User's involvement is mandatory to define requirements against business intelligence solution. Business intelligence competence centers appeared recently in companies' life. They provide business intelligence skills for maintenance and operation. IT support is not enough in this cases, one of the key question is, how to use BI tools properly in a certain business situation. Project management methods, like PRINCE2 can help a lot, to set up a proper project organization and to manage well all the previously mentioned areas.

User interfaces are becoming simpler in order to serve ad-hoc needs of users, but they have to be complex enough to provide the necessary analytical capabilities. For-medium term several business intelligence solutions developed functions, which help the integration with Microsoft Office products, e.g. with Microsoft Excel. This tendency can lower the necessary training costs. Another trend is the integrated, built-in usage of business intelligence services, like in new Microsoft Excel 2007. Business intelligence services will be used more widely, than before, which raises up new challenges. If BI tools are used widely in the organization, how we can avoid the inconsistencies and redundancies in reporting. New term namely BI 2.0, similarly to web 2.0 is used to describe the new concepts about the evolution of business intelligence. BI 2.0 services are simpler and more accessible; they provide personal analytical tools on an as-needed basis. Locating the right information to solve problems has to be supported by a semantic process, so results of semantic web can be utilized. The term is linked with real-time and event-driven BI, but it is really about the application of these technologies to business processes. Goal of BI 2.0 is to reduce the time between when an event occurs and when an action is taken - in order to improve business performance. The above discussed new tendencies transformed the business intelligence field. To sum up the most influencing ones are the following:

- built-in business intelligence services appear

- business processes and its relation to business intelligence are emphasized
- new BI governance methods are introduced
- BI solutions are offered to the whole organization, which raise new challenges, especially in data quality field
- semantic technologies are ready to be applied to enhance the potential of BI solutions.

At organizational level business intelligence is and will be glue between operative systems and decision support systems. It has a fundamental role for the whole information management. At personal level, there is growing risk of privacy and data protection. These challenges require modifications at the field of regulation (from government and from enterprises too). Individuals will have more responsibility in conscious usage of business intelligence services in near future.

## REFERENCES

Adriaans, P., & Zantige, D. (2002). *Adatbányászat*. Budapest, Hungary: Panem.

Ballard, C., Herreman, D., Bell, D. S. R., Kim, E., & Valencic, A. (1998). *Data modeling techniques for data warehousing*. IBM Corporation, International Technical Support Organization Study. Retrieved on August 21, 2008, from http://www.redbooks.ibm.com/redbooks/pdfs/sg242238.pdf

Bentley, C. (2003). *Prince 2: A practical handbook*. Oxford: Butterworth-Heinemann.

Berry, M. J. A. (2002). *Mastering data mining MS with data mining set*. New York: John Wiley.

Berry, M. J. A., & Linoff, G. (1997). *Data mining techniques:For marketing, sales, and customer support*. New York: John Wiley.

Boehm, B. W. (1988). A spiral model of software development and enhancement. [Los Alamitos, CA: IEEE Computer Society Press.]. *Computer IEEE, 21*(5), 61–72.

Codd, E. F., Codd, S. B., & Salley, C. T. (1993). *Providing OLAP (online analytical processing) to user-analysts: An IT mandate*. Codd & Date, Inc. Retrieved on August 21, 2008, from http://www.fpm.com/refer/codd.html

Davenport, T., & Prusak, L. (2000). *Working knowledge*. Boston, MA: Harvard Business School Press.

Dresner, H. (2008). *Howard Dresner predicts the future of business intelligence*. Retrieved on September 10, 2008 from http://searchdatamanagement.techtarget.com/generic/0,295582,sid91_gci1308688,00.html

Eckerson, W. (2003). Four ways to build a data warehouse. What works. *Best Practices in Business Intelligence and Data Warehousing*, 15. Chatsworth, CA: Data Warehousing Institute.

Edelstein, H. A. (1999). *Introduction to data mining and knowledge discovery* (3rd edition). Potomac, MD: Two Crows Corp.

Fernández-González, J. (2008). Business intelligence governance, closing the IT/business gap. *The European Journal for the Informatics Professional, IX*(1). Retrieved on September 25, 2008, from http://www.upgrade-cepis.org/issues/2008/1/upgrade-vol-IX-1.pdf

Gutierrez, N. (2006). *White paper: Business intelligence (BI) governance*. Retrieved on September 23, 2008, from http://www.infosys.com/industries/retail-distribution/white-papers/bigovernance.pdf

Han, J., & Kamber, M. (2004). *Adatbányászat-Koncepciók és technikák (Data mining. Concepts and techniques.)*. Budapest, Hungary: Panem.

Inmon, W. H. (2002). *Building the data warehouse* (3rd edition). New York: Wiley.

ISACA. (2007). *Top business/technology issues survey results*. Retrieved on September 26, 2008 from http://www.isaca.org/Content/ContentGroups/Research1/Deliverables/ISACA_Research_Pubs/Top_Bus-Tech_Survey_Results_1Aug08_Research.pdf

ISACA. (2008). *CISA review manual 2008*. IL: ISACA.

ITGI. OGC, & itSMF. (2005). *Aligning COBIT, ITIL, and ISO 17799 for business benefit*. Retrieved on September 18, 2008, from http://www.isaca.org/ContentManagement/ContentDisplay.cfm?ContentID=32757

ITGI. (2008). *COBIT 4.1*. Retrieved on September 16, 2008, from http://www.isaca.org/Template.cfm?Section=COBIT6&Template=/TaggedPage/TaggedPageDisplay.cfm&TPLID=55&ContentID=7981

Kantardzic, M. (2002). *Data mining: Concepts, models, methods, and algorithms*. USA: Wiley-IEEE Press.

Kimball, R., & Ross, M. (2002). *The data warehouse toolkit second edition–the complete guide to dimensional modeling*. New York: Wiley Computer Publishing.

Larson, D., & Matney, D. (2008). The four components of BI governance. Retrieved on September 17, 2008, from http://www.bibestpractices.com/view/4681

Leonard, B. (2008). *Framing BI governance*. Retrieved on September 16, 2008, from http://www.bi-bestpractices.com/view/4686

Luhn, H. P. (1958). A business intelligence system. *IBM Journal*. Retrieved on August 19, 2008, from http://www.research.ibm.com/journal/rd/024/ibmrd0204H.pdf

Martinet, B., & Marti, Y. M. (1996). *Diagnostic grid for business intelligence risks. Protecting information in business intelligence, the eyes and ears of the business.* Paris: Editions d'Organisation.

OGC (Great Britain Office of Government Commerce). (2002). *Managing successful projects with Prince2: Reference manual.* London: The Stationery Office.

Oud, E. J. (2005). The value to IT of using international standards. [ISACA.]. *Information Systems Control Journal, 3,* 35–39.

Peterson, R. R. (2003). Information strategies and tactics for information technology governance. In W. Van Grembergen (Ed.), *Strategies for information technology governance.* Hershey, PA: Idea Group Publishing.

PMI (Project Management Institute). (2003). *A guide to the project management body of knowledge* (3rd edition). Project Management Institute. Retrieved from http://hu.wikipedia.org/wiki/Speci%C3%A1lis:K%C3%B6nyvforr%C3%A1sok/193069945X

Power, D. J. (2007). *A brief history of decision support systems,* version 4.0. Retrieved on August 19, 2008, from http://dssresources.com/history/dsshistory.html

SAS. (1998). *Rapid warehousing methodology.* A SAS White Paper. Retrieved in August 2008, from http://www.sas.com

SAS. (2008). *SAS history.* Retrieved on August 19, 2008, from http://www.sas.com/presscenter/bgndr_history.html#2008

Toigo, J. W. (2003). *Disaster recovery planning: Preparing for the unthinkable* (3rd edition). USA: Prentice-Hall.

Turban, E., Aronson, J. E., & Tin-Peng, L. (2005). *Decision support systems and intelligent systems* (7th edition). Upper Saddle River, NJ: Pearson Prentice-Hall.

Van Grembergen, W., De Haes, S., & Guldentops, E. (2003). Structures, processes, and relational mechanisms for IT governance. In W. Van Grembergen (Ed.), *Strategies for information technology governance.* Hershey, PA: Idea Group Publishing.

Von Roessing, R. (2002). *Auditing business continuity: Global best practices.* USA: Rothstein Associates.

Weir, R., Peng, T., & Kerridge, J. (2002). *Best practice for implementing a data warehouse: A review for strategic alignment.* Retrieved on August 19, 2008, from, http://ftp.informatik.rwth-aachen.de/Publications/CEUR-WS/Vol-77/05_Weir.pdf

Zawada, B., & Schwartz, J. (2003). Business continuity management standards-a side-by-side comparison. *Information Systems Control Journal, 2.* Retrieved on August 21, 2008, from http://www.isaca.org/Template.cfm?Section=Home&Template=/ContentManagement/ContentDisplay.cfm&ContentID=15903

## ENDNOTES

[1]   SAS is a software company, leader in business analytics, analytical software and services. SAS stood for "statistical analysis software, was created by Jim Goodnight and N.C. State University colleagues, including John Sall, in the early 1970s to analyze agricultural-research data (SAS 2008).

[2]   Extract Transform, Load - programs periodically extract data from source systems, transform them into a common format, and

then load them into the target data source, typically to a data warehouse or data mart.

[3] ISACA stands for Information Systems Audit and Control Association, has become a global

organization for information governance, control, security and audit professionals.

# Chapter 3
# Collaborative Systems for Decision Making for Disaster Preparedness and Response

**Deirdre Hahn**
*Arizona State University, USA*

**Jessica Block**
*Arizona State University, USA*

**Mark Keith**
*Arizona State University, USA*

**Ajay Vinze**
*Arizona State University, USA*

## ABSTRACT

*Real time collaboration solutions are critical during a large scale emergency situation and necessitate the coordination of multiple disparate groups. Collaborative technologies may be valuable in the planning and execution of disaster preparedness and response. Yet, research suggests that specific collaborative technologies, such as group decision support systems, are not often leveraged for decision-making during real time emergency situations in the United States. In this chapter, we propose a theoretical model of the impact of disaster immediacy and collaboration systems on group processes and outcomes. Using a 3D model of the dimensions of space, time, and situation, we explore media richness and group polarization within the context of collaboration technologies and disaster situations. We also present the next generation of collaboration technology extensions in order to address the need for more contemporary decisional settings. This set of principles and theories suggest how collaborative technologies may be positioned to better manage future disasters.*

## INTRODUCTION

Hurricane Katrina is considered the worst natural disaster in American history, affecting 92,000 square miles of land (Moynihan, 2007) and killing 1,464 people (LA Dept of Health and Hospitals, 2006). Katrina created a situation where federal, state, and local agencies had to collaborate in an unprecedented way. Despite extraordinary response

DOI: 10.4018/978-1-60566-723-2.ch003

by both civilian and military relief organizations, the response aid to Hurricane Katrina was almost entirely a failure. No single individual or agency took charge in the beginning of the event, and the failure to establish a unified command among these organizations prohibited organized decision making and execution of relief activities. It was reported that the head of the American Red Cross was refused access to the Superdome at the height of the crisis, and that trucks with supplies donated by Walmart were turned back by security forces and local boat owners were prevented from delivering aid supplies (Mindtel, 2005).

According to government reports, the greatest failure in the emergency response to Hurricane Katrina was an astonishing lack of communication and coordination between military and local law enforcement, with civilian organizations (Moynihan, 2007). Demand for resources and services surge during a crisis, often before decision makers make the needful allocations. Decision-makers must prioritize issues in real time across multiple variables such as cost, impact, and ease of recovery while ensuring that a base level consensus is maintained. The stark reality, learned after the fact, was that the ability of the responding agencies to deal with uncertain information in a straightforward way and reach consensus hinged on the quality of collaboration of groups *prior* to the emergency. In other words, the efforts of emergency responders and aid organizations to practice group collaboration before the emergency may have created higher levels of situational awareness and, thus, more rational responses during Katrina.

Practicing complex collaboration scenarios through table top exercises or simulations prior to an emergency situation is now standard group work for most emergency aid organizations. What is not standard is an understanding of the role that collaborative systems and technology play for group settings in disaster preparedness. As exemplified during Hurricane Katrina, coordination of disparate organizations during planning

and execution can be extremely complex, and as such, it is important to examine if collaborative systems could aid in the coordination of these groups. Leveraging collaboration systems and decision support technology enhancements could change planning for disaster preparedness as well as emergency response coordination from both a theoretical and practical perspective.

## Decision Support Systems

Decision support systems (DSS) and interactive computer based information and knowledge systems, have been around for over the last 30 years to support business and organizational decision making. DSS tools allow users to make real-time decisions by organizing raw data, managing information, controlling inventory, and running models. A specialized extension of DSS, group support systems (GSS), was developed as a solution to specifically improve group decision making processes. GSS applications started to become commercialized in the late 80's and early 90's, using computer technologies specially designed to facilitate group decision making, minimize negative group dynamics and enhance positive influences of individual input within a group. Commercial examples of a GSS application include GroupSystems™, Facilitate.com, and Zing Technologies. Significant research supports the multiple collaborative benefits of computer-based GSS tools for more effective meetings and coordination of group efforts (DeSanctis & Gallupe, 1987; El-Shinnawy & Vinze, 1998; Isenberg, 1986; Nunamaker, Dennis, Valacich, Vogel, & George, 1991; Rains, 2005).

Multiple terms have been used to describe the set of technologies which facilitate group collaboration and decision making: Decision Support Systems (DSS), Group Support Systems (GSS), group decision support systems (GDSS), computer-supported collaborative work (CSCW), collaboration technology (CT). Typically, the use of CT is considered or analyzed in terms of its ability to support and facilitate the group decision-making process. This process can take place across physical space such as face-to-face (FTF) or distributed meetings, and can occur at varying times such as in synchronous or asynchronous collaboration settings (DeSanctis & Gallupe, 1987; El-Shinnawy & Vinze, 1998; Nunamaker et al., 1991; Rains, 2005).

Real time solutions are critical during a large scale emergency situation and necessitate the coordination of multiple disparate groups. When dealing with ongoing emergencies, critical time constraints exist and traditional face-to-face meetings may be impossible either before or during the emergency. Collaborative technologies may be valuable in the planning and execution of disaster preparedness and response. Yet surprisingly, research suggests that CT have not been leveraged in real time emergency situations in the United States or elsewhere (cf. GSS literature review by Rains, 2005).

The disaster preparedness and response context implies the need to consider a third dimension of CT use viewed as need for CT both *before and after* the disaster (disaster preparedness) versus *during* the disaster (disaster response). This chapter examines the specific role collaborative technologies could have for both disaster preparedness planning and emergency situations by proposing a theoretical model of group decision making before, during, and after a disaster. In this chapter, we also suggest the term *collaboration system* (CS) to refer to a set of group collaboration technology and techniques that combine the information processing capabilities needed to support collaborative group decision making.

## BACKGROUND

**Before the Storm:** In the case of Hurricane Katrina, existing relationships among responders had become fragile before the onset of the storm. Due to its incorporation with the Department of

Homeland Security, Federal Emergency Management Administration (2005), or FEMA, lost certain critical capacities to enable preparedness which limited FEMA's ability to respond and weakened critical communication pathways with other responders. The result damaged relationships with state responders (Moynihan, 2007) and created a lack of trust among those responders. Ultimately, there was an inability for the responders to collaborate successfully because of a non-existent hierarchy of command and control. In contrast, there was an overwhelming response from outside the existing network of people who urgently wanted to help. The rapidly expanding network of responders was very difficult to coordinate within the existing network of government and military responders (Moynihan, 2007). FEMA under Department of Homeland Security, was unprepared, could not comprehend the scale of the event, or coordinate the overall network of responders waiting to help.

**During the Storm:** The lack of set command and control structures during Katrina disrupted efficient information sharing once the storm made landfall. The communication network was further compromised because many of the designated first responders became victims and needed aid themselves. Critical shortcomings of collaboration and information sharing prevented real-time adaptive decision making during Hurricane Katrina. The government authorities did not have a plan in place for evacuating citizens who did not have their own transportation or alternative shelter (H.R. No. 109-396, 2006). For example, during the storm FEMA turned down the state's suggestion to use school buses for evacuation citing the lack of air conditioning as the reason. Governor Kathleen Blanco reported waiting days for the FEMA appointed buses to arrive. The Governor assumed the buses were coming from somewhere in close proximity to the city, but when the buses made it to New Orleans days later, many of the sickest and weakest were dying or already dead (Millhollon, 2005). The essential geospatial information from FEMA was not shared, preventing the governor from adapting and responding efficiently. Although preparations had been made to be ready for a category 5 hurricane, the organizations responsible for acting lacked the structures to adapt to changes in information.

Problems before the storm versus issues during the storm required different collaboration systems. Before Katrina, the organizational changes made in FEMA led to severe under-preparedness and a poor communication infrastructure among those who would need to work closely together in the event of a disaster. During Katrina, responders were hampered by a poor command and control structure and limited communication among the appropriate group members. Targeted use of collaborative technologies may have allowed group members to be better connected in real time despite damages to the communication infrastructure.

## The 3-Dimensional Domain of Group Decision-Making

In prior research, CTs are considered in terms of the four quadrants generated by the space and time dimensions: 1) same time, same place; 2) same time, different place; 3) different time, same place; 4) different time, different place. For example, in quadrant 1, groups meet FTF and may not necessitate any CT at all (or used only to reduce the negative processes that FTF groups encounter). In quadrant 2, CT is required which will allow real time communication among members in different places such as audio, video, or internet conferencing. Groups collaborating in the quadrant 3 context need CT which will store group data in a centralized and accessible location so that members can review and contribute to the group output as their schedules permit. Because of internet capabilities, many groups which would fall into the 3rd quadrant now fit quadrant 4 where CTs storing group outputs are made accessible on the Web so that members do not need to meet in a centralized location. Disasters may force groups

into suboptimal quadrants. For example, Hurricane Katrina likely prevented groups, who would have traditionally met FTF, from using conferencing technology because of obstructed roads or lack of transportation.

Figure 1 illustrates these four quadrants plus the additional quadrants generated by the disaster dimension of before/after versus during. We can further examine the implications of this additional dimension for group processes and collaborative systems through theories associated with *media richness* and the *group decision-making processes*.

## Media Richness

Media richness refers to the extent to which a particular communication medium can reproduce the information being sent over it (Daft & Lengel, 1986). The need for media richness becomes increasingly important during a disaster versus before or after. In the CT context media richness refers to how well the technology can represent the group's verbal and non-verbal cues and information. For example, FTF is often considered as the "richest" communication medium because it is synchronous and all verbal and non-verbal cues can be conveyed. At the opposite extreme, email is one of the "least rich" communication media because it is asynchronous and usually only text is shared.

Media richness theory posits that optimal performance is achieved for a group task when the demands for communication richness are met by the capabilities of the communication media used to perform the task. Highly uncertain environments require highly rich media (Daft & Lengel, 1986). Therefore, if disaster circumstances require that critical decision makers cannot meet FTF, then the CT used must provide adequate media richness to allow group members to reach decisions as quickly and efficiently as possible.

*Figure 1. The 3-dimensional domain of group decision-making for disaster preparedness and response*

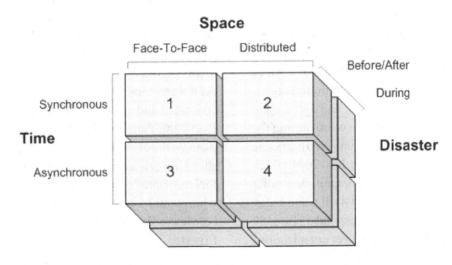

## Group Decision-Making Process

Another way to understand the implications of the dimensions in Figure 1 is in terms of how each quadrant impacts the group decision-making process. As with media richness, the process of group decision-making in disasters is heavily influenced by the time dimension.

One of the predominant themes in the literature on group decision-making is identifying the factors, and interactions among factors, that influence the group decision-making processes and outcomes. Common factors studied in the literature include: communication medium/technology used, task context, group member characteristics, group size, space and time dimensions (DeSanctis & Gallupe, 1987; El-Shinnawy & Vinze, 1998; Nunamaker et al., 1991; Rains, 2005). The group process itself is often conceptualized in terms of the persuasive arguments made before coming to a decision (El-Shinnawy & Vinze, 1998; Sai, Tan & Wei 2002). This is because *persuasive arguments theory* posits that a group's decision is determined by the persuasive arguments made among the group members (Lamm & Myers, 1978). These arguments are often based on the data and information that is available to the group. The group

decision-making process will differ before versus during a disaster in terms of: 1) the CTs needed to support the decision-making process, and 2) the ability of group members to make effective persuasive arguments.

Consider quadrant 1 of Figure 1 which represents a group collaborating FTF in a synchronous environment. Before a disaster, CT can be used to brainstorm a large number of decision alternatives which can then be considered individually. CT applications such as ThinkTank™ allow for categorization of ideas and detailed voting techniques. There are a variety of CTs which can support this type of task. Simulations via table top exercises can be performed to generate hypothetical data to augment CT application use. However, during a disaster, there is the need for immediate action and timely data-based decisions and less of a need for hypothetical brainstorming. The persuasive arguments made among group members will also differ before versus during a disaster. Before the disaster, the arguments are based on hypothetical data and simulated information, whereas during the disaster, real-time factual data and information is used. During a disaster, technologies which allow rich data processing must be made available to multiple group members and updated in real-time. This difference will likely influence the effectiveness of persuasive arguments before versus during a disaster.

The act of simulating a disaster in the field or in a virtual space can highlight the needed coordination that responders have not thought of before. It also provides a setting for multiple agencies to practice communication and agree upon the structure for command and control during the event. "Hurricane Pam," was a simulated hurricane disaster exercise carried out in July 2004 which coincidentally had assumed a magnitude similar to that of Katrina's (FEMA, 2004). It was a 5-day exercise in which emergency responders from 50 parish, state, federal, and volunteer organizations worked together to design joint response plans for a catastrophic hurricane in Louisiana (H.R. No. 109-396, 2006). The atmospheric simulation run at Louisiana State University simulated a Hurricane Pam at 120 mile per hour winds, 20 inches of rain in some parts of Louisiana, and a storm surge that topped levees in the New Orleans area (FEMA, 2004). During the Hurricane Pam simulation, participants broke into groups to design response scenarios in areas of evacuation, medical care, search and rescue, and temporary shelter. The Southeast Louisiana Catastrophic Hurricane Plan was the first product out of the workshops, which was considered the first step towards creating a comprehensive hurricane response plan. Although it was a preliminary document, participants agreed that it helped medical officials prepare and respond to Katrina. Local, state, and federal governments also agreed that the Plan helped them evacuate more people pre-landfall (H.R. No. 109-396, 2006).

Parish and state government participants saw the Hurricane Pam exercise as a contract of responsibilities. After Katrina, the same groups stated that the federal government did not carry out what it committed to doing during the exercise. The Hurricane Pam simulations did not convince all of the group members to follow through with the group decisions. This is because the persua-sive arguments made before a disaster occurs are only hypothetical. There is room for doubt among group members concerning the validity of the data and information produced by the simulation. As a result, it is more difficult to make persuasive arguments before a disaster versus during a disaster. As it were, topics such as evacuation, relocation, command and control were discussed during the Hurricane Pam simulation exercise, but further plans were not written because the follow-on workshops never occurred. The simulation workshops for Hurricane Pam were a good start in anticipating what would later occur during Katrina, but the Hurricane Pam simulation was meant only as a first step in the planning process.

In retrospect of Katrina, two critical requirements emerge for disaster preparedness and response: 1) the need for communication and collaboration between victims and responders (Comfort, 2007; Atlay & Green, 2006), and 2) the need for accurate data and information processing to coordinate and document the decisions made among collaborators (Mendonca, Beroggi, van Gent, & Wallace, 2006; Mendonca, 2007). A collaboration system would serve to bring these two requirements together in a streamlined model both before/after and during a disaster. The following section describes in greater detail two of the decision making areas such a system would need to address: 1) the group decision making process and 2) limitations to the quality of data and information used to make decisions.

## GROUP INFLUENCES

### Group Polarization

Group decision-making outcome is often framed in terms of the group's decision *polarization*. Group polarization refers to the tendency people have to make more extreme decisions when they are in a group setting versus when they are alone (Isenberg, 1986; Lamm & Meyers, 1978). Research on polarization has suggested that group discussion affects not only the extremeness of group decisions, labeled *choice shifts* (Zuber, Crott, & Werner, 1992), but also individual opinions, called *attitude shifts* (Hinsz & Davis, 1984). An example of choice shift occurs when two competing parties must come to a decision agreement that satisfies both parties, yet is more extreme than either party would have agreed to individually. Attitude shifts explain how individuals can gather useful information, but then ignore the data that doesn't support their attitude resulting in a less than optimal decision.

Isenberg's (1986) meta-analytic study revealed that the phenomenon of group polarization is driven primarily by two theories – *social comparison theory* and the *theory of persuasive arguments*. According to the theory of social comparisons (Baron & Roper, 1976; Brown, 1965), a group's decisions are affected by the social normative influences that occur because people tend to want to conform to the expectations of other members – particularly those with greater influence. In essence, as group members review the positions of others, they revise their decisions to align themselves with the social norm. As more and more group members revise their decisions, the group decision becomes polarized making the final decision appear to be far more supported than it initially was. On the other hand, the theory of persuasive arguments focuses on the collection and dissemination of information (Burnstein 1982; Heath & Gonzalez 1995; Vinokur & Burnstein, 1978) – rather than social influence. It posits that groups shift their decisions based on the relevant and factual information which are produced, presented, and shared among group members. Basically, each member collects and presents information to persuade others to agree with their decision. In general, the persuasiveness of an argument depends on its validity and degree of novelty (Burnstein 1982; Isenberg, 1986). Validity refers to how acceptable and relevant the argument is to the group discussion and novelty refers to how different or unique the

argument is from prior discussions (Vinokur & Burnstein, 1978). Therefore, the more persuasive the argument, the more a group will shift position and polarize the decision.

While there are studies to suggest that both social comparison and persuasive arguments alone are the leading indicator of choice shift (Heath and Gonzalez 1995; Paritt, 1994; Zuber et al., 1992), it is clear that both play a significant role in final group decision outcome. Collaborative technology applications, such as using GSS software and facilitation, play a role in aiding choice shift. CT can fundamentally change decision making quality by reducing the negative influence of social comparisons while enhancing the ability of members to make valid persuasive arguments using factual information (El-Shinnawy & Vinze, 1998). This is accomplished through specific tools found in GSS software. For example, brainstorming tools found in GSS software with guidance by a facilitator can provide anonymity to participant discussion inputs. Research suggests that anonymous input into decision making means that the "lowest" group member contribution is given as much attention as the "highest" authoritative figure in the group. Overall, GSS research has demonstrated that CT does help to reduce group polarization (El-Shinnawy & Vinze, 1998).

So, what could be expected to happen if CT alone is used for allocation planning before or during a disaster? In a recent study performed by the authors, approximately 144 MBA students were tasked with considering a set of public policy options for resource allocation. Participants were given a hypothetical amount of money to allocate across six different US social government programs. The purpose of the activity was to see if group polarization occurred during a decision making process if participants used a stand alone CT designed to minimize the effects of social normative influences.

Three steps were involved in the experiment. First, each participant made their resource allocation decision for the six social programs by themselves and then recorded their individual response. Second, the participants were put into small groups of six to eight members where they used the CT application ThinkTank™. This task was performed in a single room where the small groups convened in random seating arrangements and used their own laptop computers to access the ThinkTank™ software. Group members were given a fixed amount of time to discuss the six social government programs and make persuasive arguments for their discussions, through the software, about allocation of funding. The anonymity provided by the CT application meant that students were not necessarily aware of who was making the discussion contributions in their group. The group decisions were recorded using the features for polling provided by ThinkTank™. The purpose of this design was to reduce the possibility of normative influences as much as possible. Third, the small groups were combined into one large group. As a single large group, participants discussed the same six social government programs and made their own persuasive arguments concerning how the resource allocation should be distributed to the programs. Again, participant decisions were recorded through the CT polling. The results of the allocation indicated that participant decisions did change between the individual level, small group level, and large group level, becoming increasingly polarized despite the use of the tool.

Upon further examination of the actual comments and discussion recorded by ThinkTank™, it became clear to the authors that some group members found ways to exhibit normative influences despite the design of the CT tool to minimize this behavior through anonymous input. For example, participants often referred to themselves and others by name or made comments that identified the participant. More importantly, participants were making persuasive arguments based on their individual opinions as information offered by the researchers was limited regarding the social programs. The authors concluded that the use of a modern CT with anonymity and de-

tailed polling features may not effectively reduce the normative group influences when used alone and, in some cases, may actually increase group polarization—CT alone doesn't always level the playing field, so to speak. As such, any CT used for allocation decision making before or during a disaster should also be combined with other CT's that depict quality data and provide accurate information on which to base persuasive arguments. It is this combination of multiple CT's that define a collaboration system.

## Data and Information

Many existing CT's such as ThinkTank™, provide a platform for discussing and prioritizing ideas, when used alone, but do not provide a venue for viewing or analyzing critical information necessary to make the decisions. It becomes exponentially more complex to gather, transfer, and summarize data in real time from the 'field' into the decision-making arena during a disaster. For example, geographic information may be constantly changing in terms of where and how the disaster has compromised an area. Yet, this information is essential for coordinating the allocation of relief aid.

Remote sensing, global positioning systems (GPS), geographical information systems (GIS), Internet, cell phones, and traffic cameras—these are just some of the sources for data collection during a disaster. GPS is becoming standard in cars and cell phones making individuals in the field a part of the network of data collectors. Once enough people upload information of the same event, the data can be compared spatially and temporally to provide real-time comprehensive insight to the situation. With the latest technology in mobile PDA's and cell phones, the Internet can be accessed by most first responders and can be kept up to date using a common website for sharing information. During and after Hurricane Katrina made landfall the Internet was used for sharing information for missing persons and reuniting families (Mindtel, 2005). Today, the military is testing and evaluating the use of a web site hosted by Google called InRelief (http://partnerpage. google.com/inrelief.org) designed to share data between organizations involved in disaster response. However, transferring data for evaluation can still be a problem because the low bandwidth available for data sharing. Image acquisition companies are trying to solve this issue by finding new methods for transferring information in a resource limited environment. New 3G mobile networks are also becoming available to transfer data faster, such as with the new iPhone network. Ultimately, interoperability among software and data formats is the key for emergency responders be able to share each others' data.

Open source software is being explored as a venue for data sharing and for solving data interoperability issues. Open source allows users the freedom to adapt the software to their needs and also removes the interests of a private business trying to sell software. Software such as QGIS, OSSIM Planet, and Global Mapper are all geospatial data software packages that can process and visualize geographic datasets in standard formats that can be then shared among organizations. The accessibility of these free software packages continues to improve real-time data analysis capabilities.

The technologies listed above are addressing components of deficient informational influences on the decision making. Training and awareness remain an essential component to the integration to response plans. This is why simulations and table top exercises are an essential component to preparing response groups, building trust among responders, and putting in place a structure for command and control. In the case of Hurricane Katrina, responders to the disaster lacked the integration of real time data with CT decision software to create a collaboration system for use before/after and during the event.

## Model for a Collaboration System

Few studies have examined the impact of disaster response decisions when quality data and information processing capabilities is combined with CT software applications (i.e. ThinkTank™) to form a collaboration system. Furthermore, research has not demonstrated how the temporal state of an emergency situation--disaster immediacy— would change the utilization of a collaboration system. Combining prior research for CT group process (Benbasat & Lim, 1993; Dennis, Haley, & Vandenberg, 1996; Dennis, George, Jessup, Nunamaker & Vogel, 1988; El-Shinnawy & Vinze, 1998; Pinsonneault & Kraemer, 1989) within the disaster context discussed in this chapter, we propose a theoretical model of the collaboration system for disaster immediacy. See Figure 2.

As with other models, we posit that group processes (e.g. polarization, persuasive argumentation, social normative influences) and the resulting group outcome decisions are driven by the communication medium – whether it is Face To Face or through a Collaborative Technology. What is different about our model is that while the communication medium may reduce normative influences in many instances, but if it is combined with data processing capabilities CTs may change the group outcome. The driving factor in our proposed model is a disaster and how the temporal dimension of that specific event may change a group outcome decision. During the emergency planning phases before a disaster occurs, there is ample time for responder groups to brainstorm ideas, simulate multiple scenarios, consider high level strategies, and decide allocation of resources. Similarly, after the disaster–or at least at the point where danger is reduced to acceptable levels–there is time to analyze the outcomes and prepare for the future.

Conversely, during a disaster, certain CT features may become more or less important. For example, enforcing anonymity of ideas in a FTF setting to reduce social norms during group

*Figure 2. Theoretical model of the impact of disaster immediacy and collaboration system on group processes and outcomes*

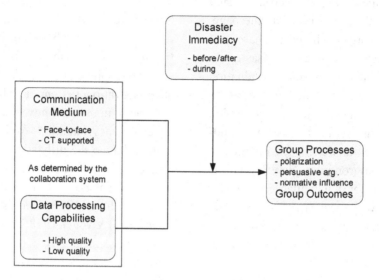

meetings may not be important. The urgency of the situation may change group member's desire to conform to social norms. Or, there may simply be no time for CT-facilitated discussions in the heat of a disaster. Controlling for data quality may be impossible. The immediacy of the disaster situation may define the success or failure of a collaborative system.

## SOLUTIONS AND RECOMMENDATIONS

### Collaboration Technology and Immediacy

An ongoing challenge for any group tasked with an emergency situation management is finding better ways to communicate as well as collect, maintain, and share essential information during the disaster event. Doing so would employ a collaboration system. However, in response to real time catastrophic events, federal, state, and local agencies are constantly looking for speed in response time and prioritization for resource allocations (Shen, Zhao & Huang, 2008). Group

outcome is directly influenced by the immediacy of need and response.

With regard to communication mediums, most CT software applications like ThinkTank™, require varying degrees of lead time which may include: set-up of a portable system, troubleshooting technology difficulties, creating an agenda and objectives, programming of activities within the tool, and training new users. Technically, CT is easy to use—even for individuals who have limited computer skills. Yet, users of CT software do require a basic level of training on how the tool functions and how to input information. The ease of use of a CT assumes access to a reliable system, readily available hardware, software and Internet access, as well as appropriate facilities for group meetings. Finally, most collaborative technologies necessitate a human facilitator who creates the group activities and maintains the integrity of the group processes and inputs. Facilitation training using CT may take several weeks to several months of practice. In a disaster situation, aligning a full CT system set up with training, access, and facilitation may not be feasible unless the CT is integrated into the planning phase—before the emergency occurs.

Of note, modern CT software applications include anonymity as a key feature of collaboration and decision making. In a standard meeting situation, concealing the identity of contributors for brainstorming and voting allows nearly equal participation and produces more unique, high quality ideas. However, in an emergency situation there is great value placed on individuals who have access to important information or specialized knowledge, thus concealing identity in a collaborative decision making exercise may seriously impede proper response (Nunamaker, Biggs, Middleman, Vogel, & Balthazard, 1996). As the immediacy of a disaster situation increases, there is less time to consider a wide range of potential solutions or to look at issues objectively from different sides (Thatcher & De La Cour, 2003).

## Collaborative Technology use During Emergency Planning

Over 25 years of research exists on the use of CT for meetings, organizational planning, teaching, training, documentation, and collaborative writing. Despite the depth of the CT research, there is virtually no research where a traditional CT was successfully deployed during a real-time disaster situation. A literature review on CTs in emergency situation planning, specifically software applications, appears to indicate that traditional CTs were not designed to support group decision-making tasks that require real-time data, effective and executable solutions during an emergency (Shen, et al., 2008).

Case in point: group of researchers have studied the use of CT for military-only efforts, as well as combined military and humanitarian exercises, during both non-emergency collaborative decision making situations and simulated emergency exercises (Adkins, Kruse, McKenna, Cuyugan, Nunamaker, Miller, Rasmussen, & Younger, 2000; Adkins, Kruse, Damianos, Brooks, Younger, Rasmussen, Rennie, Oshika, & Nunamaker, 2001; Briggs, Adkins, Mittleman, Kruse, Miller, &

Nunamaker, 1999; George, Easton, Nunamaker, & Northcraft, 1990). The researchers reported that in many cases, initial introduction of the CT tools were met with resistance from military and humanitarian groups participating in the study. The researchers found that participants required multiple successful experiences, including public testimonials and buy-in from leadership before CT was accepted by users. Once the CT tools were familiar, the researchers tended to find that military and humanitarian first responder groups reported a reduction in decision making time, acceleration in productivity, and consensus building during the planning phases for an emergency. However, the increased efficiency assumed the availability of the following: 1) ongoing scheduled meetings or advanced notice of meetings; 2) researchers to program the tools and facilitate all meetings; 3) continuity of non-researcher, trained personnel to maintain CT operations; and 4) adequate and accessible facilities and hardware.

The researchers also found that during planned military and humanitarian emergency simulation exercises, specific within and between group difficulties occurred during the use of CT tools: 1) lack of coordination between organizations whose missions were both different and unfamiliar was a challenge; 2) past interactions between some organizations created actual and perceived strains; 3) participants from different cultural backgrounds used multiple languages and acronyms which would impede communication; 3) physical barriers from extreme environmental conditions could limit access and reliability of portable CT operations; and 4) pressure to make critical life threatening decisions under time constraints could not be addressed by use of CT tools. Researchers learned that during planned simulated emergency exercises for military and humanitarian groups, critical issues required sequential conversations and significant exploration of a specific area of expertise. The researchers agreed that CT tools were not designed for those purposes (Adkins et al., 2001).

This is to be expected considering the nature

of responding to an emergency situation is essentially a judgment task requiring real-time coordination and timing among group members, as well as short term consensus on the execution of responses (Straus & McGrath, 1994). Traditional "off the shelf" CT are most often designed as a pre-planning, meeting, documentation, and decision support tool. First responder groups (i.e. military and humanitarian groups) must confer on a number of complex issues in order to reach consensus on preferred alternatives. In reality, groups such as first responders will actively change their decisions when unexpected events arise during critical decision-making emergencies, especially if the emergency is an unplanned event such as a natural disaster or terrorist attack. Therefore, feature-rich collaboration technologies (e.g. ThinkTank™) are not the right choice during a real-time emergency situation. Planning for emergency situations requires a large degree of coordination, training and practice among members' activities in order to achieve a consensus on the execution of responses.

Collaborative technologies do have an excellent track record for supporting the important processes of preparing and planning before a disaster situation. Therefore, CT can be the right choice for support of strategic approach and training groups before an emergency situation arises. For example, using CT during a table top exercise allows group members to engage in a structured and planned process while having the 'luxury' to consider a wide range of potential solutions. Using CT before a disaster may allow groups to create emergency procedure manuals which will be invaluable to first responders during a real-time disaster. Finally, collaborative technologies are equally as beneficial for use after an emergency situation. Debriefing, documentation, review of action and creating lessons learned are activities that CT tools support. After a disaster, using CT will produce outcomes which could be used to inform future iterations of strategic planning and training before the next emergency occurs.

## Data Capabilities During Emergency Planning

Innate in any disaster situation is a level of uncertainty which means first responders must depend on available data and ongoing communication to problem solve. The more ambiguous the emergency situation, the greater the need for media-rich data. The next generation of collaborative technologies is media rich—expanding into database driven visualization, simulation, semantic analysis and communication tools to create comprehensive interoperable collaboration systems. Coordinating disparate data sources and state of the art technologies with collaborative technologies is an emerging area for both corporations and universities looking for innovative methods to address emergency and disaster planning.

Emergency responders need ready access to real time data and collaboration technologies that are appropriate for ongoing situational awareness because communication with other first responders is vital to managing emergency situations. This means that key decision-makers need a means to "see" common operational picture via reliable, up-to-date information.

## Next Generation for Collaboration Systems

One example of this next generation of collaborative technologies is the Decision Theater at Arizona State University. The Decision Theater (DT) is both a physical visualization facility, as well as a set of methods that creates a unique collaboration system. It is one of the first facilities of its kind to combine multiple communication mediums with high quality data analytic technology.

The core component of the Decision Theater is the 'drum' comprising a 260-degree faceted screen, seven rear-projection passive stereo sources, tracking devices and surround sound. This enables data to be displayed and interacted with in a panoramic setting using 2D or 3D stereoscopic video. Unlike some visualization labs and flat-wall display facilities, the Decision Theater is an immersive environment designed as a collaboration system. Participants are often arranged in a conference configuration to improve human engagement with each other and to interact with the visual information around them. They combine a variety of tools to improve decision making including 3D and geospatial visualization, simulation models, system dynamics, and computer-assisted tools for collecting participant input and collaboration (CT). Participants also have access to the university's experts in policy informatics, design, geography, computational science, business, psychology and mathematics. (see Figure 3)

The facility is used by federal, state and local government agencies, community planners and policy makers in business to address complex problems ranging from hyper growth, sustainability and water resource management to disease monitoring. Similar to emergency planning, urban growth and resource management data for decision making comes from disparate sources, such as local officials, commercial imagery, on-the-

ground data, and current models. Users of this information must be able to access it in a way that meets their needs in delivering actionable intelligence. To achieve this, the DT converts data from different file formats, and translates it to one format to provide information required to obtain a common, static visualization. Yet, the DT researchers recently recognized that a dynamic and collaborative set of tools could rapidly facilitate a common operating picture and empower participants to act with increased effectiveness—fitting a timely need for expanding emergency response planning.

Recognizing the need for real-time, complex information and communications for disaster planning, the DT began to host table top exercises for emergency scenario planning in 2008. These exercises tested the core capabilities and interoperability of the DT tools, including CT's and data capabilities. Preliminary outcomes suggest that the media rich environment of the DT, combined with the collaborative technologies, make for a powerful environment to practice planning before and after emergency events. The DT has yet to be

*Figure 3. Using collaborative technologies in the decision theater*

used for a real-time emergency situation.

## FUTURE TRENDS

Much additional research needs to be completed in this area of combining process and analytics information technology. Hahn, Shangraw, Keith, and Coursey (2007) reported that highly visual, immersive conference facilities are already becoming widely available for use in urban planning, emergency planning and scientific exploration. With the increasing concern over better emergency planning and the need to integrate multiple sources and forms of communications into a single environment, many large government organizations have put into operation highly immersive command centers and advanced conference facilities. Hahn et al. (2007) reported that a number of additional research questions arise as a result from this convergence of process and analytic information technology:

- **Group collaboration and immersive environments:** How do immersive visual facilities affect group decision making? Are groups less likely or more likely to experience traditional collaboration barriers in immersive visual environments?
- **Media and immersive environments:** Do participants respond differently to group support systems, video, computer graphics, static images, animation, or other forms of visual media?
- **Content and immersive environments:** Do certain domains or types of problems generate different outcomes when communicated in an immersive environment?
- **Technology and immersive environments:** Is it possible that the introduction of a high technology environment, regardless of media, content, decision problem, etc., is independently capable of determining

perceptions and decision outcomes? In other words, do participants change their decision behavior when they are surrounded by high technology equipment? What would this mean during an emergency situation?

Communication medium combined with data capabilities as influenced by disaster immediacy is an important area of emerging research and therefore quite persuasive, but having the opportunity to examine the effects of a collaboration system during a disaster will remain the biggest challenge to this field of research. What remains important and feasible from a research perspective, is further exploration of the before/after disaster impact of a collaboration system. The next generation of decision making collaboration systems, such as the Decision Theater, will soon be commonplace in metropolitan areas, but this new approach must be further tested and adjusted well before a disaster arises.

## CONCLUSION

The disaster preparedness and response context has been proven to be an area of greater need for group collaboration and decision-making support. As CTs change and evolve, the potential for influencing group processes and outcomes changes as well. Although technologies to support group communication are widely used, more research and practice is needed to learn how to integrate these capabilities with high-quality information processing features in order to both minimize normative influences and maximize informational influences resulting in a streamlined collaboration system. In addition, research is needed to understand the value and impact of using CTs both before/after and during a disaster. In doing so, a set of principles and theories can be developed to guide the use of CTs to better manage future disasters.

# REFERENCES

Adkins, M., Kruse, J., Damianos, L. E., Brooks, J. A., Younger, R., Rasmussen, E., et al. (2001). Experience using collaborative technology with the United Nations and multinational militaries: Rim of the Pacific 2000 Strong Angel Exercise in humanitarian assistance. *Proceedings of the Hawaii International Conference on System Sciences, USA, 34*(1), 1066.

Adkins, M., Kruse, J., McKenna, T., Cuyugan, A., Nunamaker, J. F., Miller, S., et al. (2000). Experiences developing a virtual environment to support disaster relief with the United States Navy's Commander Third Fleet. *Proceedings of the Hawaii International Conference on System Sciences, USA, 33*(1), 1034.

Altay, N., & Green, W. G. (2006). OR/MS research in disaster operations management. *European Journal of Operational Research, 175,* 475–493. doi:10.1016/j.ejor.2005.05.016

Baron, R. S., & Roper, G. (1976). Reaffirmation of social comparison views of choice shifts: Averaging and extremity effects in autokinetic situation. *Journal of Personality and Social Psychology, 33,* 521–530. doi:10.1037/0022-3514.33.5.521

Benbasat, I., & Lim, L. H. (1993). The effects of group, task, context, and technology variables on the usefulness of group support sSystems. *Small Group Research, 24*(4), 430–462. doi:10.1177/1046496493244002

Briggs, R. O., Adkins, M., Mittleman, D. D., Kruse, J., Miller, S., & Nunamaker, J. F. Jr. (1999). A technology transition model derived from field investigation of GSS use aboard the U.S.S. Coronado. *Journal of Management Information Systems, 15*(3), 151–196.

Brown, R. (1965). *Social psychology.* New York: Free Press.

Burnstein, E. (1982). Persuasion as argument processing. In M. Braandstatter, J. H. Davis & G. Stocker-Kreichgauer (Eds.), *Group decision processes* (pp. 103-122). London: Academic Press.

Comfort, L. K. (2007). Crisis management in hindsight: Cognition, communication, coordination, and control. *Public Administration Review, 67*(s1), 189–197.

Daft, R. L., & Lengel, R. H. (1986). Organizational information requirements, media richness, and structural design. *Management Science, 32*(5), 554–571. doi:10.1287/mnsc.32.5.554

Dennis, A. R., George, J. F., Jessup, L. M., Nunamaker, J. F., & Vogel, D. R. (1988). Information technology to support electronic meetings. *MIS Quarterly, 12*(4), 591–624. doi:10.2307/249135

Dennis, A. R., Haley, B. J., & Vandenberg, R. J. (1996). A meta-analysis of effectiveness, efficiency, and participant satisfaction in group support systems research. In J. I. DeGross, S. Jarvenpaa, & A. Srinivasan (Ed.), *Proceedings of the Seventeenth International Conference on Information Systems,* Cleveland, OH (pp. 278-289).

DeSanctis, G., & Gallupe, R. B. (1987). A foundation for the study of group decision support systems. *Management Science, 33*(5), 589–609. doi:10.1287/mnsc.33.5.589

El-Shinnawy, M., & Vinze, A. S. (1998). Polarization and persuasive argumentation: A study of decision making in group settings. *MIS Quarterly, 22*(2), 165–198. doi:10.2307/249394

Federal Emergency Management Administration. (2004, July 23). *Hurricane Pam concludes.* Press release. Retrieved on September 1, 2008, from http://www.fema.gov/news/newsrelease.fema

Federal Emergency Management Administration. (2005, August 29). *First responders urged not to respond to hurricane impact areas unless dispatched by state, local authorities.* Press release. Retrieved on September 1, 2008, from http://www.fema.gov/news/newsrelease.fema

George, J. F., Easton, G. K., Nunamaker, J. F., & Northcraft, G. B. (1990). A study of collaborative group work with and without computer-based support. *Information Systems Research, 1*(4), 394–415. doi:10.1287/isre.1.4.394

Hahn, D., Shangraw, R. F., Keith, M., & Coursey, D. (2007). Does visualization affect public perceptions of complex policy decisions: An experimental study. *Proceedings of the Hawaii International Conference on System Sciences, USA, 40,* 96.

Heath, C., & Gonzalez, R. (1995). Interaction with others increases decision confidence but not decision quality: Evidence against information collection views of interactive decision making. *Organizational Behavior and Human Decision Processes, 61*(3), 305–326. doi:10.1006/obhd.1995.1024

Hinsz, V. B., & Davis, J. H. (1984). Persuasive arguments theory, group polarization, and choice shifts. *Journal of Personality and Social Psychology, 10*(2), 260–268. doi:10.1177/0146167284102012

H.R. No. 109-396. (2006). A failure of initiative, final report of the select bipartisan committee to investigate the preparation for and response to Hurricane Katrina.

Isenberg, D. J. (1986). Group polarization: A critical review and meta-analysis. *Journal of Personality and Social Psychology, 50*(6), 1141–1151. doi:10.1037/0022-3514.50.6.1141

Lamm, H., & Myers, D. G. (1978). Group-induced polarization of attitudes and behavior. In L. Berkowitz (Ed.), *Advances in experimental social psychology* (pp. 145-195). New York: Academic Press.

Mendonca, D. (2007). Decision support for improvisation in response to extreme events: Learning from the response to the 2001 World Trade Center attack. *Decision Support Systems, 43,* 952–967. doi:10.1016/j.dss.2005.05.025

Mendonca, D., Beroggi, G. E. G., van Gent, D., & Wallace, W. A. (2006). Designing gaming simulations for the assessment of group decision support systems in emergency response. *Safety Science, 44,* 523–535. doi:10.1016/j.ssci.2005.12.006

Millhollon, M. (2005). Blanco says feds pledged buses. *Baton Rouge Advocate,* September, 20.

Mindtel. (2005). Observations on the response to Hurricane Katrina an unclassified draft. Retrieved September 2, 2008, from http://projects.mindtel.com/2007/0508.ops-memes/

Moynihan, D. P. (2007). From forest fires to Hurricane Katrina: Case studies of incident command systems. *Robert M. LaFollette School of Public Affairs, Networks and Partnerships Series, IBM Center for the Business of Government.* University of Wisconsin at Madison.

Nunamaker, J. F., Biggs, R. O., Middleman, D. D., Vogel, D., & Balthazard, . (1996). Lessons from a dozen years of group support systems research: A discussion of lab and field findings. *Journal of Management Information Systems, 13*(3), 163–207.

Nunamaker, J. F., Dennis, A. R., Valacich, J. S., Vogel, D., & George, J. F. (1991). Electronic meeting systems to support group work. *Communications of the ACM, 34*(7), 40–61. doi:10.1145/105783.105793

Pinsonneault, A., & Kraemer, K. L. (1989). The impact of technological support on groups: An assessment of empirical research. *Decision Support Systems, 5,* 197–216. doi:10.1016/0167-9236(89)90007-9

Rains, S. A. (2005). Leveling the organizational playing field—virtually: A meta-analysis of experimental research assessing the impact of group support system use on member influence behaviors. *Communication Research, 32*(2), 193–234. doi:10.1177/0093650204273763

Sia, C. L., Tan, B. C. Y., & Wei, K. K. (2002). Group polarization and computer-mediated communication: Effects of communication cues, social presence, and anonymity. *Information Systems Research, 13*(1), 70–90. doi:10.1287/isre.13.1.70.92

Shen, H., Zhao, J., & Huang, W. W. (2008). Mission-critical group decision-making: Solving the problem of decision preference change in group decision-making using Markov chain model. *Journal of Global Information Management, 16*(2), 35–57.

Straus, & McGrath. (1994). Does the medium matter? The interaction of task type and technology on group performance and member reaction. *Journal of Applied Psychology, 79*(1), 87-97.

Thatcher, A., & De La Cour, A. (2003). Small group decision-making in face-to-face and computer-mediated environments: The role of personality. *Behaviour & Information Technology, 22*(3), 203–218. doi:10.1080/0144929031000117071

Valacich, J. S., Dennis, A. R., & Nunamaker, J. F. (1991). Electronic meeting support: The groupsystems concept. *International Journal of Man-Machine Studies, 34*(2), 261–282. doi:10.1016/0020-7373(91)90044-8

Vinokur, A., & Burnstein, E. (1978). Novel argumentation and attitude change: The case of polarization following group discussion. *European Journal of Social Psychology, 8,* 335–348. doi:10.1002/ejsp.2420080306

Zuber, J. A., Crott, H. W., & Werner, J. (1992). Choice shift and group polarization: An analysis of the status of arguments and social decision schemes. *Journal of Personality and Social Psychology, 62,* 50–61. doi:10.1037/0022-3514.62.1.50

# Chapter 4
# Principles and Experiences:
## Designing and Building Enterprise Information Systems

**Mehmet S. Aktas**
*TUBITAK (Turkish National Science Foundation), Turkey*

## ABSTRACT

*The data requirements of e-business applications have been increased over the years. These applications present an environment for acquiring, processing, and sharing data among interested parties. To manage information in such data-intensive application domain, independent enterprise e-business applications have developed their own solutions to information services. However, these solutions are not interoperable with each other, target vastly different systems, and address diverse sets of requirements. They require greater interoperability to enable communication between different systems, so that they can share and utilize each other's resources. To address these challenges, we discuss principles and experiences for designing and building of a novel enterprise information system. We introduce a novel architecture for a hybrid information service, which provides unification, federation, and interoperability of major Web-based information services. The hybrid information service is designed as an add-on information system, which interacts with the local information services and assembles their metadata instances under one hybrid architecture. It integrates different information services using unification and federation concepts. In this chapter, we summarize the principles and experiences gained in designing and building the semantics, architecture, and implementation for the hybrid information service.*

## INTRODUCTION

The data requirements of e-business applications have been increased over the years. These applications present an environment for acquiring,

DOI: 10.4018/978-1-60566-723-2.ch004

processing and sharing data among interested parties. In order to manage data in such data-intensive enterprise business application domain, Service Oriented Architecture (SOA) principles have gained great importance. A Service Oriented Architecture is simply a collection of services that are put together to achieve a common goal and that communicate with each other for either data passing or coordinating some activity. There is an emerging need for Web-based Enterprise Information Systems (EIS) that manage all the information that may be associated with wide-scale SOA-based e-business applications.

Over the years, independent enterprise e-business applications have developed their own customized implementations of Information Service Specifications. These EIS solutions are not interoperable with each other, target vastly different systems and address diverse sets of requirements (Zanikolas & Sakellariou, 2005). They require greater interoperability to enable communication between different systems, so that they can share and utilize each other's resources. Furthermore, they do not provide uniform interfaces for publishing and discovery of information. In turn, this creates a limitation on the client-end (e.g. fat client-end applications), as the users have to interact with more than one EIS implementation.

For example, large-scale e-business applications require management of large amounts of relatively slowly varying metadata. Another example, dynamic Web service collections, gathered together at any one time to perform an e-business operation, require greater support for dynamic metadata. Previous solutions do not address management requirements of both large-scale, static and small-scale, highly-dynamic metadata associated to Web Services (Zanikolas & Sakellariou, 2005). None of the existing solution enables communication between different e-business applications, so that they can share, utilize each other's resources, have unified access interface and address diverse sets of application requirements (OGF GIN-CG). We therefore see this as an important area of investigation especially for enterprise e-business applications domain.

This chapter introduces a Hybrid Service as a EIS that addresses metadata management requirements of both large-scale, static and small-scale, highly-dynamic metadata domains. The main nov-elty of this chapter is to describe the semantics, architecture, and implementation of a EIS integrating different Information Services by using unification and federation concepts. The implications of this study are two-fold. First is to describe a generic Information Service architecture, which supports one-to-many information service implementations as local data sources and integrates different kinds of Web Service metadata at a higher conceptual level, while ignoring the implementation details of the local data-systems. Second is to describe the customized implementations two widely-used Web Service Specifications: the WS-I compatible Web Service Context (WS-Context) (Bunting, et al., 2003) and Universal Description, Discovery and Integration (UDDI) (Bellwood, Clement, & von Riegen, 2003) Specifications.

The organization of this chapter is as follows. Section 2 reviews the relevant work. Section 3 gives an overview of the system. Section 4 presents the semantics of the Hybrid Service. Sections 5-6 present the architectural design details and the prototype implementation of the system. Finally, Section 7 contains a summary of the chapter.

## RELEVANT WORK

Unifying heterogeneous data sources under a single architecture has been target of many investigations (Ziegler & Dittrich, 2004). Information integration is mainly studied by distributed database systems research and investigates how to share data at a higher conceptual level, while ignoring the implementation details of the local data systems (Ozsu, 1999; Valduriez & Pacitti, 2004). Previous work on merger between the heterogeneous information systems may broadly be categorized as global-as-view and local-as-view integration (Florescu, Levy, & Mendelzon, 1998). In former category, data from several sources are transformed into a global schema and may be queried with a uniform query interface. Much work has been done on automating information federation process using global schema approach. In the latter category, queries are transformed into specialized queries over the local databases and integration is carried out by transforming queries. Although the global schema approach captures expressiveness capabilities of customized local schemas, it does not scale up to high number of data sources. In the local-as-view approach, each local-system's schema is need to be mapped against each other to transform the queries. In turn, this leads to large number of mappings that need to be created and managed.

The proposed system differs from local-as-view approaches, as its query transformation happens between a unified schema and local schemas. It utilizes and leverages previous work on global-as-view approach for integrating heterogeneous local data services. The previous work mainly focuses on solutions that automates the information federation process at semantics level. Different from the previous work, the proposed approach presents a system architecture that enables information integration at application level. To our best knowledge, the proposed system is a pioneer work, as it describes an Information Service architecture that enables unification and federation of information coming from different metadata systems. One limitation is that it does not scale to high number of local data-systems due to low-level manual semantic schema integration. To facilitate testing of our system, we did the low-level information federation manually through a delicate analysis of the structure and semantic of each target schema. Since the main focus of our research is to explore the information integration at application level, we leave out the investigation of a low-level automated information federation capability for a future study.

Locating services of interest in Web service intensive environments has recently become important, since the service oriented architecture based systems increased in numbers and gain popularity in recent years. The UDDI Specification is a widely used standard that enables services advertise themselves and discover other services. A number of studies extends and improves the out-of-box UDDI Specification (Open_GIS_Consortium_Inc.; Sycline; Galdos; Dialani, 2002; ShaikhAli, Rana, Al-Ali, & Walker, 2003; Verma, Sivashanmugam, Sheth, Patil, Oundhakar, & Miller; GRIMOIRES). UDDI-M (Dialani, 2002) and UDDIe (ShaikhAli, Rana, Al-Ali, & Walker, 2003) projects introduced the idea of associating metadata and lifetime with UDDI Registry service descriptions, where retrieval relies on the matches of attribute name-value pairs between service description and service requests. METEOR-S (Verma, Sivashanmugam, Sheth, Patil, Oundhakar, & Miller) leveraged UDDI Specification by utilizing semantic web languages to describe service entries. Grimories (GRIMOIRES) extends the functionalities of UDDI to provide a semantic enabled registry designed and developed for the MyGrid project (MyGrid). It supports third-party attachment of metadata about services and represents all published metadata in the form of RDF triples either in a database, or in a file, or in a memory. Although out-of-box UDDI Specification is a widely used standard, it is limited to keyword-based query capabilities. Neither it allows metadata-oriented queries, nor it takes into account the volatile behavior of services. The previous work on UDDI-Extensions have centralized and database-based solutions. Thus, they present low fault-tolerance and low performance as opposed to decentralized and in-memory based data-systems. The UDDI Specification is not designed to coordinate activities of Web Services participating in a work-flow style applications. Thus, it does not support data-sharing and metadata management requirements of rich-interacting systems.

The proposed system addresses the limitations of previous work by introducing an add-on architecture, which runs one layer above the implementations of UDDI and its extensions. It leverages previous work on UDDI and improves the quality of UDDI-based metadata-systems in terms of fault-tolerance and high-performance.

To our best knowledge, this approach is unique, since it improves the qualities of existing implementations of Information Services without changing their code. Different from the previous UDDI-work, the proposed system supports data-sharing and manages stateful interactions of Web Services. The proposed research also introduces semantics, communication protocols, and implementation of an extended UDDI version, which addresses metadata management requirements of aforementioned application use domains.

Managing stateful interactions of Web Services is an important problem in rich-interacting systems. There are varying specifications focusing on point-to-point service communication, such as Web Service Resource Framework (WSRF), WS-Metadata Exchange (WS-ME). The WSRF specification, proposed by Globus alliance, IBM and HP, defines conventions for managing state, so that collaborating applications can discover, inspect, and interact with stateful resources in a standard way. The WS-ME provides a mechanism a) to share information about the capabilities of participating Web Services and b) to allow querying a WS Endpoint to retrieve metadata about what to know to interact with them. Communication among services is also achieved with a centralized metadata management strategy, the Web Services Context (WS-Context) Specification (Bunting, et al., 2003). The W-Context defines a simple mechanism to share and keep track of common information shared between multiple participants in Web service interactions. It is a lightweight storage mechanism, which allows the participant's of an activity to propagate and share context information. Although point-to-point methodologies successfully manage the stateful information, they provide service conversation with metadata coming from the two services that exchange information. This is a limitation, since they become inefficient, when the number of communicating services increased. We find the WS-Context Specification as promising approach to tackle the problem of managing distributed session state, since it models a session metadata repository as an external entity, where more than two services can easily access/store highly dynamic, shared metadata. Even though it is promising, the WS-Context has some limitations as described below. Firstly, the context service has limited functionalities such as the two primary operations: GetContext and SetContext. Secondly, the WS-Context Specification is only focused on defining stateful interactions of Web Services. It does not define a searchable repository for interaction-independent information associated to the services involved in an activity. Thirdly, the WS-Context Specification does not define a data model to manage stateful Web Service information.

The proposed system differs from previous work focusing on point-to-point service communication, since it adopts a centralized metadata management strategy to regulate the interactions. It adopts the WS-Context Specification and presents an extended version of WS-Context Specification and its implementation. The prototype implementation manages dynamically generated session-related metadata. To our best knowledge, the proposed approach is unique, since none of the previous work on Information Services implemented the WS-Context Specification to manage stateful interactions of services. The proposed Hybrid Service leverages the extended WS-Context Service implementation and improves its quality in terms of fault-tolerance and high-performance.

## HYBRID SERVICE

We designed and built a novel Hybrid Information Service Architecture called Hybrid Service, which provides unification, federation and interoperability of major Information Services. The Hybrid Service forms an add-on architecture that interacts with the local information services and unifies them in a higher-level hybrid system. In other words, it provides a unifying architecture, where one can assemble metadata instances of different information services. To facilitate testing of the system, we integrated the Hybrid Service with the two local information service implementations: WS-Context and Extended UDDI. We discuss semantics of the Hybrid Service in the following section followed by a section discussing its architecture.

## SEMANTICS

The semantics of the system may be analyzed under four categories: extended UDDI, WS-Context, Unified Schema, and Hybrid Service Schema. The extended UDDI Specification extends existing out-of-box UDDI Specification to address its aforementioned limitations. The WS-Context Specification improves the existing out-of-box Web-Service Context Specification to meet the aforementioned application requirements. The Unified Schema Specification integrates these two information service specifications. The Hybrid Service Schema consists of two small schemas: Hybrid Schema and SpecMetadata Schema. These define the necessary abstract data models to achieve a generic architecture for unification and federation of different information service implementations.

### The Extended UDDI Specification

We have designed extensions to the out-of-box UDDI Data Structure (Bellwood, Clement, & von Riegen, 2003) to be able to associate both prescriptive and descriptive metadata with service entries. This way the proposed system addresses limitations of UDDI (explained in Section 2) and interoperates with existing UDDI clients without requiring an excessive change in the implementations. We name our version of UDDI as the extended UDDI.

**The Extended UDDI Schema:** The schema addresses the metadata requirements of Geo-

graphical Information System/Sensor applications by extending the out-of-box UDDI data model. It includes following additional/modified entities: a) service attribute entity (serviceAttribute) and b) extended business service entity (businessService). We describe the additional/modified data model entities as follows.

**Business service entity structure:** The UDDI's business service entity structure contains descriptive, yet limited information about Web Services. A comprehensive description of the out-of-box business service entity structure defined by UDDI can be found in (Bellwood, Clement, & von Riegen, 2003). Here, we only discuss the additional XML structures introduced to expand on existing business service entity.

These additional XML elements are a) service attribute and b) lease. The service attribute XML element corresponds to a static metadata (e.g. WSDL of a given service). A lease structure describes a period of time during which a service can be discoverable.

**Service attribute entity structure:** A service attribute (serviceAttribute) data structure describes information associated with service entities. Each service attribute corresponds to a piece of metadata, and it is simply expressed with (name, value) pairs. Apart from similar approaches (Dialani, 2002; ShaikhAli, Rana, Al-Ali, & Walker, 2003), in the proposed system, a service attribute includes a) a list of abstractAtttributeData, b) a categoryBag and c) a boundingBox XML structures: *An abstractAttributeData element* is used to represent metadata that is directly related with functionality of the service and store/maintain these domain specific auxiliary files as-is. This allows us to add third-party data models such as "capabilities.xml" metadata file describing the data coverage of domain-specific services such as the geospatial services. An abstractAttributeData can be in any representation format such as XML or RDF. This data structure allows us to pose domain-specific queries on the metadata catalog. Say, an abstractAttributeData of a geospatial service entry contains "capabilities.xml" metadata file. As it is in XML format, a client may conduct a find_service operation with an XPATH query statement to be carried out on the abstractAttributeData, i.e. "capabilities.xml". In this case, the results will be the list of geospatial service entries that satisfy the domain-specific XPATH query. *A categoryBag element* is used to provide a custom classification scheme to categorize serviceAttribute elements. A simple classification could be whether the service attribute is prescriptive or descriptive. *A boundingBox element* is used to describe both temporal and spatial attributes of a given geographic feature. This way the system enables spatial query capabilities on the metadata catalog.

**Extended UDDI Schema XML API:** We present extensions/modifications to existing UDDI XML API set to standardize the additional capabilities of our implementation. These additional capabilities can be grouped under two XML API categories: Publish and Inquiry.

The Publish XML API is used to publish metadata instances belonging to different entities of the extended UDDI Schema. It extends existing UDDI Publish XML API Set. It consists of the following functions: **save service:** Used to extend the out-of-box UDDI save service functionality. The save service API call adds/updates one or more Web Services into the service. Each service entity may contain one-to-many serviceAttribute and may have a lifetime (lease). **save serviceAttribute:** Used to register or update one or more semi-static metadata associated with a Web Service. **delete service:** Used to delete one or more service entity structures. **delete serviceAttribute:** Used to delete existing serviceAttribute elements from the service. The Inquiry XML API is used to pose inquiries and to retrieve metadata from the Extended UDDI Information Service. It extends existing UDDI Inquiry XML API set. It consists of the following functions: **find service:** Used to extend the out-of-box UDDI find service functionality. The find service API call locates specific

services within the service. It takes additional input parameters such as serviceAttributeBag and Lease to facilitate the additional capabilities. **find serviceAttribute:** Used to find the aforementioned serviceAttribute elements. The find serviceAttribute API call returns a list of serviceAttribute structure matching the conditions specified in the arguments. **get serviceAttributeDetail:** Used to retrieve semi-static metadata associated with a unique identifier. The get serviceAttributeDetail API call returns the serviceAttribute structure corresponding to each of the attributeKey values specified in the arguments. **get serviceDetail:** Used to retrieve service entity structure associated with a unique identifier.

**Using Extended UDDI Schema XML API:** Given the capabilities of the Extended-UDDI Service, one can simply populate metadata instances using the Extended-UDDI XML API as in the following scenario. Say, a user publishes a new metadata to be attached to an already existing service in the system. In this case, the user constructs a serviceAttribute element. Based on aforementioned extended UDDI data model, each service entry is associated with one or more serviceAttribute XML elements. A serviceAttribute corresponds to a piece of interaction-independent metadata and it is simply expressed with (name, value) pair. We can illustrate a serviceAttribute as in the following example: ((throughput, 0.9)). A serviceAttribute can be associated with a lifetime and categorized based on custom classification schemes. A simple classification could be whether the serviceAttribute is prescriptive or descriptive. In the aforementioned example, the throughput service attribute can be classified as descriptive. In some cases, a serviceAttribute may correspond to a domain-specific metadata where service metadata could be directly related with functionality of the service. For instance, Open Geographical Concorcium compatible Geographical Information System services provide a "capabilities.xml" metadata file describing the data coverage of geospatial services. We use an abstractAttributeData element to represent such metadata and store/maintain these domain specific auxiliary files as-is. As the serviceAttribute is constructed, it can then be published to the Hybrid Service by using "save_serviceAttribute" operation of the extended UDDI XML API. On receiving a metadata publish request, the system extracts the instance of the serviceAttribute entity from the incoming requests, assigns a unique identifier to it and stores in in-memory storage. Once the publish operation is completed, a response is sent to the publishing client.

## The WS-Context Specification

We have designed extensions and a data model for the WS-Context Specifications to tackle the problem of managing distributed session state. Unlike the point-to-point approaches, WS-Context models a third-party metadata repository as an external entity where more than two services can easily access/store highly dynamic, shared metadata.

**The extended WS-Context Schema:** The schema is comprised of following entities: sessionEntity, sessionService and context.

**Session entity structure:** A sessionEntity describes a period of time devoted to a specific activity, associated contexts, and serviceService involved in the activity. A sessionEntity can be considered as an information holder for the dynamically generated information. An instance of a sessionEntity is uniquely identified with a session key. A session key is generated by the system when an instance of the entity is published. If the session key is specified in a publication operation, the system updates the corresponding entry with the new information. When retrieving an instance of a session, a session key must be presented. A sessionEntity may have name and description associated with it. A name is a user-defined identifier and its uniqueness is up to the session publisher.

A user-defined identifier is useful for the information providers to manage their own data. A description is optional textual information about a session. Each sessionEntity contains one-to-many context entity structures. The context entity structure contains dynamic metadata associated to a Web Service or a session instance or both. Each sessionEntity is associated with its participant sessionServices. The sessionService entity structure is used as an information container for holding limited metadata about a Web Service participating to a session. A lease structure describes a period of time during which a sessionEntity or serviceService or a context entity instances can be discoverable.

**Session service entity structure:** The sessionService entity contains descriptive, yet limited information about Web Services participating to a session. A service key identifies a sessionService entity. A sessionService may participate one or more sessions. There is no limit on the number of sessions in which a service can participate. These sessions are identified by session keys. Each sessionService has a name and description associated with it. This entity has an endpoint address field, which describes the endpoint address of the sessionService. Each sessionService may have one or more context entities associated to it. The lease structure identifies the lifetime of the sessionService under consideration.

**Context entity structure:** A context entity describes dynamically generated metadata. An instance of a context entity is uniquely identified with a context key, which is generated by the system when an instance of the entity is published. If the context key is specified in a publication operation, the system updates the corresponding entry with the new information. When retrieving an instance of a context, a context key must be presented.

A context is associated with a sessionEntity. The session key element uniquely identifies the sessionEntity that is an information container for the context under consideration. A context has also a service key, since it may also be associated with a sessionService participating a session. A context has a name associated with it. A name is a user-defined identifier and its uniqueness is up to the context publisher. The information providers manage their own data in the interaction-dependent context space by using this user-defined identifier. The context value can be in any representation format such as binary, XML or RDF. Each context has a lifetime. Thus, each context entity contains the aforementioned lease structure describing the period of time during which it can be discoverable.

**WS-Context Schema XML API:** We present an XML API for the WS-Context Service. The XML API sets of the WS-Context XML Metadata Service can be grouped as Publish, Inquiry, Proprietary, and Security.

**The Publish XML API:** The API is used to publish metadata instances belonging to different entities of the WS-Context Schema. It extends the WS-Context Specification Publication XML API set. It consists of the following functions: **save session:** Used to add/update one or more session entities into the hybrid service. Each session may contain one-to-many context entity, have a lifetime (lease), and be associated with service entries. **save context:** Used to add/update one or more context (dynamic metadata) entities into the service. **save sessionService:** Used to add/update one or more session service entities into the hybrid service. Each session service may contain one-to-many context entity and have a lifetime (lease). **delete session:** Used to delete one or more sessionEntity structures. **delete context:** Used to delete one or more contextEntity structures. **delete sessionService:** Used to delete one or more session service structures. The Inquiry XML API is used to pose inquiries and to retrieve metadata from service. It extends the existing WS-Context XML API. The extensions to the WS-Context Inquiry API set are outlined as follows: **find session:** Used to find sessionEntity elements. The find session API

call returns a session list matching the conditions specified in the arguments. **find context:** Used to find contextEntity elements. The find context API call returns a context list matching the criteria specified in the arguments. **find sessionService:** Used to find session service entity elements. The find sessionService API call returns a service list matching the criteria specified in the arguments. **get sessionDetail:** Used to retrieve sessionEntity data structure corresponding to each of the session key values specified in the arguments. **get contextDetail:** Used to retrieve the context structure corresponding to the context key values specified. **get sessionServiceDetail:** Used to retrieve sessionService entity data structure corresponding to each of the sessionService key values specified in the arguments. The Proprietary XML API is implemented to provide find/add/modify/delete operations on the publisher list, i.e., authorized users of the system. We adapt semantics for the proprietary XML API from existing UDDI Specifications. This XML API is as in the following: **find publisher:** Used to find publishers registered with the system matching the conditions specified in the arguments. **get publisherDetail:** Used to retrieve detailed information regarding one or more publishers with given publisherID(s). **save publisher:** Used to add or update information about a publisher. **delete_publisher:** Used to delete information about a publisher with a given publisherID from the metadata service. The Security XML API is used to enable authenticated access to the service. We adopt the semantics from existing UDDI Specifications. The Security API includes the following function calls. **get_authToken:** Used to request an authentication token as an 'authInfo' (authentication information) element from the service. The authInfo element allows the system implement access control. To this end, both the publication and inquiry API set include authentication information in their input arguments. **discard_authToken:** Used to inform the hybrid service that an authentication token is no longer required and should be considered invalid.

**Using WS-Context Schema XML API:** Given the capabilities of the WS-Context Service, one can simply populate metadata instances using the WS-Context XML API as in the following scenario. Say, a user publishes a metadata under an already created session. In this case, the user first constructs a context entity element. Here, a context entity is used to represent interaction-dependent, dynamic metadata associated with a session or a service or both. Each context entity has both system-defined and user-defined identifiers. The uniqueness of the system-defined identifier is ensured by the system itself, whereas, the user-defined identifier is simply used to enable users to manage their memory space in the context service. As an example, we can illustrate a context as in ((system-defined-uuid, user-defined-uuid, "Job completed")). A context entity can be also associated with service entity and it has a lifetime. Contexts may be arranged in parent-child relationships. One can create a hierarchical session tree where each branch can be used as an information holder for contexts with similar characteristics. This enables the system to be queried for contexts associated to a session under consideration. This enables the system to track the associations between sessions. As the context elements are constructed, they can be published with save_context function of the WS-Context XML API. On receiving publishing metadata request, the system processes the request, extracts the context entity instance, assigns a unique identifier, stores in the in-memory storage and returns a respond back to the client.

## The Unified Schema Specification

This research investigates a system architecture that would support information federation and unification at application-level. To facilitate testing of such system architecture, a unified schema is needed. We achieved semantic-level unification manually through a delicate analysis of the structure and semantics of the two schemas: extended UDDI and WS-Context. We introduced an abstract

data model and query/publish XML API and named it as the Unified Schema Specification.

We begin unification by finding the mappings between the similar entities of the two schemas. First mapping is between ExtendedUDDI.businessEntity and WS-Context.sessionEntity: The businessEntity is used to aggregate one-to-many services and sites managed by the same people. The sessionEntity is used to aggregate session services participating to a session. Therefore, businessEntity (from ExtendedUDDI) can be considered as matching concepts with the sessionEntity (from WS-Context schema) as their intentional domains are similar. The cardinality between these entities differs, as the businessEntity may contain one to may sessionEntities. The second mapping is between: ExtendedUDDI.service and WS-Context.sessionService: These entities are equivalent as the intentional domains that they represent are the same. The cardinality between these entities is also the same. In the integrated schema, we unify these entities as service entity. The third mapping is between ExtendedUDDI.metadata and WS-Context.context: These entities are equivalent as the intentional domains that they represent are the same. The cardinality between these entities is also the same. We continue unification by merging the two schemas based on the mappings that we identified and create a unified schema. The Unified Schema unifies matching and disjoint entities of the two schemas.

The Unified Schema is comprised of the following entities: businessEntity, sessionEntity, service, bindingTemplate, metadata, tModel, publisherAssertions. A businessEntity describes a party who publishes information about a session (in other words service activity), site or service. The publisherAssertions entity defines the relationship between the two businessEntities. The sessionEntity describes information about a service activity that takes place. A sessionEntity may contain one-to-many service and metadata entities. The service entity provides descriptive information about a Web Service family. It may contain one-to-many bindingTemplate entities that define the technical information about a service end-point. A bindingTemplate entity contains references to tModel that defines descriptions of specifications for service end-points. The service entity may also have one-to-many metadata attached to it. A metadata contains information about both interaction-dependent, interaction-independent metadata and service data associated to Web Services. A metadata entity describes the information pieces associated to services or sites or sessions as (name, value) pairs.

**The Unified Schema XML API:** To facilitate testing of the federation capability, we introduce a limited Query/Publish XML API that can be carried out on the instances of the parts of the Unified Schema. We can group the Unified Schema XML API under two categories: Publish and Inquiry.

**The Publish XML API:** This API is used to publish metadata instances belonging to different entities of the Unified Schema. It consists of the following functions: **save business:** Used to add/update one or more business entities into the hybrid service. **save session:** Used to add/update one or more session entities into the hybrid service. Each session may contain one-to-many metadata, one-to-many service entities and have a lifetime (lease). **save service:** Used to add/update one or more service entries into the hybrid service. Each service entity may contain one-to-many metadata element and may have a lifetime (lease). **save metadata:** Used to register or update one or more metadata associated with a service. **delete business:** Used to delete one or more business entity structures. **delete session:** Used to delete one or more sessionEntity structures. **delete service:** Used to delete one or more service entity structures. **delete metadata:** Used to delete existing metadata elements from the hybrid service. **The Inquiry XML API** is used to pose inquiries and to retrieve metadata from service. It consists of following functions: **find business:** This API call locates specific businesses within the hybrid services. **find session:** Used to find sessionEntity elements. The find session API

call returns a session list matching the conditions specified in the arguments. **find service:** Used to locate specific services within the hybrid service. **find metadata:** Used to find service entity elements. The find service API call returns a service list matching the criteria specified in the arguments. **get businessDetail:** Used to retrieve businessEntity data structure of the Unified Schema corresponding to each of the business key values specified in the arguments. **get sessionDetail:** Used to retrieve sessionEntity data structure corresponding to each of the session key values specified in the arguments. **get serviceDetail:** Used to retrieve service entity data structure corresponding to each of the service key values specified in the arguments. **get metadataDetail:** Used to retrieve the metadata structure corresponding to the metadata key values specified.

**Using the Unified Schema XML API:** Given these capabilities, one can simply populate the Hybrid Service with Unified Schema metadata instances using its XML API as in the following scenario. Say, a user wants to publish both session-related and interaction-independent metadata associated to an existing service. In this case, the user constructs metadata entity instance. Each metadata entity has both system-defined and user-defined identifiers. The uniqueness of the system-defined identifier is ensured by the system itself, whereas, the user-defined identifier is simply used to enable users to manage their memory space in the context service. As an example, we can illustrate a context as in the following examples: a) ((throughput, 0.9)) and b) ((system-defined-uuid, user-defined-uuid, "Job completed")). A metadata entity can be also associated with site, or sessionEntity of the Unified Schema and it has a lifetime. As the metadata entity instances are constructed, they can be published with "save_metadata" function of the Unified Schema XML API. On receiving publishing metadata request, the system processes the request, extracts the metadata entity instance, assigns a unique identifier, stores in the in-memory storage and returns a respond back to the client.

## The Hybrid Service Semantics

The Hybrid Service introduces an abstraction layer for uniform access interface to be able to support one-to-many information service specification (such as WS-Context, Extended UDDI, or Unified Schema). To achieve the uniform access capability, the system presents two XML Schemas: a) **Hybrid Schema** and b) **Specification Metadata (Spec-Metadata) Schema**. The Hybrid Schema defines the generic access interface to the Hybrid Service. The SpecMetadata Schema defines the necessary information required by the Hybrid Service to be able to process instances of supported information service schemas. We discuss the semantics of the Hybrid Schema and the SpecMetadata Schema in the following sections.

## The Hybrid Schema

The Hybrid Schema is designed to achieve a unifying access interface to the Hybrid Service. It is independent from any of the local information service schemas supported by the Hybrid Service. It defines a set of XML API to enable clients/providers to send specification-based publish/query requests (such as WS-Context's "save_context" request) in a generic way to the system.

The Hybrid Service XML API allows the system support one-to-many information service communication protocols. It consists of the following functions: **hybrid_service:** This XML API call is used to pose inquiry/publish requests based on any specification. With this function, the user can specify the type of the schema and the function. This function allows users to access an information service back-end directly. The user also specifies the specification-based publish/query request in XML format based on the specification under consideration. On receiving the hybrid_function request call, the system handles the request based on the schema and function specified in the query. **save_schemaEntity:** This API call is used to save an instance of any schema entities of a given

specification. The save_schemaEntity API call is used to update/add one or more schema entity elements into the Hybrid Information Service. On receiving a save_schemaEntity publication request message, the system processes the incoming message based on information given in the mapping file of the schema under consideration. Then, the system stores the newly-inserted schema entity instances into the in-memory storage. **delete_schemaEntity:** The delete_schemaEntity is used to delete an instance of any schema entities of a given specification. The delete_schemaEntity API call deletes existing service entities associated with the specified key(s) from the system. On receiving a schema entity deletion request message, the system processes the incoming message based on information given in the mapping file of the schema under consideration. Then the system, deletes the correct entity associated with the key. **find_schemaEntity:** This API call locates schemaEntities whose entity types are identified in the arguments. This function allows the user to locate a schema entity among the heterogeneous metadata space. On receiving a find_schemaEntity request message, the system processes the incoming message based on information given in the schema mapping file of the schema under consideration. Then the system, locates the correct entities matching the query under consideration. **get_schemaEntity:** The get_schemaEntityDetail is used to retrieve an instance of any schema entities of a given specification. It returns the entity structure corresponding to key(s) specified in the query. On receiving a get_schemaEntityDetail retrieval request message, the system processes the incoming message based on information given in the mapping file of the schema under consideration. Then the system retrieves the correct entity associated with the key. Finally, the system sends the result to the user.

Given these capabilities, one can simply populate the Hybrid Service using the "save_schemaEntity" element and publish metadata instances of the customized implementations of information service specifications. The "save_schemaEntity" element includes an "authInfo" element, which describes the authentication information; "lease" element, which is used to identify the lifetime of the metadata instance; "schemaName" element, which is used to identify a specification schema (such as Extended UDDI Schema); "schemaFunctionName", which is used to identify the function of the schema (such as "save_serviceAttribute"); "schema_SAVERequestXML", which is an abstract element used for passing the actual XML document of the specific publish function of a given specification. The Hybrid Service requires a specification metadata document that describes all necessary information to be able to process XML API of the schema under consideration. We discuss the specification metadata semantics in the following section.

## The SpecMetadata Schema

The SpecMetadata XML Schema is used to define all necessary information required for the Hybrid Service to support an implementation of information service specification. The Hybrid System requires an XML metadata document, which is generated based on the SpecMetadata Schema, for each information service specification supported by the system. The SpecMetadata XML file helps the Hybrid System to know how to process instances of a given specification XML API. The SpecMetadata includes **Specname**, **Description**, and **Version** XML elements. These elements define descriptive information to help the Hybrid Service to identify the local information service schema under consideration. **The FunctionProperties XML element** describes all required information regarding the functions that will be supported by the Hybrid Service. The FunctionProperties element consists of one-to-many FunctionProperty sub-elements. The FunctionProperty element consists of function name, memory-mapping and information-service-backend mapping information. Here the memory-

mapping information element defines all necessary information to process an incoming request for in-memory storage access. The memory-mapping information element defines the name, user-defined identifier and system-defined identifier of an entity. The information-service-backend information is needed to process the incoming request and execute the requested operation on the appropriate information service backend. This information defines the function name, its arguments, return values and the class, which needs to be executed in the information service back-end. **The MappingRules XML element** describes all required information regarding the mapping rules that provide mapping between the Unified Schema and the local information service schemas such as extended UDDI and WS-Context. The MappingRules element consists of one-to-many MappingRule sub-elements. Each MappingRule describes information about how to map a unified schema XML API to a local information service schema XML API. The MappingRule element contains the necessary information to identify functions that will be mapped to each other.

Given these capabilities, one can simply populate the Hybrid Service as in the following scenario. Say, a user wants to publish a metadata into the Hybrid Service using WS-Context's "save_context" operation through the generic access interface. In this case, firstly, the user constructs an instance of the "save_context" XML document (based on the WS-Context Specification) as if s/he wants to publish a metadata instance into the WS-Context Service. Once the specification-based publish function is constructed, it can be published into the Hybrid Service by utilizing the "save_schemaEntity" operation of the Hybrid Service Access API.

As for the arguments of the "save_schemaEntity" function, the user needs to pass the following arguments: a) authentication information, b) lifetime information, c) schemaName as "WS-Context", d) schemaFunctionName as "save_context" and e) the actual save_context document which was constructed based on the WS-Context Specification. Recall that, for each specification, the Hybrid Service requires a SpecMetadata XML document (an instance of the Specification Metadata Schema). On receipt of the "save_schemaEntity" publish operation, the Hybrid Service obtains the name of the schema (such as WS-Context) and the name of the publish operation (such as save_context) from the passing arguments. In this case, the Hybrid Service consults with the WS-Context SpecMetadata document and obtains necessary information about how to process incoming "save_context" operation. Based on the memory mapping information obtained from user-provided SpecMetadata file, the system processes the request, extracts the context metadata entity instance, assigns a unique identifier, stores in the in-memory storage and returns a response back to the client.

## ARCHITECTURE

We designed and built a Hybrid Information Service (Hybrid Service) to support handling and discovery of metadata associated with Web Services. The Hybrid Service is an add-on architecture that interacts with the local information systems and unifies them in a higher-level hybrid system. It provides a unifying architecture where one can assemble metadata instances of different information services.

### Abstraction Layers

Figure 1 illustrates the detailed architectural design and abstraction layers of the system. (1) The Uniform Access layer imports the XML API of the supported Information Services. It is designed as generic as possible, so that it can support one-to-many XML API, as the new information services are integrated with the system. (2) The Request-processing layer is responsible for extracting incoming requests and process operations

on the Hybrid Service. It is designed to support two capabilities: notification and access control. The notification capability enables the interested clients to be notified of the state changes happening in a metadata. It is implemented by utilizing publish-subscribe based paradigm. The access control capability is responsible for enforcing controlled access to the Hybrid Information Service. The investigation and implementation of access control mechanism for the decentralized information service is left out for future study. (3) TupleSpaces Access API allows access to in-memory storage. This API supports all query/ publish operations that can take place on the Tuple Pool. (4) The Tuple Pool implements a lightweight implementation of JavaSpaces Specification (Sun_Microsystems, 1999) and is a generalized in-memory storage mechanism. It enables mutually exclusive access and associative lookup to shared data. (5) The Tuple Processor layer is designed to process metadata stored in the Tuple Pool. Once the metadata instances are stored in the Tuple Pool as tuple objects, the system starts processing the tuples and provides the following capabilities. The first capability is the LifeTime Management. Each metadata instance may have a lifetime defined by the user. If the metadata lifetime is exceeded, then it is evicted from the TupleSpace. The second capability is the Persistency Management. The system checks with the tuple space every so often for newly added /updated tuples and stores them into the database for persistency of information. The third capability is the Fault Tolerance Management. The system checks with the tuple space every so often for newly-added/updated tuples and replicates them in other Hybrid Service instances using the publish-subscribe messaging system. This capability also provides consistency among the replicated datasets. The fourth capability is the Dynamic Caching Management. With this capability, the system keeps track of the requests coming from the pub-sub system and replicates/ migrates tuples to other information services where the high demand is originated. (6) The Filtering

*Figure 1.*

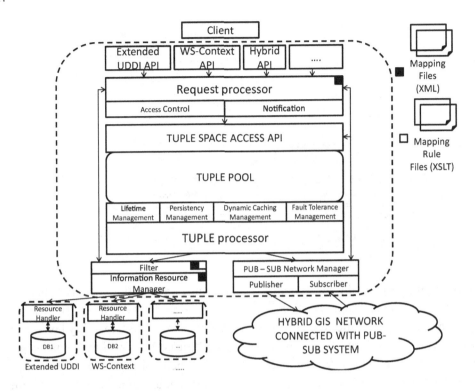

layer supports the federation capability. This layer provides filtering between instances of the Unified Schema and local information service schemas such as WS-Context Schema based on the user defined mapping rules to provide transformations. (7) The Information Resource Manager layer is responsible for managing low-level information service implementations. It provides decoupling between the Hybrid Service and sub-systems. (8) The Pub-Sub Network layer is responsible for communication between Hybrid Service instances.

## Distribution

Figure 2 illustrates the distribution in Hybrid Service and shows N-node decentralized services from the perspective of a single service interacting with two clients. To achieve communication among the network nodes, the Hybrid Service utilizes a topic-based publish-subscribe software

multicasting mechanism. This is a multi-publisher, multicast communication mechanism, which provides message-based communication. In the prototype implementation, we use an open source implementation of publish-subscribe paradigm (NaradaBrokering (Pallickara & Fox, 2003)) for message exchanges between peers.

## Execution Logic Flow

The execution logic for the Hybrid Service happens as follows. Firstly, on receiving the client request, the request processor extracts the incoming request. The request processor processes the incoming request by checking it with the specification-mapping metadata (SpecMetadata) files. For each supported schema, there is a SpecMetadata file, which defines all the functions that can be executed on the instances of the schema under consideration. Each function defines the

*Figure 2. Distributed hybrid services*

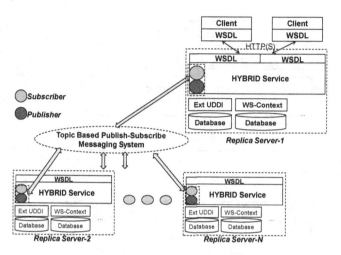

required information related with the schema entities to be represented in the Tuple Pool. (For example; entity name, entity identifier key, etc...). Based on this information, the request processor extracts the inquiry/publish request from the incoming message and executes these requests on the Tuple Pool. We apply the following strategy to process the incoming requests. First off all, the system keeps all locally available metadata keys in a table in the memory. On receipt of a request, the system first checks if the metadata is available in the memory by checking with the metadata-key table. If the requested metadata is not available in the local system, the request is forwarded to the Pub-Sub Manager layer to probe other Hybrid Services for the requested metadata. If the metadata is in the in-memory storage, then the request processor utilizes the Tuple Space Access API and executes the query in the Tuple Pool. In some cases, requests may require to be executed in the local information service back-end. For an example, if the client's query requires SQL query capabilities, it will be forwarded to the Information Resource Manager, which is responsible of managing the local information service implementations.

Secondly, once the request is extracted and processed, the system presents abstraction layers

for some capabilities such as access control and notification. First capability is the access control management. This capability layer is intended to provide access controlling for metadata accesses. As the focus of our investigation is distributed metadata management aspects of information services, we leave out the research and implementation of this capability as future study. The second capability is the notification management. Here, the system informs the interested parties of the state changes happening in the metadata. This way the requested entities can keep track of information regarding a particular metadata instance.

Thirdly, if the request is to be handled in the memory, the Tuple Space Access API is used to enable the access to the in-memory storage. This API allows us to perform operations on the Tuple Pool. The Tuple Pool is an in-memory storage. The Tuple Pool provides a storage capability where the metadata instances of different information service schemas can be represented.

Fourthly, once the metadata instances are stored in the Tuple Pool as tuple objects, the tuple processor layer is being used to process tuples and provide a variety of capabilities. The first capability is the LifeTime Management. Each metadata instance may have a lifetime defined by the user. If the metadata lifetime is exceeded, then it is evicted from the Tuple Pool. The second capability is the Persistency Management. The system checks with the tuple space every so often for newly-added / updated tuples and stores them into the local information service back-end. The third capability is the Dynamic Caching Management. The system keeps track of the requests coming from the other Hybrid Service instances and replicates/migrates metadata to where the high demand is originated. The fourth capability is the Fault Tolerance Management. The system again checks with the tuple space every so often for newly-added / updated tuples and replicates them in other information services using the pub-sub system. This service is also responsible for providing consistency among the replicated datasets. As the main focus of this paper is to discuss information federation in Information Services, the detailed discussion on replication, distribution, consistency enforcement aspects of the system is left out as the focus of another paper (Aktas, Fox, & Pierce, 2008).

The Hybrid Service supports a federation capability to address the problem of providing integrated access to heterogeneous metadata. To facilitate the testing of this capability, a Unified Schema is introduced by integrating different information service schemas. If the metadata is an instance of the Unified Schema, such metadata needs to be mapped into the appropriate local information service back-end. To achieve this, the Hybrid Service utilizes the filtering layer. This layer does filtering based on the user-defined mapping rules to provide transformations between the Unified Schema instances and local schema instances. If the metadata is an instance of a local schema, then the system does not apply any filtering, and backs-up this metadata to the corresponding local information service back-end.

Fifthly, if the metadata is to be stored to the information service backend (for persistency of information), the Information Resource Management layer is used to provide connection with the back-end resource. The Information Resource Manager handles with the management of local information service implementations. It provides decoupling between the Hybrid Service and sub-systems. With the implementation of Information Resource Manager, we have provided a uniform, single interface to sub-information systems. The Resource Handler implements the sub-information system functionalities. Each information service implementation has a Resource Handler that enables interaction with the Hybrid Service.

Sixthly, if the metadata is to be replicated/stored into other Hybrid Service instances, the Pub-Sub Management Layer is used for managing interactions with the Pub-Sub network. On receiving the requests from the Tuple Processor, the Pub-Sub Manager publishes the request to the corresponding topics. The Pub-Sub Manager may also receive key-based access/storage requests from the pub-sub network. In this case, these requests will be carried out on the Tuple Pool by utilizing TupleSpace Access API. The Pub-Sub Manager utilizes publisher and subscriber sub-components in order to provide communication among the instances of the Hybrid Services.

## PROTOTYPE IMPLEMENTATION

The Hybrid Information Service prototype implementation consists of various modules such as Query and Publishing, Expeditor, Filter and Resource Manager, Sequencer, Access and Storage. This software is open source project and available at (Aktas). The Query and Publishing module is responsible for processing the incoming requests issued by end-users. The Expeditor module forms a generalized in-memory storage mechanism and provides a number of capabilities such as persistency of information. The Filter and Resource Manager modules provide decoupling between the Hybrid Information Service and the sub-systems. The Sequencer module is responsible for labeling each incoming context with a synchronized timestamp. Finally, the Access and Storage modules are responsible for actual communication between the distributed Hybrid Service nodes to support the functionalities of a replica hosting system.

**The Query and Publishing module** is responsible for implementing a uniform access interface for the Hybrid Information Service. This module implements the Request Processing abstraction layer with access control and notification capabilities. On completing the request processing task, the Query and Publishing module utilizes the Tuple Space API to execute the request on the Tuple Pool. On completion of operation, the Query and Publication module sends the result to the client. As discussed earlier, context information may not be open to anyone, so there is a need for an information security mechanism. We leave out the investigation and implementation of this mechanism as a future study. We must note that to facilitate testing of the centralized Hybrid Service in various application use domains, we implemented a simple information security mechanism. Based on this implementation, the centralized Hybrid Service requires an authentication token to restrict who can perform inquiry/publish operation. The authorization token is obtained from the Hybrid Service at the beginning of client-server interaction. In this scenario, a client can only access the system if he/she is an authorized user by the system and his/her credentials match. If the client is authorized, he/she is granted with an authentication token which needs to be passed in the argument lists of publish/inquiry operations. The Query and Publishing module also implements a notification scheme. This is achieved by utilizing a publish-subscribe based messaging scheme. This enables users of Hybrid Service to utilize a push-based information retrieval capability where the interested parties are notified of the state changes. This push-based approach reduces the server load caused by continuous information polling. We use the NaradaBrokering software (Pallickara & Fox, 2003) as the messaging infrastructure and its

libraries to implement subscriber and publisher components.

**The Expeditor module** implements the Tuple Spaces Access API, Tuple Pool and Tuple-processing layer. The Tuple Spaces Access API provides an access interface on the Tuple Pool. The Tuple Pool is a generalized in-memory storage mechanism. Here, to meet the performance requirement of the proposed architecture, we built an in-memory storage based on the TupleSpaces paradigm (Carriero & Gelernter, 1989). The Tuple-processing layer introduces a number of capabilities: LifeTime Management, Persistency Management, Dynamic Caching Management and Fault Tolerance Management. Here, the LifeTime Manager is responsible for evicting those tuples with expired leases. The Persistency Manager is responsible for backing-up newly-stored/updated metadata into the information service back-ends. The Fault Tolerance Manager is responsible for creating replicas of the newly added metadata. The Dynamic Caching Manager is responsible for replicating/migrating metadata under high demand onto replica servers where the demand originated.

**The Filtering module** implements the filtering layer, which provides a mapping capability based on the user defined mapping rules. The Filtering module obtains the mapping rule information from the user-provided mapping rule files. As the mapping rule file, we use the XSL (stylesheet language for XML) Transformation (XSLT) file. The XSLT provides a general purpose XML transformation based on pre-defined mapping rules. Here, the mapping happens between the XML APIs of the Unified Schema and the local information service schemas (such as WS-Context or extended UDDI schemas).

**The Information Resource Manager module** handles with management of local information service implementations such as the extended UDDI. The Resource Manager module separates the Hybrid System from the sub-system classes. It knows which sub-system classes are responsible for a request and what method needs to be executed by processing the specification-mapping metadata file that belongs the local information service under consideration. On receipt of a request, the Information Resource Manager checks with the corresponding mapping file and obtain information about the specification-implementation. Such information could be about a class (which needs to be executed), it's function (which needs to be invoked), and function's input and output types, so that the Information Resource Manager can delegate the handling of incoming request to appropriate sub-system. By using this approach, the Hybrid Service can support one-to-many information services as long as the sub-system implementation classes and the specification-mapping metadata (SpecMetadata) files are provided. The Resource Handler is an external component to the Hybrid Service. It is used to interact with sub-information systems. Each specification has a Resource Handler, which allows interaction with the database. The Hybrid System classes communicate with the sub-information systems by sending requests to the Information Resource Manager, which forwards the requests to the appropriate sub-system implementation. Although the sub-system object (from the corresponding Resource Handler) performs the actual work, the Information Resource Manager seems as if it is doing the work from the perspective of the Hybrid Service inner-classes. This approach separates the Hybrid Service implementation from the local schema-specific implementations.

**The Resource Manager module** is also used for recovery purposes. We have provided a recovery process to support persistent in-memory storage capability. This type of failure may occur if the physical memory is wiped out when power fails or machine crashes. This recovery process converts the database data to in-memory storage data (from the last backup). It runs at the bootstrap of the Hybrid Service. This process utilizes user-provided "find_schemaEntity" XML documents to retrieve instances of schema entities from the information

service backend. Each "find_schemaEntity" XML document is a wrapper for schema specific "find" operations. At the bootstrap of the system, firstly, the recovery process applies the schema-specific find functions on the information service backend and retrieves metadata instances of schema entities. Secondly, the recovery process stores these metadata instances into the in-memory storage to achive persistent in-memory storage.

In order to impose an order on updates, each context has to be time-stamped before it is stored or updated in the system. The responsibility of the Sequencer module is to assign a timestamp to each metadata, which will be stored into the Hybrid Service. To do this, the Sequencer module interacts with Network Time Protocol (NTP)-based time service (Bulut, Pallickara, & Fox, 2004) implemented by NaradaBrokering (Pallickara & Fox, 2003) software. This service achieves synchronized timestamps by synchronizing the machine clocks with atomic timeservers available across the globe.

## CONCLUSION

This chapter introduced the principles and experiences of designing and building a web-based Enterprise Information Service. Within this emphasis, it also introduced a novel architecture for an Enterprise Information Service, called Hybrid Service, supporting handling and discovery of not only quasi-static, stateless metadata, but also session related metadata.

The Hybrid Service is an add-on architecture that runs one layer above existing information service implementations. Although, it mainly manages metadata that maybe associated to Web Services, it can also be used to manage any metadata about Web resources on the Internet. It provides unification, federation and interoperability of Enterprise Information Services. To achieve unification, the Hybrid Service is designed as a generic system with front and back-end abstraction layers supporting one-to-many local information systems and their communication protocols. To achieve federation, the Hybrid Service is designed to support information integration technique in which metadata from several heterogeneous sources are transferred into a global schema and queried with a uniform query interface. To manage both quasi-static and dynamic metadata and provide interoperability with wide-range of Web Service applications, the Hybrid Service is integrated with two local information services: WS-Context XML Metadata Service and Extended UDDI XML Metadata Service. The WS-Context Service is implemented based on WS-Context Specification to manage dynamic, session related metadata. The Extended UDDI Service is implemented based on an extended version of the UDDI Specification to manage semi-static, stateless metadata.

# REFERENCES

Aktas, M. S. (n.d.). Fault tolerant high performance information service-FTHPIS-hybrid WS-context service Web site. Retrieved from http://www.opengrids.org/wscontext

Aktas, M. S., Fox, G. C., Pierce, M. E. (2008). Distributed high performance grid information service. Submitted to *Journal of Systems and Software*.

Bellwood, T., Clement, L., & von Riegen, C. (2003). *UDDI version 3.0.1: UDDI spec technical committee specification*. Retrieved from http://uddi.org/pubs/uddi-v3.0.1-20031014.htm

Bulut, H., Pallickara, S., & Fox, G. (2004, June 16-18). Implementing a NTP-based time service within a distributed brokering system. In *ACM International Conference on the Principles and Practice of Programming in Java*, Las Vegas, NV.

Bunting, B., Chapman, M., Hurley, O., Little, M., Mischinkinky, J., Newcomer, E., et al. (2003). *Web services context (WS-context) version 1.0*. Retrieved from http://www.arjuna.com/library/specs/ws_caf_1-0/WS-CTX.pdf

Carriero, N., & Gelernter, D. (1989). Linda in context. *Communications of the ACM, 32*(4), 444–458. doi:10.1145/63334.63337

Dialani, V. (2002). *UDDI-M version 1.0 API specification*. Southampton, UK: University of Southampton.

Florescu, D., Levy, A., & Mendelzon, A. (1998). Database techniques for the World Wide Web: A survey. *SIGMOD Record, 27*(3), 59–74. doi:10.1145/290593.290605

Galdos. *Galdos Inc.* Retrieved from http://www.galdosinc.com

GRIMOIRES. (n.d.). UDDI compliant Web service registry with metadata annotation extension. Retrieved from http://sourceforge.net/projects/grimoires

MyGrid. (n.d.). UK e-science project. Retrieved from http://www.mygrid.org.uk

OGF Grid Interoperation Now Community Group (GIN-CG). (n.d.). Retrieved from https://forge.gridforum.org/projects/gin

Open_GIS_Consortium_Inc. (2003). *OWS1.2 UDDI experiment. OpenGIS interoperability program report OGC 03-028*. Retrieved from http://www.opengeospatial.org/docs/03-028.pdf

Ozsu, T. P. V. (1999). *Principles of distributed database systems*, 2nd edition. Prentice Hall.

Pallickara, S., & Fox, G. (2003). NaradaBrokering: A distributed middleware framework and architecture for enabling durable peer-to-peer grids. In *Proceedings of ACM/IFIP/USENIX International Middleware Conference Middleware-2003*, Rio Janeiro, Brazil.

Pallickara, S., & Fox, G. (2003). NaradaBrokering: A middleware framework and architecture for enabling durable peer-to-peer grids. (LNCS). Springer-Verlag.

ShaikhAli. A., Rana, O., Al-Ali, R., & Walker, D. (2003). UDDIe: An extended registry for Web services. In *Proceedings of the Service Oriented Computing: Models, Architectures, and Applications,* Orlando, FL. SAINT-2003 IEEE Computer Society Press.

Sun_Microsystems. (1999). JavaSpaces specification revision 1.0. Retrieved from http://www.sun.com/jini/specs/js.ps

Sycline. *Sycline Inc.* Retrieved from http://www.synclineinc.com

Valduriez, P., & Pacitti, E. (2004). Data management in large-scale P2P systems. *Int. Conf. on High Performance Computing for Computational Science (VecPar2004).* ( [). Springer.]. *LNCS, 3402,* 109–122.

Verma, K., Sivashanmugam, K., Sheth, A., Patil, A., Oundhakar, S., & Miller, J. (n.d.). METEOR–S WSDI: A scalable P2P infrastructure of registries for semantic publication and discovery of Web services. *Journal of Information Technology and Management.*

Zanikolas, S., & Sakellariou, R. (2005). A taxonomy of grid monitoring systems. *Future Generation Computer Systems, 21*(1), 163–188. doi:10.1016/j.future.2004.07.002

Ziegler, P., & Dittrich, K. (2004). Three decades of data integration-all problems solved? In *WCC,* 3-12.

# Chapter 5
# Optimization of Enterprise Information System through a 'User Involvement Framework in Learning Organizations'

**Sumita Dave**
*Shri Shankaracharya Institute of Management & Technology, India*

**Monica Shrivastava**
*Shri Shankaracharya Institute of Management & Technology, India*

## ABSTRACT

*Enterprise resource planning (ERP) today is being adopted by business organizations worldwide with a view to maximize their capabilities. But more often than not the expected outcomes are not delivered due to inaccurate calculations with respect to the organization's ability to adapt to the change. Although the benefits of enterprise information systems in streamlining the functions of the organization cannot be questioned, preparing the organization to adopt the new system needs more focused efforts. In order to ensure that the existing capabilities of the organizations are an enabler and not an inhibitor in the adoption process, they need to be learning organizations. A study was conducted in Bhilai Steel Plant (BSP), one of the leading steel manufacturing public companies in India, where ERP is to be adopted. In spite of the fact that it has a strong backbone of resources in terms of information technology (IT) infrastructure, the implementation process is virtually on a standstill. In this chapter, an evaluation of the psychological capabilities of the organization is done. This can be evaluated through the mindset of the workforce and the willingness with which they are ready to adopt change.*

## INTRODUCTION

### Information Technology

Information Technology is the key driver for change and is instrumental in the creation of lean organizations where technology fully supports the implementation of quality enhancement techniques to meet the growing demands of competition. Moreover the competitive pressures and escalating maintenance costs is pressuring organizations to replace the legacy system of operations. The envisioned benefits of IT enabled change is the

DOI: 10.4018/978-1-60566-723-2.ch005

enhancement of competitive ability through the networking of geographically distant work groups and a more effective utilization of man, material and machine.

While evaluating the benefits of enterprise information systems, the explicit outcome is change in the organization's system as a whole to implement the new practices and processes and ideas. With the introduction of a knowledge base, the challenge for the organization gets magnified as the perceived flexibility when evaluated in physical terms may be accurate but may fall short in meeting the much needed psychological flexibility. Hence, ERP and other forms of IT enabled solutions, which are being widely adopted with a view to maximize capabilities, are not able to deliver the expected outcomes due to such inaccurate calculations.

The implementation of any IT enabled operations systems requires a systematic approach which includes the evaluation of the organization's learning capabilities. Hammer and Champy (1993) focused on IT based organizational reengineering. Their vision can be summarized along the following points.

1.  Radical transformation: It is time consuming and does not happen overnight.
2.  Changes come from a clean slate through the conceptualization of gradual work arrangements unlike total quality management.
3.  The focus of change should be process based.
4.  The change needs to be initiated at the top and then directed downwards throughout the organization. and
5.  Seamless access to information to one and all.

Hence, in order to ensure that the IT enabled change acts as an enabler of growth, it becomes necessary to evaluate the firm's learning capabilities. Organizational learning takes place when successful organization learning is transferred to

an organization's shared beliefs. Learning is the key competency required by any organization that wants to survive and thrive in the new knowledge economy. As organizations grow old though they accumulate competencies, resources and knowledge, there is a possibility that their structures become a hindrance to their ability to respond to the challenges posed by the competition. A constructivist-learning environment is a place where people can draw upon resources to make sense out of things and construct meaningful solutions to problems. It emphasizes the importance of meaningful, authentic activities that help the learner to construct understandings and develop skills relevant for solving problems.

"Make learning part of every day office environment" is the mantra to survive in this competitive world. The Learning Organization is one that learns continuously and transforms itself. Learning takes place in individuals, teams, the organizations, and even the communities with which the organizations interact. Learning results in changes in knowledge, beliefs, and behaviors. Learning also enhances organizational capacity for innovation and growth. The Learning Organization has embedded systems or mechanisms to capture and share learning. Thus organizational learning is an important part of **Organizational Transformation process**.

## Enterprise Information System

An Enterprise Information System (EIS) is a type of management information system made to facilitate and support the information and decision making needs of senior executives by providing easy access to both internal and external information relevant to meeting the strategic goals, of the organization. It is commonly considered as a specialized form of a Decision support system. EISs are defined as computerized information systems designed to be operated directly by executive managers without the need of any intermediaries. Their aim is to provide fast and easy access to information from a variety of sources (both internal and external to the organisation). They are easily customizable and can be tailored to the needs and preferences of the individual executive using it. They deliver information of both soft and hard nature. This information is presented in a format that can be easily accessed and most readily interpreted. This is usually achieved by the utilization of multiple modes of accessing data and the use of Graphical User Interfaces (GUIs).

Choosing the appropriate software is vital to designing an effective EIS. Therefore, the software components and how they integrate the data into one system are very important. According to the Wikipedia, the basic software needed for a typical EIS includes four components:

1. Text base software. The most common form of text is probably documents;
2. Database. Heterogeneous databases residing on a range of vendor-specific and open computer platforms help executives access both internal and external data;
3. Graphic base. Graphics can turn volumes of text and statistics into visual information for executives. Typical graphic types are: time series charts, scatter diagrams, maps, motion graphics, sequence charts, and comparison-oriented graphs (i.e., bar charts);
4. Model base. The EIS models contain routine and special statistical, financial, and other quantitative analysis.

Enterprise Resource Planning (ERP) helps to cater to the changing information requirements of the Enterprise Information System very efficiently and effectively. An EIS can provide key indicators of company performance, based on the information in ERP database and external factors.

## LEGACY SYSTEMS

The phrase "legacy replacement" has crept its way into almost everyone's vocabulary throughout both the business and technical ranks. Generally legacy systems replacement term is used to imply improvement, or elimination of the negative or obsolete. According to the dictionary, replace means "provide an equivalent for" but the new 'IT' based solutions provide much more than the older systems. Enterprise wide system replacements can be extremely disruptive to the entire organization, with catastrophic results if not well implemented. Flexibility, speed, immediate access and anywhere-anytime computing are no longer luxuries. They are now the necessities of interacting with customers in an on-line environment. Use of internet and the availability of information online have left no stones unturned to increase customer expectations for immediate service and this relatively new expectation has left many businesses scrambling to adopt modern technology like ERP in order to meet the demand.

During the past few years, business houses have gone through a technology and process learning curve to respond to these new service demands. For a multitude of technical reasons, these legacy systems simply cannot be adequately retrofitted to address current and future business requirements in a cost- or time-effective manner.

## Success Story Due to Legacy Systems

Bhilai Steel Plant, a unit of Steel Authority of India Limited (SAIL), a Navratna, is one of the most profits making steel industry in India. It was established in the year 1958. Many legacy systems are working in the organization presently, some of which are going to be replaced by the ERP system soon. (see Figure 1)

*Figure 1. (Adapted from C&IT Dept, Bhilai Steel Plant)*

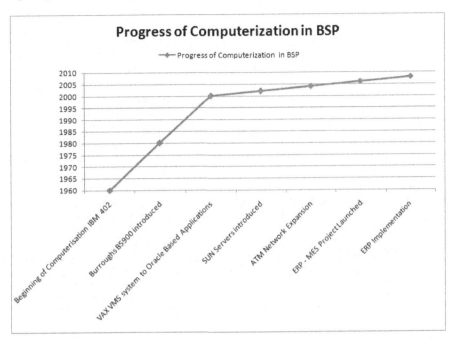

Studies have revealed that the rate of success of IT enabled change is rather low. Although, IT enabled change has significantly altered the managerial paradigms within the organization with a view to raise the organization to a higher plane of performance through a greater involvement of the employees at large, by functionally integrating the various departments, it was found in a study conducted by us that success begets success may not always hold true.

Some of the areas where legacy systems are currently working and running successfully in BSP are shown in Table 1.

Over the years substantial data has been collected which is helping the decision making with respect to different business processes. One of the most extensive System of Bhilai Steel Plant is the Materials Management System. This system is as old as computerization in BSP. It started with IBM mainframes and tape drives and graduated to VAX VMS based system, developed with the help of the Digital Company, got transformed on introduction of SUN Servers, Oracle database

and Developer 2000 and finally went on the web with Oracle 10g, Apache Web Servers and JSP, all developed in-house.

The Materials Management System was developed to take care of procurement of Stores and Spares, quality management, logistics management, bill processing, bill payment and inventory management of these procured items. To facilitate the system, masters like material master, vendor master, etc were extensively developed and sections identified to maintain them.

With the introduction of ATM network across the Plant, the systems were extended beyond the boundaries of Materials Management, to the end users. Planning sections across the Plants were able to prepare Purchase Requisitions and send them online through the approval process to the Purchase Department for procurement action. Customized forms were developed in Legacy system to cater to this. They were also able place reservations for items lying in the central stores. Various queries were provided to end users thereby improved the visibility of stock and reduced over indenting of

*Table 1.*

| Groups | Areas | Benefits |
|---|---|---|
| Financial Management | Finance, VMS, Oprn. A/c, RMBA, EFBS, Cost Control, Assets, Braman, ORAMS, E-Payment etc. | Timely closing of accounts, online details of financial Transactions, Online CPF Loan, Faster & accurate payment to parties through e-payment, Advance processing of Employee Tours etc. |
| Sales and Order progressing | OASIS, CISF Manpower Deployment System, PRAHARI, VATACS etc. | Online Invoice Preparation Vehicle monitoring, Daily Duty Chart for CISF, etc |
| Employee and Estate Services | Payroll for regular & DPR employees, Estate Services, CPF & Allied Jobs, Time Offices, Leave Accounting, VRS Module, Final Settlement module etc. | Qtr allotment, Salary payment on time, e-TDS, HB Advances and other Loans & recoveries, CPF Ledger, Estate Third Party Billing, Incentives Calculation, VRS details etc |
| Personnel Administration and Hospital Management and Web Services | HRIS, HRD, HMS, Contract Mgmt, Contract Labour System, UDAN, DATES, PADAM, DBA Activities, Assignment Monitoring System, Web Services etc. | Personal details, LTC/LLTC details, Training Details, Patients & Pharmacy accounting, All details & monitoring of Contacts in non works areas, Registration & online attendance system, Various departmental home pages etc |
| Networking, Hardware and Procurement | H/w Maintenance, Planning & Procurement, Networking and Computer Operation. | Hardware Complaints & monitoring, Procurement of Computer Assets and consumables including stationeries, 24 x 7 computer operation and monitoring of servers, Various reports for Users and Top Management etc. |

stores and spares. This had a tremendous impact on the inventory turnover ratio which has considerably gone down.

With the introduction of the concept of Door Delivery through the Store Issue Note Generation System (SINGS), a number of material chasers were redeployed for other jobs in the shops as the responsibility of delivery of stores and spares was shifted to the stores department which carried out this function centrally. The vehicles used by various shops were redeployed. Thus due to introduction of this system there was substantial reduction of manpower and vehicle requirement in the shops.

With the complete Purchasing activity on the system, the Purchasing lead time got considerably reduced. The introduction of in-house E – Procurement system was a major step forward for the Materials Management System as with this the legacy system was treading into the challenging Internet world where encryption, security & transparency were the new challenges. This again was successfully implemented and has gone a long way in reducing the Purchasing Lead time thereby saving a lot of revenue for the company. Other

units of SAIL have outsourced this application through a company Metal Junction. The in-house development and maintenance of the E – procurement solution has saved a lot of outflow of revenue of the company. About 65% of the total volume of procurement is being carried out through the E – procurement route.

Computerization of Store Bills and Store Accounting section and linking it to the Materials Management System lead to a huge reduction of manpower who were required before to process bills manually. The payment lead time also got considerably reduced thereby winning the goodwill of the suppliers of the company. The introduction of E – Payment has further reduced the lead time and the manpower required.

With the built-up of database of transactions and historical data, a number of analyses are helping the company take correct decisions. Inventory analysis, ABC analysis, XYZ analysis, lead time of procurement of items, analysis of non moving items and slow moving items has helped in reducing inventory and also take informed decisions during procurement.

Lately the control of Procurement Budget and Consumption Budget has been strengthened and regular monitoring is being done by the higher management. Another area of concern of the management – Shop Inventory has been addressed by a legacy system which monitors the shop floor inventory of BSP. All these are possible only due to the strong legacy system in Bhilai Steel Plant.

With the introduction of various legacy systems in the company, executives and non executives were forced to take up learning computers. This has improved the skill set of employees and also of the developers of the legacy systems who have to continuously upgrade themselves to match the pace with the industry. With the introduction of E – procurement, even the small suppliers too have taken up computers and are hugely benefitting out of this.

## Limitations of the Present System in BSP

The legacy systems being used in the plant are able to help meet the demands of the plant in the present scenario, but in days to come with the advent of newer technologies and new competition the present system will not be that effective. Hence, the management has decided to implement Enterprise Resource Planning in order to meet the changing demands of the market.

The present systems have been made to cater to demands of a particular area and hence are not holistic in nature. Because of this, there is no centralized database and the systems are not integrated, resulting in less user involvement and interaction with the system.

## Need for Change

Most organizations across the world have realized that in a rapidly changing environment, it is impossible to create and maintain a custom designed or tailor made software package which will cater to all their requirements and also be completely up-to-date. Realizing the requirement of such organizations, software like Enterprise Resource Planning solution incorporating best business practices have been designed, which will offer an integrated software solution to all the business functions of an organization.

In the ever growing business environment the following demands often plague an organization:

- Cost control initiatives
- Need to analyze costs or revenues on a product or customer basis
- Flexibility to respond to ever changing business requirements
- More informed management decision making by seamless information flow
- Changes in ways of doing business
- Simulate the complexity of variables effecting businesses

Difficulty in getting accurate data, timely information and improper interface of the complex natured business functions have been identified as the hurdles in the growth of any business. Time and again depending upon the speed of the growing business needs, many solutions have come up and ERP is one of such solution.

Some of the features of ERP which are compelling organizations to make it part and parcel of their business activities are:

- It facilitates company-wide Integrated Information System covering all functional areas like Manufacturing, Selling and distribution, Payables, Receivables, Inventory, Accounts, Human resources, Purchases etc.,
- It performs core activities and increases customer service.
- It bridges the information gap across the organisation i.e. results in seamless flow of information.

- It supports multiple platforms, multiple currency, multimode manufacturing and is multi-linguistic in nature.
- It provides for complete integration of Systems not only across the departments in a company but also across the companies under the same management.
- It allows automatic introduction of latest technologies like Electronic Fund Transfer, Electronic Data Interchange (EDI), Internet, Intranet, E-Commerce etc.
- It not only addresses the current requirements of the company but also provides the opportunity of continually improving and refining business processes.
- It integrates all the levels of information system and provides business intelligence tools like Decision Support Systems (DSS), Executive Information System (EIS), management dashboards, and strategic enterprise management, Reporting, Data Mining and Early Warning Systems (Robots) for enabling people to make better decisions and thus improve their business processes.
- It also enables collaborative processes with business partners and links suppliers, organization and customers more effectively.

In order to reap the benefits and implement change effectively the companies need to be learning organizations.

## Organization Learning

*"Organizations where people continually expand their capacity to create the results they truly desire, where new and expansive patterns of thinking are nurtured, where collective aspiration is set free, and where people are continually learning to learn together" (Peter Senge, 1990)*

*Table 2. (Adapted from FORUM Journal Volume 93.1)*

| Learning Organizations |
|---|
| Respond to environment change |
| Tolerate stress |
| Compete |
| Exploit new niches |
| Take risks/ mutate |
| Develop symbiotic relationships |

Learning organizations are those that have in place systems, mechanisms and processes, that are used to continually enhance their capabilities and those who work with it or for it, to achieve sustainable objectives - for themselves and the communities in which they participate. (see Table 2)

According to Mr. Udai Parekh, "The concept of learning organization is a natural extension of organizational learning". Organizations today are changing in terms of values, structures, processes and expectations. We need to help the employees prepare for the living in the new organizations. In the new organizations, it is expected that employees have substantial content knowledge in their work specialization and be well prepared in the process and behavioral dimensions of their experiences in the changing organizations. The process and behavioral dimensions such as effective communication skills and negotiation skills are attributes that play a vital role in individual and group learning. Individuals at all levels in the organization must combine the mastery of some technical expertise with the ability to interact effectively with customers and clients, work productively in teams and critically reflect upon and then change their own original practices.

Learning organizations creates a language that is ideal, an approach, a vision to move towards a type of organization that one wants to work in and which can succeed in the world of increasing change and interdependency. A learning organization requires a basic shift in how we think and interact and these changes go to bedrock assumptions and habits of our culture.

## Key Variables

According to Mr. Udai Parekh, the key variables which play a very important role during organization learning are:-

1.  Holistic frame $(X_1)$
2.  Strategic thinking $(X_2)$
3.  Shared vision $(X_3)$
4.  Empowerment $(X_4)$
5.  Information Flow $(X_5)$
6.  Emotional maturity $(X_6)$
7.  Learning $(X_7)$
8.  Synergy $(X_8)$

**Holistic framework $(X_1)$:** Learning should be done within holistic framework, i.e, by taking into account the environment in which the organization functions, putting emphasis on the causatives of the problem rather than the symptoms, learning not just for short term gains but for a vision, by understanding the relationships and interrelations between the various facets of an organization.

**Strategic thinking $(X_2)$:** careful strategies should be design in terms of which areas to be targeted first, what would be the implications of each step, clearly defining the roles and policies of the organization, creating an environment which will support learning. The strategy should be well communicated at all levels to ensure its success.

**Shared vision $(X_3)$:** Vision should be developed by employee's participation. Communicating vision and freezing it is also an important aspect, which needs to be taken into consideration. The top management must lay emphasis on the creating an environment full of transparency, motivation and help nurture creativity and leadership traits.

**Empowerment $(X_4)$:** creating an environment where there are decentralized structures which enable more participation, more power, a culture of trust, faster decision making, rewards and incentives is very important aspect and cannot be ignored.

**Information Flow $(X_5)$:** Transparency in working, seamless flow of information, sharing of critical information at all levels, minimum grapevine, encouraging development by sharing is a very important aspect.

**Emotional maturity $(X_6)$:.** An environment where integrity, discipline, devotion, teamwork, transparency, mutual respect and moral responsibility should be created which will help to evolve a culture of trust thus, enabling the employees to be more loyal, committed, able to control their emotions and keep the organizations achievement a step higher than their own personal achievements.

**Learning $(X_7)$:** A learning environment encourages self-development allowing space for discussions, enquiries, freedom of speech and reward schemes. The management should felicitate people who are ready to accept the change.

**Synergy $(X_8)$:** The dynamic energetic atmosphere is created when participants interact and productively communicate with each other and in groups. The cooperative efforts of the participants create an enhanced combined effect compared to the sum of their individual effects. An effort for coordinated activities, enhanced teamwork, cross-functional teams, is a must for the organizations to be called learning organizations.

Bhilai Steel Plant, a unit of SAIL with strength of 34,800 employees, is an integrated steel plant with end-to-end processes of generation of Raw Materials to selling the finished goods. Different departments have different systems with less of integration resulting into duplicity and limited information flow. With the competitive business scenario and the need of advanced functionalities like Strategic Enterprise Management, Business

Information Warehousing, Business Process Simulation, etc. the need of a standard world-class product is being felt which could enhance effectiveness of the processes and functions within the system. The existing bureaucratic culture is impairing holistic framework, empowerment, organization climate, shared vision, which is making employees feel less motivated and hence the overall learning process has taken a backseat. The major players of learning process, namely structure, processes and information flow in the current scenario is becoming a deterrent in making the company, outsmart its competitors and face the change in economy.

Hence an LOP survey was done on BSP to identify the key areas where improvement is possible to enhance the learning capabilities of the organization so as to facilitate a smooth adoption of technologies.

## Research Methodology

**Sampling:** Simple Random sampling was undertaken on Bhilai Steel Plant and five (5) major departments namely; materials management, plant maintenance, purchase, finance and quality management were covered.

**Sample Size**: 50 Executives.

**Data Collection Period**: Prior to the implementation of ERP.

**Statistical Instruments Used**: Single factor ANOVA to test whether the 8 parameters are significantly different or not.

**Level of Consideration**: 5% level of significance

## Hypothesis

$H_0$: All parameters have the same potential according to the employees

$(X_1=X_2=X_3=X_4=X_5=X_6=X_7=X_8)$

$H_1$: All the parameters do not have the same potential according to the employees.

$(X_i \neq X_j)$, (where i, j =1,2,3,4,5,6,7,8)

*Table 3. ANOVA: Single factor*

| For Elements $X_1$, $X_3$ and $X_6$ | | | | | | |
|---|---|---|---|---|---|---|
| SUMMARY | | | | | | |
| **Groups** | Count | Sum | Average | Variance | | |
| $X_1$ | 50 | 1463 | 29.26 | 100.32 | | |
| $X_3$ | 50 | 1411 | 28.22 | 125.28 | | |
| $X_6$ | 50 | 1409 | 28.18 | 99.46 | | |
| ANOVA | | | | | | |
| **Source of Variation** | SS | df | MS | F | P-value | F crit |
| Between Groups | 37.49 | 2 | 18.75 | 0.17 | 0.84 | 3.06 |
| Within Groups | 15927.58 | 147 | 108.35 | | | |
| Total | 15965.07 | 149 | | | | |

$H_0$: Accepted Conclusion: $X_1$, $X_3$ and $X_6$ are not significantly different at 5% level of significance

## Assumption

30 points are assumed to be the standard value of parameters (where x >= 30) (see Table 3)

## Findings

The $X_1$, $X_3$ and $X_6$ (Holistic framework, shared vision, emotional maturity) parameters are below 30 (all respondents hold the same opinion.)

**Inference**

It is concluded that parameters $X_1$, $X_3$ and $X_6$ are really below the assumed value indicating that they are weak parameters. All the employees support this opinion (refer to table 1).

The rest five parameters (strategic thinking, empowerment, information flow, emotional maturity, learning and synergy) are above 30 (all respondents hold the same opinion.) (see Table 4)

**Inference**

It is further concluded that parameters $X_2$, $X_4$, $X_5$, $X_7$, $X_8$, are the strong parameters and all the employees support this.

It can be supported by table –3 where all parameters are taken together and all the employees have different opinions which suggests that there is bipolarization of opinion. (see Table 5)

**Inference**

From 1-8 parameters, if ANOVA is conducted at a time all employees hold different opinions about different parameters.

It can be observed that BSP lacks

1. A holistic framework of operations
2. Shared vision – free flow of communication, hence transparency and
3. Emotional maturity – Poor teamwork and lack of commitment and mutual respect

## Suggestions

In order to overcome the identified deficiencies and to induce organization learning in a better way, it is essential that BSP adopts practices in order to make ground more fertile to adopt ERP thus, initiate the process of transformation. It needs to

*Table 4.*

| For Elements $X_2$, $X_4$, $X_5$, $X_7$, and $X_8$ | | | | | | |
|---|---|---|---|---|---|---|
| SUMMARY | | | | | | |
| **Groups** | **Count** | **Sum** | **Average** | **Variance** | | |
| $X_2$ | 50 | 1657 | 33.14 | 89.43 | | |
| $X_4$ | 50 | 1614 | 32.28 | 135.96 | | |
| $X_5$ | 50 | 1561 | 31.22 | 165.73 | | |
| $X_7$ | 50 | 1858 | 37.16 | 217.16 | | |
| $X_8$ | 50 | 1588 | 31.76 | 181.66 | | |
| ANOVA | | | | | | |
| **Source of Variation** | **SS** | **df** | **MS** | **F** | **P-value** | **F crit** |
| Between Groups | 1124.344 | 4 | 281.09 | 1.78 | 0.13 | 2.41 |
| Within Groups | 38706.520 | 245 | 157.99 | | | |
| Total | 39830.864 | 249 | | | | |

$H_0$: Accepted
Conclusion: $X_2$, $X_4$, $X_5$, $X_7$ and $X_8$ are not significantly different at 5% level of significance

*Table 5.*

| For All Elements from $X_1$ to $X_8$ | | | | | | | |
|---|---|---|---|---|---|---|---|
| SUMMARY | | | | | | | |
| **Groups** | **Count** | **Sum** | **Average** | **Variance** | | | |
| $X_1$ | 50 | 1463 | 29.26 | 100.32 | | | |
| $X_2$ | 50 | 1657 | 33.14 | 89.43 | | | |
| $X_3$ | 50 | 1411 | 28.22 | 125.28 | | | |
| $X_4$ | 50 | 1614 | 32.28 | 135.96 | | | |
| $X_5$ | 50 | 1561 | 31.22 | 165.73 | | | |
| $X_6$ | 50 | 1409 | 28.18 | 99.46 | | | |
| $X_7$ | 50 | 1858 | 37.16 | 217.16 | | | |
| $X_8$ | 50 | 1588 | 31.76 | 181.66 | | | |
| ANOVA | | | | | | | |
| **Source of Variation** | **SS** | **df** | **MS** | **F** | **P-value** | **F crit** | |
| Between Groups | 3110.0975 | 7 | 444.30 | 3.19 | 0.003 | 2.03 | |
| Within Groups | 54634.1000 | 392 | 139.37 | | | | |
| Total | 57744.1975 | 399 | | | | | |

$H_0$: Rejected Conclusion: Elements from $X_1$ to $X_8$ are significantly different at 5% level of significance

1.  Search for novel solutions
2.  Give and seek information
3.  Honour the contributions of others
4.  Seek and give evaluation
5.  Question basic assumptions and practices

In order to encourage experimental learning and collaborative teamwork which is both problem finding as well as problem solving, suggested methods to stimulate creative learning include

1.  RAT (Role Analysis Transaction)
2.  Diagnostic Window

**RAT** is a tool for improving the effectiveness of work groups. It helps to clarify the role expectations; i.e. the expectations the members of the work group have for their own performance and for the performance of other group members. The role requirements are determined by consensus, which ultimately results in more effective and mutually satisfactory performance. It enhances participation and collaboration, hence enhanced

holistic framework, shared vision and emotional maturity.

**Diagnostic Window** – It helps the groups to identify important issues and problems. The issues are discussed according to the following quadrants shown in Table 6.

The idea is to reach a consensus on issues and the likelihood of change where it is required and help the group to define some action plans to address the needed change. This activity not only encourages participation and communication but also enhances commitment thus stimulating critical thinking about the organization needs and priorities.

RAT and Diagnostic window can be most helpful in conditions of structural change such

*Table 6.*

| Amenable to change | Potential | Operational |
|---|---|---|
| Not Amenable to change | Disaster | Temporary |

as that of BSP as they help to address personal and behavioral adjustments to the creation of change.

## CONCLUSION

To be able to maintain the market share there is a definite need for change and the organizations with is capable of learning are able to implement the same in more effective manner. Change is accompanied by resistance which can be managed by proper user training and communication. Thus, although it is very necessary for organizations to adopt IT enabled operations; a proper analysis of the existing legacy system needs to be done in the light of the existing system so as to ensure full and timely acceptability of the new technology.

## REFERENCES

Amburgey, T., Kelly, D., & Barnett, W. P. (1993). Resetting the clock: The dynamics of organization change and failure. *Administrative Science Quarterly, 38*, 51–73. doi:10.2307/2393254

Argyris, C. (1982). *Reasoning learning and action: Individual and organizational.* Jossey Bass.

Argyris, C. (1991). Teaching smart people how to learn. *Harvard Business Review.*

Baron, J. N., Burton, D. M., & Hannan, M. T. (1996). *The road taken: Origins and evolution of employment.*

Booth, W. C., Williams, J. M., & Colomb, G. G. (2003). *The craft of research.* University of Chicago.

Bordens, K. S. (2005). *Research design methods*, 6th edition. Bruch & Abbot, TMH.

Coulsin-Thomas, C. (1996). Business process reengineering: Myth and reality. London: Kogna Page.

Courtney, N. (1996). BPR sources and uses. In C. Coulsin-Thomas (Ed.), Business *process engineering: Myth and reality* (pp. 226-250). London: Kogna Page.

Davenport, T. H. (1996). *Process innovation: Reengineering work through information technology.*

Dayal, I., & Thomas, J. M. (1968). Role analysis technique, operation KPE: Developing a new organization. *The Journal of Applied Behavioral Science, 4*(4), 473–506. doi:10.1177/002188636800400405

Garwin, D. A. (1993). Building a learning organization. *Harvard Management Review*, 88-91.

Gupta, V. (2004). *Transformative organizations: A global perspective.* Response Books.

Hammer, M., & Champy, J. (1993). *Reengineering the corporation: A manifesto for business revolution.* New York: Harper Collins.

Hammer, M., & Stanton, S. A. (1995). *The reengineering revolution handbook.* London: Harper Collins.

Leedy, P. D., & Ormrod, J. E. (2004). *Practical research: Planning and design.* PHI.

Linden, R. (1984). *Seamless government: A practical guide to reengineering in public sector.*

Lyons, P. (1999). *Assessment techniques to enhance organization learning.* Opinion papers.

Pareek, U. (2002). *Training instruments in HRD & OD*, 2nd edition. TMH.

Ruma, S. (1974). *A diagnostic model for organizational change, social change* (pp. 3-5).

Seinge, P. (1991). An interview with Peter Seinge: Learning organizations made plain. Training and Development.

Senge, P. (n.d.). *The fifth discipline: The art and practice of learning organizations*. Doubleday/Currency.

Shajahan, S. (2005). *Research methods for management*, 3rd edition. Jaico Publishing House.

Vaughan, D. (1997). The trickle down effect: Policy decisions, risky work, and the challenge tragedy. *California Management Review, 39*(2), 80–102.

# Chapter 6

# Always–On Enterprise Information Systems with Service Oriented Architecture and Load Balancing

**Serdal Bayram**
*Siemens, Turkey*

**Melih Kırlıdoğ**
*Marmara University, Turkey*

**Özalp Vayvay**
*Marmara University, Turkey*

## ABSTRACT

*In today's world, it is essential for a business to provide a seamless and continuous service to its customers. Such an always-on service is required, not only for the strong competitive environment but also because of the fact that most the customers also have to offer seamless and continuous service to their own customers. In this chain, failure of one of the systems even for a short time can result in a disaster in the entire service chain. A wise approach to provide a continuous service should consider all possible failure areas in a computer-based information system. Since hardware and software are vulnerable to a myriad of problems that can halt the normal operation of a system, an ideal solution should not only consider both of these two components, but also should seek to find ways for them to work in support of each other against a malfunction. This chapter is an attempt to develop a model that provides this functionality. Service oriented architecture (SOA) is implemented in the model due to its tenets that are suitable for such functionality.*

## INTRODUCTION

Due to the ever-increasing reliance of the society on the Enterprise Information Systems (EIS), these systems need to be up and running all the time. Malfunction even for a short time can have disastrous consequences in many environments such as banks where almost all of the processes are performed through the IS round-the-clock. This situation is aggravated by the competitive environment where

DOI: 10.4018/978-1-60566-723-2.ch006

service consumers have the power of shifting into another service provider in the slightest flaw of satisfaction. The activities and services can be easily imitated by competitors thanks to the ever-increasing standardization of IS that perform these activities and services.

Hence, offering a continuous service is of utmost importance for today's businesses where undisruptive service means lack of failure of IS on which the services depend. However, due to the inherent fragility of IS, there are myriad of factors that have the potential of disrupting the smooth running of these systems. Since IS have mainly two distinct components, namely hardware and software, it is plausible to scrutinize potential failure reasons in these two distinct components where potential failure areas are different from each other. This chapter proposes a model that aims continuous EIS operation in terms of hardware and software components where these components work in tandem. The model uses Service Oriented Architecture (SOA) as an important component of the software side of the model. This chapter is organized as follows: SOA, which is implemented as the main software component of the model is described in the following section. That section will also cover the Quality of Service (QoS) and Enterprise Service Bus (ESB) concepts of SOA due to their relevancy to the proposed model. Hardware component of the model and the Load Balancer will be described in the following section which will be followed by the section which describes the tandem working of SOA and Load Balancer. A case study that has been developed by the model will be explained next and the chapter will terminate with the conclusion.

## SOFTWARE COMPONENT: SERVICE ORIENTED ARCHITECTURE

Although SOA can be defined in several ways, all definitions can be categorized in two main perspectives, namely business perspective and technical perspective. Business perspective can be analyzed in terms of business processes and business services, whereas technical perspective can be analyzed in terms of software components and operational resources. The two perspectives, their components, and their interrelationships are illustrated in the Figure 1.

*Figure 1. SOA with Technical and Business Perspective (adapted from OMG)*

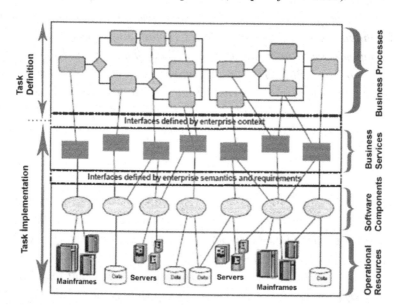

From the business perspective, which is seen as top level in the figure, SOA is an architectural style that guides all aspects of creating and using business processes (Newcomer & Lomow, 2005). In this view, business processes and their management are highlighted and Business Process Management (BPM) concept arises. BPM can be defined as the method of efficiently aligning an organization with the wants and needs of clients. Business perspective contains the interaction between business services and business processes. A business process can contain one or more business services, and a business service can be used in one or more business processes.

The technical perspective is depicted in the lower half of the figure. According to this perspective, SOA can be defined as a kind of distributed computing that is designed to allow the communication of software components, namely services, across a network. In this view, services are performed by software components and SOA contains interactions of these software components in a distributing computing environment. Under services, there are some operational resources such as database servers or mainframes. At a higher level of abstraction, business processes and services are implemented through the technical level which contains software components and operational resources.

In this environment, SOA can be defined as follows:

*"A service-Oriented Architecture (SOA) is a software architecture that is based on the key concepts of an application frontend, service, service repository, and service bus. A service consists of a contract, one or more interfaces, and an implementation" (Krafzig, Banke & Dirk, 2005, p.57).*

According to this definition, there are four main elements of SOA: Application frontend, service, service repository, and service bus. Application frontend is the component that is used to initiate, control, and receive the results. For example, it can be the interfaces that have been designed through GUI concepts or batch program triggers which invoke the services. It can also be used for controlling the execution of services.

The second element in definition of SOA is the service. A service can be described as "a component capable of performing a task" (Sprott & Wilkes, 2004, p.2). Although a service can be seen as a task or an activity, it is more complicated than these concepts. This is due to the fact that every service has a contract, an interface, and an implementation routine. Josuttis (2007) argues that a service has the following attributes:

- **Self-contained:** Self-contained means independent and autonomous. Although there can be exceptions, a service should be self-contained. In order for the services to be self-contained, their inter-dependencies should be kept in a minimum level.
- **Coarse-grained:** This indicates the implementation detail level of services for consumers. Implementation details are hidden for a service consumer because the consumer doesn't care about such details.
- **Visible/Discoverable:** A service should be visible and easily reachable. This is also important for reusability which means that a service can be used multiple times in multiple systems.
- **Stateless:** Services, ideally, but not always, should be stateless. This means that a service request does not affect another request because service calls don't hold invocation parameters and execution attributes in a stateless service. On the other hand, sometimes a service can be stateful, such as shopping-chart services because they have to hold service invocation sticky attributes, like products that are put in to the shopping-basket.
- **Idempotent:** This means the ability of redo or rollback. In some case, while a service is

executing, a bad response can be returned to the service consumer. In such a case service consumers can rollback or redo the service execution.

- **Composable:** For a composable service, the service can contain several sub-services where they can be separated from the main service. A composable service can call another composable service.

- **QoS and Service Level Agreement (SLA)-Capable:** A service should provide some non-functional requirements such as runtime performance, reliability, availability, and security. These requirements are important for QoS and SLA.

- **Pre- and Post-Conditions:** These specify the constraints and benefits of the service execution. Pre-condition represents the state before the service execution. Post-condition represents the state after the service execution.

- **Vendor Diverse:** SOA is neither a technology nor a product. It is also platform (or vendor) independent. This means that a SOA platform can be implemented by different products and one does not need to be familiar with the technology used for the service.

- **Interoperable:** Services should be highly interoperable. They can be called from any other systems. Interoperability provides the ability of different systems and organization to work together. In other words, services can be called from any other system regardless of the types of environment for them.

The third element of SOA is the Service Repository. As explained above, a service should be easily discoverable. This requirement is realized by the Service Repository. All required information when calling a service such as arguments, operation service provider, access rights, and QoS values can be retrieved from the Service Repository. Service Repository holds meta-data about services and it provides service dictionary to the systems.

The last element of SOA is the Service Bus. Service Bus is used to connect the service consumer and service provider. Through the Service Bus, the concepts of connectivity (interconnections between the components of an SOA system) and heterogeneity of technology (communication of a variety of technologies among themselves) are achieved.

SOA offers several advantages some of which are explained below:

- **Distributed Computing:** Distributed Computing is an old concept that has been developed in the last 30 years. Goff (2004) describes a distributed system as "embedded in a single device or can operate within cluster of devices in which the nodes work together to appear as a single node, offering a unified view of system resources to the application". In the SOA perspective, a service does not need to reside on the same physical machine as the calling client (frontend). The capability of calling a program (or service) from another service which is located on a different server in another physical location is one of the main tenets of SOA. From this point of view, SOA is well-suited to dealing with complex distributed systems which are becoming more and more common in today's world.

- **Loose Coupling:** This is another key concept in SOA which is essential to minimize the impact of modifications and failures on the whole system which is usually made up of several components. Coupling refers to degree of dependency between any two systems (Papazoglou, 2008). In a loosely coupled system failure of a component has minimal effect on other components thereby preventing the failure of the entire system. This concept is also useful in a dynamic business environment where existing requirements often change and frequently new requirements are introduced. The minimal level of coupling between the components is a real advantage in such an environment, because it provides easy maintainability and flexibility. In the SOA, modules and services are loosely coupled by using physical connections via a mediator. On the contrary, physical connections are established with point-to-point communication in a tightly coupled system.

- **Heterogeneous Systems:** An important tenet of today's complex world is the heterogeneity of components in a software system. A complex distributed system should be able to run across a range of different platforms such as different operating systems, databases, and application servers. Although interoperability of heterogeneous systems is not a goal in SOA *per se*, SOA provides an excellent environment for such a system through the concept of loose coupling.

## Quality of Service in Service Oriented Architecture

According to Choi *et al.* (2007), QoS is determined by non-functional requirements of service such as availability, performance, reliability, usability, discoverability, adaptability, and composability (Figure 2).

These attributes are ideally included in the service contract. Although QoS attributes are hidden to service consumers due to the black-box nature of SOA, they are important to provide the continuity and smooth running of the system. Availability and reliability are of utmost importance in providing the continuity of the system and performance is important due to its relation with service quality. Hence, these three particularly important attributes for an always-on system will be elaborated:

- **Availability** is the degree accessibility for a service by the service requestors. In order for a service to be available, it must be operational as a prerequisite. Relation between these two concepts can be formulated as follows:

$$Availability\ of\ Service = \frac{Service\ Operating\ Time}{Service\ Operating\ Time + Service\ Reparing\ Time}$$

In this formula Service Operating Time is uptime of the service and Service Repairing Time is down-time. The range of availability is 0..1 where higher value means higher availability of service.

- **Performance** is the capability of service to provide appropriate response and processing times and throughput rates when performing its function under stated conditions. Service Response Time (SRT) and Throughput (TP) of a service are the metrics of the performance. SRT is calculated as follows:

SRT = (Time when service consumer finishes sending request to the service) – (Time when service consumer starts receiving response from service)

SRT is always greater than zero and a low SRT means high performance.

The other performance metric, Throughput represents the number of service requests at unit time and it can be calculated as follows:

$$Thoughput\ (TP) = \frac{Number\ of\ Completed\ Service\ Requests}{Unit\ Time}$$

High Throughput indicates high performance.

- **Reliability** is the ability of a service to keep operating with specified level of

*Figure 2. Service quality model in SOA environment (adapted from Choi et al., 2007)*

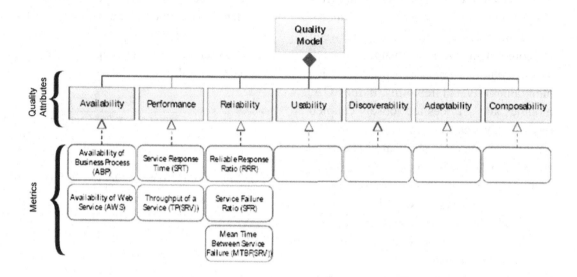

performance over time. Since services are reusable and can be used in multiple applications in a SOA environment, the reliability of a service can affect several applications. The metrics of reliability are Reliable Response Ratio (RRR), Service Failure Ratio (SFR), and Mean Time Between Service Failure (MTBSF). RRR can be calculated as:

$$RRR = \frac{Number\ of\ Reliable\ Response}{Total\ Number\ of\ Requests}$$

SFR can be calculated as:

$$SFR = \frac{Number\ of\ Failures}{Time\ Period}$$

Lower SFR means higher reliability. The third metric, MTBSF, can be calculated as:

$$MTBSF = \frac{Summation\ of\ Time\ Between\ Failures}{Time\ Number\ of\ Failures}$$

MTBSF represents the average time between two failures and high MTBSF means higher reliability.

## Enterprise Service Bus in Service Oriented Architecture

ESB is a kind of SOA based software infrastructure for business application integration (or Enterprise Application Integration (EAI)). As seen in the Figure 3, main responsibility of ESB is to enable service consumers to call the services provided. Today's complex business structures demand several platforms to interoperate. This means that ESB should provide an environment where the system would be technology-independent. In other words, ESB should work like a medium for smooth operation of services originating from a diverse range of sources. Josuttis (2007) lists some functionalities of ESB:

- **Providing Connectivity:** As explained before, the main purpose of the ESB is to provide connectivity. Not only different hardware and software platforms but also distinct implementation of services can be connected via ESB. The ESB works like a universal language.
- **Data Transformation:** The ESB can also be used for data transformation. In some cases, extracted data from the source is not fit to the destination system because formats are different. ESB deals with this problem and it translates the data as required. For example, let's say that a source service has the Name and Surname as different fields and the destination service has these combined. In such a case ESB concatenates the fields as:

"Name", "Surname" → *(ESB transformation)* → "Name, Surname"

(see Figure 3)

- **Intelligent Routing:** The ESB routes requests to the service according to pre-defined rules. According to data from the service requester, a service provider can be chosen via the ESB. This is an important capability for providing a continuous operation because through Intelligent Routing the load might be shifted from an ailing unit to another one automatically when required. This can be possible by making the Intelligent Routing work in tandem with the Load Balancer. Whenever a service fails or has too much load, ESB routes the request to another service or unit according to the load balancing algorithm. In order for this to be realized, there should be replicated services in the system. As illustrated in the Figure 4, whenever a service consumer requests a service, ESB invokes the Load Balancer which directs the request to the idle service. The Load Balancer also continuously monitors the availability of each

*Figure 3. Example of enterprise service bus*

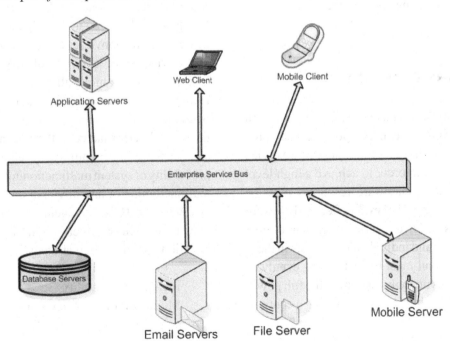

*Figure 4. An ESB with a load balancer for provided services (adapted from Josuttis, 2007)*

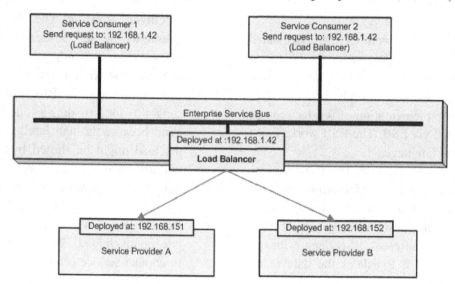

service and whenever a service that is consumed is down for any reason it directs the request to another service that is available at that time. In such a case the interrupted work is rolled-back and restarted by the new available service. (see Figure 4)

- ESB also provides additional functionalities for security, service management, service monitoring and logging.

## HARDWARE COMPONENTS

The responsiveness is the most important health factor of a SOA system. Responsiveness is the level of availability and timeliness of a service when requested. In order to achieve a high level of responsiveness hardware resources must be utilized effectively. The key for effective hardware utilization is to have a series of resource units such as servers and individual processors in these servers. The load must be distributed evenly to these resources not only for getting the full power of the hardware, but also for providing a continu-

ous service in case of a hardware malfunction. In the proposed system this is achieved through a software component called Load Balancer.

## Load Balancer

SOA enables a distributed system. Like all distributed systems it is likely that some components are more heavily loaded when some others are lightly loaded or even idle. In the SOA terminology unit in the above sentence can be translated as a service. Since it is desirable to distribute the workload evenly among all the services, an agent responsible for this task is required. Effective operation of such a service will not only increase the overall performance of the system but it will also increase its reliability by eliminating the probability of system malfunctioning as a result of malfunctioning of an individual unit or service.

The Load Balancer agent has the following objectives each of which might have some implications on the design strategy:

- Increased Reliability
- Minimization of response time

- Maximization of throughput
- Predictability of response times
- Balanced distribution of work load
- Shifting the process to other resources in case of a malfunction

A load distribution plan must decide where and when a given service should be executed in order to increase performance and make the system available and reliable. There are mainly two types of load distribution policies, namely static policy and dynamic policy. In static polices, load is distributed without taking into consideration of the current state of the system. On the other hand, dynamic policies use the system-state information to make load distribution decisions, so they have the potential to perform better than static polices by the improved quality of their decisions. Another advantage of the dynamic policies is their capability to perform through monitoring the long-term status of the components and deciding accordingly so that they are not affected by short-term load surges. Although dynamic policies consume some system resources for such a monitoring task, this cost can be justified when compared by the advantages provided.

In order to realize the objectives of the Load Balancer there are several commonly used algorithms of load distribution such as Round Robin Algorithm (RRA), Random Load Balancing Algorithm (RLBA), Weight-Based Algorithm (WBA), and Hardware-Awareness Minimum Load Algorithm (HAMLA). Although these algorithms are mainly used for load distribution among particular servers, they can also be used for load distribution among particular services in a SOA environment. Since the proposed model uses all these algorithms they need to be explained:

- **RRA:** In the Round-Robin Algorithm, where static load distribution policy is employed, there is a list of server resources and they are selected one at a time in order. The advantages of the round-robin

algorithm are that it is simple, cheap, and very predictable. None of the servers have priority to the others. RRA is advantageous in cases where the work loads of the tasks and capacities of servers are close to each other. In cases where opposite is true, i.e., where there are major variations in workloads and server capacities RRA might not be effective. For example, the tasks executed on a comparably less powerful server will take more time than the others, resulting in the overall degrade of the system performance.

- **RLBA:** In Random Load Balancing Algorithm service requests are routed to servers randomly. The algorithm is also good in cases where the power of servers is close to each other. Otherwise, the problem described in the RRA is also applicable for RLBA. RLBA also employs static load distribution policy.

- **WBA:** Weight-Based Load Balancing bears a resemblance to the RRA and it also employs static load balancing policy. The only difference with the RRA is that a pre-assigned weight for each server is taken into account when distributing the load. The weight usually varies between 1 and 100 and it determines the load capacity of each server compared to the others. Load distribution is made according to the weight, i.e., a server that has twice the weight of another one can bear twice as much as the other. Hence, WBA is finely applicable for heterogeneous systems where server capacities vary.

- **HAMLA:** In Hardware-Awareness Minimum Load Algorithm the Load Balancer selects the minimum loaded server to route the request. In order to perform this, the balancer has to consider several hardware parameters such as CPU usages, memory usages, and/or I/O operations. This algorithm is more complicated than the others and it uses some models such as Service Level Checker (Polling System) and Service Status Monitoring System. These models are as follows:

- **Service Level Checker System:** In order to have real-time information about the work load of individual servers they are continuously monitored by a polling system. This system produces historical availability information that can be used by the Load Balancer to gain an insight for the behavior of the system. This information can be used as a basis for the Service Level Agreement (SLA) between service requestor and service provider in the SOA.
- **Service Status Monitoring System:** Service Status Monitoring System provides the following system information for the Load Balancer:
  - **CPU idle ratio:** Calculated as 1-CPU usage ratio. The load balancer tends to choose the server that has the maximum CPU idle ratio for the next request.
  - **Available Memory Ratio:** Calculated as available memory divided by the system maximum memory. The load balancer tends to choose the server that has the maximum AMR for the next request.
  - **Disk I/O intensity:** Defines the disc usage at real time with information such as read bytes and write bytes. Load Balancer tends to choose the server that has the minimum disk I/O for the next request.
  - **Open Sessions:** The number of connected users at a specific time. When the number of active (open) sessions increases, server consumption increases. Load Balancer tends to choose the server that has the minimum open session number for the

next request.

Parameters of Service Level Checker System and Service Status Monitoring System are used by HAMLA not only for diverting the requests to the idle services, but also for informing the operators about the problems of the services.

## SOA AND LOAD BALANCER WORKING IN TANDEM FOR CONTINUITY

As explained in the previous sections, SOA has the capability of providing continuity from the software side and Load Balancer can do that from the hardware side. This section will explain the suggested model that uses these components that work in tandem to provide an environment where probability for failure will be minimum.

In order to explain the main tenets of the model, consider the following simple scenario: We have a small service organization where only four roles exist. Let this be an accounting company which lodges tax files for individual customers. The first role is the customer to be served. The second role is the one that is performed by the experts of the company who actually fill in the tax forms for the client. The third role is performed by the manager that assigns tasks to the experts who perform the second task. The last role is performed by the supervisor who continuously monitors the current and the future work load of the experts. In other words, the supervisor is knowledgeable for the tax files of each expert that is currently processed as well as that are waiting in the queue. The supervisor is also knowledgeable about the competence level of each expert in terms of speed and accuracy.

According to the sample scenario, as illustrated in the Figure 5 below, the customer sends the tax lodging request to the manager. After accepting the task, the manager then asks the supervisor which expert is most suitable for the new task in terms of work load. The supervisor checks the experts' current workload and the works of each that wait in the queue. S/he then chooses the most suitable expert for the new task and informs the manager about it. The process of choosing the most suitable expert for the new task is performed by the supervisor through a specific algorithm. The manager then assigns the new task to the expert pointed by the supervisor.

Translating this scenario to the SOA terminology, the customer is the service consumer, the manager is the ESB, and the experts are individual services. The supervisor performs the task of the Load Balancer in the model. In other words, the three roles of the model are performed in terms of SOA concept and the fourth one, which is the supervisor's role, is performed outside SOA.

This scenario can further be elaborated in terms of the proposed model in Figure 6. Service Consumers correspond to customers of Figure 5, the main ESB performs the task of the manager, Service Providers correspond to the tax experts,

and Load Balancer Component corresponds to the supervisor.

In the model, the requests of the service consumers are first confronted by the main ESB at the top. The key task performed here by the main ESB is to route the requests to the most convenient algorithm. In order to accomplish this task, the main ESB invokes the Load Balancer Component which is responsible for selecting the most suitable algorithm. Load Balancer then selects the appropriate service through that algorithm. This process is performed by invoking the Service Router ESB which is responsible by routing the task to the previously selected service provider.

Although choosing the most appropriate Load Balancer algorithm can be performed through Artificial Intelligence methods, the proposed model currently does not support such a method. Instead, this task is currently performed manually.

The four service selectors in the Load Balancer component are based on the four algorithms ex-

*Figure 5. The scenario for load balancing with SOA*

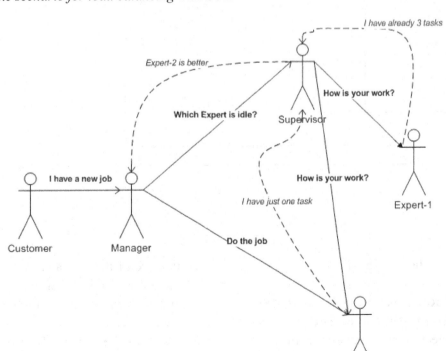

*Figure 6. The proposed model with SOA roles and load balancer*

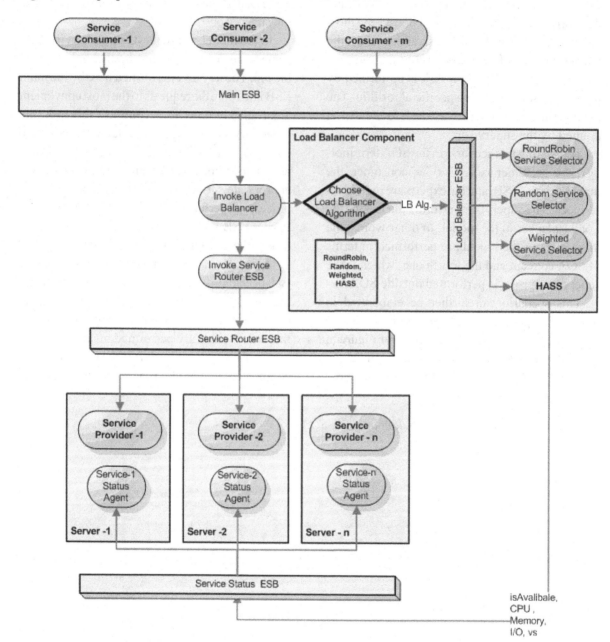

plained above. They are as follows:

• **Round Robin Service Selector (RRSS):**
This service selector is based on RRA which means that all requests are distributed to the services equally without regarding

the size of the task and the power of the service provider. When service resources and tasks are homogenous RRSS is a good alternative.

• **Random Service Selector (RSS):**
Random Service Selector runs the RLBA.

A service request is routed to a random service provider. This selector also works best when service resources and tasks are homogeneous.

- **Weighted Service Selector (WSS):** This selector is based on WBA described in Load Balancer algorithms. Every service has a pre-defined weight as load factor. The requests are routed according to this weight. For example, if the weight ratio is 1:2 for two services the number of requests that are routed to the second service will be as twice as the number for the first service provided that both tasks are of equal size. WSS is suitable for both heterogonous and homogonous capacity resources.

- **Hardware Awareness Service Selector (HASS):** This is based on HAMLA explained above. It chooses the most appropriate service provider according to the parameters of the hardware like CPU, memory, and I/O. Additionally, availability of the service provider is also considered. This relationship is shown in Figure 6 with the connection between Service Status ESB and HASS. As an example, if all of service providers are available but memory of the server of the first service provider is higher than the others and all other system values are equal then the selector chooses this service for routing the next request. The service selector gets the service state information from Service Status ESB that collects the status information from service agents.

After getting the right service for the current request from Load Balancer Component, Service Router ESB (SR-ESB) is invoked. SR-ESB is used to direct the request to the relevant service. Each candidate service runs on a different server container. This is an essential requirement for the proposed model, because as explained above, a computer system may cease to function as a result of either hardware or software resources.

On the software side services are monitored by Service Status Agents. The agents contain Service Status Monitoring and Service Level Checker Systems which are explained in Load Balancer. The agents are aware of the availability and work load of their relevant services through the Service Level Checker and the Service Status Monitoring Systems. When a service selector like HASS needs this information, SS-ESB makes this information available to the service selector.

If the system did not use the SOA concept, all connections would be point-to-point where there would be tight coupling among different components of the system. In such a case malfunction of a single unit would have adverse effects on the entire system. SOA and the concept of ESB in load balancing process provides loose coupling where malfunction of a unit (other than ESB, of course) simply results in shifting the load to another unit.

Additionally, loose coupling enables easier maintenance and enhancement of the system when business conditions dictate such cases. In essence, loose coupling can only be possible by a modular approach where hardware and software resources are self-contained in an SOA environment.

This environment is quite suitable for providing not only continuity, but also flexibility and agility in business. When requirements change, as it is frequent in a business environment, it is easy to insert a new load balancer selector service. It is also flexible with the "Choose Load Balancer Algorithm" decision activity which can be easily made. For example, a day can be divided into time slices where peak hours, normal workload hours, and idle hours are identified. In these slices different Load Balancer algorithms which fit best to each slice can be used. Most probably, HASS would be more suitable in peak hours where many heavy requests have to be responded and system resources have to be used in a most effective way. On the contrary RRA would probably be more convenient for idle hours such as midnight.

The proposed model offers the SOA's QoS

attributes such as availability, performance, and reliability. Each of these attributes is crucially important in providing business continuity and they deserve further elaboration:

- **Increased availability:** Replicated services can continue to function even in the face of server down time due to hardware failure or maintenance. With a simple calculation, if there are three replicated services and all services have the same availability of 95%, overall system availability can be calculated as (1 – *overall system failure*) which is $(1 – 0.05*0.05*0.05) = 99.9875\%$ provided that the services are stateless, i.e., they do not interfere with each other.

  In cases where even higher availability is required this can be simply accomplished by adding new hardware which hosts additional services.

- **Increased performance:** The service requests which have to be processed simultaneously can easily be performed by the proposed model. Since there are several hardware resources, each of which supporting a service stateless tasks can be processed in parallel by services. This results in reduced processing time for large tasks which involve several sub-tasks.

- **Increased reliability:** As stated above, the degree of reliability can be measured by MTBSF. Reliability of a system is strongly related with the availability of it. The main difference between these concepts is the unit of measure where availability is measured in terms of ratio of time and reliability is measured in terms of time. Since reliability is measured as total time between failures (up time) divided by number of failures, reduced failures through higher availability will result in higher reliability.

## CASE STUDY

The proposed model is applied in a case study. The study employs Oracle SOA Suite which makes use of graphical symbols for service activities and processes. Without actually writing code, Oracle SOA Suite provides tools and techniques to develop a service-based system graphically.

The case study implements the Business Process Execution Language (BPEL) which is a language for specifying business processes in SOA environment. BPEL is an XML-based flow language for the formal specification of business processes and interaction protocols (Papazoglou, 2008).

Normally, service consumers directly connect to service providers in a SOA environment. The difference of the proposed model in this aspect is that the connection is established through the Load Balancer. The implementation of the proposed model is seen in the Figure 7. The figure illustrates the main process of the model which contains the activities of services. There are totally seven activities in the model. The process starts with the Service Consumer's request that targets the Receive_Input activity. Control is then transferred into the Assign_LB_Algorithm activity which is, in the BPEL terminology, an assign activity. These activities are used for assigning values to variables. Assign_LB_Algorithm is used for manually assigning the name of the Load Balancer algorithm intended to be used. The model contains a number of load balancer algorithms which are explained above as RRSS, RSS, WSS, and HASS. After the Load Balancer algorithm is selected, the algorithm is notified to the Load Balancer ESB which is responsible for calling the previously preferred Load Balancer algorithm. This task is accomplished by the Invoke_LB-ESB activity which is an invoke activity in BPEL terminology. Invoke activities are used for calling or invoking a service, LoadBalancerESB service in the model (Figure 8).

*Figure 7. Service routing and load balancer*

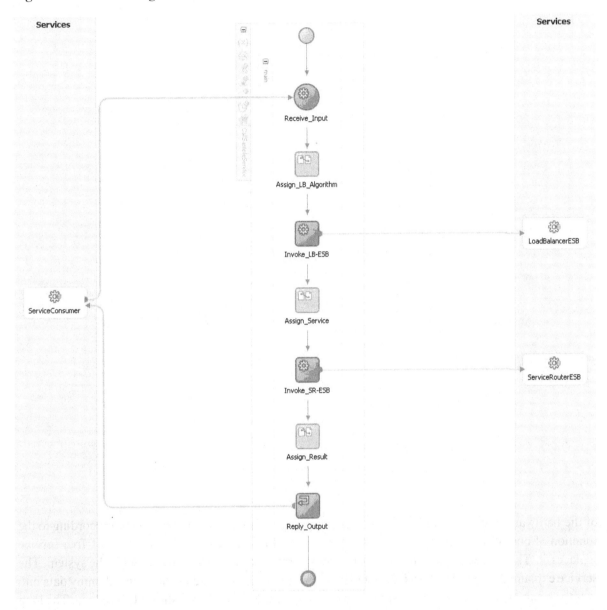

LoadBalancerESB connects the service selectors to the main process. The service selectors choose the service based on their own algorithms. For example, if the selected algorithm in the Assign_LB_Algorithm activity is the Round-Robin then RRSS service will be invoked by the LoadBalancerESB (Figure 8). The LoadBalancerESB also has an output for the selected service name which will be used for routing the request to the relevant service. This output is used as an input for the Assign_Service activity which starts the Invoke_SR-ESB activity which, in turn, invokes the ServiceRouterESB service. This service is used to connect the Service Providers to the model (Figure 8). There are two Service Providers in the model and each of them uses different hardware resources. The Service Status Monitoring System explained above continuously monitors the health

*Figure 8. Load Balancer and Service Router ESBs*

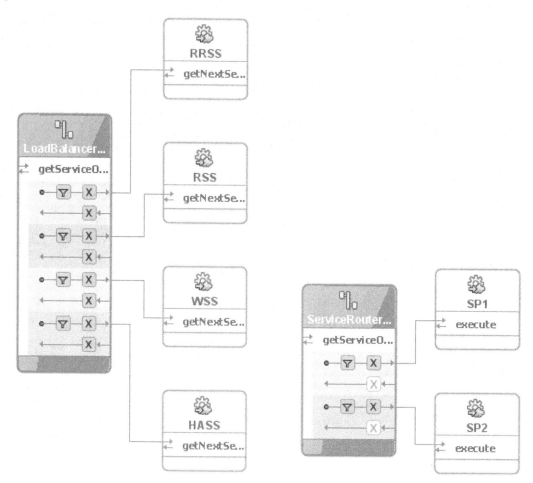

of the hardware resources and in case of a malfunction of one of the resources the second one replaces it. This is accomplished by the HASS service explained above. The ServiceRouterESB gets the result of the execution of the service from the relevant service provider and transfers this value to the Assign_Result activity. The process ends with the transfer of this value to the consumer via the Reply_Output activity.

In order to show the expediency of the model, it was tested with test data. Two rounds of tests were performed, first without the Load Balancer and with only one service working on a single server. The second round was performed with the Load Balancer and in that test two servers were

used. Both tests were performed according to the following scenario: An average of five service requests in a second were sent to the system. The requests involved loading some dummy data into the memory through the CPU by a loop. The loop iterated 100 to 1000 times at each request depending on the load factor of 1 to 10 respectively. Each request was assigned a random load factor. Each test lasted 24 hours which is 1440 minutes. The tests aim to find out the number of failures in a given time due to insufficiency of resources such as memory. The requests load data into the memory and the Garbage Collection service continuously deletes the data loaded by the requests. Failure occurs whenever the system attempts to load data into the memory that is full. In such a case the computer cannot respond to the service requests and the system is regarded to be down until the Garbage Collector clears the memory. Results of the tests in terms of Availability of Service and MTBSF, explained above, are as follows:

In the first test where no Load Balancer was used the down-time of the system was 171 minutes and 87 failures were encountered. This means that uptime of the system was 1269 minutes and the Availability of Service and MTBSF values were calculated as follows:

Availability of Service = 1269 minutes / (1269 minutes +171 minutes) = 0.881

which means that the system was 88.1% available in this case.

MTBSF = 1269 minutes / 87 failures =14.59 minutes / failure.

In the second round the system was tested with the Load Balancer and two separate servers. In this case the down-time of the system was reduced to 39 minutes and 20 failures were encountered which means that uptime was 1401 minutes. The Availability of Service and MTBSF values were calculated as follows:

Availability of Service = 1401 minutes / (1401 minutes + 39 minutes) = 0.973

which means that the system was 97.3% available in this case.

MTBSF = 1401 minutes / 20 failures = 70.05 minutes / failure

The improvement provided by the Load Balancer is from 88.1% to 97.3% in terms of Availability of Service and from 14.59 minutes/ failure to 70.05 in MTBSF. These figures will be much better with increasing number of additional

servers. Although it is impossible to provide 100% availability in theory by this method an acceptable level of high availability can be accomplished.

## CONCLUSION AND FUTURE WORKS

Availability and reliability of a computer system depend on both of the components of the system, namely hardware and software and both of these components are prone to malfunctions and failures. This chapter asserts that one of the ways of developing a highly available and reliable system is to consider the potential failure possibilities not only in hardware or not only in software, but in both of them. Although hardware failures are inevitable, the most plausible way to reduce their impact is to backup them so that if one piece of hardware fails some other can assume its workload. SOA can be helpful in this aspect by having a number of identical services each working on separate hardware. This provides an ideal environment for substituting the service of a healthy hardware instead of an ailing one. SOA can also be helpful in the software side by some its main tenets. Unlike the traditional software where components are tightly coupled in a point-to-point architecture, SOA is based on distributed and heterogeneous architecture and offers loose coupling. Distributed computing allows services to be distributed to different resources thereby enhancing the backup logic, and loose coupling minimizes the impact of modifications and failures on the whole system when there is a problem in one component. The support of SOA for heterogeneous systems is also important in today's world where systems are increasingly large and involving heterogeneous components. In short, the main tenet of model proposed in this chapter is to backup hardware and to support this task with the software. SOA provides an ideal environment for this support.

These arguments are supported by the case study where notable improvements in availability and reliability are achieved by using additional hardware and a SOA-based Load Balancer. However, it must also be acknowledged that using the proposed approach for every task is impossible because the requirement for additional hardware becomes unacceptable after some point. Hence, only key services that allocate main part of the system can be modeled.

The model uses a manual command for choosing the Load Balancing algorithm. As a future work, this may be done automatically through a software agent which has learning capability from the effectiveness of past choices. Such a component should increase the usability of the model.

## REFERENCES

Choi, S. W., Her, J. S., & Kim, S. D. (2007). Modeling QoS attributes and metrics for evaluating services in SOA considering consumers' perspective as the first class requirement. In the *2nd IEEE Asia-Pacific Services Computing Conference* (pp. 398-405). Seoul, Korea: IEEE Computer Society.

Goff, M. K. (2004). *Network distributed computing: Fitscapes and fallacies.* Santa Clara, CA: Prentice Hall.

Josuttis, N. M. (2007). *SOA in practice.* Sebastopol, CA: O'Reilly.

Krafzig, D., Banke, K., & Dirk, S. (2005). *Enterprise SOA: Service-oriented architecture best practices.* Upper Saddle River, NJ: Prentice Hall.

Newcomer, E., & Lomow, G. (2005). *Understanding SOA with Web services.* Upper Saddle River, NJ: Pearson Education.

OMG. (n.d.). *The OMG and service-oriented architecture.* Retrieved on September 10, 2008, from http://www.omg.org/attachments/pdf/OMG-and-the-SOA.pdf

Papazoglou, M. P. (2008). *Web services: Principles and technology.* Harlow/England: Pearson Education Limited.

Sprott, D., & Wilkes, L. (2004). *Understanding service-oriented architecture.* CBDI Forum. Retrieved on October 10, 2008, from http://www.msarchitecturejournal.com/pdf/Understanding_Service-Oriented_Architecture.pdf

# Chapter 7
# Challenges of Data Management in Always-On Enterprise Information Systems

**Mladen Varga**
*University of Zagreb, Croatia*

## ABSTRACT

*Data management in always-on enterprise information systems is an important function that must be governed, that is, planned, supervised, and controlled. According to Data Management Association, data management is the development, execution, and supervision of plans, policies, programs, and practices that control, protect, deliver, and enhance the value of data and information assets. The challenges of successful data management are numerous and vary from technological to conceptual and managerial. The purpose of this chapter is to consider some of the most challenging aspects of data management, whether they are classified as data continuity aspects (e.g., data availability, data protection, data integrity, data security), data improvement aspects (e.g., coping with data overload and data degradation, data integration, data quality, data ownership/stewardship, data privacy, data visualization) or data management aspect (e.g., data governance), and to consider the means of taking care of them.*

## INTRODUCTION

In everyday business we may notice two important data characteristics:

- **Every business is an information business:** All business processes and important events are registered by data and, eventually, stored in an enterprise information system's data base. In other words: if it is not registered by data, it has not happened.

- **Data is registered in digital form:** The majority of important business data is registered in digital form, e.g. the sales data collected at point of sale, the transaction data at automated teller machine, etc. They are all memorized in digital form in various data bases.

The underlying task of an enterprise information system (EIS) is to link processes on the operational,

DOI: 10.4018/978-1-60566-723-2.ch007

management and decision-making level so as to improve performance efficiency, support good quality management and increase decision-making reliability (Brumec, 1997). The EIS's database, specifically its organization and functionality, play a critical role for the functional use of data and information assets in an organization.

Data management involves activities linked with the handling of all organization's data as information resource. The Data Management Association (DAMA) Data Management Body of Knowledge (DAMA, 2008) defines data management as "the development, execution and supervision of plans, policies, programs and practices that control, protect, deliver and enhance the value of data and information assets."

Always-on EIS supports business agility which is the ability to make quick decisions and take actions. "Agility is the ability of an organization to sense environmental change and respond efficiently and effectively to that change" (Gartner, 2006, p. 2). The measurable features that enable a business system to increase the agility of its performance can be defined as follows:

- **Awareness is knowing what is going on:** Awareness level can be determined by answering these questions: Do end users see the right information at the right time? Is the information easily accessible to the right people?
- **Flexibility is the ability to respond appropriately to expected changes in business conditions.**
- **Adaptability is the ability to respond appropriately to unexpected change:** Does the structure of business data promote or prevent flexibility and adaptability is the key question regarding adaptability and flexibility.
- **Productivity is the ability to operate effectively and efficiently:** It is important to establish whether or not business data increase the efficiency and effectiveness of business operations and decisions.

Effective data management in an EIS is essential to fulfil these tasks. This chapter considers various aspects, possibly not all, of data management that seem to be important for running an

*Table 1. Data management aspects and challenges*

| | Aspect | Challenge |
|---|---|---|
| Data continuity | Data availability | Is data available all the time? |
| | Data integrity | Is data integrity compromised? |
| | Data security | Is data secure enough? |
| Data improvement | Data overload | Can we cope with all that data? |
| | Data integration | How to integrate data?<br>Could the data integrate the business?<br>Do we know organization's data?<br>Do we know how to use organization's data? |
| | Data quality | Do we know what quality data is?<br>Are we aware that the quality of data is degradable? |
| | Data ownership/stewardship | Who is the owner/steward of the data? |
| | Data privacy | Is data privacy a concern? |
| | Data visualization | Could we amplify cognition of data? |
| Data management | Data management | Do we need data governance? |

EIS. Table 1 shows the considered aspects and challenges classified as data continuity aspects, data improvement aspects, and data management aspects.

The challenges of successful data management vary from technological to conceptual. Technological aspects of data management help business continuity by making EIS data available, complete, consistent, correct and secure. The aspects addressing the problem of EIS data continuity are described in the section on data continuity.

Once the technological aspects are solved, business may run smoothly. Nevertheless, the business may run even better if it is innovated constantly and persistently. Conceptual aspects deal with important data management issues that can improve business data: coping with data overload, solving data integration problems, improving data quality, assigning data ownership/stewardship, maintaining data privacy, and improving insight into data. In fact, these aspects address the issue of EIS data improvement and are dealt with in the section on data improvement.

## DATA CONTINUITY

### Data Availability

#### Challenge: Is Data Available All the Time?

Enterprises use their EIS based on information technology (IT) infrastructure to increase process productivity, empower users to make faster and more informed decisions, and consequently provide a competitive advantage. As a result, the users are highly dependent on EIS. If a critical EIS application and its data become unavailable, the entire business can be threatened by loss of customers and revenue. Building of EIS that ensures high data availability is critical to the success of enterprises in today's economy.

Data availability is the degree of availability of data upon demand through application, service or other functionality. Data availability importance varies among applications. It is more important if an organization depends on data to provide business service to its customers. Data availability is always measured at an applications' end and by end users. When data is unavailable the users experience the downtime of their applications. Downtime leads to lost business productivity, lost revenue and it ruins customer base. The total cost of downtime is not easy to determine. Direct cost, such as lost revenue and penalties when service level agreement (SLA) objectives are not met, can be quantified but the effects of bad publicity and customer dissatisfaction are hard to determine.

Setting up a data availability strategy may help to define the aims and procedures to achieve the required high data availability. The steps of data availability strategy involve determining data availability requirements, planning, designing and implementing required data availability. Data availability requirements analysis begins with a rigorous business impact analysis that identifies the critical business processes in the organization. Processes may be classified into a few classes:

• Processes with the most stringent high data availability requirements, with recovery time objective (RTO) and recovery point objective (RPO) close to zero, with the system supporting them on a continuous basis, such as internet banking. RTO (Oracle, 2008; IBM, 2008) is maximum amount of time that a business process can be down before the organization begins suffering unacceptable consequences, such as financial loss. RPO is the maximum amount of data a business process may lose before severe harm to organization results. RPO is a measure for data-loss tolerance of a business process. It is measured in terms of time, for example one hour data loss.

- Processes with relaxed data availability and RTO and RPO requirements, with the system that does not need to support extremely high data availability, such as supply chain.
- Processes that do not have rigorous data availability requirements, such as internal organization's business processes.

The challenge in designing a highly available IT infrastructure is to determine all causes of application downtime. Causes of downtime may be planned, such as system or database changes, adding or removing processor or node in cluster, changing hardware configuration, upgrading or patching software, planned changes of logical or physical data structure; and unplanned, such as computer and storage failure, data corruption in database, human errors etc.

Important factors that influence data availability are:

- **Reliability of hardware and software components of the EIS:** hw/sw reliability
- **Recoverability from failure if it occurs:** data protection
- **Timely availability problem detection:** data problem detection

## Hw/Sw Reliability

Storage management is very important because data resides on storage media or storage devices. Disk drives or various disk subsystems, such as RAID (Redundant Array of Independent Disks) or JBOD (Just Bunch Of Disks), are dominant storage media. Although disk drives are very reliable (Mean Time Before Failure - MTBF is almost one million hours) their mechanical nature makes them the most vulnerable part of a computer system. If a storage system includes hundreds or thousands of disk drives, data availability problem becomes very severe. Secondary storage media for backup and archive purposes include removable storage,

optical storage, non-volatile storage, solid state disks, and tape devices.

Modern IT architecture, referred to as cluster or grid computing, has a potential to achieve data availability. Cluster/grid computing architecture effectively pools large numbers of servers and storage devices into a flexible computing resource. Low-cost blade servers, small and inexpensive multiprocessor servers, modular storage technologies, and open source operating systems such as Linux are raw components of this architecture.

High hw/sw reliability may be achieved by using many features. To give some indication on them and not intending to diminish the features of other vendors, here is a non-exhaustive list of Oracle's features (Oracle, 2008):

- **Efficient storage management, such as Oracle's Automatic Storage Management:** The feature spreads database files across all available storage and simplifies the database files management.
- **Redundant storage with high availability and disaster-recovery solution that provides fast failover, such as Oracle's Data Guard:** The feature maintains standby databases as transactionally consistent copies of the primary or production database. When the primary database becomes unavailable the feature switches any standby database to the primary status, minimizing the downtime. It may be used with traditional backup and restore.
- **Fine replication, such as Oracle's Streams:** The feature includes fine-grained replication, many-to-one replication, data transformation etc.
- **Cluster or grid management, such as Oracle's Real Application Clusters and Clusterware:** The features allow the database to run any application across a set of clustered servers. This provides a high level of availability and scalability. In the case that a server fails the database continues to

run on the surviving servers. Also, a new server can be added online without interrupting database operations.

## Data Protection

The main aim of data protection is to recover data from failure if it occurs. High data availability and data vitality can only be ensured using a comprehensive and reliable database backup and recovery strategy, and the ways to locate media loss or corruption. Again, some of Oracle's (Oracle, 2008) features essential to data protection are:

- **Backup and recovery management, such as Oracle's features Secure Backup, and Recovery Manager:** The backup feature must include all modern techniques of local or remote tape devices backup, either on calendar based scheduling or on demand. Data may be encrypted as well. Database recovery is a very demanding job and a good recovery management tool is absolutely necessary. Such a tool may be designed to determine an efficient method of executing backup, restoration or recovery, for example online or offline backup of the whole database or its constituent parts (files, blocks), fast incremental backups (only changed blocks are backuped), and incrementally updated backups (on-disk image copy backups are rolled forward in-place using incremental backups), automatic recovery to control or in time points, etc.
- **Recovery intelligence tool, such as Oracle's Data Recovery Advisor:** The tool which is able to automatically diagnose disk data failures, present repair options and run them.
- **Logical recovery features, such as Oracle's Flashback Technologies:** The feature may analyze and recover data on the row and table level and do fine granular repair, or rewind the entire database to

undo extensive logical errors. It includes a fast database point-in-time "rewind" capability, historical viewing and quick recovery.

Continuous data protection (CDP), also called continuous backup or real-time backup, offers some advantages over traditional data protection. CDP data is continuously backuped by saving a copy of every data change, in contrast to traditional backup where the database is backuped at discrete points of time. In CDP, when data is written to disk, it is also asynchronously written to a second (backup) location over the network, usually another computer. Essentially, CDP preserves a record of every transaction and captures every version of the data that the user saves. This eliminates the need for scheduled backups. It allows restoring data to any point in time, while traditional backup can only restore data to the point at which the backup was taken. Furthermore, CDP may use multiple methods for capturing continuous changes of data, providing fine granularity of restorable objects. In the growing CDP products market the leaders are, among others, IBM Tivoli Continuous Data Protection for Files, Microsoft System Center Data Protection Manager, and Symantec Backup Exec.

In fact, CDP does complete journaling, which is essential for high availability (Schmidt, 2006). Journaling is a property of a database system where changes are first written to a non-volatile area before the database I/O operation has finished. Nevertheless, journaling may be restricted by aggressive cashing techniques where write operation places changes in the RAM and cache management eventually writes the data to disk. Thus, DBMS that resides on a database server, shown in Fig. 1 (Schmidt, 2006), employs persistent storage for actual data (data store), cashing for needed performance and persistent storage for auxiliary data such as logs or journaling.

A relational database supports transactions as the basic units of works. A transaction consists of a series of low-level operations that are all success-

*Figure 1. DBMS and the types of storage*

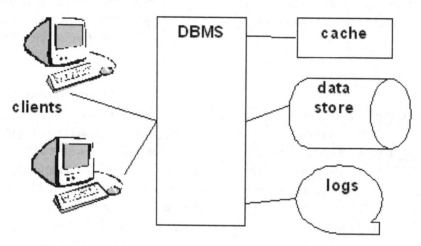

fully executed or not executed at all. Transactions possess ACID properties: *Atomicity* (transaction is either done completely or not at all), *Consistency* (the database does not violate any integrity constraints when a transaction begins and when it ends), *Isolation* (every transaction behaves as if it accesses the database alone) and *Durability* (the successful transaction results are not lost, but remain). In the high-availability environment durability requires special attention. It may be reduced during disaster recovery.

## Data Problem Detection

High data availability can only be achieved as a result of preventive action and early data problem detection. It is advisable to use some of the intelligent tools that automatically diagnose data failures, inform users about them, and assess the impact of the failure, such as Oracle's Data Recovery Advisor.

## Data Integrity

### Challenge: Is Data Integrity Compromised?

Protecting data integrity means ensuring that data is complete, consistent and correct both on physical and logical level. Physical integrity means physical protection from malicious, accidental or natural damage. Logical integrity is preserved if only the permitted combination of data is registered in the data base, in keeping with the data description in the metadata repository.

Data integrity is in an always-on EIS environment, as important as data availability. Data integrity can be compromised in a number of ways. Storage media failure, including cache and controller failures, may cause corruption of data that can be more dangerous than a failure that causes storage to be offline. Corrupted data may be copied during backup operation to backup media without being detected. Consequently, it is extremely important to check data integrity and detect data corruption before it is too late.

Human and logical errors are always possible. For example, a user or application may erroneously modify or delete data. In contrast to physical media corruption, logical errors are difficult to isolate because the database may continue to run without any alerts or errors. Focused repair techniques are thus necessary to combat logical errors.

Repair technology may use the same features that are used in data protection. Again, some of Oracle's features (Oracle, 2008) are:

- Intelligent tool that automatically diagnoses data failures, presents recovery options, and executes recovery, such as Oracle's Data Recovery Advisor.
- Backup and recovery management, such as Oracle's features Secure Backup, and Recovery Manager.
- Logical recovery features, such as Oracle's Flashback Technologies.
- Auditing tool, such as Oracle's Logminer, which can be used to locate changes in the database, to analyse data in the database, and to provide undo operation to rollback logical data corruptions or user errors?

## Data Security

### Challenge: Is Data Secure Enough?

Data security must ensure that access to data is controlled and that data is kept safe from corruption. The broader and more commonly used term is information security, which is the process of protecting information, and information systems, from unauthorized access, use, disclosure, destruction, modification, disruption or distribution (Allen, J. H., 2001). Protection of confidential data, and information, is in many cases a legal issue (e.g. bank accounts data), ethical issue (e.g. information about personal behaviour of individuals), and business issue (e.g. business enterprise customers' data). For individuals, information security has a significant effect on privacy, which is described in the section on data privacy.

The key features of information security are confidentiality, integrity and availability. *Confidentiality* means that the system must not present data to an unauthorized user or system. Confidentiality is usually enforced by encrypting data during transmission, by limiting the number of places where data might appear, and by restricting access to the places where data is stored. *Integrity* means that data cannot be modified without authorization. *Availability* means that data must be available when it is needed. High availability systems aim to remain available at all times, preventing service disruptions due to power outages, hardware failures, and system upgrades.

Data Protection Act is used to ensure that personal data is accessible only to the individuals concerned. Data should be owned or stewarded so that it is clear whose responsibility it is to protect and control access to data. In the security system where the user is given privileges to access and maintain an organization's data, the principle of least privilege should never be overlooked. This principle requires that a user, i.e. user's programs or processes, is granted only the privileges necessary to perform tasks successfully. Organizations must regularly update their user's privileges database, especially when the user is moved to a new job or leaves the organization.

Due to high probability that security threats will appear during EIS lifecycle it is absolutely necessary to establish a security policy, develop and implement security plans and programs, and manage security risks. Many security techniques are standardized. International Standardization Organization (ISO), the world's largest developer of standards, published the following standards: ISO-15443: Information technology - Security techniques - A framework for IT security assurance; ISO-17799: Information technology - Security techniques - Code of practice for information security management; ISO-20000: Information technology - Service management; and ISO-27001: Information technology - Security techniques - Information security management systems. Professional knowledge may be certified as Certified Information Systems Security Professional (CISSP), Information Systems Security Architecture Professional (ISSAP), Information Systems Security Engineering Professional (ISSEP), Information Systems Security Management Professional (ISSMP), and Certified Information Security Manager (CISM).

## DATA IMPROVEMENT

### Data Overload: Exploding Data

#### Challenge: Can We Cope with All that Data?

(IDS, 2008) gives the forecast of worldwide information growth through 2011. It estimates that the digital universe in 2007 numbers $2.25 \times 10^{21}$ bits, and by 2011 it will be 10 times the size it was in 2006. Approximately 70% of the digital universe is created by individuals, but enterprises are responsible for the security, privacy, reliability, and compliance of 87% of the digital universe. The amount of data content is increasing to the point that we individually and collectively suffer from data overload.

Experiments and experience in decision making processes show that data overload negatively impacts decision performance. Decision makers face three problems:

- **problem of timeliness:** high volumes of data constrain them if they are performing both sense making and decision making tasks,
- **problem of throughput:** high volumes of data overwhelm and distract them during sense making tasks, causing "analysis paralysis" and lowering the overall performance, and
- **problem of focus:** decision makers have a finite amount of attention that may be distributed across tasks.

Data fusion is an example of a technique to cope with data overload. By means of fusion, different sources of information are combined to improve the performances of a system (Hall & Mcmullen, 2004). The most obvious illustration of fusion is the use of various sensors, typically to detect a target. The different inputs may originate from a single sensor at different moments (fusion in time) or even from a single sensor at a given moment. In the latter case several experts process the input (fusion on experts).

As a response to the question "Can we ever escape from data overload?" Wood, Paterson & Roth (2002) suggest that the problem can be resolved by cognitive activities involved in extracting meaning from data. They argue "that our situation seems paradoxical: more and more data is available, but our ability to interpret what is available has not increased" (p 23). We are aware that having greater access to data is a great benefit, but the flood of data challenges our ability to find what is informative and meaningful.

Reduction or filtration of data does not seem to solve the problem of data overload. Data which is evaluated as unimportant and non-informative and thus eliminated may turn out to be critically important and informative in another particular situation. Ironically, if the benefit of technology is increased access to data, reduction of data discards some of accessed data.

Data are informative by relationship to other data, relationships to larger frames of reference, and relationships to the interests and expectation of the observer. "Making data meaningful always requires cognitive work to put the datum of interest into the context of related data and issues" (Wood, Paterson & Roth, 2002, p. 32). Therefore, all approaches to overcome data overload must involve some kind of selectivity. Between positive or negative selectivity we must choose positive. "Positive selectivity facilitates or enhances processing of a portion of the whole" (Wood, Paterson & Roth, 2002, p. 32). Negative selectivity or filtering, which is commonly used, inhibits processing of non-selected areas. "The critical criterion for processes of selection, parallel to human competence, is that observer need to remain sensitive to non-selected parts in order to shift focus fluently as circumstances change or to recover from missteps" (Wood, Paterson & Roth, 2002, p. 32). In conclusion, data overload can only be effectively resolved using a positive form of selectivity and techniques that support focus shifting over the field of data. Consequently, in order to overcome data overload, data processing should create context sensitivity rather than insist of data finesse.

## Data Integration

In the eighties of the 20th century we all hoped for a single integrated enterprise's database that would be based on a stable schema. These hopes have never been realised in practice and probably never will be. Data integration techniques are gaining increased importance as a result. Data integration, in a broad sense, is a process of integrating mutually related data which resides at autonomous and heterogeneous sources, and providing a unified view of integrated data through a unified global schema (Halevy, 2001). The need of data integration increases with the overall need to share existing data. The exploding abundance of data and new business needs requires the data to be integrated in order to extract new information and gain new knowledge. Data integration aims to answer complex questions, such as how some market factors influence the marketing strategy of certain products. From the managerial view, data integration is known as Enterprise Information Integration.

## Challenge: How to Integrate Data?

Although the data integration problem has been theoretically extensively considered both in business and science, many problems still remain to be solved in practice. Nonetheless, we may recognize three basic types of data integration approach: federation approach, warehouse approach and mediator approach.

In *federation approach* each of data sources talks independently through wrapper to other data sources in order to be mutually "integrated".

*Data warehouse approach*, which is frequently and successfully used in many commercial systems

*Figure 2. Data warehouse approach*

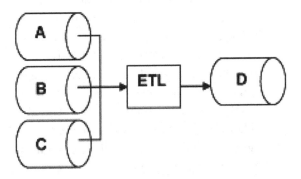

oriented on data analysis and decision support, is shown in Fig 2. Information is extracted from source databases A, B and C to be transformed and loaded into the data warehouse D by the process known as ETL. Each of data sources A, B or C has its own and unique schema. After extracting data from A, B and C, data may be transformed according to business needs, loaded into D and queried with a single schema. The data from A, B and C are tightly coupled in D, which is ideal for querying purposes.

Nevertheless, the freshness of data in D constitutes a problem as the propagation of updated data from the original data source to D takes some time, called latency time. As business becomes more real-time, the system that supports it needs to be more real-time. The challenge is how to make a real-time data warehouse. Here are some techniques for making data warehouse more or less real-time (Langseth, 2004):

- **"Near real-time" ETL:** The oldest and easiest approach is to execute the ETL process again. For some applications, increasing the frequency of the existing data load may be sufficient.

- **Direct trickle feed:** This is a true real-time data warehouse where the data warehouse is continuously fed with new data from data sources. This is done either by directly inserting or updating fact tables in the data warehouse, or by inserting data into separate fact tables in a real-time partition.

- **Trickle and feed:** The data is continuously fed into staging tables and not directly into the actual data warehouse tables. Staging tables are in the same format as the data warehouse actual tables. They contain either a copy of all the data or a copy of the data of current period of time, such as day. At a given period the staging table is swapped with the actual table so the data warehouse becomes instantly up-to-date. This may be done by changing the view definition where the updated table is used instead the old one.

- **External real-time cache:** this is a variant of trickle and feed where the real-time data are stored outside the data warehouse in an external real-time cache, avoiding potential performance problems and leaving the data warehouse largely intact.

Full integration of the data in the business sense is achieved by the warehouse approach supported by an active data warehouse. The *active data warehouse* represents a single, canonical state of the business, i.e. a single version of the truth. It represents a closed loop process between the transactional (operational) system and data warehousing (analytical) system. The transactional system feeds the data warehouse, and the

data warehouse feeds back the transactional system in order to drive and optimize transactional processing. Thus, the data warehouse is active if it automatically delivers information to the transactional system.

Recent trends towards *mediator approach* try to loosen the coupling between various data sources and thus to avoid the problem of replicated data and delayed update in the data warehouse architecture. This approach (Fig. 3) uses a virtual database with mediated schema and wrapper, i.e. adapter, which translates incoming queries and outgoing answers. A wrapper wraps (Ullman, 1997) an information source and models the source using a source schema. The situation emerges when two independent data sources have to be merged or combined into one source, such as integration of two similar databases when two organizations merge or integration of two document bases with similar structure content.

The users of the integrated system, i.e. data source D, are separated from the details of the data sources A, B and C at the schema level, by specifying a mediated or global schema. The *mediated schema* is a reconciled view of data in sources A, B and C, so the user needs to understand the structure and semantics of the mediated schema in order to make a meaningful query (Lu, 2006). The task of the data integration system is to isolate the user from the knowledge of where data are, how they are structured at the sources, and how they are reconciled into the mediated schema.

*Figure 3. Mediator approach*

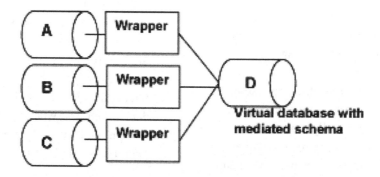

The source databases are approachable through a wrapper code which transforms the original query into a specialized query over the original databases A, B or C. This is a view based query because each of the data sources A, B or C can be considered to be a view over the virtual database D. The first step in the approach involves setting up the mediated schema either manually or automatically (Rahm & Bernstein, 2001). The next step involves specifying its relationships to the local schemas in either Global As View (GAV) or Local As View (LAV) fashion.

In the GAV or global-centric approach the mediated or global schema is expressed in terms of the data sources, i.e. to each data element of the mediated schema, a view over the data sources must be associated. In the GAV approach mediator processes queries into steps executed at sources. Changes in data sources require revising of the global schema and mapping between the global schema and source schemas. Thus, GAV is sensitive on scalability of global model.

In the LAV or source-centric approach the mediated or global schema is specified independently from the sources but the sources are defined as views over the mediated schema. LAV is better at scalability because the changes in data sources require adjusting only a description of the source view. Nevertheless, query processing in LAV is more difficult. Some approaches try to combine the best of GAV and LAV approach (Xu & Embley, 2004; Cali, De Giacomo & Lenzerini, 2001).

The query language approach propagates extending query languages with powerful constructs to facilitate integration without the creation of the mediated or global schema. SchemaSQL (Laksmanan, Sadri & Subramanian, 2001) and UDM (Lu, 2006) are examples of this approach. They serve as the uniform query interface (UQI) which allows users to write queries with only partial knowledge of the "implied" global schema.

An issue of growing interest in data integration is the problem of elimination of *information conflicts* among data sources that integrate.

*Intensional inconsistencies*, often referred to as semantic inconsistencies, appear when the sources are in different data models, or have different data schemas, or the data is represented in different natural languages or in different measures. For example: "Is 35 degrees measured in Fahrenheit or in Centigrade?" this type of inconsistencies may be resolved by the usage of ontologies which explicitly define schema terms and thus help to resolve semantic conflicts. This is also called ontology based data integration.

*Extensional inconsistencies*, often referred to as data inconsistencies, are factual discrepancies among the data sources in data values that belong to the same objects. Extensional inconsistencies are visible only after intensional inconsistencies are resolved. (Motro & Anokhin, 2006, p.177) argue that "all data are not equal", and "that data environment is not egalitarian, with each information source having the same qualification". In a diverse environment "the quality" of information provider's data is not equal. Many questions arise, such as: Is data enough recent or is outdated? Is the data source trustworthy? Is data expensive? An interesting approach is suggested by (Motro & Anokhin, 2006). In Internet era when the number of alternative sources of information for most applications increases, users often evaluate information about data sources. The meta data, such as timestamp, cost, accuracy, availability, and clearance, whether provided by the sources themselves or by a third-party dedicated to the ranking of information sources, may help users judge the suitability of data from the individual data source.

## Challenge: Could the Data Integrate the Business?

A business process is a structured, measured set of activities designed to produce a specific output for a particular customer or market (Davenport, 1993). Even though most organizations have a functional structure, examining of business processes provides a more authentic picture of the way business is run.

A good information system relies on Enterprise Resource Planning system (ERP) which uses a multitude of interrelated program modules that process data in individual functional areas. In Figure 4, ERP is exemplified by three basic functions: supply, manufacturing and sales. They stretch from the top to the bottom of the pyramid. If a program module covers the whole function, it runs through all management levels: operational, tactical and strategic.

ERP is often supplemented by program modules for analytical data processing which is characteristic for data warehousing and decision support systems. As a result it is perceived as an Enterprise Information system (EIS) or simply an Enterprise System (ES) that represents complete operational and analytical program solutions.

According to business process approach, some typical process lines may be used:

- **Financial and Business Performance Management:** a set of processes that help organizations optimize their business or financial performance
- **Customer Relationship Management:** a set of processes utilized to provide a high level of customer care
- **Supply Chain and Operations:** a set of processes involved in moving a product or service from supplier to customer

A vertically integrated information system connects activities on the lowest level of a particular function (e.g. a process of transactional retailing) with data analysis and data representation on the decision-making level (e.g. reports on sales analysis for the general manager).

A horizontally integrated information system enables a systematic monitoring of specific business process from end to end. For instance, as soon as a purchase order arrives, an integrated

*Figure 4. Enterprise Resource Planning (ERP) system*

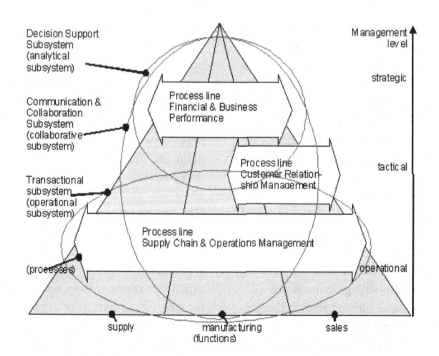

information system can receive it, forward it "automatically" to sales and delivery process which will deliver the goods to the customer and send the invoice to his information system, open a credit account; record the quantity of goods delivered in warehouse evidence; in case that goods first need to be produced in a manufacturing plant the system will issue a work order to manufacture the required quantity of goods; the production process can be supplied by a production plan; sales results will be visible to the sales manager and analysed using analytical tools of the information system; etc. An integrated information system enables recording of all business events so that the data can be used an analysed effectively throughout the organization.

Let us mention some problems related to integrated data:

- If the vertical coverage of data from a particular functional area is insufficient, data does not comprise all levels of this functional area. This is the case when, for example, only operational sales data exist, whereas sales data for the tactical and strategic level of decision-making are missing due to the lack of appropriate sales reports or if there is no possibility to interactively analyse sales data.
- Insufficient horizontal integration of different functional areas results when functional areas are not integrated. In case that production data are not visible in sales application, or they need to be re-entered (although they already exist in production application), operational sales data will not be well integrated with operational production data.
- Finally, if data in an information system are not sufficiently integrated, the information system will be comprised of isolated information (data) islands. An information system is not integrated unless individual functional areas are mutually integrated

with other functional areas by data. For instance, sales data may not be integrated i.e. connected with production data; or they may be integrated in indirect and complicated ways. Problem occurs because some older applications were designed for individual functional areas without concern for other functional areas.

## Challenge: Do We Know Organization's Data?

If we do not know organization's data well enough, we will use them rarely and poorly. Users often do not know what information is available and, as a consequence, they do not use the information system frequently enough. Users should be briefed about the information system and the ways to use it. A (central) *data catalogue* should be provided to present the complete data repertoire.

## Challenge: Do We Know How to Use Organization's Data?

If we do not know how to use the information system well enough, we will not use it sufficiently and we will not exploit all of its capabilities. Even if users know that the organization has data, they may not know how to use it. Therefore, the information system should be documented and ways of using it described in a *catalogue of functions*.

## Data Quality

## Challenge: Do We Know What the Quality Data is?

(Juran & Godfrey, 1999) defines data to be of high quality if the data is fit for their intended uses in operations, decision making and planning, i.e. if it correctly represents the real world to which it refers. Among various categories of attributes describing data quality the most commonly used are *accuracy* (degree of conformity of the data to the actual or true value to which it refers), *completeness* (if nothing needs to be added to it), *relevance* (the data is pertinent and adequate to the context and the person who use it) and *timeliness* (the data is given in timely manner). Naturally, it is desirable that the data supported by EIS fulfil the mentioned quality characteristics.

(Bocij, Chaffey, Greasley & Hickie, 2006) gives a few additional lists of categories of data quality concerning time dimension (timeliness, currency, frequency, time period), content dimension (accuracy, relevance, completeness, conciseness, scope), form dimension (clarity, detail, order, presentation, media) etc. However, the end user of data requires quality data in quantities that support the decision-making process. Too much data can be a burden for the person who needs to make a decision.

Most companies view data quality control as a cost problem, but in reality it can drive revenue. The problem of data quality drives the companies to set up a data governance function whose role it is to be responsible for data quality.

## Challenge: Are We Aware that the Quality of Data is Degradable?

Many databases behave as growing organism. Data is added, updated or deleted. Due to new applications the structure of a database may be altered to meet new business requirements. During the database lifetime many alternations keep the database functional. But over time, with continuing alterations to its structure and content, the logical integrity of the database can be so degraded that it becomes unreliable. It often happens that data integration is negatively affected by the lack of proper documentation regarding changes, the fact that the people responsible for the application have moved on, or that the vendor of the application no longer exists. In many cases the organization does not realize that the database has been degraded until a major event, such as data integration, occurs. It is time to determine the true quality of

data in the database.

(Healy, 2005) suggests that the only reliable way to determine the true nature of data is through a *data audit*, involving thorough data analysis or profiling. There are manual and automated methods of data profiling. In manual data profiling analysts assess data quality using the existing documentation and assumptions about the data to anticipate what data problems are likely to be encountered. Instead of evaluating all data they take data samples and analyze them. If such an analysis discovers wrong data, the appropriate programs have to be written to correct the problems. The manual procedure can be a very costly and time-consuming process requiring a number of iterations. The more efficient and accurate way of examining data is to use an automated data profiling tool that is able to examine all the data. Data profiling tools can identify many problems resident in the data and provide a good picture of data structure including metadata descriptions, data values, formats, frequencies, and data patterns. Automated data profiling solutions offer to correct data errors and anomalies more easily and efficiently.

## Data Ownership/Stewardship

## Challenge: Who is the Owner/ Steward of the Data?

Data ownership refers to both the possession of and responsibility for data. Ownership implies power over and control of data. Data control includes the ability to access, create, modify, package, sell or remove data, as well as the right to assign access privileges to others. This definition probably implies that the database administrator is the "owner" of all enterprise data. Nevertheless, this is not true and must not be true. The right approach to ownership aims to find the user who will be responsible for the quality of the data.

According to (Scofield, 1998), telling a user that he/she "owns" some enterprise data is a dangerous thing. The user may exercise the "ownership" to inhibit the sharing of data around the enterprise. Thus, the term "data stewardship" is better, implying a broader responsibility where the user must consider the consequences of changing "his/her" data. Data stewardship may be broken into several stewardship roles. For example, definition stewardship is responsible to clearly define the meaning of data and may be shared between analyst, database administrator and key user. Access stewardship is responsible to permit or prevent access to enterprise's data. Quality stewardship is responsible to fulfil the broad term "quality data" and may be shared between analyst and key user. Thus, data stewardship may be seen as distributed responsibility, shared between IT people (analyst, database administrator) and key users. Responsibilities assigned to all data stewardship actors, i.e. data stewards, must be registered in a data catalogue.

## Data Privacy

### Challenge: Is Data Privacy a Concern?

Data privacy is important wherever personally identifiable information (in digital or other form) is collected and stored. Data privacy issues arise in various business domains, such as healthcare records, financial records and transactions, criminal justice records, residence records, ethnicity data, etc. Information that are sensitive and need to be confidential are, for example, information about person's financial assets and financial transactions.

The challenge in data privacy is to share data while protecting personally identifiable information. Since freedom of information is propagated at the same time, promoting both data privacy and data openness might seem to be in conflict. Data privacy issue is especially challenging in the internet environment. Search engines and data mining techniques can collect and combine

personal data from various sources, thus revealing a great deal about an individual. The sharing of personally identifiable information about users is another concern.

Data protection acts regulate the collecting, storing, modifying and deleting of information which identifies living individuals, sometimes known as data subjects. This information is referred to as *personal data*. The legal protection of the right to privacy in general, and of data privacy in particular, varies greatly in various countries. The most regulated are data privacy rights in the European Union (EU), more restrictively than in the United States of America. Data protection in EU is governed by Data protection Directive 95/46/EC (EU, 1995), where personal data is defined as "any information relating to an identified or identifiable natural person". Personal data must be, according to the Directive "(a) processed fairly and lawfully; (b) collected for specified, explicit and legitimate purposes and not further processed in a way incompatible with those purposes; (c) adequate, relevant and not excessive in relation to the purposes for which they are collected and/or further processed; (d) accurate and, where necessary, kept up to date; every reasonable step must be taken to ensure that data which are inaccurate or incomplete, having regard to the purposes for which they were collected or for which they are further processed, are erased or rectified; and (e) kept in a form which permits identification of data subjects for no longer than is necessary for the purposes for which the data were collected or for which they are further processed."

Privacy and data protection are particularly challenging in multiple-party collaboration. If heterogeneous information systems with differing privacy rules are interconnected and information is shared, privacy policy rules must be mutually communicated and enforced. Example of a platform for communicating privacy policy in the web-services environment is Web Services Privacy (WS-Privacy). P3P (W3C, 2008) is a system for making Web site privacy policies machine-readable. P3P enables Web sites to translate their privacy practices into a standardized, machine-readable XML format that can be retrieved automatically and easily interpreted by a user's browser. Translation can be performed manually or with automated tools. Eventually, the Web site is able to automatically inform P3P user agents of site privacy practices in both machine- and human-readable formats. On the user side, P3P user agent may read P3P site's privacy policy and, if appropriate, automate decision-making based on this practice.

## Data Visualization

### Challenge: Could We Amplify Cognition of Data?

Many data acquisition devices, such as various measure instruments, scanners etc. generate large data sets, which data is collected in large databases in textual, numerical or multimedia form. The results of data analysis of the large data sets are not acceptable and attractive to the end users without good techniques of interpretation and visualization of information.

Information visualization is a rapidly advancing field of study both in academic research and practical applications. (Card, Mackinlay & Shneiderman, 1999, p.8) define information visualization, as "the use of computer-supported, interactive, visual representations of abstract data to amplify cognition. Cognition is the acquisition or use of knowledge. The purpose of the information visualization is insight, not picture. The goal of the insight is discovery, decision making and explanation. Information visualization is useful to the extent that it increases our ability to perform this and other cognitive activities."

Information visualization exploits the exceptional ability of human brain to effectively process visual representations. It aims to explore large amounts of abstract, usually numeric, data

to derive new insights or simply make the stored data more interpretable. Thus, the purpose of data visualization is to communicate information clearly and effectively through graphical means, so that information can be easily interpreted and then used.

There are many specialized techniques designed to make various kinds of visualization using graphics or animation. Various techniques are used for turning data into information by using the capacity of the human brain to visually recognize data patterns. Based on the scope of visualization, there are different approaches to data visualization. According to (VisualLiteracy, 2008) the visualization types can be structured into seven groups: *sketches* ("Sketches are atmospheric and help quickly visualize a concept. They present key features, support reasoning and arguing, and allow room for own interpretation. In business sketches can be used to draw on flip charts and to explain complex concepts to a client in a client meeting."), *diagrams* ("Diagramming is the precise, abstract and focused representation of numeric or non-numeric relationships at times using predefined graphic formats and/or categories. An example of a diagram is a Cartesian coordinate system, a management matrix, or a network. Diagrams explain causal relationships, reduce the complexity to key issues, structure, and display relationships."), *images* ("Images are representations that can visualize impression, expression or realism. An image can be a photograph, a computer rendering, a painting, or another format. Images catch the attention, inspire, address emotions, improve recall, and initiate discussions."), *maps* ("Maps represent individual elements (e.g., roads) in a global context (e.g., a city). Maps illustrate both overview and details, relationships among items, they structure information through spatial alignment and allow zoom-ins and easy access to information."), *objects* ("Objects exploit the third dimension and are haptic. They help attract recipients (e.g., a physical dinosaur in a science museum), support learning through constant presence, and allow the integration of digital interfaces."), *interactive visualizations* ("Interactive visualizations are computer-based visualizations that allow users to access, control, combine, and manipulate different types of information or media. Interactive visualizations help catch the attention of people, enable interactive collaboration across time and space and make it possible to represent and explore complex data, or to create new insights."), and *stories* ("Stories and mental images are imaginary and non-physical visualizations. Creating mental images happens trough envisioning."). Each of mentioned visualization types has its specific area of application.

## DATA MANAGEMENT

DAMA's functional framework (DAMA, 2008) suggests and guides management initiatives to implement and improve data management through ten functions:

- **Data Governance:** planning, supervision and control over data management and use
- **Data Architecture Management:** as an integral part of the enterprise architecture
- **Data Development:** analysis, design, building, testing, deployment and maintenance
- **Database Operations Management:** support for structured physical data assets
- **Data Security Management:** ensuring privacy, confidentiality and appropriate access
- **Reference & Master Data Management:** managing versions and replicas
- **Data Warehousing & Business Intelligence Management:** enabling access to decision support data for reporting and analysis
- **Document & Content Management:** storing, protecting, indexing and enabling access to data found in unstructured sources (electronic files and physical records)

- **Meta Data Management:** integrating, controlling and delivering meta data
- **Data Quality Management:** defining, monitoring and improving data quality

Using DAMA's functional framework (DAMA, 2008) each function may be described by seven environment elements: goal and principles of the function, activities to be done in the function (i.e. planning, control, development and operational activities), deliverables produced by the function, roles and responsibilities in the function, practices and procedures used to perform the function, technology supporting the function; and organization and culture.

A similar term is enterprise information management. (Gartner, 2005) defines it as an organizational commitment to define, secure and improve the accuracy and integrity of information assets and to resolve semantic inconsistencies across all boundaries to support the technical, operational and business objectives of the company's enterprise architecture strategy.

## Challenge: Do We Need Data Governance?

According to DAMA (DAMA, 2008), the beginning and central data management activity is data governance which is exercise of authority, control and decision-making over the management of organization's data. It is a high-level planning and control mechanism over data management. (IBM, 2007, p.3) defines data governance as "a quality control discipline for adding new rigor and discipline to the process of managing, using, improving, monitoring and protecting organizational information". It may be a part of organization's IT governance.

All organizations take care of data governance, whether formally or informally. Tendency is to manage data governance more formally. The objectives of data governance are implemented by various data governance programs or initiatives. Factors driving data governance programs include the need for implementation of EIS as a core system with a consistent enterprise-wide definition of data, the problems of organization's data overload, data integration, data security etc. Some external drivers are regulatory requirements for more effective controls for information transparency, such as Basel II and Sarbanes-Oxley, the need to compete on market using better analytics and having the right information to provide reliable insights into business.

Data governance is not a typical IT project as it is declared at the first Data Governance Conference in 2006. Based on the experience of successful data governance programs it is agreed that data governance is more than 80 percent communication and that data governance must focus on people, process and communication before considering any technology implementation. Organization's data governance body may consist of executive leadership, line-of-business and project managers, and data stewards.

Data governance must follow a strategic approach considering first the current state, devising a future state and designing an implementation plan to achieve the future state. A data governance project may be difficult, often with the tough task to change the culture of an organization. Therefore, a phased approach should be applied. Each step must be small enough to be successfully and relatively quickly implemented, the achieved results analysed and lessons learned implemented in the following steps.

According to the well known Software Engineering Institute, Capability Maturity Model for organization's software development process which describes five-level graduated path from initial (level 1), managed (level 2), defined (level 3), quantitatively managed (level 4) to optimizing (level 5) (IBM, 2007) describes a similar data governance maturity model. The model measures data governance competencies of an enterprise based on 11 domains of data governance maturity: organizational structures and awareness, steward-

ship, policy, value creation, data risk management and compliance, information security and privacy, data architecture, data quality management, classification and metadata, information lifecycle management; and audit information, logging and reporting.

## CONCLUSION

Challenges of successful data management are numerous and diverse, varying from technological to conceptual. The chapter presented the most challenging aspects of data management classified into three classes. The first combines data availability, data integrity and data security, which serve as data continuity aspects that are important for the continuous provision of data in business processes and for decision-making purposes. The aspects in the second class enable innovative, better, more efficient and more effective data usage. The problems of data overload, data integration, data quality, data degradation, data ownership or stewardship, data privacy, and data visualization are described. The last aspect is of managerial nature. Data governance is important for planning, supervising and controlling of all management activities exercised to improve organizational data and information.

It is been shown that data management challenges are numerous. A data management analysis in a typical organization will most probably reveal that some data management aspects are more problematic than others and resolving data management issues can be dynamic. Consequently, data governance will constantly need to discover novel and innovative ways to deal with data management problems.

# REFERENCES

W3C. (2008). Platform for privacy preferences (P3P) project. Retrieved on September 2, 2008, from www.w3.org/P3P/

Allen, J. H. (2001). *The CERT guide to system and network security practices.* Boston: Addison-Wesley.

Bocij, P., Chaffey, D., Greasley, A., & Hickie, S. (2006). *Business information systems.* Harlow, UK: Prentice Hall Financial Times.

Brumec, J. (1997). A contribution to IS general taxonomy. *Zbornik radova, 21*(22), 1-14.

Cali, A., De Giacomo, G., & Lenzerini, M. (2001). Models for information integration: Turning local-as-view into global-as-view. In *Proc. of Int. Workshop on Foundations of Models for Information Integration, 10th Workshop in the Series Foundations of Models and Languages for Data and Objects.* Retrieved on August 16, 2008, from www.dis.uniroma1.it/~degiacom/papers/2001/CaDL01fmii.ps.gz

Card, S. K., Mackinlay, J. D., & Shneiderman, B. (1999). *Readings in information visualization: Using vision to think.* San Francisco: Morgan Kaufmann.

DAMA. (2008). *DAMA-DMBOK: Functional framework*, version. 3. Retrieved on August 16, 2008, from http://www.dama.org/files/public/DMBOK/DI_DAMA_DMBOK_en_v3.pdf

Davenport, T. H. (1993). *Process innovation: Reengineering work through information technology.* Boston: Harvard Business School Press.

EU. (1995). *Directive 95/46/EC of the European Parliament and the council on the protection of individuals with regard to the processing of personal data and on the free movement of such data.* Retrieved on September 2, 2008, from http://ec.europa.eu/justice_home/fsj/privacy/docs/95-46-ce/dir1995-46_part1_en.pdf

Gartner. (2005). *Business drivers and issues in enterprise information management.* Retrieved on September 2, 2008, from http://www.avanade.com/_uploaded/pdf/avanadearticle4124441.pdf

Gartner Inc. (2006). *Defining, cultivating, and measuring enterprise agility.* Retrieved on September 15, 2008, from http://www.gartner.com/resources/139700/139734/defining_cultivating_and_mea_139734.pdf

Halevy, A. Y. (2001). Answering queries using views: A survey. *The VLDB Journal, 10*(4), 270–294. doi:10.1007/s007780100054

Hall, D., & McMullen, S. H. (2004). *Mathematical techniques in multisensor data fusion.* Norwood, USA: Artech House.

Healy, M. (2005). *Enterprise data at risk: The 5 danger signs of data integration disaster* (White paper). Pittsburgh, PA: Innovative Systems. Retrieved on August 22, 2008, from http://www.dmreview.com/white_papers/2230223-1.html

IBM. (2007). *The IBM data governance council maturity model: Building a roadmap for effective data governance.* Retrieved on August 22, 2008, from ftp://ftp.software.ibm.com/software/tivoli/whitepapers/LO11960-USEN-00_10.12.pdf

IBM. (2008). *RPO/RTO defined.* Retrieved on September 15, 2008, from http://www.ibmsystemsmag.com/mainframe/julyaugust07/ittoday/16497p1.aspx

IDS. (2008). *IDS white paper: The diverse and exploding digital universe.* Framingham: IDC.

Juran, J. M., & Godfrey, A. B. (1999). *Juran's quality handbook.* McGraw-Hill.

Lakshmanan, L. V., Sadri, F., & Subramanian, S. N. (2001). SchemaSQL: An extension to SQL for multidatabase interoperability. *ACM Transactions on Database Systems, 26*(4), 476–519. doi:10.1145/503099.503102

Langseth, J. (2004). *Real-time data warehousing: Challenges and solutions*. Retrieved on August 29, 2008, from http://DSSResources.com/papers/features/langseth/langseth02082004.html

Lu, J. J. (2006). *A data model for data integration.* (ENTCS 150, pp. 3–19). Retrieved on August 16, 2008, from http://www.sciencedirect.com

Motro, A., & Anokhin, P. (2006). Fusionplex: Resolution of data inconsistencies in the integration of heterogeneous information sources. [from http://www.sciencedirect.com]. *Information Fusion, 7*, 176–196. Retrieved on August 16, 2008. doi:10.1016/j.inffus.2004.10.001

Oracle. (2008). *Oracle® database high availability overview 11g release 1 (11.1)*. Retrieved on September 8, 2008, from http://download.oracle.com/docs/cd/B28359_01/server.111/b28281/overview.htm#i1006492

Rahm, E., & Bernstein, P. A. (2001). A survey of approaches to automatic schema matching. *The VLDB Journal, 10*(4), 334–350. doi:10.1007/s007780100057

Schmidt, K. (2006). *High avalability and disaster recovery*. Berlin: Springer.

Scofield, M. (1998). Issues of data ownership. *DM Review Magazine*. Retrieved on August 29, 2008, from http://www.dmreview.com/issues/19981101/296-1.html

Ullman, J. D. (1997). Information integration using local views. In F. N. Afrati & P. Kolaitis (Eds.), *Proc. of the 6th Int. Conf. On Database Theory* (ICDT'97). (LNCS 1186, pp. 19-40). Delphi.

VisualLiteracy. (2008). *Visual literacy: An e-learning tutorial on visualization for communication, engineering, and business*. Retrieved on September 3, 2008, from http://www.visual-literacy.org/

Woods, D. D., Patterson, E. S., & Roth, E. M. (2002). Can we ever escape from data overload? A cognitive systems diagnosis. *Cognition Technology and Work, 4*, 22–36. doi:10.1007/s101110200002

Xu, L., & Embley, D. W. (2004). Combining the best of global-as-view and local-as-view for data integration. *Information Systems Technology and Its Applications, 3rd International Conference ISTA'2004* (pp. 123-136). Retrieved on September 2, 2008, from www.deg.byu.edu/papers/PODS.integration.pdf

# Chapter 8
# Continuous Database Availability

**Dražena Tomić**
*Faculty of Economics, Mostar, Bosnia and Herzegovina*

**Brano Markić**
*Faculty of Economics, Mostar, Bosnia and Herzegovina*

## ABSTRACT

*In today's business environment, it is usual that data relevant to business is stored on different hardware, inside different databases, different data warehouses, inside as well as outside of the organization. Accuracy, quality, timeliness, and especially availability of such distributed data make crucial role in the process of business managing. Now, one of the biggest challenges is to ensure continuous availability of that data, even in critical and disaster situations. This chapter gives a short overview of the most used solutions for database availability that have become industry standards and gives examples of implementation of these standards by, in this moment, three main database vendors: Oracle (Oracle 11g), IBM (DB2 Version 9.5) and Microsoft (SQL Server 2008).*

## INTRODUCTION

The main characteristics of today's business, mostly owing to Internet and web technologies, are globalization and continuous availability (24/7/365). Although information technology (IT) is the one of the main driving forces in enabling such a business, ensuring continuous business availability is still one the biggest challenge for IT itself.

This chapter presents necessity of enabling continuous database availability and different approaches used in ensuring this. Today's huge amount of different variety of data stored in voluminous databases and data warehouses has to be readily accessible by Internet and sophisticated communications network. Gathering customer data, vendor information, minute financial measurements, product data, retail sell-through data and manufacturing metrics become one of the most important organization goals. The final result is that organization had to accumulate terabytes of data on increasingly large storage systems, with the main purpose to enable users who by different software applications use that data in order to improve their

DOI: 10.4018/978-1-60566-723-2.ch008

business activities and resolve potential business problems.

During last four decades, with great thanks to rapid development of IT, business decision making has become more complex than ever. Today, organizations no longer rely primarily on local or regional sources for inputs, work force to complete production or consumers to purchase their products. This means that decision makers must be aware of trends, activities, customs and regulations around the world and therefore must have easy access to considerably more information and from considerably more sources. At the same time, development of IT, especially related to communications and Internet has enabled 24/7/365 access to digitally stored data. Data relevant to business are stored on different hardware, inside different databases, different data warehouses, inside as well as outside of organization (public databases, web pages, Internet and so on). Accuracy, quality, timeliness and especially availability of such distributed data make crucial role in the process of business managing. Now, one of the biggest challenges is to ensure continuous (24/7/365) access to that data, even in critical and disastrous situations.

With the growing understanding of how incredibly valuable organization data is, there is a new focus on protecting and accessing data. As organizations received hard-earned lessons on what can happen when data is destroyed, damaged, or unavailable, more focus has been placed on protecting mission-critical information than on simply accumulating it. As data volumes continue to grow, organizations are dealing with larger and larger databases. Forrester estimates that 80% of the enterprises supporting terabyte-size databases in production will encounter tremendous challenges in backup and recovery (Otey & Otey, 2005). Large database backups require a scalable solution that includes appropriate hardware infrastructure. As enterprises deploy new applications, including applications related to Web services and content management, they are poised to support databases that run well into hundreds of terabytes. Therefore, backup and recovery administration challenges will come in phases, with enterprises pushing for higher thresholds and vendors trying to deliver scalable database backup solutions.

For mission-critical applications, the database and servers that support full 24/7/365 database availability need to be available during the times that users require those data. The requirements for achieving the necessary levels of availability in the enterprise today extend far beyond the simple data protection provided by traditional backup and restore technologies. Creating a high-availability environment for business continuity is a complex undertaking because it touches so many different areas in the organization. It is also influenced by many factors, including technological challenges and capabilities as well as human and organizational factors that extend beyond the realm of pure technology into operations. This chapter is focused on only one, but extremely important, part of the availability story – database availability. The aim of the chapter is to explain different approaches and solutions that IT community developed and used in order to protect data and enable its continuous availability. Among standard approaches there are those using high availability (HA) devices with redundant systems, backing up data regularly to tape and data duplication techniques. There are also some more sophisticated methods, including remote mirroring and remote copy (data vaulting), hot (near-line) backup, Data Lifecycle Management (DLM), Information Lifecycle Management (ILM) and so on.

## BACKGROUND

Shifting business models, driven by increased customer expectations for 24/7/365 access to different services, changing regulatory requirements and new networking technologies make business continuity increasingly important. Also, downtime costs modern, Internet oriented, organization more than it used to. The average number of downtime hours, experienced each year, ranges from about 300 in logistics to nearly 1,200 in financial services, with the bulk coming from outages (IBM, 2006). Some analysis show that downtime costs financial organizations as much as 16 percent of their revenue, annually (IBM, 2006), without counting the damage to organizations' brand, especially if it depends on the Internet for business.

In the past decade organizations all around the world faced different threats to their existence, like natural (weather) disasters, terrorist's attacks, civil unrest and others. Owing to that, ensuring business continuity has become one of the top issues, especially related to IT support. A lot of books, covering this topic, have been published and some of them made outset in preparing this chapter (Schmidt, 2006; Marcus & Stern, 2003; Snedaker, 2007; Wallace & Webber, 2004).

In these books, authors proposed theirs definitions of business continuity. For the purpose of this chapter IBM definition (IBM, 2006) has been adopted where business continuity and resilience is defined as a combination of proactive and reactive strategies that keep organization's critical business processes available, practically without interruption—while improving their operational efficiency. It means that availability solutions should help reduce the chances that a system failure will force organization to declare a disaster and can bring business processes back online faster if a serious disruption does occur.

Also, over the last decade there almost has been no book or DBMS handbook related to database administration without at least one chapter dedicated to techniques and solutions related to high database availability (Hart&Jesse, 2004; Hirt, 2007; IBM, 2008; Oracle, 2007; Microsoft, 2008).

Looking from the IT point of view, availability can be defined as the time in which a system or resource, in this case database, is available for use. The level of availability is typically measured according to its percentage of absolute availability

where 100% means that the resource is available all of the time and there is no downtime (Otey & Otey, 2005). But, it is important to stress that 100% availability is used as ideal situation that is almost impossible to achieve in practice. Instead, the closest practical measure of very high availability is five 9s or 99.999%. Expressed mathematically, availability can be defined as (Otey & Otey, 2005):

Percentage of availability (%) = ((total elapsed time – sum of downtime)/total elapsed time)

If each year has a total of 8,760 hours (24 hours per day times 365 days per year) of available uptime, it means that a total of 8,760 hours of uptime could be translated to 100% of the available uptime for that year.

Different factors could influence on decreasing of the availability percentage. For example, it is common for a system to have one working day (eight hours) of scheduled downtime for monthly maintenance so that IT staff can perform hardware upgrades, apply system patches, or perform other routine maintenance activities. In this scenario, the percentage of availability of the system is shown in the following expression:

$$98.9 = ((8760 - (8 \times 12)/8760)$$

In other words, eight hours of downtime per month results in an overall availability number of 98.9 percent. It is obvious that one working day of downtime per month results in an overall availability of 98.9 percent which rates at one 9 out of a possible five 9s. One day per month is not a great deal of downtime and for some organizations this level of availability would be adequate. However, there are many organizations, especially those with their business related to Internet, where that level of availability is not enough. The Table 1. (Otey & Otey, 2005) shows the amount of downtime that is associated with each successive increase in the level of availability.

*Table 1. Downtime and level of availability*

| Number of 9s | Percentage Availability | Downtime per Year |
|:---:|:---:|:---:|
| 1 | 98.9% | 3 days, 18 hours, 20 minutes |
| 2 | 99.0% | 3 days, 15 hours, 36 minutes |
| 3 | 99.9% | 8 hours, 46 minutes |
| 4 | 99.99% | 53 minutes |
| 5 | 99.999% | 5 minutes |

It is obvious (Table 1.) that at the highest level of availability (five 9s of availability), the downtime per year must be less than .09 hours or about 5 minutes of downtime per year. Achieving these higher levels of availability with today's database platforms is possible but it cannot be accomplished using technology only. Instead, the highest level of availability can only be accomplished by harnessing a combination of people, processes, and technological factors.

## THREATS TO CONTINUOUS DATABASE AVAILABILITY

One of the challenges in designing a high (continuously) available database is examining and addressing all the possible causes of downtime. There are different classifications of downtime, according to:

- That if the downtime is planned or unplanned (Oracle, 2008)
- The source of downtime, e.g. network, hardware, software, DBMS, human error, natural disaster, or other causes (Mullins, 2002)
- The relative value of data to the business (Leung & Rhodes, 2003)
- The critical data security requirements (Petrocelli, 2005).

Planned downtime is related to regular database maintenance activities such as backups, hardware and software upgrades, applying system patches and other.

Unplanned downtime is primarily the result of some kind of failure, either computer (hardware failure), communication or data failure.

Focus on the source of downtime makes distinguish between causes of database unavailability. Namely, it is clear that availability of database depends, not only on proper functioning of database management system (DBMS), but also on properly network and hardware functioning, software availability and human barrier.

The relative value of data for the business is related to implementation of data lifecycle management solutions which enable organization to assemble the appropriate combination of storage devices, media types and network infrastructure in order to ensure a proper balance of performance, data accessibility and easy retrieval cost.

Classification process, made according to the critical data security requirements, is related to implementation of information lifecycle management that offers organization to define an appropriate security approach designated to incorporate IT processes and vendor security offerings that will support and strengthen data security.

The classification, used in this chapter, is based on combination of the type and source of downtime. The main threats to continuous database availability are grouped into four categories: network, hardware, software and DBMS, but inside each category there is a distinction between planned and unplanned threats (downtime). Table 2. summarized the proposed classification of

*Table 2. Classification of threats to continuous database availability*

| Category | | Threat |
|---|---|---|
| Network | Planned | Adding new network nodes<br>Adding new network components/devices<br>Replacing existing network components/devices<br>Network tuning |
| | Unplanned | Network node failure<br>Network devices failure |
| Hardware | Planned | Adding memory to system<br>Adding storage to system<br>Adding new hardware devices<br>Replacing hardware components or complete systems |
| | Unplanned | Memory failure<br>Storage failure<br>Hardware device failure |
| Software | Planned | Applying operation system patch<br>Replacing operation system with new one<br>Applying application-level service pack<br>Replacing application with new one<br>Adding new applications |
| | Unplanned | Operation system failure<br>Application software failure |
| DBMS | Planned | Backups<br>Online schema and data reorganization<br>Database tuning |
| | Unplanned | Data corruption / Inconsistency<br>DBMS failure |

threats to continuous database availability.

In proposed downtime classification human errors are purposely omitted. The reason is that in each proposed category of threats (Table 2.) human error could appear as one of the causes. Research in David Patterson's study (Patterson, 2002), shows that 53 percent of downtime is the result of human error. Other similar researches published in the "Disaster Recovery Journal" showed that human error accounted for 36 percent of the data loss that occurs in an organization.

Clearly, overcoming the people barrier is one of the biggest steps toward achieving higher

availability. It only takes a few minutes of operator or user error to corrupt a database while it can take hours or days to recover or restore the data. Those recovery hours can be both costly and avoidable.

There is no way to avoid human errors, but steps can be taken proactively to minimize downtime and recover from these errors. Human error can be introduced from two main sources: user error and operator error. If allowed, users can wreak havoc with company information by inadvertently deleting important data or incorrectly updating the database with the wrong information. Training, the creation of adequate application documentation, and the establishment of regular procedures are some of the best defenses against user errors. One of the most important steps to curtail possible downtime because of user error is to restrict each user's access to data and services to just what is essential to them.

Operator or application developer errors can also have a huge impact on database and application availability. For example, deleting an incorrect table from the database or coding an error that results in incorrect data being written to the database can adversely affect application availability. A good way to prevent these types of errors is to increase staff awareness, especially upper management staff, about the complexities and responsibilities that are associated with continuous information availability. This translates to increasing training budgets and spending time and resources to develop operational guidelines as well as developing and implementing disaster recovery plans.

## SOLUTIONS TO CONTINUOUS DATABASE AVAILABILITY

There are different high-availability solutions that provide varying degrees of protection from threats to continuous database availability summarized in Table 2. These solutions could be viewed from two standpoints: a narrow and broad one.

Narrow approach is focused on solutions provided by information technology (IT), while broad approach IT support sees only as a part of broader environment that includes business processes, management of complete data and information lifecycle, additional education and training of users and IT staff, establishing disaster recovery strategies and action plans.

Table 3 summarizes the proposed classification of solutions for continuous database availability.

## BACKUP AND RECOVERY

Database backup refers to the copying of data stored in database, usually to media different from that where original data is stored, so that these copies may be used for database restoring after any disastrous event. Backups are typically that last line of defense against data loss, and consequently the least granular and the least convenient to use. The backup copy can include important parts of the database, such as the control file and datafiles. Backups could be divided into physical backups

*Table 3. Classification of solutions for continuous database availability*

| Category | | Solution |
|---|---|---|
| Narrow view | DBMS | Backup and recovery Clustering Log shipping Stand by Replication Mirroring |
| | Software | Automated software applications |
| | Network | Remote data movement / Replication |
| | Hardware | Virtualization |
| Broad view | | Data Lifecycle Management (DLM) Information Lifecycle management (ILM) |

and logical backups. Physical backups, which are the primary concern in a backup and recovery strategy, are copies of physical database files. In contrast, logical backups contain logical data (for example, tables and stored procedures) and they can be used to supplement physical backups. Also, backups could be divided into complete (or full) database backup and incremental backup. A full database backup is a backup of every datafile in the database, including and the control file, while incremental backup copies the transaction log file since the most recent full backup. Also, database backups can be performed while the database is being actively accessed – online ("hot" backup) or when the database is shutdown – offline ("cold" backup). From the high availability point of view, online backup is the most interesting one. Online backups or so called "hot" backups, means that during the backup users could normally work with database. They ensure protection against media (disk) failures by maintaining a change log on a separate device. Like offline backup, restore for online backup begins by restoring the database from the backup copy. This returns the active database to its initial state. Restore for online backup then processes the roll forward journal and applies all committed changes made since the initial backup. This returns the active database to its latest state (Figure 1.).

It is important to be aware of these differences among different kinds of backups when one plans out backup and recovery strategy because the type of backup directly influences the possibilities and duration of recovery if recovery is necessary.

IBM's Online Backup facility provides continuous backup that is always active. The purpose of this facility is to protect the physical database against loss of information due to permanent or transient errors in the storage media. Online Backup solves the problem of lost changes in offline backup by providing a continuous backup that is always active. Like offline backup, Online Backup begins by taking a snapshot backup of the current database. During subsequent runs,

*Figure 1. Online backup*

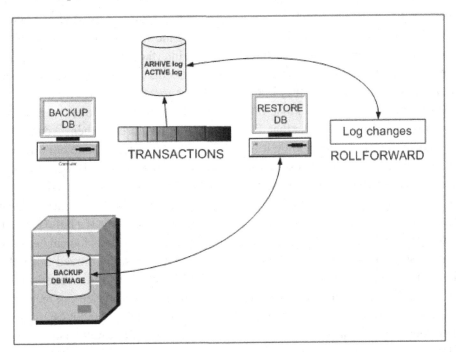

the DBMS logs all committed changes to a roll forward journal on an independent device. Each run appends its changes to the journal. To ensure full synchronization between the journal and the database, the DBMS flushes all changes to the journal as part of transaction commit. The data in the roll forward journal reflects the current (committed) state of the live database, during runs and between runs. A recovery process can return the database to its current state by restoring the backup snapshot and applying the changes in the roll forward journal (IBM, 2008).

The most of database vendors, besides standard backup and recovery routines, use automated software tools in order to ensure faster backup and recovery. For example, in earlier versions, the smallest piece of an Oracle Recovery Manager (Oracle RMAN) backup was an entire file. Because Oracle datafiles can be up to 128TB in size, it is not feasible to back up a very large file. In Oracle Database 11*g*, however, Oracle RMAN can break up a single large file into sections and back up

and restore them independently. The SECTION SIZE parameter in the BACKUP command tells Oracle RMAN to create a backup set in which each backup piece contains blocks from one file section, enabling the backup of large files to be parallelized across multiple channels. Restoring a multisection backup in parallel is automatic (Oracle, 2007). Also, Oracle Flashback Transaction enables the changes made by a transaction to be undone, optionally undoing changes made by dependent transactions. This recovery option uses undo data to create and execute corresponding compensating transactions that make the affected database revert to its original state (Oracle, 2007).

## CLUSTERING

While today's server hardware is highly reliable and all of the tier-one hardware vendors offer many redundancy features for the primary system components, hardware and operating system maintenance and upgrades remain an unavoidable fact of life. For example, if user has an application that requires 24/7/365 availability, that application can be implemented on a database platform using one of these multiserver clusterings. In that case, when IT needs to perform maintenance, they initiate a manual failover to switch the workload off the node that requires maintenance. After that, IT can repair, upgrade, or patch the node while it is offline. The remaining cluster node(s) or standby server will assume the workload during the time the node that is being maintained is unavailable. Therefore, there is no loss of application availability. When the procedure is finished, IT can restore the node to the cluster and fail back to ordinary operations. IT can repeat this process for the other cluster nodes if needed. This ability to perform rolling upgrades eliminates the planned downtime associated with routine maintenance.

These failover strategies are based on clusters of systems where a cluster is a group of connected systems that work together as a single system. Each physical machine within a cluster contains one or more logical nodes. Clustering allows servers to back each other up when failures occur, by picking up the workload of the failed server.

A cluster, when used for high availability, consists of two or more machines, a set of private network interfaces, one or more public network interfaces, and some shared disks (Figure 2.). This special configuration allows a data service to be moved from one machine to another. By moving the data service to another machine in the cluster, it should be able to continue providing access to its data. Moving a data service from one machine to another is called a failover, as illustrated in Figure 2.

IBM DBMS DB2 ensures clustering through HADR (High Availability Disaster Recovery) database replication feature. HADR is a high availability solution that protects against data loss by replicating changes from a source database, called the primary database, to a target database, called the standby database.

The private network interfaces are used to send heartbeat messages, as well as control messages, among the machines in the cluster. The public network interfaces are used to communicate directly with clients of the HA cluster. The disks in an HA cluster are connected to two or more machines in the cluster, so that if one machine fails, another machine has access to them. A data service running on an HA cluster has one or more logical public network interfaces and a set of disks associated with it. The clients of an HA data service connect via TCP/IP to the logical network interfaces of the data service only. If a failover occurs, the data service, along with its logical network interfaces and set of disks, are moved to another machine (IBM, 2008). One of the benefits of an HA cluster is that a data service can recover without the aid of support staff, and it can do so at any time. Another benefit is redundancy. All of the parts in the cluster should be redundant, including the machines themselves. The cluster should be able to survive any single point of failure. Even though highly available data services can be very different in nature, they have some common requirements. Clients of a highly available data service expect the network address and host name of the data service to remain the same, and expect to be able to make requests in the same way, regardless of which machine the data service is on.

Oracle Real Application Clusters (RAC) enables the enterprise to build database servers across multiple systems that are highly available and highly scalable. In a RAC environment Oracle runs on two or more systems in a cluster while concurrently accessing a single shared database. RAC also enables enterprise Grids that are built out of large configurations of standardized, commodity-priced components: processors, servers, network, and storage. RAC is technology that can harness these components into useful processing system for the enterprise. Dynamic provisioning of nodes, storage, CPUs, and memory allow service levels to be easily and efficiently maintained while lowering cost still further through improved utilization.

*Figure 2. Example of failover*

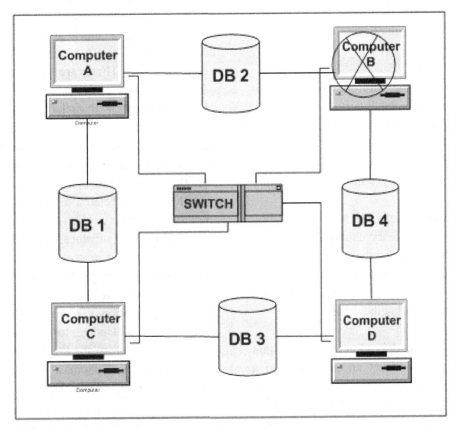

In addition, RAC is completely transparent to the application accessing the RAC database and does not need to be modified in any way to be deployed on a RAC system (Oracle, 2007).

Microsoft Windows Clustering Services and Oracle's RAC both support the ability to perform rolling upgrades that enable IT staff to manually take either one system in the cluster or a group of systems offline to perform routine maintenance.

Microsoft cluster solution is the combination of SQL Server 2008 and Windows Server 2005 in such a way that using an N+1 configuration (N active nodes with 1 spare node) provides a very flexible and cost effective clustering scenario to enable highly available applications. For example, with an eight-node cluster in an N+1 configuration, user can have seven of the eight nodes set up to actively provide different services while the eighth

node is a passive node that is ready to assume the services of any of the seven active nodes in the event of a server failure (Microsoft, 2008).

## STANDBY

A standby database is a complete system that is running at a secondary location, waiting to replace, in case of downtime, the primary database server. This inherently means that the standby database must be kept up to date with data and as close to real time to the primary database as possible in order to enable a quick switch over of operations. Secondary location, e.g. location of the standby database could be at the same (local) site or at different one than primary database. It is obvious that if the standby database is located at a different site than the primary database, recovery from a disaster is enhanced.

Software component of standby environment should ensure (Figure 3.):

- Almost real time data copying from primary to standby database.
- In case that primary database is down fast switchover to the target copy of data on standby database. It means that standby database takeover the role of primary database.
- When primary database is up, rebuilding it again as a primary database means applying to primary database all data changes that occur during its downtime.
- Fast switch currently primary database back to the standby database.

Oracle Data Guard is Oracle solution that provides the ability to set up and maintain a standby copy of production database. Data Guard provides a comprehensive set of services that create, maintain, manage, and monitor one or more standby databases to enable production Oracle databases to survive disasters and data corruptions. A Data Guard configuration consists of one primary database and up to nine standby databases. The databases in a Data Guard configuration are connected by Oracle Net and may be dispersed geographically. There are no restrictions on where the databases are located as long as they can communicate with each other. If the primary database becomes unavailable, Data Guard can switch any standby database to the production role, thus minimizing the downtime associated with the outage (Oracle, 2007).

IBM solution related to standby database is the DB2 Data Server High Availability Disaster Recovery (HADR) feature. It is a database replication feature that protects against data loss by replicating data changes from a source database, called the primary, to a target database, called the standby. Applications can only access the current primary database. Updates to the standby database occur by rolling forward log data that is generated on the primary database and shipped to the standby database. HADR can redirect the clients that were using the original primary database to the standby database (new primary database) by using automatic client reroute or retry logic in the application (IBM, 2008).

*Figure 3. Standby database*

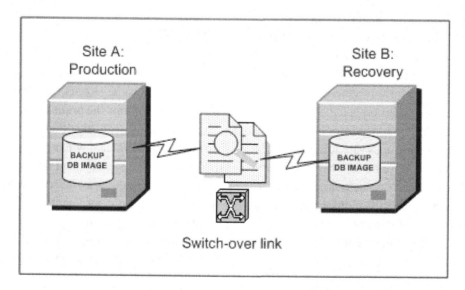

## LOG SHIPPING

Log shipping is the process of copying whole log files to a standby machine either from an archive device, or through a user exit program running against the primary database. The standby database is continuously rolling forward through the log files produced by the production machine. When the production machine fails, a failover occurs and the following takes place: The remaining logs are transferred over to the standby machine. The standby database rolls forward to the end of the logs and stops. The clients reconnect to the standby database and resume operations. The standby machine has its own resources (for example, disks), but must have the same physical and logical definitions as the production database. When using this approach the primary database is restored to the standby machine, by using restore utility or the split mirror function (IBM, 2008).

## MIRRORING

Data mirroring is the process based on copying all data in real time to a second storage location and keeping them synchronized. Copying data in real time ensures that the information stored from the original location is always an exact copy of the data from the production device. Data mirroring can be implemented locally or remote e.g. at a completely different location.

Mirroring can be organized as hardware (using RAID – Redundant Array of Independent Disks) or software (at the level of operation system or DBMS) solution.

RAID is a hard disk technology which is used to speed up data manipulation and provide disk redundancy. RAID provides these features by using more than one hard disk at a time. There are several variations of a RAID configuration known as levels. RAID 0 uses a technique called data striping (writing and reading data sequentially to/from more than one storage device) and requires at least 2 hard disks. RAID 1 level uses a pair of hard disks at a time to provide fault tolerance (there is no performance benefit) and requires at least 2 hard disks. Using a disk mirroring the same data is written to both disks at a time, so if one hard disk crashes then the same data is available from the remaining hard disk. RAID 2 configuration uses data striping and a fault tolerance technique called parity and it requires at least 3 disks. RAID 2 strips the data into bits which is why RAID 3 is a better implementation as it strips the data into bytes instead. RAID 4 strips the data into blocks and uses a parity drive for fault tolerance, at least 3 drives are required.

RAID 5 is a very popular RAID configuration using at least 3 drives. Data is striped across the drives in bytes, the parity data for one particular drive is stored on another drive allowing the data to be rebuilt using the parity technique.

Oracle Automatic Storage Management (ASM) mirrors at the file level, unlike operating system mirroring, which mirrors at the disk level. The mirrored copy of each file extent is always kept on a different disk from the original copy. If a disk fails, ASM can continue to access affected files by accessing mirrored copies on the surviving disks in the disk group. ASM supports 2-way mirroring, where each file extent gets one mirrored copy, and 3-way mirroring, where each file extent gets two mirrored copies (Oracle, 2007).

IBM uses online split mirror handling, that is, splitting a mirror without shutting down the database. A split mirror is an "instantaneous" copy of the database that can be made by mirroring the disks containing the data, and splitting the mirror when a copy is required (IBM, 2008).

The new database mirroring capability in SQL Server 2008 is another important option that enables guarding against unplanned downtime cause by a server or database failure. Unlike Windows Clustering Services which work at the server level, database mirroring is implemented at the database level. In the event when the primary database fails, Database Mirroring enables a second standby database located on a secondary SQL Server system to be almost instantly available. Database Mirroring can be set up for a single database or it can be set up for multiple databases on the same server. It provides zero data loss. The secondary database will always be updated with the current transaction that's being processed on the primary database server (Microsoft, 2008).

## REPLICATION

Data replication is copying of data into multiple locations, using DBMS, in order to support distributed application (Goodman, 2005). Replication can be either synchronous or asynchronous. Synchronous data replication means that data is written to all storage devices at the same time, and the write operation could not be completed until all devices have successfully completed writing. Asynchronous replication does not need confirmation that write operation is completed on all storage devices (data is written to all storage devices at once, although the write operation is considered complete when the primary storage device has completed writing).

Synchronous replication is the most effective type of replication for high-availability clusters and server failover in a LAN environment, since the data is completely identical at all times between the primary and other storage servers (Goodman, 2005). However, the characteristics of synchronous replication that make it great for high-availability applications are the same characteristics that make it a poor choice for remote data protection. Namely, synchronous replication works well in high-bandwidth network environments but when the primary and other storage servers are separated by more than a few miles, network latency can cause serious performance problems for the storage application (Goodman, 2005).

Asynchronous replication is not limited by the same latency and distance constraints of synchro-

nous replication, because the new or changed data does not need to be sent to the other devices at the same time it is written to the primary storage. This characteristic candidate asynchronous replication as a solution for disaster recovery across a WAN and for long distance disaster recovery, but it is not the best choice for high-availability failover. Latency and security concerns limit clustered servers from being spread over a WAN, preventing long distance automated failover.

The preferred solution for remote data management is point-in-time or scheduled, asynchronous replication. Point-in-time, asynchronous replication offers an excellent compromise between system-level and file-level data protection and provides the flexibility needed for remote office data protection and data management. Replication jobs are run on a scheduled basis, bringing the target storage server up-to-date at preset intervals and based on corporate policies that can be tailored to each type of data that needs to be protected.

In this sense, point-in-time replication acts more like a backup than a mirror, except that it stores the copied data in its original format so it can be accessed immediately without the need for recovery and rebuilding. Remote offices any distance away can be protected since point-in-time replication does not suffer from distance limitations and data consolidation and distribution can be scheduled as needed to most efficiently use limited network resources (Goodman, 2005).

WebSphere® Information Integrator and the DB2 database system include SQL replication and Q replication solutions that can also be used in some configurations to provide high availability. These functions maintain logically consistent copies of database tables at multiple locations (IBM, 2008).

Oracle Streams is database feature to implement fine-grained replication, multimaster replication, many-to-one replication, data transformation, hub and spoke replication, and message queuing. Using Streams, each unit of shared information is called a message, and user can share these messages in a stream. The stream can propagate information within a database or from one database to another. The stream routes specific information to specific destinations. The result is a feature that provides greater functionality and flexibility than traditional solutions for capturing and managing messages, and sharing the messages with other databases and applications. Streams provide the capabilities needed to build and operate distributed enterprises and applications, data warehouses, and high availability solutions (Oracle, 2007).

SQL Server 2008 replication uses a publishing industry metaphor to represent the components in a replication topology, which include Publisher, Distributor, Subscribers, publications, articles, and subscriptions. Although the magazine metaphor is useful for understanding replication, it is important to note that SQL Server replication includes functionality that is not represented in this metaphor, particularly the ability for a Subscriber to make updates and for a Publisher to send out incremental changes to the articles in a publication (Microsoft, 2008).

There are three types of replication in SQL Server 2008: transactional replication, merge replication, and snapshot replication. All of these types rely on a number of standalone programs, called agents, that carry out the tasks associated with tracking changes and distributing data.

In addition to replication, in SQL Server 2008, user can synchronize databases by using Microsoft Sync Framework and Sync Services for ADO. NET. Sync Services for ADO.NET provides an intuitive and flexible API that can be used to build applications that target offline and collaboration scenarios.

## AUTOMATED SOFTWARE APPLICATIONS

Comprehensive database tuning tools are also featured in each of the database solutions to enhance performance even as user load and queries change over time. Those tools advise the database administrator how to use configuration settings in the best way by, for example, monitoring and analyzing the operations of query statements and monitoring disk I/O subsystem performance.

Flashback is unique to the Oracle Database and supports recovery at all levels including the row, transaction, table, tablespace and database wide. Oracle 10$g$ Flashback technology includes Flashback Database, Flashback Table, Flashback Drop, Flashback Versions Query, and Flashback Transaction Query. Flashback Database quickly rewinds an Oracle database to a previous time, to correct any problems caused by logical data corruptions or user errors. Flashback Database is like a 'rewind button' for database. It provides database point in time recovery without requiring a backup of the database to be restored first. Flashback revolutionizes recovery by operating on just the changed data. A single command surgically repairs corruptions from human errors. Flashback technology removes the complexity of recovery while decreasing the time it takes to recover from unpredictable human errors (Oracle, 2007).

IBM ensure failover support through platform-specific software (IBM2, 2008):

- Tivoli[R] System Automation for Linux[TM].
- High Availability Cluster Multi-Processing, Enhanced Scalability (HACMP/ES), for AIX[R].
- Microsoft[R] Cluster Server (MCS), for Windows operating systems
- Sun Cluster, or VERITAS Cluster Server, for the Solaris operating system.
- Multi-Computer/ServiceGuard, for Hewlett-Packard.

The SQL Server 2008 Policy Management feature, which was actually called Declarative Management Framework in the Community Technology Previews (CTPs), allows you to create and execute configuration policies against one or more database servers.

The Data Collector is a built-in mechanism that eases the task of collecting management-related data. It allows you to use the SQL Server Agent and SQL Server Integration Services (SSIS) to create a framework that collects and stores your data while providing error handling, auditing, and collection history (Microsoft, 2008).

## VIRTUALIZATION

Virtualization is a broad term encompassing a set of server deployment and management features and could be defined as a technique used to abstract the physical characteristics of the resources of a system from other systems, applications, or users interacting with those resources (IBM, 2008). The main advantage of virtualization is that it could make a single physical resource appear to be multiple logical resources, or multiple physical resources appear to be a single logical resource.

Virtualization could be viewed as software, storage or desktop virtualization. Software virtualization enables users to use today's more-efficient, high-performance hardware to support hundreds of applications and several operating systems in a single system. Storage virtualization enables users to centralize data storage to protect data, improve security and disaster recovery, and accelerate data backups, while desktop virtualization enables moving of data, applications, and processing away from desktop PCs onto secure, cost-efficient virtualized network resources, replacing expensive PCs with virtualized thin-client computers (Moore, 2006).

Storage virtualization is commonly used in file systems, storage area networks (SANs), switches and virtual tape systems. Users can implement storage virtualization with software, hybrid hardware or software appliances.

Storage virtualization enables the pooling of multiple physical resources into a smaller number of resources or even a single resource, which reduces complexity. Also, policy-driven virtualization tools automate many time-consuming tasks.

Oracle VM is server virtualization software that fully supports both Oracle and non-Oracle applications. It is a single point of enterprise-class support for their entire virtualization environments, including the Linux operating system, Oracle Database, Fusion Middleware, and Application software. Oracle VM solution combines the benefits of server clustering and server virtualization technologies to deliver integrated clustering, virtualization, storage, and management for Grid Computing (Oracle, 2007).

With Windows Server 2008, everything needed to support server virtualization is available as an integral feature of the operating system—Windows Server 2008 Hyper-V. Hyper-V enables users to make the best use of their server hardware investments by consolidating multiple server roles as separate virtual machines (VMs) running on a single physical machine and also efficiently run multiple different operating systems—Windows, Linux, and others—in parallel, on a single server, and fully leverage the power of x64 computing (Microsoft, 2008).

IBM makes virtualization possible by a layer called IBM POWER Hypervisor™ (PHYP), which provides an abstract view of system hardware resources to the operating system of the shared processor partition. Virtualization features, such as IBM Micro-Partitioning™, virtual I/O (VIO), and virtual ethernet, deliver value through methods such as resource sharing, workload management, and dynamic resource allocation without operating system instance reboots (dynamic logical partitioning). Running in a partitioned environment, VIO can also alleviate storage administration overhead by providing a centralized focal point (IBM, 2008).

## DATA LIFECYCLE MANAGEMENT (DLM)

Data life cycle management (DLM) is a policy-based approach to managing the flow of an information system's data throughout its life cycle: from creation and initial storage to the time when it becomes obsolete and is deleted. DLM products automate the processes involved, typically organizing data into separate tiers according to specified policies, and automating data migration from one tier to another based on those criteria. As a rule, newer data, and data that must be accessed more frequently, is stored on faster, but more expensive storage media, while less critical data is stored on cheaper, but slower media (Hough, 2008).

Data life cycle management architectures would typically include an archiving system that indexes all critical and compliance-related information, backs it up and stores it where it can't be tampered with and can be discovered and accessed in a reliable and timely fashion. Deduplication and compression of all files ensure efficient usage of available storage space.

Unfortunately, many business DLM deployments have stalled, primarily because companies have failed to define adequate archiving and data migration policies. Since those policies need to reflect business and regulatory priorities, in their defining it is necessary collaborative work involving not just different profiles of IT staff, but also different profiles of business staff.

The easiest criterion for migrating information to cheaper storage is age. However, companies in highly regulated industries often want to go further, classifying data by how quickly or often it needs to be accessed, on the basis of who sent or received it, or on the basis of keywords or number strings. But, the real challenge is defining them and ensuring that they remain viable over time, with little or no human intervention.

## INFORMATION LIFECYCLE MANAGEMENT (ILM)

Information life cycle management (ILM) is a comprehensive approach to managing the flow of an information system's data and associated metadata from creation and initial storage to the time when it becomes obsolete and is deleted. Unlike earlier approaches to data storage management, ILM involves all aspects of dealing with data, starting with user practices, rather than just automating storage procedures and in contrast to older systems (for example hierarchical storage management – HSM), ILM enables more complex criteria for storage management than data age and frequency of access. (SearchStorage, 2004).

It is important to stress that ILM is not just technology. ILM integrates business processes and IT in order to determine how data flows through an organization, enabling users and managers to manage data from the moment it is created to the time it is no longer needed

Although terms data life cycle management (DLM) and information life cycle management (ILM) are sometimes used interchangeably, ILM is often considered as a more complex.

Data classification by business value is an integral part of the ILM process. Namely, the ILM approach recognizes that the importance of any data does not rely solely on its age or how often it is accessed. ILM expects that users and managers specify different policies for data that declines in value at different rates or that retains its value throughout its life cycle. A path management application, either as a component of ILM software or working in conjunction with it, makes it possible to retrieve any data stored by keeping track of where everything is in the storage cycle (Duplessie et al., 2003).

Successful and efficient implementation of IML needs that organization identifies critical data security requirements and includes them in their data classification processes. Data users, both individuals and applications, should be identified and categorized on the basis of the needs associated with their function.

Some of best practices related to IML implementation include (SUN, 2006):

- Focus on user productivity in order to gain strategic advantage through access to needed data.
- Protect data from theft, mutilation, unintended disclosure, or deletion.
- Create multiple layers of security, without creating excessive management complexity.
- Ensure that security processes are incorporated into overall business and IT processes.
- Use established standards and models as references in order to meet the organization's unique security needs.

Of course, each organization will need to develop and implement its own unique storage security solution, which must continue to evolve, adapting to new opportunities, threats, and capabilities.

Microsoft Identity Lifecycle Manager provides an integrated and comprehensive solution for managing the entire lifecycle of user identities and their associated credentials. It provides identity synchronization, certificate and password management, and user provisioning in a single solution that works across Microsoft Windows and other organizational systems.

IBM solutions for information life cycle management are grouped under five categories (IBM, 2008): E-mail archive (IBM DB2 CommonStore, VERITAS Enterprise Vault, OpenText-IXOS Livelink), application and database archive (Princeton Softech's Active Archive), data lifecycle management (IBM's TotalStorage SAN File System), content management (Content management repository, DB2 Content Manager), retention management (IBM DB2 Records Manager).

The Oracle ILM Assistant is a GUI based tool for managing ILM environment. It provides the ability to create lifecycle definitions, which are assigned to tables in the database. Then based on the lifecycle policy, the ILM Assistant advises when it is time to move, archive or delete data. It will also illustrate the storage requirements and cost savings associated with moving the data. Other capabilities include the ability to show how to partition a table based on a lifecycle definition and to simulate the events on a table if it were partitioned (Oracle, 2008).

From the previous overview, it is clear that ensuring continuous (high) database availability has been a fundamental offering from most database vendors over the last decade.

Table 4. presents summarized overview of specific DBMS vendors solutions, by three the most used DBMS, for ensuring high database availability. From the table 4. is obvious that each vendor also uses very automated tools or wizards in order to make the routine activities more easier for DBA.

It is clear that DBMS could not influence on, or completely avoid computer failures, they only could have implemented mechanisms for data protecting, e.g. they have to ensure that data could not be lost because of computer failures. One of the first steps in protection against hardware failure is to invest in a hardware platform that provides redundancy of key components (hot-swappable RAM and RAID drives, redundant power supplies, built-in Uninterruptible Power Supply – UPS and so on). But in case of hardware, or any other failure, DBMS have to enable very efficient and quick data recovery in order to ensure its availability.

Presented brief overview of different vendor solutions for ensuring high level database availability shows that each of the compared enterprise-level database platforms is able to deliver similar levels of high availability by using a somewhat different combination of their own methods and technologies. As it might be expected, the differ-

*Table 4. Summary of vendor solutions for downtime threats*

| Type of solution | Specific DBMS vendors' solutions | | |
|---|---|---|---|
| | **DB2 Version 9.5** | **Oracle 11g** | **SQL Server 2008** |
| Backup and Recovery | DB2 Backup and recovery Multiple database partitions back-ups with single system view (SSV) backup Rollforward recovery | Oracle Backup and recovery Data recovery advisor Health monitor Oracle Recovery Manager (Oracle RMAN) Oracle Flashback Transaction Oracle Secure Backup | MS Backup and recovery Automatic recovery Fast recovery File group restore |
| Clustering | DB2 High Availability Disaster Recovery (HADR) Tivoli System Automation for Multiplatforms High Availability Cluster Multipro-cessing (HACMP) | Grid clusters Real Application Cluster (RAC) | Microsoft Windows Clustering services N-way clustering |
| Log shipping | Log shipping | RMAN Flashback | Log shipping Log shipping with delay |
| Stand by | DB2 High Availability Disaster Recovery (HADR) | Data Guard | |
| Replication | IBM Replication | Oracle replication Oracle Advanced Replication Management | MS Replication Database snapshot |
| Mirroring | Split mirror and suspended I/O support | Automatic Storage Management (ASM) | Database mirroring |
| Virtualization | Tivoli Workload Automation software | Oracle VM | Hyper-V |
| ILM | IBM DB2 CommonStore, VERI-TAS Enterprise Vault, OpenText-IXOS Livelink, DB2 Content Manager | Oracle ILM Assistant | MS Identity Lifecycle Manager |

ent high-availability solutions provide varying degrees of protection from server failure and data corruption, and each method incurs different costs in terms of both the technology required to purchase the solution as well as the staffing costs that are a necessary part of implementing and operating the solution.

## FUTURE TRENDS

The previous overview of different solutions to continuous database availability used classification of these solutions based on the differentiation between technical (narrow) and business (broad)

approach to this problem (see Table 3.). According to that, it could be assumed that future trends, especially in near future, will also follow that kind of classification. It means that two main directions in development of solutions to continuous database availability could be recognized: one primarily based on IT development (technical direction) and other concentrated more on management of complete data and information lifecycle (business direction). Technical direction expects further improvement of existing IT solutions in ensuring database availability (backup, mirroring, standby, replication and so on) and developing of new solutions at all levels of IT support, starting form hardware (new generations of disk controllers, hard disks, processors and so on), network (new generations of network devices), operating systems, automated software and DBMS.

But, in order to move to a more automated, services-oriented platform for database availability, however, a paradigm shift is needed. What has been missing thus far was a simple, yet scalable way to offer continuous database availability through core disaster recovery data services from within the storage network fabric that connects all critical servers with their underlying network storage subsystems (Poelker, 2008).

The IT solution, that is on the best way to ensure this, is virtualization. Virtualization has made it possible for organizations to adopt this type of services-oriented platform to leverage services available from within the fabric, whenever they need them. Providing the intelligence for core data services at the fabric layer rather than within the storage itself or on the host provides multiple benefits including (Poelker, 2008):

- Simplification of the infrastructure
- Standardization of operations
- Higher service quality
- Reductions in overall IT capital and operating expenses
- More unified provisioning of services and storage capacity
- High levels of availability and functionality across bulk storage
- Protection across heterogeneous storage arrays
- Closer integration with applications for more consistent, rapid recovery.

New developments in virtualization are mostly related to storage virtualization and machine virtualization. Implementation of solution based on virtual network for storage virtualization could enable creation of storage framework where all storage is visible no matter whether it is fibre channel or iSCSI SAN connection in question.

Implementation of machine virtualization could ensure moving of logical machines dynamically and without disrupt.

The new generation of virtual servers and storage virtualization delivered via an intelligent switch could offer a way to effectively and efficiently implement database continuity and disaster recovery without the expense and need for proprietary storage architectures (Tchang, 2008)

Business direction in further improvement and development of solutions to continuous database availability is focused on stronger connection of database availability with business processes, meaning that IT support is only one part of the successful and efficient solution to database high availability. The other, crucial part of that integral solution is strongly related to business processes, users' and managers' awareness of necessity of their involvement in data classification and data management.

Namely, the costs of ensuring continuous database availability can be greatly reduced with the proper classification of data. Unless IT understands the real value of data within the environment, it remains difficult to determine how to best assign storage resources for its placement. Once the data has been assigned a value, the storage resource should also be assigned a value. By properly placing data (the proper data value on the proper value array), IT can more effectively distribute data across multiple resources, which should lead to better utilization and cost savings. (Duplessie et al., 2003)

Information life cycle management (ILM) is solution that could offer through including users and managers, resolving of problems like the cost of managing storage, ineffective use of storage, storage growth related to data backup, replication, disaster recovery continuance and so on. The importance of ILM for organization is in the same rank of the importance as CRM and ERP

Organizations can actually use ILM processes to more effectively implement CRM and ERP solutions, ensuring that critical data is given top-priority storage resources and is always available. ILM is an ever-growing and evolving process. In order to realize the benefits of the ILM process, organization should continuously review the usage patterns of its storage resources and ensure adherence to policies and procedures (Duplessie et al., 2003).

But, it is important to stress that there is a mutual dependence between the development of more business oriented and more technical oriented solutions. For example, new advances in ATA and SATA disk will play an important role in helping IT administrators with ILM, giving them the ability to stage backups and snapshots inexpensively.

So, in the future, one could expected that these two directions of development solutions to continuous database availability will converge to integral solutions, meaning solutions that fully integrated the IT support with business process and overall business continuity.

## CONCLUSION

This chapter is focused only on one - database aspect of continuous data availability. Presented overview of solutions shows that different approaches and techniques could be used for enabling database continuous availability. Main classification of these solutions is based on the differentiation between narrow and broad approach to this problem. While narrow approach is focused on IT solutions (backup and recovery, clustering, replication, mirroring), broad approach IT solution sees only as a part of broader context that includes business processes, management of complete data and information lifecycle, additional education and training of users and IT staff, establishing disaster recovery strategies and action plans (DLM, ILM).

In the chapter it is stressed that there is a strong dependency between development of technical and business solutions and that they could not be discussed separately. In the future development it could be expected that technical and business solutions will converge to integral solution. That integral solution should have taken the best of both approaches and offers methodology and technical framework for further development of efficient and business oriented solutions to, not only continuous database availability, but continuous business availability at all.

## REFERENCES

Duplessie, S., Marrone, N., & Kenniston, S. (2003). The new buzzwords: Information lifecycle management. Retrieved on February 18, 2008, from http://www.computerworld.com/action/article.do?command=viewArticleBasic&articleId=79885&pageNumber=2

Goodman, J. H. (2005). Data protection and disaster recovery of local and remote file servers. *Computer Technology Review, 25.* Retrieved on June 5, 2008, from http://findarticles.com/p/articles/mi_m0BRZ/is_5_25/ai_n15786523/print?tag=artBody;col1

Hart, M., & Jesse, S. (2004). *Oracle database 10g high availability with RAC, flashback, and data guard (Osborne ORACLE Press Series).* Emeryville: McGraw-Hill Osborne Media.

Hirt, A. (2007). *Pro SQL server 2005 high availability.* New York: Apress.

Hough, G. (2008). *Future trends in dana lifecycle management.* Retrieved on September 3, 2008, from http://www.continuitycentral.com/feature0314.htm

IBM. (2006). *Panic slowly. Integrated disaster response and built-in business continuity.* Retrieved on January 14, 2007, from http://www-935.ibm.com/services/us/bcrs/pdf/wp_integrated-disaster-response.pdf

IBM. (2008). *Data recovery and high availability guide and reference–DB2 version 9.5 for Linux, UNIX, and Windows*. Retrieved on May 12, 2008, from http://www-01.ibm.com/ support/docview. wss?rs=71&uid=swg27009727

Leung, A., & Rhodes, G. (2003). Best practices for implementing data lifecycle management solutions–tape/disk/optical storage. *Computer Technology Review*, 5. Retrieved on September 19, 2007, from http://findarticles.com/p/articles/ mi_m0BRZ/is_7_23 /ai_108112613/pg_4

Marcus, E., & Stern, H. (2003). *Blueprints for high availability*. Indianopolis, IN: Wiley Publishing, Inc.

Microsoft. (2008). *SQL server 2008 books online*. Retrieved on August 28, 2008, from http://technet. microsoft.com/en-us/library/ms190202.aspx

Moore, F. G. (2006). Storage virtualization for IT flexibility. Retrieved on May 15, 2008, from http://www.sun.com/storage/virtualization/Stg-VirtWP.pdf

Mullins, C. S. (2002). *Database administration–the complete guide to practices and procedures*. Indianapolis, IN: Addison-Wesley.

Oracle. (2007). *Oracle database high availability overview 11g release 1 (11.1)*. Retrieved on June 15, 2008, from http://www.oracle.com/technology/documentation/database.html

Oracle. (2008). *Oracle database 11g high availability–overview*. Retrieved on August 12, 2008, from http://www.oracle.com/technology/deploy/availability/htdocs/HA_Overview.htm

Otey, M., & Otey, D. (2005). *Choosing a database for high availability: An analysis of SQL server and oracle*. Redmond: Microsoft Corporation.

Patterson, D. A. (2002). *A simple way to estimate the cost of downtime*. Retrieved on June 22, 2007, from http://roc.cs.berkeley.edu/papers/Cost_Downtime_LISA.pdf

Petrocelli, T. (2005). *Data protection and information lifecycle management*. Upper Saddle River, NJ: Prentice Hall.

Poelker, C. (2008). Shifting the emphasis: Disaster recovery as a service. *Disaster Recovery Journal, 21*. Retrieved on September 20, 2008, from http://www.drj.com/index.php?option = com _content &task=view&id=2237&Itemid=429

Schmidt, K. (2006). *High availability and disaster recovery: Concepts, design, implementation*. Berlin/Heidelberg, Germany: Springer.

SearchStorage. (2004). *Information lifecycle management*. Retrieved on May 10, 2008, from http:// searchstorage.techtarget.com/sDefinition/0,sid5_ gci963635,00.html#

Snedaker, S. (2007). *Business continuity and disaster recovery planning for IT professionals*. Burlington: Syngress Publishing, Inc.

Tchang, K. (2008). Implementing a disaster recovery strategy that's not an IT disaster. *Disaster Recovery Journal, 21*. Retrieved on September 20, 2008, from http://www.drj.com/ index. php?option=com_content&task=view&id=223 6&Itemid=419&ed=47

Wallace, M., & Webber, L. (2004). *The disaster recovery handbook: A step-by-step plan to ensure business continuity and protect vital operations, facilities, and assets*. New York: AMACOM.

# Chapter 9

# Some Aspects of Implementing Always–On IT–Solutions and Standards in Banking Sector:
## The Case of Croatia

**Mirjana Pejić Bach**
*Faculty of Economics and Business Zagreb, Croatia*

**Martina Draganić**
*Faculty of Economics and Business Zagreb, Croatia*

**Božidar Jaković**
*Faculty of Economics and Business Zagreb, Croatia*

## ABSTRACT

*The growing competition in the banking sector, resulting in growing demands of the customers, requires from the banks a 24 hour availability of services. The technological development is accompanied by the increase in technologically sophisticated forms of fraud. The answer to these challenges is a more efficient use of information technology. The use of new technologies, besides the defense from unauthorized access into the bank's information system, abuse of information technology, and damage that can be caused, represents the basis for the new service offer which has an important role in market positioning of the banks. An empirical research was conducted in order to determine the level of influence of the information technology to the payment transactions. The results suggest that the level of influence is important due to the enlargement of product range and communication channels with clients, expense reduction for the costumers and the bank, as well as the increase of the business security.*

## INTRODUCTION

With the reform of the payment system in Croatia, during which payment operations and accounts of the participants of the payment system, bank depositors, are transferred from the Payment Operations Institute (Zavod za platni promet - ZAP) to commercial banks, banks as depository institutions became main bearers of the payment system.

DOI: 10.4018/978-1-60566-723-2.ch009

The payment system is a significant segment of banking business from the aspect of substantial revenues for the banks, as well as from the aspect of the bank's interest in collecting deposits, granting of loans and other banking activities. Due to the significance of the payment system for their business activity, banks need to invest in its development. The basis for the development can be provided by information technologies, which themselves are developing on a daily basis. The development of information technology initiated the development of new forms of banking activities though direct distribution channels.

The development of the Internet thus enabled the banks to connect with the large number of users (from other financial institutions and business subjects to individual users of financial services) and a higher level of security of the bank information system, but problems in ensuring the communication between the client and the bank arose as well.

## PAYMENT SYSTEM

The payment system[1], according to the Committee on Payment and Settlement Systems of G-10 countries (CPSS[2]) acting within the Bank for International Settlements (BIS) in Basel, is a system which consists of sets of instruments, procedures, rules and systems of interbank funds transfer, used to enable the circulation of money within the country.

Shortly, the payment system implies the transfer of a payment order from the payer to the payee, i.e. debiting of the payer's account and crediting of the payee's account.

The payment system includes all payments between legal persons and individuals with the aim of settling monetary debts or collection of monetary claims. Aforementioned payments represent a way of settlement of monetary obligations, which can be cash (cash delivery) or cashless (transfer from one account to the other, i.e. accounting transfer of money amounts from the debtor to the creditor).

A large proportion of the payment system consists of cashless domestic payments within the bank itself. Payment orders on paper are performed by a commercial bank transferring the money from one account to another within the same bank. If the account in favor of which the transfer is being made is open in another bank, the transfer is made through a central bank.

Payments from one account to another managed in different banks are performed through systems for settlement of interbank funds transfer. Payment systems serve the purpose of collecting orders and performing settlements.

Depending on the payment methods in interbank transfer systems, there are gross settlement systems and net settlement systems.

**Gross settlement system**[3] is a system in which every payment order is performed separately and in the given amount. The bank-entries are simultaneously done at the account of the receiving bank and the one of the sending bank. In these systems payments are performed in real-time[4].

**Net settlement system** is a system in which payments are recorded during the whole work day but they are performed at a time of the work day where final settlements are completed. The final settlement is the moment where final and non-revocable transfer of funds is made to the accounts of the banks within the central bank.

There are two forms of net settlements: bilateral and multilateral net settlements.

In the bilateral net settlement system a net position of each pair of direct participants is calculated and in the multilateral net settlement system a net position of each direct participant is calculated in relation to all other participants in the system, which means in relation to the whole system.

The division of payment systems to gross and net settlement systems can be viewed as large value payment systems and retail payment systems.

The names for the two systems origin from the size of individual amounts ordered for execution.

**Large value payment system** is mostly used for relatively large amounts and in principle between the banks. As payments/offsets are made in real-time, these systems are also called Real Time Gross Settlement systems (RTGS).

**Retail payment systems** are used for ordering payments of relatively small amounts and are therefore used mainly by physical persons and for payments between clients and the bank (i.e. between any buyer and supplier). In these systems, offsets are made at the end of a cycle, and if there are several cycles during the work day, payments can be performed during or at the end of the work day.

An example of a retail payment system is a **multilateral net settlement system** (MNS), in which offsets are made at the end of a clearing cycle. In clearing, only the differences of net positions are being processed and not individual payment messages. As the name of the system suggests, it involves a multilateral principle of net settlement. The risk of this system arises from the uncertainty if an ordered debit will be credited to the other account.

Within the reform of the payment system in Croatia, a system of net settlements based on the multilateral principle called the **National clearing system (NCS)** began to operate on 5 February 2001. The final settlement of a net position from the National clearing system at the end of the work day is performed by the Croatian National Bank (CNB) through Croatian Large Value Payments System[5] (RTGS[6]) by a direct transfer from the bank's account in the central bank.

An example of a large value payment system is a **real time gross settlement system** (RTGS), in which each payment message is performed individually and immediately after receipt. As offsets are made immediately after receipt of a payment message, it means that it is performed in real-time, distinct from MNS where its per-

formance would have to wait for the end of the clearing cycle.

Within the reform of the payment system in Croatia, a system of gross settlements called the **Croatian Large Value Payments System** (CLVPS) began to operate on 6 April 1999. The owner and operational manager of the system is the Croatian National Bank.

CLVPS is Croatian RTGS, which is clear from the definition of CLVPS in Article 2 of the *Regulation on the Croatian Large Value Payments System and offsets on banks' accounts at the Croatian National Bank*[7] from CNB (issued on 31 January 2002), which defines CLVPS as a settlement system for real-time interbank transactions according to the gross principle.

Measures to decrease the risk[8] in gross settlement systems include accession criteria, i.e. capital, organizational and technological requests that future participants need to fulfill, and the time of settlement. The settlements are performed in real time and the cost of delay[9] in settlement is borne by the participant.

The transfer of the commercial and savings banks' account to the central bank allows the central bank to follow daily banking sector liquidity and the transfer of clients' accounts to commercial banks allows the commercial banks to follow their own daily liquidity, which significantly lowers liquidity risk.

The liquidity risk is also reduced in case of existing reserves which are deposited at the central bank.

Additional risk protection, in case a bank cannot fulfill its obligation, consists in blocking the banks' account for settlement, which means that a bank cannot perform other payments until the settlement of the liability received earlier.

Since illiquidity and credit risks are minimal (due to risk protection measures), there is no systematic settlement risk (risk of payment performance), because no payment can be performed if there is no coverage at the bank's account.

In past, large and small payments were performed within the same system, but after the payment system reform they have been split: small payments are performed within CNB and large payments through CLVPS.

NCS is a settlement system based on multilateral principle, and CLVPS is a gross settlement system[10].

At its session held on 4 January 1995, the Council of the Croatian National Bank adopted a document *Fundamentals of improvement of the national payment system*[11], which was the origin of the payment system reform. The bases of organization and functioning of the payment system drafted in that document are still valid, only in the meantime the system has developed.

The results of the reform were made visible when CLVPS began to operate in April 1999, and NCS in February 2001. The first approvals to commercial banks for managing legal subjects' accounts followed in July 2001, and in October of the same year the Unified Register of Business Entities' Accounts (URBEA) was established. The National Payment System Act[12] entered into force in April 2002, and in June 2003 Foreign Exchange Act[13].

The aims of the payment system reform were the following[14]:

- abolish monopoly in payment operations and enable competition (by separating operations that were conducted by the Payment Operations Institute)
- enable legal persons a freedom of choice of depositary institutions which will manage their accounts
- transfer the managing of the accounts of participants in the payment system, including legal persons, exclusively to depository institutions (commercial and savings banks) which will conduct payment operations in their own name and for their own account, whereas non-depository institutions will conduct payment operations only

in the name and for the account of depository institutions
- strengthen the role of the CNB in the payment system and
- separate operations of account management and settlement accounting where accounts of the payment system participants will be managed by depository institutions, settlement accounting through NCS and offsets at the accounts of depository institutions performed in CNB (through CLVPS).

The technological infrastructure of the new Croatian payment system after the reform is composed by interbank payment systems: CLVPS, as a gross settlement system and NCS as a net settlement system, Unified Register of Business Entities' Accounts and cash centres.

They began to operate in the same order: CLVPS on 6 April 1999, NCS on 5 February 2001, URBEA on 15 October 2001 and cash centres on 1 April 2004.

The record of all business entities' accounts forms the **Unified Register of Business Entities' Accounts** which began to operate on 15 October 2001 in the Croatian National Bank and as of 1 November 2002 it is kept by the Financial Agency (FINA).

The Unified Register of Business Entities' Accounts is established with the aim of blockade implementation of all the business entities' accounts.

The banks are supplied with cash through 22 cash centres.

The transfer of the commercial banks' accounts, due to the reform, from the Payment Operations Institute to Croatian National Bank (CLVPS began to operate on 6 April 1999) and the transfer of the business subjects' accounts from the Payment Operations Institute to commercial banks (at the latest by 1 March 2002 according to the new National Payment System Act[15]), prevented the clients to overdraft the business bank's account. While the banks' and business entities' accounts were managed by the Payment Operations Institute, the banks did not have insight into the balance of their clients and the clients could, in the total sum of their balances, create a negative balance at the bank's account. After the reform, this situation cannot occur because commercial banks know the balance of their clients and they will not approve of payments from the client's account if it is not covered, which means that the negative balance will not be created (clients cannot spend more than they have at the account).

Additionally, due to the Unified Register of Business Entities' Accounts, used by all the banks, blockade of all the business entities' accounts can be implemented (which means in all the banks), if there is no cover for the performance of an order, i.e. orders that include legal obligations and public revenues, orders for collection of securities and payment guarantee instruments (e.g. bonds), payment orders based on court decisions implementation and other distraint documents.

As the banks did not have insight into the account balance of their clients' during the work day, they did not have insight into their own liquidity which led to a great risk of claims settlement[16]. In these circumstances, a bank needed to cover for payment settlement ordered by clients, and if it did not do it, the central bank would, by emergency loans (additional issue of cash), create cover for the bank's negative balance. However, this process made the central bank's monetary policy questionable.

Now a bank through CLVPS can, at any time, see the balance of its account, follow its own liquidity and the liquidity of clients as well as manage its liquidity.

Transferring of the business entities' accounts from the Payment Operations Institute to commercial banks as a part of the payment system reform (except abolishing Payment Operations Institute's monopoly and introducing competition into the payment system) encouraged the development of banking operations through direct distribution channels, i. e. to the development of

new services (especially Internet banking), based on new information technologies.

The second important prerequisite for the development of modern channels for performing financial transactions are regulations, which means laws regulating internal payment system, payment system with foreign countries, electronic signature, data privacy, etc.

Besides the transfer of business entities' accounts from the Payment Operations Institute to commercial banks, the reform enabled the transfer of the commercial and savings banks' accounts to CNB, and CNB can follow banks' daily liquidity and thus systematic risk has been abolished. The Croatian Large Value Payments' System, through which payments of large sums are performed almost at the moment of the order, prevents the execution of payments without cover and such payments are, at the end of the work day, returned to the sender.

Additional security lies in the fact that the CNB can block the commercial bank's accounts in case of obligations at the cost of the bank account which it cannot settle.

Besides the setting up of the modern infrastructure of the payment system, which consists of interbank payment systems (CLVPS and NCS), Unified Register of Business Entities' Accounts and cash centres, the reform of the payment system enabled the minimization of the systematic settlement risk (risk of payment execution) and better liquidity management.

CNB was enabled to monitor commercial banks' daily liquidity (by transferring all commercial and savings banks' accounts to CNB after the payment system reform) and the liquidity risk in CLVPS is lowered.

The transfer of the business entities' accounts[17] from the Payment Operations Institute to commercial banks led to the abolishment of the monopoly of the Payment Operations Institute and thus the prerequisites for the development of the payment system on market principles were created. Further development of the payment system (like Internet banking, deposit ATM machines, prepaid, debit and credit cards (business cards) for business subjects) and banks can follow business activities of their clients and manage liquidity at the level of the bank better.

## NEW TECHNOLOGIES

Each bank wishes to offer to its clients a service which is attractive from the point of view of price and quality and represents a value because of which they will not go to the competition. Today it cannot be done by means of classic business, without information technologies. Transformation of business (from classic way to development of direct distribution channels) and transformation of the banks' role (from the place for processing of transactions to financial adviser) are necessary in the modern banking business.

The bank seeks to keep existing clients and attract the new ones (even from foreign markets), and offer them the best possible quality of financial services through many different distribution channels, by fulfilling their specific needs, establishing quality relationships with clients (acquiring their trust and gathering knowledge on their needs, by means of Customer Relationship Management - **CRM**), preventing to lose customers to competition and being the first to offer certain products or services at the market, by which it creates a recognizable name and becomes more present at the market.

The purpose of the CRM is to increase banks' revenues and profitability, identify non-profit products and services and create a comprehensive knowledge base including existing and potential clients in order to develop a better relationship and connection with customers.

A bank can increase revenues and profits by keeping existing clients and attracting the new ones as well as by decreasing mass marketing costs and turning to individual selling, offering its clients the products that might interest them[18].

As the banks try to be improve client service, they introduce free information lines, information centres (centres for informing on banks' services), complaints centres, credit card centres, Internet banking support centres, general clients' support centres (help desks), which develop into contact centres offering support for all above mentioned functions.

**Contact centres** represent a unit within the company where a coordinated group of people during the majority of their working hours remotely communicates with clients, via one of communication channels such as telephone, mobile phone (SMS, Internet access thorough a mobile phone), fax, Internet (web pages), electronic mail, i. e. any channel except personal contact.

Permanent availability to clients and a quick response to their requests have become a significant tool in achieving customer satisfaction. The telephone and the Internet represent the most important channels used by a bank to contact clients (informing customers, help in service use, quick problem solving and dealing with reclamations and orders) and distribute bank services.

In developing advantage over competition, a bank, through its contact centre, tries to reduce transaction costs, *increase the rapidity of service*, *improve service quality* and adapt the service to customers.

The reason for investing into direct distribution channels are already mentioned reduced business costs, which will be above the average in comparison with the competition if a bank does not offer communication services through direct channels, especially the Internet, and make it non-competitive.

If a bank does not offer new business services, and the competition does, a bank may face client drain. Customers will accept innovations at competitive banks or at least reduce the use of classical business services.

A contact centre may be a market differentiation means in terms of the quality of customer communication as well as the quality of service. The customers are enabled simple access to the bank and in one place they can quickly get an answer to all their questions. As a supporting sales and claims' collection channel, a contact centre has an important role in the growing competition in the banking sector.

Due to the advancement of information technology, a personal contact with the bank clerk is no longer a prerequisite for customer communication with the bank. In order to facilitate client communication, banks develop new direct distribution channels based on new technologies.

In Croatia, the following direct distribution channels are offered: ATM machines, Electronic Funds Transfer at Point of Sale terminals, Internet banking, phone banking, SMS services, mobile banking.

The development of direct distribution channels allows reducing the crowds in the bank offices and the portion of transactions made through direct distribution channels in the total number of performed transactions is still growing. The trend can be illustrated by the data from Zagrebačka banka on the portion of the number of transactions through direct distribution channels: in 2001[19] it was 40%, and in 2004[20] it grew to 70% and in 2005[21] to 75%. Branches now become a place where clients can consult the bank on investment, crediting and deposit term possibilities.

The portion of electronic transactions in the total number of transactions in Croatia is 12%, and in the Financial Agency[22] is 3%.

## ATM Machines

ATM machines, as a direct distribution channel, enable the clients to see their account balance, to collect and deposit cash (deposit ATM machines, ATM machines with the feature to accept deposit of bulk notes (Bulk Note Acceptor – BNA)).

Unlike the deposit ATM machines, where the payments become visible only after the verification of the paid cash amount (in an envelope or a bag – envelope or business deposit) and after

the night-safe procedure has been done, the BNA machines allow for account deposit at once.

The importance of BNA machine introduction and, generally, the importance of ATM machines as a direct distribution channel, can be seen from the transactions volume on Zagrebačka banka ATM machines in 2005, when it amounted to HRK 19 billion, and in the first five months of 2006, when it was HRK 8.1 billion.

Cash handling is in this way enabled without waiting in the bank, which reduces crowds in the bank offices and makes business substantially easier for legal entities. Citizens now less and less come to bank offices for information on their account balance and cash collection up to the daily limit, which makes the offices to focus more on advisory role for their clients.

For any ATM machine transaction, clients need a current account card (citizens), or a card related to the business account (giro-account for legal entities). They identify themselves with a personal identification number - PIN.

## EFT POS Terminals

EFT POS terminals (Electronic Funds Transfer at Point of Sale) are electronic devices that enable the stores to accept debit and credit cards.

The invoice payment transaction with a debit card is made by choosing the transaction type by the salesman, e.g. purchase of goods, purchase of a mobile phone prepayment card (depending on the POS device application, not necessary), entering the amount that will be charged to the debit card and getting the card through the slot at the machine (whereat the user's data and the service code giving the information on the type of the card – debit or credit, VISA, MasterCard, Maestro - is read from the magnetic tape on the card). After that, the debit card user authorizes the payment by entering the PIN.

The authorization is made by sending a request, containing data from the magnetic tape on the card and the entered PIN, from the POS to the bank for authorization. The bank replies (accepts or rejects the transaction) and then the transaction result is printed on the slip. In case the card was not issued by the bank owning the POS device, the request does not go directly to the bank, but it goes through the Europay network to the bank that issued the card. At the bank, in order to accept the payment, the card expiry date is verified (the card's validity date), the status of the card (valid, blocked for overdraw or because it was stolen), account balance (if there are sufficient funds to cover that transaction) and it is verified if the entered PIN is correct.

The transaction of an invoice payment in a store or elsewhere with a credit card is only different from payment with a debit card in two elements: instead of the account balance check, only the limit of the card is verified – if this limit would be overdraft with that particular transaction – and the user does not enter the PIN in the POS device since the authorization is not made by PIN, but by the card holder's signature; thus, the PIN verification is not done.

From the security perspective, debit cards are safer than credit cards in particular due to the cardholder identification. A person who stole a credit card can simulate the signature from the back of the card, whereas a person who stole a debit card must know the cardholder's PIN in order to be able to use the card.

POS devices contribute to the significance of the card business, which encompasses both payment on points of sale and various loans on cards.

## Internet Banking

An unavoidable part of the banking offer and a segment of the banking business that shows major raise in terms of the number of users, number of transactions performed and the total turnover is Internet banking.

The share of payments made through Internet services in banks is between 30% and 60%.

The acceptance of online banking services has been rapid in many parts of the world, and in the leading ebanking countries the number of e-banking contracts has exceeded 50 percent[23] Banks offer two kinds of Internet banking: for legal entities and for individuals.

Internet banking for legal entities enables businesses to perform payments around the clock, while accessing from any place in the world where there is a computer and Internet access (which makes them more mobile). This way, they save time (avoiding waiting in bank offices) and money (costs for payments through the Internet banking are lower than the ones in the bank offices due to lower bank fees).

Since the banks are always improving their payment transactions software applications for clients, businesses can enter the forms from bank software to their own software. This enables them automatization of their business process and additional time saving.

Internet banking for individuals is even more mobile since banks offer simpler and more mobile way of Internet banking user authentication for individuals than for the legal entities. The example for this is individual's authentication by PIN or token, whereas legal entities perform authentication by a smart card.

Benefits for banks arising from use of Internet banking is represented in fewer clients in bank offices, which requires fewer employees per office and reduced need for business space. This also reduces the bank's costs. Acceptance of payment orders filled in by clients and automatized entering of those orders to the bank system reduces bank's mistakes and potential costs caused by possible mistakes.

As the services via online distribution channels mature and more consumers will go online, characteristics of online delivery will have to change to accommodate these consumers' preferences in regard to the „touch and feel" of banking services. As in face-to-face transactions, where the employee knows what needs to be done for the customer and uses pre-selection to serve customer needs, social presence and communication effectiveness for customers means that personal preference profiles are incorporated in a personal Web-site. A more sophisticated technological platform providing additional information about the service and company could assist the user in what they perceive as a more complex task (gathering information and making decision regarding an intangible banking service)[24].

## Phone Banking

Phone banking service in Croatian banks is not so different in terms of the financial service offer itself, as it is in terms of the identification form or the security level.

A telephone bank user is in Erste & Steiermärkische bank and Hypo Alpe Adria bank identified with the PIN (provided in the bank for that purpose), whereas a client of the Raiffeisen bank Austria and Zagrebačka banka is identified with the token, used as an identification device.

To businesses, telephone banking offers the information on the account balance only, whereas a broader service package (information on account balance or transaction on kuna payment accounts, possibility to make payments from any place at any time from a mobile of fixed telephone line) is only offered to individuals who perform a registered business activity. Any telephone banking service starts with the client's call to the bank and his/her identification to the bank.

## Mobile Banking and SMS Services

Only rather recently have Croatian banks recognized the advantages of mobile phones as a distribution channel. While some banks offer information on account balance and its changes only, others have developed a complete financial service through that channel. The information on the account balance itself is very significant for preventing frauds, i.e. abuse of cards.

MBU Ltd. for informatics engineering and interbank services, a company that authorizes transactions made by cards for 19 banks, uses the MBSMS service to provide banks to send to their clients information on transactions made and account balance changes. In addition to the possibility to send various requests via SMS and receive replies from the system, clients receive information on authorizations made for their cards, which enables them to discover abuse of their cards; thus, this represents a significant contribution in fighting frauds.

The term *m-pay* or *m-payment* means a service of paying for goods or services by a mobile phone.

Within this PBZ's service, invoices are paid by sending SMSs, whereas the money spent is directly taken off the user's bank account or credit cards. Among banking transactions, only the insight in the account balance is possible. The service is only enabled to T-mobile's clients and holders of at least one account opened in Privredna banka Zagreb, or to holders of at least one PBZ Card card.

RBA mDIREKT is similar to PBZ's mPay, since it is generally limited to one mobile operator only, in this case VIPnet, and it offers the same possibilities of payment of invoices for facilities and those at points of sale. However, instead of the T-Mobile invoice, the user can pay VIPnet's invoice for service, as well as buy VIPme prepaid vouchers. Also, in both cases the user's bank account of credit card is charged (within mPay in PBZ, within mDIREKT in Raiffeisen bank).

RBA mDIREKT comprises 5 types of services accessible through a mobile phone: "mDIREKT account balance" and "mDIREKT credit card" that are at the disposal of any mobile network users through SMS, whereas other services are accessible by VIPnet users only: "mDIREKT invoice payment" and "mDIREKT money transfer" through SMS, and "mDIREKT transactions review" through WAP (Wireless Application Protocol – means of Internet access via mobile phone).

Almost all banks offer the service of sending account balance reports via SMS; however, the mobile banking implies a supply of the complete financial service.

Mobile banking or m-banking, as a term, comprises all banking services performed via mobile phones.

Unlike PBZ's mPay and RBA's mDIREKT, Erste mBanking (mobile banking by Erste & Steiermärkische bank, which was introduced to the market at the end of 2005) does not depend on the mobile operator and it offers a complete access to financial services via mobile phone, making it the first complete m-banking service in Croatia. The service offers an overview of all user's accounts balance, transfers from one account to another, performing of all kinds of payments to the account and from the account, deposit terming, payment of invoices, order of checks, contracting stand-by loans (allowed overdraw), review of recorded transactions archive. This makes this service – in terms of its scope - the same as Internet banking. In order to be able to perform all mentioned transaction, the user must be in an area covered by GSM[25] signal, he must dispose with a GSM mobile phone with Java application, whereas the data transfer is made through GPRS[26].

The advantage of this service in relation to Internet banking is the simpler use and higher mobility. With Internet banking the client must use a computer (which is less accessible than a mobile phone) and Internet (connection to which is not as broadly disposable as GSM signal) and he needs to have at least basic technical education. Due to the low data volume that can be transferred, GPRS cost charged by the mobile operator to the user is minimal, which makes this service acceptable in terms of price.

Out of other direct distribution channels, businesses are – in addition to ATM machines for payments to accounts and from accounts and day/night safes for cash transactions – offered self-use devices for acceptance of payment orders – these are order machines for non-cash payment.

## Identification Forms

Information, as any company's, as well as any financial institution's, strategic resource, has its value and must be appropriately protected, irrespective of the form of information and the path it uses to get through (post, telephone, fax, Internet). Protection of information reduces business risks, which has a positive influence on the company's image and, accordingly, new potential contracts and the company's future profit

Business through the Internet made security of information traveling through the net the number one issue. The term security comprises secrecy, integrity and accessibility of information. Secrecy means access to the information by authorized persons only (classified information), integrity means completeness and reliability of information (it must not be changed in relation to its original form), whereas accessibility means that the information must be at authorized persons' disposal whenever they need it.

Security threats can be unauthorized access to information (including also physical safety of informatics resources), disclosure of information (e.g. by the competitors), disabling of operations (e.g. in the form of Denial of Service attack, that can be represented in network overload with useless packages, overload of the server with senseless requests, speed reduction due to uploaded viruses – shortly, any attacks where the network and computers providing service are not accessible to clients), which influences bank's productivity and profit.

In line with the mentioned threats, it is crucial to protect the information system. Depending on the type of business and the value of the data, a company has the choice of using virtual private networks, digital certificates, data encryption, and network operating systems to protect their data while in transit, ensure the identity of a user, and mask the data from unauthorized eyes[27].

Terms of user's authentication and authorization are related to this issue, as well as to the issue of data protection and their encrypting.

**Authentication**[28] is a process of identifying a person (identity determination), i.e. determining if a person is the one he/she claims to be. However, this process does not define the user's access rights. Identification of a person is performed on the basis of the information he/she knows or possesses: username and password, biometric characteristics, identification device such as a token or a smart card (where various data can be comprised: from PIN to certificate).

Cryptography has become an essential feature for many current technological applications. Cryptographic methods are usually divided into private-key (or symmetric) and public-key (or asymmetric) algorithms[29]. **Authorization** is a process of giving a person access to system elements based on the person's identity determined within the authentication process.

**Data encrypting is** transferring of data to a secret code (based on a cipher or algorithm), which can only be read by the one possessing the secret key or password enabling decryption of the code.

The cipher is an algorithm used to transform the data from the readable form into a secret form. The cipher's integral part is the key – agreed symbol or procedure. Modern encrypting methods are based on publicly known algorithm (e.g. on a certain mathematical method – computation of factorial[30] for large numbers, e.g. within RSA algorithm) and the secret key.

Depending on whether the decrypting key is the same of different from the encrypting key, there are two encrypting types: symmetric encrypting (encrypting with one secret key) and asymmetric encrypting (also known as encrypting with a public key).

When **symmetric encrypting** or symmetric algorithm (traditional cryptography is based on them) is concerned, the same key is used for both encrypting and decrypting. Accordingly, this key must be secret – this is why these algorithms are also called algorithms with a secret key.

Examples of symmetric algorithms are DES[31] (Data Encryption Standard) and IDEA[32] (International Data Encryption Algorithm).

The problem with symmetric encrypting is exchange of the secret key between two parties, especially on a public network such as Internet.

**Asymmetric encrypting**, or asymmetric algorithms, are used for encrypting and decrypting of various keys. Accordingly, the encrypting key can be made public (where the title of this algorithm origins – public key algorithm), since the decrypting key cannot be known from it and must remain secret. Broadly known examples of asymmetric algorithms are RSA[33] (Rivest, Shamir, Adleman), Diffie-Hellman[34] and PGP[35] (Pretty Good Privacy).

Due to their slowness, asymmetric algorithms (RSA, Diffie-Hellman) are usually used for exchange of symmetric keys (e.g. for DES symmetric algorithm), since symmetric algorithms are up to 100.000 times faster.

In the payment transactions context, special care is given to the security of payment messages transfer. This encompasses authentication of the sender and receiver, preservation of the message's integrity (original form of the message sent) and privacy (ensured by the encrypting process), as well as inability of the sender to claim that he never sent and signed the message.

The simplest authentication form is representation of the user by the user name and **password** (secret line of symbols).

According to certain studies, 80% of security holes are a result of poor passwords. Since the information system accessible with passwords is the most vulnerable (easiest to be broken through), it is useful to consider more secure access protection forms.

Due to the above-mentioned reason, the use of **PIN** is not acceptable as an authentication method in Internet banking, especially if the actual possibility of PIN interception in Internet transfer is taken into account. As the PIN is always the same, the interceptor can use the PIN at any time later and identify himself as the user. Also, since the PIN is the only identification element, the bank cannot distinguish the interceptor from the user. This way, the interceptor can easily cause damage to the user without being obstructed.

PIN as the identification element is also present in combination with transaction numbers (Transactions Number - **TAN**). For the registration in Internet banking, the Erste & Steiermärkische bank provides the user – along with the PIN – with a list of TANs used for additional authorization. PIN is always the same, but with this negative feature the problems lays also with TAN, although it is always different. Due to the fact that TAN is long, and there are a number of them, the user cannot memorize them, but has to carry the TANs list with him. In case it is stolen, the system is open for abuse by stealers.

**Token**, as an authentication form, is a small device, size of a credit card, looking similar to a calculator, which generates and displays always different identification codes (ID code). The user must first enter the password (PIN) to register with the token, then the token shows the generated number that can be used for registration with the network, in the application or else. Generated IDs have limited duration - 40 seconds, irrespective of whether they are used or not.

When used for identification, the token generates a random number (one-time password), whereas the identical calculation is performed at the main computer for user identity verification. Should the algorithm in the token and at the authentication computer achieve the same result, the user is authenticated and access is allowed.

Croatian banks use tokens as an authentication device in telephone and Internet banking.

Due to its size and the fact that it does not require additional installation software at the user's personal computer, the token enables mobility to the user and allows for telephone banking usage from any (fixed or mobile) telephone in the world, as well as the possibility to use Internet banking from any computer with Internet access and with an installed browser that is supplied with the operative system.

In order to keep the token ready for use, the bank must first perform the initialization and personalization of the token. Initialization comprises entering to the token those keys or parameters that are necessary for encrypting; this will enable unique connection of generated codes of one-time passwords (One time password - OTP) and authentication of message codes (Message Authentication Code - MAC) with the token. In this way, two various tokens are disabled to generate the same OTP or MAC. The token personalization is a process of allocation of the token to the user; in the sense of bank's evidences, and an unambiguous relation user-token is created.

Ensuring this unambiguous user-token relation, as well as OTP-token and MAC-token, the use of the token enables that the identity of the bank service user is reliably determined and so is the integrity of the message (it remains unchanged), i.e. financial data comprised in it. For the registration to the application, the user enters OTP, whereas for the payment authorization (financial transaction performance) he enters MAC.

**Smart card**[36] is a small electronic device, size of a credit card, containing electronic memory. It is most frequently used as digital cash storage (e-wallet) and for generating of identification codes. A smart card reader (for reading the information from the device or adding information to the chip in the card) is needed for the use of smart cards. It is a small device where the smart card is plugged in.

In the Croatian banking system, the smart card mostly used for authentication in Internet banking (the client introduces himself with the certificate stored in the smart card and digitally signs the transaction).

Digital transaction[37] is a digital code added to the electronically transmitted message, whose aim is to unambiguously identify the sender, in order to guarantee that the sender is the one he claims to be.

In exchange of payment messages its goal is to ensure[38]:

- message privacy protection,
- integrity of messages (original/authentic/ non-changed and integral message),
- prove of the sender's identity,
- inability for the sender to deny that the message was sent.

There are four kinds of operations[39] performed: encrypting and decrypting, as well as digital signing of messages and verification of the signature on the messages, where:

1.  the message privacy is ensured by encrypting of messages,
2.  the message integrity is ensured by creating the "hash" and by digital signing of the message,
3.  the sender's identity is provable in the authentication process thanks to the digital signature,
4.  due to the digital signature, the sender cannot deny the fact that he sent the message he signed.

When the symmetric encrypting is used, the sender encrypts the message with a secret key. The message, encrypted this way, goes to the recipient, who decrypts the message with that same key. Should the asymmetric encrypting be used, the sender encrypts the message with the recipient's public key, whereas when the message is received, the recipient decrypts it with his secret key. The

prerequisite for this is the sender's knowledge of the recipient's public key.

The sender of the payment message creates a summary of the original message (hash) applying the hash function on the payment message, encrypts (i.e. signs) this summary with his private key and sends the signed summary together with the original message. Since it is impossible to achieve the same random value by applying the same function to different texts, the application of hashing[40] enables for checking if the message has been changed during its transfer through the network.

Once the message is received, the recipient verifies the sender's identity by verifying his digital signature with the sender's public key. By verifying the signature, i.e. by decrypting the message's hash, the sender receives the sent summary. Authenticity[41] of the message is verified by letting the message through the same hush function the sender had used. Accordingly, he receives the summary of the message (a line of symbols) that needs to be compared with the received summary. If the summaries are identical, the message has not been changed during its transfer through the network, which means that it is authentic.

If the message is encrypted, it is recommendable that encrypting is performed with the keys that are different than those used to sign the message summary (the ones used for digital signing). This is not the case with the **digital envelope**, where the combination of symmetric and asymmetric algorithm is applied. For encrypting a payment message (with the aim to preserve its secrecy), symmetric encrypting is used (as much faster[42]) with a randomly generated one-time key (session key), whereas for the exchange of symmetric key and for efficient digital signing the asymmetric encrypting is used. This resolves the problem of exchange of keys through the public network of Internet needed at symmetric encrypting, as well as the problem of slowness at asymmetric encrypting.

*Figure 1. Review of the activities of an SSL sender and SSL recipient – application of digital envelope at SSL protocol[43]*

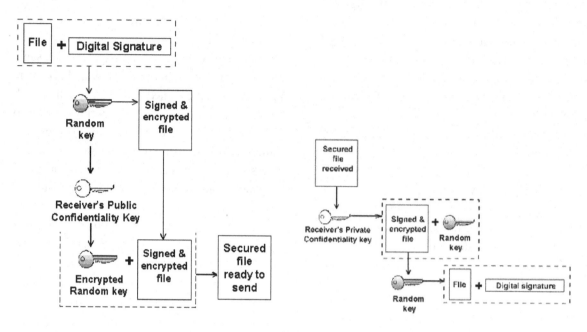

A practical application of the digital envelope is seen at the Secure Socket Layer (SSL) protocol (Figure 1), which represents a standard for message encrypting in transfer through the Internet.

One of the future identification forms will surely rely on biometry. **Biometry** is a discipline which studies measurable biological characteristics that can be automatically verified. There are two types of biometric protection: static and dynamic. It is common for both of them that the characteristics they verify are unique for the particular individual, which makes him different than anyone else.

Static biometric protection for users' identification examines physical characteristics that the individual has, such as fingerprint, eye's retina or cornea, print and geometry of the fist, facial lines, layout of veins in the finger. On the other hand, the dynamic biometric protection is based on examination of characteristic "behavior" (dynamic characteristics), such as handwriting, own signature, voice, way of walk, way of writing on a keyboard etc.

In line with the request for increased security, along with usage of the SSL connection, some authors mention the usage of two-factor authentication. The term two-factor authentication[44] designates something that the user has (e.g. token, smart card), something he is (e.g. fingerprint) and something he knows (e.g. PIN).

The advantages of the information technology are within the protection of the information system it offers in the form of anti-virus programs, systems for detection of intruders, unauthorized invasions and unauthorized actions in the network (Intrusion Detection System - IDS), system for disabling of unauthorized access to a certain network implemented as a combination of hardware and software (firewall) and requested user's authentication at any access to the information resource.

Unfortunately, every progress also brings potential abuse. Thus, technological frauds become more and more sophisticated. In addition to viruses, there are more sophisticated frauds, such as steal of identity through phishing. Phishing is attracting or remonstrating users to send their personal information via e-mail, web-page or Internet generally; such information would then be used for false identification in a legal business.

The authentication of the bank or the bank's web page plays an important role in fraud prevention like phishing (where the user receives false mail on behalf of the bank with a link to a false bank web-page that belongs to the intruder). In order for the user to be able to verify if he is at the bank's web-page prior to the registration with Internet banking, the bank should receive a certificate from one of the world's recognized authority for certificates (e.g. VeriSign, Thawte) and put its sign on the page. By clicking the authority's sign, the user verifies the name of the bank's server, i.e. if the name in the opened window under "site name" corresponds to the name in the address field of the user's Internet browser.

The security of Internet banking service comprises various aspects[45]:

1. authentication (identity determination) of the user (by PIN, OTP, certificate),
2. authentication of the bank, i.e. the bank's web-page (by the bank's certificate),
3. data protection during the Internet transfer (by SSL protocol between the client and the bank),
4. payment authorization (by the user's signature of data from the payment order with MAC or the user's certificate),
5. bank's information system protection (from unauthorized access it is secured by firewalls (from attacks from the Internet), physical protection of the information resources and authentication and authorization of the users who wish to access the resources).

## EMPIRICAL RESEARCH

### Research Methods

Empirical research was conducted by the survey method at the sample of Croatian banks. The aim of this paper was to analyze the influence of information technology on the payment system and describe different forms of payment transactions supported by the information technology. Attitudes of computer and banking experts towards this problem were researched by means of a survey.

A sampling frame was not used since on 3 August 2006 in Croatia there were 35 banks[46]. Instead, the goal was to gather the answers from as many banks as possible. Out of 35 banks, 14 participated in the research (40%), which is acceptable in this type of study[47].

Forms of payment transactions (supported by information technology) were researched by the method of secondary research of secondary and professional literature and sources from the Internet pages. The characteristics of the users' identification forms (in direct distribution channels) were analyzed and compared. Based on the results, an evaluation of identification forms was performed.

A questionnaire was used in order to research the offer of payment system services in Croatian banks as well as the influence of information technology on the offer. The questionnaire was addressed to directors of information sector in various banks and the results were analyzed by the methods of inferential statistics (t-test for differences between two populations). The conclusions were drawn on the basis of the results by inductive and deductive method.

## Results

The results of the survey show that 93% of participants think that the influence of information technology to the payment system is important and that banks' creativity in creating and developing different forms of payment transactions is based on these technologies (Table 1).

This view, i.e. a claim that the development of information technology enables greater diversity of forms of payment transactions (direct distribution channels through which payment system is in

*Table 1. Influence of information technology to the payment system*

| Likert Scale | No of banks | % |
|---|---|---|
| Strongly Agree | 8 | 57,1 |
| Agree | 5 | 35,7 |
| Neither agree nor disagree | 0 | 0 |
| Disagree | 1 | 7,2 |
| Strongly disagree | 0 | 0 |
| **Sum** | **14** | **100** |

*Table 3. Customer acceptance of new technologies*

| Customer structure | No of banks | % |
|---|---|---|
| 0-10% | 4 | 28,6 |
| 10-25% | 2 | 14,3 |
| 25-50% | 3 | 21,4 |
| 50-75% | 5 | 35,7 |
| 75-100% | 0 | 0 |
| **Sum** | **14** | **100** |

place) is supported by the fact that functioning of direct distribution channels would not be possible without information technology, by a current bank offer through direct distribution channels (93% of the banks offer Internet banking service, 86% ATM machines, 57% phone banking service and 50% mobile banking and EFT POS terminals – Table 2) and by the fact that customers have accepted new technologies (in 36% of banks 50-75% of customers accept new technologies, in 29% of banks less than 10% of customers accept new technologies, in 21% of banks 25-50% of customers and in 14% of banks 10-25% of customers accept services based on new technologies). (see Table 3)

The contribution of information technology to the increased security of payment system is reflected by the results on the ways of reducing the risk of fraud by means of information technology. Almost two-thirds of the banks (64.3%) think that information technology reduces the risk of fraud in the payment system and contributes to a greater

business protection "from the outside" (through physical security due to less work with cash, through communication between the customer and the bank protected from the assault by the third person and through payment irrevocability). More than two-fifths (43%) out of 14 banks consider that information technology is useful for them in order to prevent fraud "from the inside", i.e. by bank employees (Table 4).

As there is an increase in the number of frauds, banks consider that the development of information technology, which protects business "from the outside" as well as "from the inside", contributes to greater business security and reduces the risks of payment system operations.

In order to assess the influence of information technologies to the market positioning of the banks, it was necessary to relate services enabled by information technology and client satisfaction with these services. Customers appear to become

*Table 2. Distribution channels based on new information technology*

| Distribution Channel | No of banks | % |
|---|---|---|
| ATM machines | 12 | 85,7 |
| EFT POS terminals | 7 | 50 |
| Phone banking service | 8 | 57,1 |
| Internet banking service | 13 | 92,9 |
| Mobile banking service | 7 | 50 |

*Table 4. The ways of reducing the risk of fraud by means of information technology*

| Phone banking service | No of banks | % |
|---|---|---|
| Less work with cash | 9 | 64,3 |
| Communication between the customer and the bank protected from the assault by the third person | 9 | 64,3 |
| Payment irrevocability | 9 | 64,3 |
| Prevent fraud "from the inside", i.e. by bank employees | 6 | 42,9 |

increasingly sophisticated and their expectations regarding interaction with their service providers are not only driven by direct competitors but also by theri encounters with providers from other industries (e.g. telecommunications)[48]. Therefore, the survey included questions on which bank services are the most important for the client choice and which characteristics are crucial for his acceptance or refusal of Internet banking, as a representative direct distribution channel. An average value was calculated describing the influence of different bank services on the client choice of the bank, i.e. acceptance of Internet banking, where value 1 indicates "influences at least" and value 5 indicates "influences the most" (Table 5).

The highest average value (the highest importance of a bank service for the client choice) is attributed to credit cards (average value 4.5) and overdraft limit related to the current account (4.4), which is probably a consequence of the citizens' bad economic status, followed by the functions enabled by Internet banking: update on the balance in the account (3.8), insight in the account balance and transactions (3.7), 24 hour service availability (3.4) and a possibility of the control of expenses (3.2).

As far as the importance of individual factors on the client decision to use of Internet banking,

the highest value refers to the following: simplicity of the service use (average value 4.3), followed by 24 hour service availability, increased business efficiency for business entities and decreased transaction charges (all averages values above 4.1), time savings (4.0). Lower values refer to the size of the bank and control of expenses (both with the average value 3.4), service safety (3.0) and good marketing (2.9) – Table 6.

The above mentioned values indicate that the clients, according to the assessment of the participant of the study, besides service simplicity and availability at any time, value more time and money savings (business efficiency for business entities), than the way of marketing Internet banking service. However, one needs to take into account the fact that commercials influence customers without their awareness, but that issue should be investigated in another study.

The client's decision not to use Internet banking service is in the first place influenced by the client's computer literacy (average value 4.3), customer's age (3.7), education level (3.2), service safety (2.9) and customer's revenues (2.2) – Table 7.

Although the development of information technology provided for the characteristics of Internet banking which are crucial for the customer's

*Table 5. The influence of different bank services on the client choice of the bank*

| Bank service | Average value | Standard deviation |
|---|---|---|
| credit cards | 4,5 | 0,8 |
| overdraft limit related to the current account | 4,4 | 0,9 |
| update on the balance in the account | 3,8 | 0,8 |
| insight in the account balance and transactions | 3,7 | 1,3 |
| 24 hour service availability | 3,4 | 1,4 |
| possibility of the control of expenses | 3,2 | 1,1 |

*Table 6. The importance of individual factors on the client decision to use of Internet banking*

| Factor | Average value | Standard deviation |
|---|---|---|
| Simplicity of the service use | 4,3 | 1 |
| 24 hour service availability | 4,1 | 1,3 |
| Increased business efficiency for business entities | 4,1 | 1 |
| Decreased transaction charges | 4,1 | 1,1 |
| Time savings | 4 | 1,2 |
| Size of the bank | 3,4 | 0,5 |
| Control of expenses | 3,4 | 1,1 |
| Service safety | 3 | 1,3 |
| Good marketing | 2,9 | 1,4 |

*Table 7. The client's decision not to use Internet banking service*

| Factor | Average value | Standard deviation |
|---|---|---|
| client's computer literacy | 4,3 | 1 |
| customer's age | 3,7 | 1,3 |
| education level | 3,2 | 1,1 |
| service safety | 2,9 | 1,4 |
| customer's revenues | 2,2 | 1,3 |

*Table 8. The importance of the safety for conducting business through direct distribution channels*

| Likert Scale | No of banks | % |
|---|---|---|
| Strongly Agree | 10 | 71,5 |
| Agree | 2 | 14,3 |
| Neither agree nor disagree | 0 | 0 |
| Disagree | 1 | 7,1 |
| Strongly disagree | 1 | 7,1 |
| **Sum** | **14** | **100** |

acceptance of that service (with high average of the following: simplicity of use, 24 hour service availability, affordable charges, efficient business and time savings), the same information technology represents an obstacle to the customer's acceptance of Internet banking, because it requires computer literacy (assessed by the high value of 4.3), and is connected to the age factor (3.7) and the education level (3.2) of the user which influence the computer literacy. Therefore we can conclude that banks' investment into the development of information technologies (through the new services offer and 24 hour availability) has a double impact on attracting new clients and keeping the existing ones – there is a positive correlation but only in those clients who have higher level of computer literacy.

The analysis of the data regarding the importance of the safety for conducting business through direct distribution channels (Table 8) revealed that almost 86% of the customers have confidence in the safety of these services based on information technology. A significantly higher number of customers (six times more customers) have confidence in the security of bank services based on information technologies then the number of clients who are not confident. The customers' confidence in the security of these services is a basis for their acceptance, i. e. use of these services. Other reasons for accepting bank services based on information technology are usefulness of these services for the customers, i.e. advantages that

these services offer. Naturally, a bank also needs to have benefits from information technology in order to be motivated to invest in the development of these services.

As major benefits from information technology for the banks (Table 9), participants of the study stated the following: faster processing of larger number of transactions (for 64% of participants), expense reduction (50% of participants), other responses (which include expanding the range of services, lower operative business risk, freeing the bank clerk's time for counseling and selling purposes, better, faster and cheaper reporting, controlling and availability of bank services outside the working hours of branches), development of new products and distribution channels (for 29% of participants) and greater customer satisfaction with better services (for 14% of participants).

According to the survey, the greatest threats related to information technology for the banks are the following (Table 10): threats related to the abuse of information technology by employees, which can be called assault "from the inside" (for 57% of the participants), followed by loss of the direct contact with customers (for 42% of the participants), danger of Internet assault, which can be considered as an assault "from the outside" (for 36% of the banks participating in the survey), followed by 14% of the bank which indicated the risk from unskilled use of information technology,

*Table 9. Major benefits from information technology for the banks*

| Benefits | No of banks | % |
|---|---|---|
| 1st reason | | |
| Faster processing of larger number of transactions | 6 | 42,9 |
| Expense reduction | 5 | 35,7 |
| 2nd reason | | |
| Faster processing of larger number of transactions | 3 | 21,4 |
| Expanding the quality of service | 2 | 14,3 |
| Expense reduction | 2 | 14,3 |
| Expanding the range of services | 1 | 7,1 |
| Lower operative business risk | 1 | 7,1 |
| 3rd reason | | |
| Development of new products and distribution channels | 4 | 28,6 |
| Freeing the bank clerk's time for counseling and selling purposes | 1 | 7,1 |
| Better, faster and cheaper reporting | 1 | 7,1 |
| Controlling | 1 | 7,1 |
| Availability of bank services outside the working hours of branches | 1 | 7,1 |

*Table 10. The greatest threats related to information technology for the banks*

| Threat | No of banks | % |
|---|---|---|
| 1st reason | | |
| Danger of Internet assault | 4 | 28,6 |
| Danger of Information technology misuse | 4 | 28,6 |
| Loss of the direct contact with customers | 2 | 14,3 |
| Unskilled use of information technology | 1 | 7,1 |
| 2nd reason | | |
| Loss of the direct contact with customers | 3 | 21,4 |
| Danger of Information technology misuse | 3 | 21,4 |
| Reputation risk connected to technical problems | 2 | 14,3 |
| Danger of Internet assault | 1 | 7,1 |
| 3rd reason | | |
| Higher costs without a guarantee for return of investment | 2 | 14,3 |
| Loss of the direct contact with customers | 1 | 7,1 |
| Danger of Information technology misuse | 1 | 7,1 |
| Unskilled use of information technology by clients | 1 | 7,1 |

reputation risk connected to technical problems and higher costs without a guarantee for return of investment.

The fact that the participants consider that the greatest danger of information technologies comes from the assault "from the outside" (the Internet) and "from the inside" (abuse by employees), confirms the importance of the safety as a prerequisite for successful business through direct distribution channels, among which a special challenge is Internet banking.

In order to determine if a development of the payment system, as a consequence of the development of information technology, has an influence on the increased profitability for the banks, two groups of banks were formed: banks offering more then 10 services based on information technology and banks offering less then 10 such services. For both groups of banks return of average assets rate (ROAA) and return of average equity rate (ROAE) were calculated. The data referred to 2004 and they were gathered through the banks' web pages or in contact with their Public Relations Department.

Return of average assets rate (ROAA), as a ratio between a net profit (profit after tax) and average assets, represents a measure of profits relative to the assets of a business. As ROAA expresses gained profit per kuna of asset, shares of the bank represent a profitable investment if ROAA rate is greater then one[49].

Return of average equity rate (ROAE), as a ratio between net profit and average stockholders equity, is an indicator of profitability on the bank's invested own capital[50], whose value is shown in the final account (book value, not the market value of shares). As ROAE expresses the size of the financial result, available for accumulation and dividends, per one unit of the invested share capital, it gives the information to the stockholders on the value of profit the bank's management succeeded to achieve per kuna of their share in the bank's capital[51]. In order for the stockholders not to be at loss, ROAE indicator needs to be at least equal to the inflation rate or higher.

Box plot diagram of ROAE indicators for the banks with regard to the use of IT services (Figure 2) shows that the banks offering a larger number of services with the use of information technology have greater average ROAE, but with greater variability (shown by the size of the square which covers the central 50% of the distribution). The banks offering fewer services with the use of information technology have lower ROAE but with less variability.

In order to verify if the differences revealed by the box plot diagram are statistically significant, a t-test was performed to compare medians of the two groups. As a t-test can be performed with equal or different variances, an F-test was first performed to compare variances of the two groups. The F-test showed that with 10% probability (p=0.08) a hypothesis that variances of ROAE rates are different can be accepted. Therefore, a t-test was performed with the assumption of unequal variances. The t-test showed that the ROAE of the banks offering less IT services (9.27) is significantly lower then the ROAE of the banks offering a larger number of IT services (15.10), and the difference is statistically significant (two tailed p=0.04).

Box plot diagram of ROAA for the banks with regard to the number of IT services (Figure 3) shows that the banks offering more IT services have a slightly higher ROAA, but with significantly less variability (shown by the size of the square which covers the central 50% of the distribution).

In order to test if the difference revealed by the box plot diagram is statistically significant, a t-test was performed to compare medians of the two groups. In order to choose the type of t-test, an F-test was performed and it showed that a hypothesis on different variances of the two groups of banks cannot be accepted (p=0.15). A t-test was than performed with the assumption of equal variances. The t-test showed that ROAA of the banks offering a larger number of IT services

*Figure 2. Box plot diagram of ROAE indicators for the banks with regard to the number of IT services*

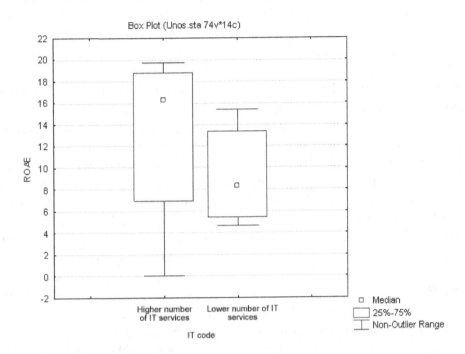

*Figure 3. Box plot diagram of ROAA indicators for the banks with regard to the number of IT services*

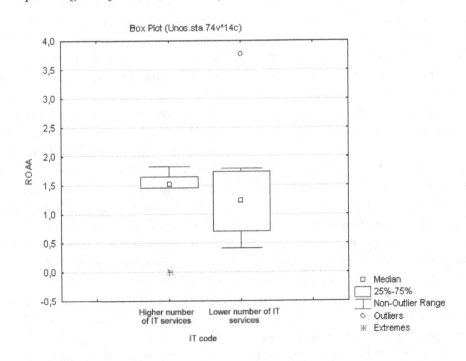

is 1,44 and the ROAA of the banks offering a fewer number of IT services is 1.32 and that the difference is not statistically significant (two tailed p=0.83) and a hypothesis on the different ROAA cannot be accepted.

These results suggest that the banks offering a larger number of IT services (>10) have in average greater profitability measured by ROAA and ROAE. The difference between these rates is statistically significant only for ROAE, so the influence of the development of the payment system (as a consequence of the development of information technology) on the increase of the bank profitability is only partial.

## CONCLUSION

On the bases of the conducted research it can be concluded that, due to customer demand and strong competition, banks need to invest in new information technologies in order to develop new communication channels with their clients, not only for keeping advantage over competition but to survive at the market.

To meet customer needs, keep up with competitors, or improve efficiency, new technologies such as advanced computer operating systems, wide and local area networks (WAN, LAN), and the Internet, are becoming significant strategic arcas for financial institutions. The overall impact of technology on the banking industry is positive[52].

The customers demand that financial services be not limited by the space and time. This demand can be satisfied if the bank offers them more flexible ways of performing operations in the payment system and better service quality.

Under the influence of the market, reducing the costs is an imperative for all sectors, including banking. The new direct distribution channels enable lower transaction costs (for the bank and for the customer as payment transaction charges) and the increase of non-interest incomes of the bank

through payment transaction charges).

By determining a target group of potential future clients, the banks should chose in which direct distribution channel they will invest. They should certainly invest in the development of Internet banking, with an appropriate protection of the communication between the bank and the customer and a reliable authentication through advanced forms as tokens.

The banks should also invest in the development of the services through self-service devices for performance of payment orders as such services do not require informatics' knowledge and are thus suitable for customers who are not computer literate. In this way, these clients would also have access to this service outside working hours which would relieve the branches and in time decrease their number and the bank costs.

As the results of the study suggest, the level of acceptance of the new distribution channels by the clients depends on the simplicity of the created service and on the stimulation of the clients by lower transaction costs in these channels.

Basel II already requires banks to perform a thorough analysis of the risks resulting from their business and the solutions of risk management. This includes operational risks containing the risks of the information system. The study showed that information technology can help in reducing risks through data access control and risk management (data collection and statistical analysis), but can also be a risk source: the risk of an unskilled use of information technology and the reputation risk (in case of technical failure or employees' abuse if the controls are not implemented).

In the future, even greater importance of the influence of the information technology on the development of different forms of payment transactions can be expected as well as the increase in the number of banks offering payment transaction services based on information technology.

A further development of the offer of different forms of payment transactions is to be expected, influenced by the development of information technology, competition and the need for the banks and the customers to decrease their costs.

# REFERENCES

Barbaroša, N. (2004). Platni sustav u Hrvatskoj: institucionalni, tehnički i pravni aspekt, HNB.

Committee on Payment and Settlement Systems., (2006, January). *General guidance for national payment system development,*. CPSS Publications No. 70,. Basel: Bank for International Settlements,. Basel, January 2006

Ćurković, P. (2004). *Platni promet: pojmovi, vrste namirenja, rizici, standardi, inicijative*, HNB, str. 7, 18. Definicija autentikacije, http://insideid. webopedia.com/TERM/A/authentication.html

Definicija smart kartice, http://insideid.webopedia.com/TERM/S/smart_card.html

Hawkins, S., Yen, D. C., Chou, D. C. (2000). Awareness and challenges of Internet security

Hrvatska narodna banka. (1997). Sažetak godišnjeg izvješća za 1996. godinu.

Hrvatska narodna banka. (2002). *Odluka o Hrvatskom sustavu velikih plaćanja i o namiri na računima banaka u Hrvatskoj narodnoj banci*, Retrieved from http://www.nn.hr/clanci/sluzbeno/2002/0359.htmhttp://www.nn.hr/clanci/sluzbeno/2002/0359.htm

International Journal of Bank Marketing. *Volume: 21* Issue: (1); 2003. Research Paper.

Johnson, O. E. G., Abrams, R. K., Destresse, J.-M., Lybek, T., Roberts, N. M., & Swinburne, M. (1998). *Payment systems, monetary policy, and the role of the central bank*. Washington, D.C.: International Monetary Found, Washington D.C.

Joyce, E. (2006). Q&A with Neal Creighton, CEO, GeoTrust. Retrieved from, http://www.insideid.com/credentialing/article.php/3589686http://www.insideid.com/credentialing/article.php/3589686

Jurković, P., et al. (1995). *Poslovni rječnik*, Masmedia, Zagreb.

Kalton, G. (1983). *Introduction to survey sampling*, London: SAGE Publications, London.

Lang, B., & Colgate, M. (2003). Relationship quality, on-line banking, and the information technology gap. *International Journal of Bank Marketing; Volume: 21* Issue: (1).; 2003 Research paper.

Lassar, W. M., & Dandapani, K. (2003). Media perceptions and their impact on Web site quality.

Panian, Ž. (2002). *Izazovi elektroničkog poslovanja*, Narodne novine d.d., Zagreb, str. 236, 417.

Panian, Ž. (2005). *Englesko-hrvatski informatički enciklopedijski rječnik*, Europapress holding d.o.o., Zagreb.

Pavković, A. (2004). *Instrumenti vrednovanja uspješnosti poslovnih banaka*, Zbornik radova Ekonomskog fakulteta u Zagrebu, 2(1), str. 179-191.

Pikkarainen, T., Pikkarainen, K., Karjaluoto, H., & Pahnila, S. (2004). Consumer acceptance of online banking: aAn extension of the technology acceptance model. *Internet Research; Volume: 14* Issue: (3). 2004 Research paper.

Pujol, F. A., Mora, H., Sánchez, J. L., & Jimeno, A. (2008). A client/server implementation of an encryption system for fingerprint user authentication. *Kybernetes;, Volume: 37* Issue: (8).; 2008

*Revidirani rezultati poslovanja Grupe Zagrebačke banke za 2001. godinu*, http://www.zaba.hr/info/abo/news/press/habo_press125.htm

*Revidirani rezultati poslovanja Grupe Zagrebačke banke za 2004. godinu,* http://www.zaba.hr/info/abo/news/press/habo_press269.htm

*Revidirani rezultati poslovanja Grupe Zagrebačke banke za 2005. godinu,* http://www.zaba.hr/info/abo/news/press/habo_press341.htm

Šarić, J. (2001). *Upravljanje sigurnošću informacija*, magistraski rad, Sveučilište u Zagrebu, Ekonomski fakultet, Zagreb, str. 124.

Schneier, B. (1996). *Applied cryptography*, New York: John Wiley & Sons, New York, 1996.

Vintar, T. (2006). *Ove godine Fina očekuje 12000 korisnika e-kartice*, Lider, God. 2, broj 17, str. 54-55. y. *Information Management & Computer Security;, Volume: 8* Issue: (3); 2000.

Zakon o deviznom poslovanju, Narodne novine, br. 96/03 (2003).

Zakon o platnom prometu u zemlji, Narodne novine, br. 117/01 (2001).

Žgela, M. (2000). *Some Ppublic kKey Ccryptography Iissues in Ee-business*, Međunarodni simpozij IIS, Varaždin.

Žgela, M. (2004). Trendovi – platni sustavi i Internet, pametne kartice i beskontaktna plaćanja, HNB, str. 16.

Zhu, Z., Scheuermann, L., & Babineaux, B. J. (2004). Information network technology in the banking industry. *Industrial Management & Data Systems; Volume: 104* Issue: (5).; 2004 Research paper.

## ENDNOTES

[1] Committee on Payment and Settlement Systems, *General guidance for national payment system development*, CPSS Publications No. 70, Bank for International Settlements, Basel, January 2006

[2] CPSS, through specific studies, contributes to strengthening the infrastructure of the financial market by promoting efficient payment systems and serving as a forum to central banks of G-10 countries.

[3] Ćurković, P. *Platni promet: pojmovi, vrste namirenja, rizici, standardi, inicijative*, HNB, 2004., p. 7

[4] Real-time transactions are those transactions made in the moment where they actually happen.

[5] Croatian Large Value Payments System is a gross settlement system, which means: each payment order is performed individually and in real time.

[6] Real Time Gross Settlement is a large value payment system in which the settlement is performed in real-time, i.e. each payment message is executed individually and immediately after receipt.

[7] Definition of the Croatian Large Value Payments System, http://www.nn.hr/clanci/sluzbeno/2002/0359.htm

[8] Ćurković, P. *Platni promet: pojmovi, vrste namirenja, rizici, standardi, inicijative*, HNB, 2004., p. 18

[9] In case there is no money on the offset account, orders wait to be performed in the payment quest. As payments need to be performed a few seconds after the order, the bank owning the account with no cover must pay for this waiting for payment execution.

[10] Two systems, one for netting, and other RTGS system exist in the United States, Germany and France whereas in Japan since 1988. there is only one system - BOJ-NET. Source: Johnson, O.E.G., Abrams, R.K., Destresse, J-M., Lybek, T., Roberts, N.M., Swinburne, M. *Payment Systems, Monetary Policy, and the Role of the Central Bank*; International Monetary Fond, Washington D.C., 1998.

[11] Hrvatska narodna banka, *Sažetak godišnjeg izvješća za 1996. godinu*, 1997.

[12] Official Gazette 117/01 (2001)

[13] Official Gazette 96/03 (2003)

[14] Barbaroša, N. *Platni sustav u Hrvatskoj: institucionalni, tehnički i pravni aspekt*, HNB, 2004.

[15] Official Gazette 117/01 (2001)

[16] Reduction of the systematic risk of settlement (payment execution) was one of the targets of establishment of the CLVPS. Source: Barbaroša, N. *Platni sustav u Hrvatskoj: institucionalni, tehnički i pravni aspekt*, HNB, 2004.

[17] A business entity is a legal person, government authorities, government administration bodies, local and district (regional) government units and natural persons (entrepreneurs) undertaking registered activities in accordance with regulations.

[18] Panian, Ž. *Izazovi elektroničkog poslovanja*, Narodne novine d.d., Zagreb, 2002., p. 236

[19] Revised business results of Zagrebačka banka Group in 2001, http://www.zaba.hr/info/abo/news/press/habo_press125.htm

[20] Revised business results of Zagrebačka banka Group in 2004, http://www.zaba.hr/info/abo/news/press/habo_press269.htm

[21] Revised business results of Zagrebačka banka Group in 2005, http://www.zaba.hr/info/abo/news/press/habo_press341.htm

[22] Vintar, T. Ove godine Fina očekuje 12.000 korisnika e-kartice, Lider, God. 2, no 17, 2006., pp. 54-55

[23] Pikkarainen, T., Pikkarainen, K., Karjaluoto, H., Pahnila, S., *Consumer acceptance of online banking: an extension of the technology acceptance model*. Internet Research; Volume: 14 Issue: 3; 2004 Research paper

[24] Lassar, W.M., Dandapani, K. *Media perceptions and their impact on Web site quality*. International Journal of Bank Marketing; Volume: 21 Issue: 1; 2003 Research Paper

[25] General System for Mobile Communications.

[26] General Packet Radio Service is a standard for wireless communication, faster from GSM, supporting broadband transmission; it is suitable for transmission of large data quantities and for receiving and sending smaller data groups, such as web browsing results or e-mail (Panian, Ž. *Englesko-hrvatski informatički enciklopedijski rječnik*, Europapress holding d.o.o., Zagreb, 2005.).

[27] Hawkins, S., Yen, D.C., Chou, D.C. *Awareness and challenges of Internet security* Information Management & Computer Security; Volume: 8 Issue: 3; 2000

[28] Definition of authentication, http://insideid.webopedia.com/TERM/A/authentication.html

[29] Pujol, F.A., Mora, H., Sánchez, J.L., Jimeno, A. A client/server implementation of an encryption system for fingerprint user authentication. Kybernetes; Volume: 37 Issue: 8; 2008

[30] Times whole numbers

[31] DES is an algorithm developed in the seventies of the last century; it uses a key of 56 bit, easy to be broken through with a fast computer, first public algorithm. Today, as a safer version, the triple DES algorithm is used (DES algorithm used three times in an encrypting sequence with two or three different non-connected keys).

[32] IDEA is an algorithm developed in 1990 in Zurich; it uses the key of 128 bit, one of the best publicly available algorithms, not yet broken through.

[33] RSA is an algorithm named after its authors, developed in 1977, patented in the U.S.A., uses keys of 512 bit to 2048 bit, quite safe when keys longer than 1024 bit are used.

[34] Diffie-Hellman algorithm is based on mathematic problem of logarithm computation and it is quite safe if a key long enough is

used and if the size of the secret exponent is sufficiently large.

[35] PGP developed in 1991 in the U.S.A. by Phil Zimmermann, published on the Internet as freeware (motivated by the human right to communication privacy, as a reply to FBI's wish to supervise citizen communications), uses public and private keys for electronic mail messages encrypting, very secure, easy to use, and the only problem is the fact that one must know the public key of the person who wishes to send the message.

[36] The definition of the smart card, http://insideid.webopedia.com/TERM/S/smart_card.html

[37] Panian, Ž. *Englesko-hrvatski informatički enciklopedijski rječnik* Europapress holding d.o.o., Zagreb, 2005.

[38] Žgela, M. (2000). *Some Public Key Cryptography Issues in E-business*, International Symposium IIS, Varaždin

[39] Panian, Ž. *Izazovi elektroničkog poslovanja*, Narodne novine d.d., Zagreb, 2002., p. 417

[40] Panian, Ž. *Englesko-hrvatski informatički enciklopedijski rječnik* Europapress holding d.o.o., Zagreb, 2005.

[41] Schneier, B. *Applied Cryptography*, John Wiley & Sons, New York, 1996.

[42] Typically, today's symmetric keys are of 128 bit, whereas the asymmetric are of 1024 bit. Since the key length slows down the encrypting process, symmetric encrypting are, accordingly, much faster than the asymmetric.

[43] Žgela, M. *Trendovi – platni sustavi i Internet, pametne kartice i beskontaktna plaćanja*, HNB, 2004., p. 16

[44] Joyce, E. *Q&A with Neal Creighton, CEO, GeoTrust*, http://www.insideid.com/credentialing/article.php/3589686, 2006.

[45] Šarić, J. *Upravljanje sigurnošću informacija*, MA thesis, University of Zagreb, Business School of Economics, 2001., p. 124

[46] Source: http://www.hnb.hr, 2006.

[47] Kalton, G. *Introduction to Survey Sampling*, SAGE Publications, London, 1983.

[48] Lang, B., Colgate, M., *Relationship quality, on-line banking and the information technology gap.* nternational Journal of Bank Marketing; Volume: 21 Issue: 1; 2003 Research paper

[49] Pavković, A. *Instrumenti vrednovanja uspješnosti poslovnih banaka*, Zbornik radova Ekonomskog fakulteta u Zagrebu, 2(1), pp. 179-191, 2004.

[50] Since the banks are joint stock companies, their own capital is the share capital.

[51] Jurković, P. et al. *Poslovni rječnik*, Masmedia, Zagreb, 1995.

[52] Zhu, Z., Scheuermann, L., Babineaux B.J., *Information network technology in the banking industry.* Industrial Management & Data Systems; Volume: 104 Issue: 5; 2004 Research paper

# Chapter 10
# Leagility in Manufacturing and Procurement:
## A Conceptual Framework

**Sumeet Gupta**
*Shri Shankaracharya College of Engineering and Technology, India*

**Miti Garg**
*The Logistics Institute – Asia Pacific, Singapore*

**Mark Goh**
*The Logistics Institute – Asia Pacific, Singapore*

**Maya Kumar**
*The Logistics Institute – Asia Pacific, Singapore*

## ABSTRACT

*A combination of lean and agile concepts, leagility has gained ground in recent years. While it has found widespread applications in the domain of manufacturing, other domains such as procurement can also benefit from the principles of leagility. We study the application of concepts of leagility in PC manufacturing through the case of Dell and based on our experience with a worldwide retailer, we develop a conceptual framework in this paper which can be used as the basis for applying the principles of leagility in the domain of procurement. The framework would be of particular significance to academics as it extends the field of leagility to procurement. At the same time, manufacturing and retail firms can derive benefits by downsizing their inventory using the principles and conceptual framework discussed in this chapter.*

## INTRODUCTION

The pressure of increasing global competition and shift of power from suppliers to buyers has spurred many manufacturers to adopt a lean production philosophy which ties closely with the tenets of just-in-time philosophy. Lean paradigm is about eliminating wastes from the supply chain with the ultimate objective of cutting costs. On the other hand, the increasingly demand-driven marketplace (and the consequent demand volatility) is motivat-

DOI: 10.4018/978-1-60566-723-2.ch010

ing companies to adopt an agile approach. In the agile paradigm, a company attempts to make its processes flexible so as to cater to the fluctuating and volatile customer demand.

Traditionally, the lean and agile manufacturing paradigms have been viewed in a progression and in isolation of each other but not together (Naylor et al., 1999). Using the principles of leagility, both lean and agile paradigms can be applied together successfully for achieving maximum efficiency. According to Naylor et al. (1999), both lean and agile paradigms can be combined with a total supply chain strategy particularly considering market knowledge and positioning of the decoupling point as agile manufacturing is best suited to satisfying a fluctuating demand and lean manufacturing requires a level schedule. In fact, for success in global markets a firm must be both lean (so as to reduce its inventory and wastes) as well as agile (to be market responsive). When lean and agile paradigms are applied together, the approach is known as leagility (lean+agile).

The concept of leagility has been adopted mostly by manufacturing firms. Retailers can also benefit from the principles of leagility, by improving their procurement. This paper discusses the application of principles of leagility to procurement based on the authors experience with a world-wide retailer and develops a conceptual framework which can be used by retailing firms in procurement.

The paper is organized as follows. In the next section (literature review) we discuss separately the lean supply chain paradigm, agile supply chain paradigm and the combination of two (i.e., the leagile supply chain paradigm). Then we discuss the application of leagile supply chain paradigm in case of PC manufacturing through the case study of dell in the third section. In the fourth section we discuss how these principles can be applied in case of procurement. In the last section we conclude the chapter with a brief discussion and conclusion.

## LITERATURE REVIEW

### Lean Supply Chain Paradigm

The lean supply chain modeling approach, first introduced by Womack et al. (1990), calls for the elimination of all waste in the supply chain (Harris, 2004/05). In the lean paradigm, activities that consume resources but generate no redeeming value in the eyes of the consumer are waste that must be eliminated (Womack & Jones, 1996). The wastes can be classified into seven basic forms, namely, defects in production, overproduction, inventories, unnecessary processing, unnecessary movement of people, unnecessary transport of goods, and waiting by employees (Ohno, 1988). A lean enterprise is one that seeks out the value inherent in specific products, identifies the value stream for each product, supports the flow of value, allows the customer to extract value from the producer, and pursues perfection (Womack & Jones, 1996).

The epitome of the lean supply chain is Toyota, where manufacturing reacts to a combination of dealer orders and sales forecasts provided by Toyota Motor sales. The focus of Toyota production system (TPS) was on the reduction and elimination of waste or muda. Toyota's manufacturing responds to the demand signal emitted by the next-stage customer who is rarely the end user. Thus, the principle behind lean enterprise is pull replenishment from the next-stage customer and not the end user. (see Figure 1)

### Agile Supply Chain Paradigm

The concept of agile manufacturing was put forward by Iaccoca Institute of Lehigh University in 1991. The agile manufacturing focuses on the ability to respond rapidly to changes in demand, both in terms of volume and variety. The origins of agility as a business concept lie in flexible manufacturing systems (FMS). Flexibility is one of the key characters of an agile organization (Qi

*Figure 1.*

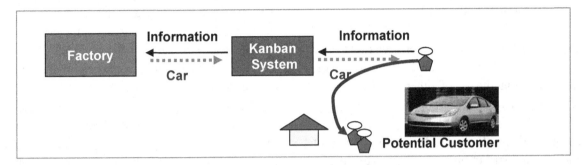

et al., 2007).

While lean management emphasizes the pursuit of process efficiency – generating the greatest outcome from the least input through the minimization of waste, agility refers to effective, flexible accommodation of unique customer demands (Christopher, 2000). An agile enterprise is one that "[uses] market knowledge and a virtual corporation to exploit profitable opportunities in a volatile marketplace" (Naylor et al., 1999). Instead of relying on speculative notions of what might be demanded, the quantity of demand, and the location of that demand, agility employs a wait-and-see approach to demand, not committing to products until demand becomes apparent and known. Key to providing this agile response is flexibility throughout the supply chain. For agility to happen, supply should be located nearby, and information sharing among the parties in the supply chain must be open and frequent (Christopher & Towill, 2001). Many companies already realize that the costs and risks associated with holding speculative inventories are too great (Goldsby et al., 2006). This is particularly true with products that have short life cycles (such as consumer electronics) or erratic demand (such as fashion apparels), where the risk of obsolescence is also high.

A well known example of an agile supply chain is that of Dell's direct-to-consumer business model. Dell holds minimum inventories of component parts such as hard drives, processors,

memory storage media, monitors, speakers, and a host of other supplies close to its assembly and testing locations. Many of Dell's local suppliers are located in the vicinity and some of them replenish parts as frequently as every two-hourly (Hoffman, 2004). Dell uses these supplies and quickly configures the components into finished desktop and laptop computers that meet customer-specific orders. The make-to-order approach requires that the consumer waits, as opposed to pre-positioned finished good inventories found in make-to-stock operations. Dell and other agile companies bank on the customer's willingness to wait for products that meet their specific requirements.

Therefore, while lean management typically calls for make-to-stock replenishment driven by short-term forecasts, agile supply chains tend to employ make-to-order provisions, producing only what has already been sold or pre-committed in the marketplace. Though, lean and agile supply chain strategies are often pitted as diametric paradigms, they share a common objective: meeting customer demands at the least total cost (Goldsby et al., 2006). It is on the nature of that demand and the basis of meeting customer demands that these two approaches differ. Researchers (e.g., Harris, 2004/05; Naylor et al., 1999) in recent years have even suggested that the two approaches need not necessarily represent opposing points of view. Rather, they may be merged in a variety of ways to create the so-called leagile (lean + agile) approach.

## Leagile (Lean + Agile) Supply Chain Paradigm

Naylor et al. (1999) coined the term leagile to refer to the hybrid of the lean and agile approaches. They argue that the use of either paradigm has to be combined with a total supply chain strategy, one that considers intimate market knowledge and strategic positioning of the decoupling point since agile distribution is best suited to satisfying a fluctuating demand and lean manufacturing requires a level schedule. Building on the concept of the blended strategy set forth by Naylor et al. (1999), Christopher and Towill (2001) have conceived three distinct hybrids which are elaborated below.

*The Pareto curve approach*: Many companies manufacturing or distributing a range of products will find that the Pareto Law applies and can be exploited to determine the best supply strategy (Koch, 1997). Indeed, it is safe to note that 80 percent of total volume will be generated from just 20 percent of the total product line. Naturally, the way in which these 20 percent are managed should probably be quite different from the way the remaining 80 percent are managed. For example, it could be argued that there is a layer of family of products (say top 20 percent) sold by volume that are likely to be predictable by demand and hence they lend themselves to lean principles of manufacturing and distribution. The slow moving 80 percent, on the other hand, will typically be less predictable and will require an agile response.

In the adoption of personalized production, BMW discovered that a relatively small number of variants in color and make accounted for most of the demand. Most of these are in a way predictable, and can be made ahead of demand. By centralizing their inventory instead of pushing it to the dealers, BMW has ensured availability. This was the lean part of BMW's supply chain. For the agile part, where forecasting was impossible, priority was given to these product categories in manufacturing. In the part where forecasting is impossible or poor, companies observe that the base differs from the surge demand, it is better to outsource the surge demand, using the principles of both lean and agile instead of lean or agile supply chain management. This can be achieved by decoupling.

*The de-coupling point approach*: This approach involves creation of a 'de-coupling' point by placing strategic inventory to meet the needs of peak demand. The idea is to hold inventory in some generic or modular form and only complete the final assembly or configuration when the precise customer requirement is known. An example is the customized PC (Christopher & Towill, 2000). Utilizing this concept of postponement, companies may utilize lean methods up to the de-coupling point and agile methods beyond it. Companies such as Hewlett-Packard have successfully employed such strategies to enable products to be localized much closer in time to actual demand (Feitzinger & Hau, 1997). The ability to base replenishment decisions on real demand clearly contributes to supply chain agility and flexibility. This approach works best when goods can be developed from common materials or components into a near-finished state with final touches to the product providing for a diverse assortment that still accommodates distinct customer needs.

*Separation of base and surge demands*: This strategy involves having temporary capacity to meet the needs of peak demand and is based on separating demand patterns into base and surge elements. Most companies experience a base level of demand over the course of a year. Base demand can be forecasted on the basis of past history whereas surge demand typically cannot be forecasted. Base demand can be met through the classical lean procedures to achieve economies of scale whereas surge demand is provided through more flexible, and probably higher cost processes, albeit shorter time. This strategy is increasingly being employed in the fashion industry where the base demand can be sourced in low cost countries and the surge demand 'topped up' locally nearer to the market. Even though the unit cost of manufacturing in the local markets will be higher than sourcing from low cost locations, the supply chain advantage can be considerable. Alternatively, arrangements can be made for dealing with both base and surge demands either by separation in space (via separate / dedicated production lines) or in time (by using slack periods to produce base stock).

## LEAGILITY IN PC MANUFACTURING (CASE STUDY OF DELL)

"The PC industry is one of the strangest in the world. There is probably no other type of product that is so technologically sophisticated, sells for so much money, and yet is sold by so many companies for a very little profit (Yashuhi, 2004)." PC manufacturing requires a supply chain that needs to be agile to respond to the rapid obsolescence of the PCs as well as lean to hold only the required amount of inventory. According to IDC, about 75 percent of the U.S. population has a computer as compared to 5.1 percent in India and 9 percent in China[1]. On one hand, the low PC ownership amongst the most populous Asian economies should be a cause of much cheer amongst PC manufacturers. On the other hand, intensive global competition, continual price cuts, shortening product lifecycles and uncertainty in fluctuations in demand threaten the major players in the market[2]. The industry faces severe price erosion and price fluctuations. On average PC prices fall 1% every week (Callioni et al., 2005). PC prices have fallen 55 percent in the last ten years. Prices for computer components are generally dropping rapidly. Inventory which was available at X dollar may actually lose value and fall to X/2 dollars within a week, leading to immense losses to component manufacturers and PC vendors. Vendors generally do not stock parts and finished goods that they sell. This results in frequent stock outs especially when there is high demand. In such a scenario a business model which supports low inventory and high inventory turnover is suited to this product.

## PC Market: An Overview

The first personal computer invented by Charles Babbage, occupied an area the size of a football field. Innovation in personal computing is one of the miracles of the industrial age. The latest personal computer can be integrated with your hand held and operates at the touch of your finger tip. The PC market resembles the car market, in the sense that it is more of a replacement market than a growth market; the mobile computing segment has been experiencing steady growth in the past few years (Hugos 2006). Laptops are being used by people from every walk of life – students, small businesses and large corporate. From tech-savvy Generation Y'ers and their soccer moms to IT professionals upgrading the last cycle of PCs for sleek business executives, laptop computers are becoming increasingly popular with everyone. The drivers of this phenomenon include the obvious portability of laptops, the narrowing of the price-performance gap, and laptop technology becoming comparable or even surpassing desktop computers.

There is severe price competitiveness in the market. The commoditization of the personal computer and the ease with one which one can be assembled without much expertise has lead to a spate of PC manufacturers in the industry. Global competition is cited as the main reason for the problems that the PC manufacturers face. PC manufacturers sell computers at margins as low as 10 percent or 100 dollars per PC.

Dell, the second largest personal computer company for home, office and data centers, has turned its focus to this market, claiming that "For every person, there's a Dell." In fact, Dell is the only PC manufacturer selling computers at a profit! Founded in 1984, by Michael Dell in his dormitory room in the University of Texas, with a start-up capital of $1000, Dell Computer Corporation has grown to become a Fortune 500 company and one of the largest PC manufacturers in the world within 20 years of its conception. Dell achieved sales of US $61 Billion in 2008. Dell Computers can be found everywhere-libraries, offices, homes, you name a place and a Dell PC can be found there. Every 1 in 4 computer sold in the US is manufactured by Dell. Here, we study the case of DELL who has epitomized the application of leagile principles in PC manufacturing. A quick look at Dell's current lean supply chain DNA is followed by an attempt to understand today's computer supply chain management challenges as competition becomes more heated.

Dell serves the following customer segments-

- Relationship Customers (Large customers with turnover> USD 1M/yr)
- Transaction Customers (Home and small business customers)
- Public Sector (Government and educational customers)

Dell offers a wide portfolio of products. It operates in the following market segments-

- Enterprise Systems (Servers, storage, work stations, networking products)
- Client Systems (notebook and desktop computers)
- Printing and imaging systems
- Software and peripherals and global services

## Dell's Global (Yet Local) Supply Chain

Dell has a global footprint that covers three continents. In Asia Pacific and Japan, Dell has a presence in India, China, Malaysia, Singapore, Taiwan and Japan. Dell hires 32,100 people in this region. The regional headquarters are located in Singapore. Manufacturing facilities are located in China, India and Malaysia. Dell has the most comprehensive presence in India outside of the US, with 14,000 employees who serve on teams in domestic sales, research and development, manufacturing, customer support, services and analytics. Customer contact centers in Bangalore, Hyderabad, Chandigarh and Gurgaon support customers around the world. The India Research and Design Center in Bangalore, established in 2001 provides end-to-end server design for enterprise products, software development, server development, test engineering, documentation, and international product support[3]. Dell analytics in Bangalore develops unique solutions for financial services, database marketing, e-business, logistics, services and business analytics. A manufacturing facility was set up in Sri Perumbudur in 2007 in South India. Dell was No. 4 in India and grew the fastest amongst the top 10 companies in 2006.

In China, Dell is the third largest computer provider. China is Dell's third largest customer. Dell's largest design center outside of US was established in 2000 in Shanghai and employs more than 6000 people, of whom 600 are engineers who design desktops, mobiles computers and peripherals. Dell's manufacturing facility in Xiamen, China shipped its 10 millionth computer in 2005.

The Penang facility in Malaysia supports 95 percent of the manufacturing of notebooks for Dell customers worldwide. Penang regional center is the regional center for manufacturing, software development, engineering logistics and quality management.

Dell established a Design Center in Singapore focusing on Dell Displays and Dell Imaging in 2005. These business lines include Dell's TVs, projectors, displays, printers and related software[4]. Dell Japan employs 14000 employees in sales, marketing and customer contact. Since 2003, Taipei has housed a sales office and Dell's design center focusing on laptop and server development, as well as data center solutions. Headquartered in Sydney, Australia; Dell Australia performs sales and marketing functions. In all, regional offices are located in 13 countries in the Asia Pacific Region. Dell holds third position in Asia Pacific.

Products for Australia, Japan and other Asia Pacific nations are manufactured, customized and installed with software at the Asia Pacific Customer Center (APCC) in Malaysia, from where they are flown to Japan. In Japan, computers are transported to a Dell Logistics Center (DLC) where peripherals are added. Then these are distributed to the customers. 90% of the customers receive products within 2 days of shipping from Malaysia. In China, Dell has established the China Customer Center to replicate the manufacturing functions found at APCC (Yashuhi, 2004, 82-83). Dell manufactures and sells computers with a "Made in India" tag from its Sri Perumbudur facility in India.

In Americas, Dell is headquartered in Round Rock, Texas and has hired 39,500 people. It has 4 manufacturing facilities in the United States and Brazil. In USA, Dell's manufacturing facilities are located in Austin, Texas and Winston-Salem, N.C. and Nashville, Tenn. The Austin Design Center focuses on computers (both laptops and desktops), server and storage system development, and related software development[5]. It is the No. 1 PC provider in United States, with every 1 in 4 PC sold in US is a Dell. Dell opened its manufacturing center in El Dorado do Sul, Brazil, in November 1999. It launched another manufacturing facility in Hortolandia, Sao Paulo in May 2007. Dell is the largest supplier to corporate customers in Brazil. In Canada, Dell hired 3000 people in its customer contact centers; however this facility was closed down due to high labor costs. Dell enjoys the No. 1 position in this region with regional offices in 14 countries.

In Europe, Dell's headquarters are located in Bracknell, U.K. Dell employs 17,500 people across its facilities in UK. Manufacturing facilities are located in Ireland and Poland. There are regional offices in 30 countries in Europe. Germany has over 60 million internet users and Dell is one of the large businesses in Germany. Dell is one of the top 5 employers in Germany. Dell started its international expansion in UK in 1987 and is Dell's largest PC market in Europe. Sales and support center is located at Glasgow. Dell's manufacturing facility in Ireland is located in Cherrywood Co., Dublin and Limerick. Dell hires more than 4500 people who support 93 countries and manufacture 7 different product lines. Dell is the market leader across Ireland for desktops and laptops.

## Dell's Leagile Supply Chain Practices

What led to the astounding success of Dell Computer Corporation? The secret lies in its unique and novel supply chain model which follows principles from lean and agile supply chain management.

Dell Computer Corporation has made ordering a laptop, an expensive and highly technical product as easy as ordering a pizza. Instead of the choice of toppings, customers chose the size of the memory, processor type, hard disk size and screen specifications- *online, by phone or by fax.* After customizing the desktop or laptop according to their choice, and the latest promotions advertised on the website, customers pay for their purchase by credit card. The desktop/laptop is delivered within 1-2 weeks depending on the location of the customer by a third party logistics service provider. "The direct model has become the backbone of our company, and the greatest tool in its growth."- according to Michael Dell, the CEO and founder of Dell Computers[6]. The direct delivery model eliminates the bricks and mortar retail format replacing it with a clicks and order e-commerce format. It allows Dell to receive payment from the customer immediately by credit card. Since Dell pays its suppliers 36 days after it receives payment from the customer it operates on a negative working capital and eliminates the need to finance its operations. As compared to its competitors such as HP and IBM which operate on positive cash cycles and turns inventory 8.5

to 17.5 times a year, Dell turns inventory 107 times a year.

*Procurement and Inventory Management:* The e-commerce model also eliminates the need for storing excess inventory at Dell's warehouses. In fact Dell does not have warehouses. The storage areas are called "revolvers". By starting to build computers only after receiving the customer order, Dell employs postponement strategies and delays the final configuration of the product for as long as possible. Once the customer places an order for a laptop he activates the supply chain and initiates a series of events. As new orders come into the plant (over the internet, by fax or by phone every 20 seconds. Orders are consolidated every 15 minutes) manufacturing signals its core suppliers, which stage the components in "revolvers", small warehouses located near the Dell assembly line. The inventory is vendor managed. Suppliers share the rent for the warehouses with Dell. Suppliers have 90 minutes to truck their parts to the assembly line. In case of a change in demand, inventory can easily be replaced with the one that is needed. If there is a supply disruption, it is the supplier who is stuck with the inventory not Dell.

Dell operates on 'zero inventory', its clout with its suppliers epitomized by thin white lines which circle the cargo bays on the floor of the manufacturing plant[7]. The white line demarcates Dell's entire supply chain. When the assembly line runs low on a certain part it emits a signal. A forklift crosses the white line and retrieves parts that are required. Only when the scanned information enters the system does Dell accept ownership of the parts. Suppliers hold 20-80 days worth of total inventory. Dell holds inventory for six to eight hours it takes to travel across the assembly line and 18 hours it takes to send a completed CPU to the merge center, where the unit is bundled with a monitor and shipped off- a total of 2 to 3 days. Its competitors- HP and IBM hold finished inventory for an average of 30-45 days.

*Supplier Management:* Suppliers are selected carefully. Supplier performance is measured on cost, technology, supply predictability and service. Suppliers are provided feedback at annual events such as quarterly business reviews and ranked according to their performance. There is a direct connection between their performance and Dell's profit and loss.

*Manufacturing:* Information related to the purchase such as the specifications, model type are conveyed through a sheet known as the 'traveler.' Once the traveler is pulled, all the internal parts and components are assembled, picked and placed together in a tote. A team of workers snap together the modular parts and create a built-to-order product. Modularity allows computer manufacturer to fit together parts from different suppliers into the CPU casing. "Speed is at the core of everything we do" according to Dick Hunter, the company's supply chain czar for the Americas (Yashuhi, 2004, pg. 82-83). By studying videotapes of the manufacturing process, Dell has streamlined its manufacturing process to reduce the number of times a worker touches the computer and designed its components to snap into place. Dell produces 700 consumer and corporate desktops in an hour. The final product is customized to the individual's tastes and preferences much like a Mercedes car is customized to suit the requirements of the individual. The system is extensively tested by using the Dell Diagnostics and standard software and hardware are added. The final product is boxed and shipped along with manuals and documentation to the customer. The customer can track the entire process online.

*Demand Shaping:* Dell uses demand shaping effectively to keep its customers hooked when it has run out of stock of a particular configuration. Dell keeps its sales informed of which part may run out. Depending on this, Dell runs a promotion on a part of equal or greater quality for its customers. If on the other hand, there is a part for which there is excess inventory Dell promotes its sales by slashing costs. Dell also foresees the spikes in demand and works on smoothing these by working with its sales staff on preventing back logs.

*Learning:* Through this well known example of Dell's direct-to-consumer business model we demonstrate the working of an agile supply chain. To summarize, Dell holds minimum inventories of component parts such as hard drives, processors, memory storage media, monitors, speakers, and a host of other supplies close to its assembly and testing locations. Many of Dell's local suppliers are located in the vicinity and some of them replenish parts as frequently as every two-hourly (Hoffman, 2004). Dell uses these supplies and quickly configures the components into finished desktop and laptop computers that meet customer-specific orders. The make-to-order approach requires that the consumer waits, as opposed to pre-positioned finished good inventories found in make-to-stock operations. Dell and other agile companies bank on the customer's willingness to wait for products that meet their specific requirements.

In summary, we see the applications of leagility in case of Dell's supply chain everywhere from supplier management to manufacturing to delivery and logistics. Everywhere Dell has minimized inventory holding (requirement of lean paradigm) as well as made its manufacturing agile to such an extent that it consolidates demand every 15 minutes and ensures delivery of the customized product in 2 days. The supply chain is thus extremely agile to respond to demand changes and at the same time with minimum inventory holding and still keeping the delivery quick.

Now, we study how companies can gain by applying the leagile paradigm to procurement (in case of a retailer).

## APPLYING LEAGILITY IN PROCUREMENT

While lean and agile strategies have received widespread application in manufacturing, they can be equally well applied to other domains, such as the procurement of a retail firm. A retail firm's product line consists of a variety of products which differ in demand and time characteristics. The product line may range from low seasonal products such as liquor, watches, travel accessories, tobacco to highly seasonal products such as cosmetics, fashion garments and so on. A firm with such a varied product line can benefit from prudent application of the principles of leagility in its procurement strategy.

Consider the example of Marks and Spencer, most profitable retailer over a decade ago (Harris, 2004/05). To cope with high costs of sourcing garments from the UK and Ireland, it moved its sourcing to locations in South-East Asia. However, this increased the lead time from weeks to around a year (Harris, 2004/05). The incorrect application of lean principles actually resulted in weaknesses in Marks & Spencer's supply chain capability, leaving it vulnerable in an increasingly fashion-oriented marketplace that required agility.

For a retail firm, postponement is difficult to achieve and hence the procurement challenge is to react and execute (Harris, 2004/05). How can a retail firm apply both the lean and agile principles in their procurement strategy? Table 1 shows the general application of principles of leagility to procurement. The fundamental question that begs an answer is gross margin return on investment (GMROI) of the retailer's products. However, GMROI should be seen in conjunction with retailer's total volume traded as for some products margin may be higher but the trade volume might be quite low. Pareto rule states that around 20% of the products contribute 80% to gross profits. Once these products are identified, a retailer can then think of divesting the rest of the product portfolio. However, we recognize that in reality it may not be possible as the other products act as fillers for selling the main products.

Once the focal products are identified, the next step is to identify the strategy for procuring these products. A retail firm can either pursue a lean procurement strategy or agile procurement strategy or both. The break-even point is decided by means of de-coupling approach. The supply

*Table 1. Principles of leagility in procurement*

| Principle | Application to Procurement |
|---|---|
| Pareto Rule | • Procure products that contribute maximally to total volume and gross margin return on investment (GMROI).<br>• Procure products from few vendors that supply and contribute maximally to total volume. |
| De-coupling approach | • Lean procurement strategy for products with long supply lead times and those that contribute greatly to total volume and GMROI.<br>• Agile procurement strategy for products with short supply lead times and those that contribute poorly to total volume. |
| Base and Surge demands | • Lean procurement strategy for products with low changes in demand and seasonality.<br>• Agile procurement strategy for products with high fluctuations in demand and seasonality. |

lead time for procurement is an important factor in deciding the decoupling point. A general rule would be to procure products with long supply lead times according to lean procurement strategy and products with short supply lead times according to agile procurement strategy.

The third principle of leagility - *base and surge demand* - should also be considered in deciding the retail firm's procurement strategy. Some products, such as flowers and boutiques, are seasonal in nature. For such products, a retail firm would naturally adopt an agile strategy. There are other products whose demand is quite variable or seasonal. For products that are demand variable or seasonal, the retail firm should adopt an agile procurement strategy and for products that are less susceptible to demand and/or seasonality the retail firm should adopt lean procurement strategy. The exhibit shows the various means of

consolidation, a retail firm can adopt to apply the leagility principles in its procurement strategy. (see Table 2)

Thus, based on the three factors, namely, contribution to firm's value, supply lead time for procurement, and product and demand seasonality, we develop the retail firm's procurement framework (Figure 2).

Figure 2 is a 2-dimensional representation of a 3-dimensional framework. The 3-dimensions are lead time (short and long), GMROI (low and high) and seasonality (low and high). Combining these three dimensions we obtain a 2x2x2 framework. The framework yield 8 combinations viz., (i) long lead time, low GMROI, low seasonality; (ii) long lead time, high GMROI, low seasonality; (iii) long lead time, low GMROI, high seasonality; (iv) long lead time, high GMROI, high seasonality; (v) short lead time, low GMROI, low seasonality;

*Table 2. Consolidation modes for applying the principles of leagility*

| To apply the principles of leagility, a retail firm would benefit by applying following principles: |
|---|
| *Product consolidation* Consolidating procurement to products that contribute a huge chunk of firm's total volume and gross profits is the first step in Leagile procurement strategy. |
| *Vendor/Supplier consolidation* A retail firm would benefit by sourcing products from a few key vendors which form almost 80% of firm's total supply of a particular product. |
| *Transportation Mode consolidation* Sometimes a small percentage of a product is transported by various modes (air and sea). A retail firm would benefit from leagility principles by consolidating the modes of transportation to a single mode. |
| *Place consolidation* In cases where there are many vendors/suppliers from the same location, a retail firm could shorten supply lead times and transportation costs by consolidating the products of various vendors and transporting them at the same time. |
| *Time consolidation* Retail firms would also benefit by consolidating the time of ordering the products, so that they can be transported at the same time. |

*Figure 2. Leagility framework for retail firm's procurement*

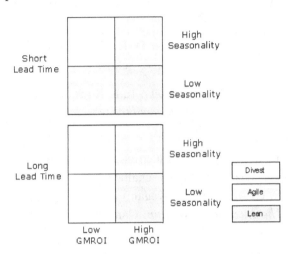

(vi) short lead time, high GMROI, low seasonality; (vii) short lead time, low GMROI, high seasonality; (viii) short lead time, high GMROI, high seasonality.

Lean procurement strategy would be best for products that yield high gross profits and are low in seasonality. Supply lead time is not a driver in lean procurement strategy. Example of such products would include liquor and tobacco. The supply lead time for products like liquor could be long due to the restriction on their transportation mode (air transportation of liquor is restricted). An agile procurement strategy would be ideal for products that are highly seasonal in nature (e.g., boutiques), yield high profits, and have a short supply lead time. For some seasonal products, such as fresh produce, the supply lead time could be high if they are sourced from a distant location. As fresh produce are usually low value products, air transportation would be less feasible as it adds considerably to transportation costs. Therefore, for such products, it is best that they be sourced from nearby locations, or transported via air to a nearby central location from which redistribution can take place. The products which contribute poorly to gross profits and are highly seasonal in nature can be divested. However, some products

(e.g., pens, lighters, travel accessories) which contribute poorly to gross profit margin, act as fillers so as to attract the customers to store. Such products, if they have shorter supply lead times and low seasonality, can be sourced using an agile procurement strategy.

## CONCLUSION

In this paper we discussed the principles of leagility in manufacturing and procurement. Leagility can benefit a firm by making it responsive to customer demand as well as minimizing the loss in inventory. Dell PC manufacturing epitomizes the principles of leagility. The same can be applied to procurement based on the supply lead time to procure the products, product's GMROI as well as the total volume traded and seasonality of the product. In the age of globalization and cut-throat competition, a retail firm would benefit by applying the principles of leagility and become more efficient and responsive. We developed a framework based on the three dimensions (lead time, GMROI and seasonality) through which retailers can decide the strategy to adopt for a particular product. Moving forward, this framework can be applied to provide the appropriate space and time utility in the supply chain.

## REFERENCES

Callioni, G., de Montgros, X., Slagmulder, R., Van Wassenhove, L. N., & Wright, L. (2005). Inventory-driven costs. *Harvard Business Review*, *83*(3), 135–141.

Christopher, M. (2000). The agile supply chain: Competing in volatile markets. *Industrial Marketing Management*, *29*(1), 37–44. doi:10.1016/S0019-8501(99)00110-8

Christopher, M., & Towill, D. R. (2000). Supply chain migration from lean and functional to agile and customized. *International Journal of Supply Chain Management, 5*(4), 206–213. doi:10.1108/13598540010347334

Christopher, M., & Towill, D. R. (2001). An integrated model for the design of agile supply chains. *International Journal of Physical Distribution and Logistics Management, 31*(4), 235–246. doi:10.1108/09600030110394914

Feitzinger, E., & Hau, L. L. (1997). Mass customization at Hewlett-Packard: The power of postponement. *Harvard Business Review, 75*(1), 116–121.

Goldsby, T. J., Griffis, S. E., & Roath, A. S. (2006). Modeling lean, agile, and leagile supply chain strategies. *Journal of Business Logistics, 22*(1), 57–80.

Harris, A. (2004). Reaping the rewards of agile thinking. *Power Engineering, 18*(6), 24–27. doi:10.1049/pe:20040605

Hoffman, W. (2004). Dell gets domestic. *Traffic World* (online edition). Retrieved on March 15, 2007, from www.trafficworld.com/news/log/12904a.asp

Hugos, M. (2006). *Essentials of supply chain management,* 2nd edition (p. 40). Wiley.

Koch, R. (1997). *The 80/20 principle: The secret of achieving more with less.* London: Nicholas Brealey.

Naylor, J. B., Mohamed, M. N., & Danny, B. (1999). Leagility: Integrating the lean and agile manufacturing paradigms in the total supply chain. *International Journal of Production Economics, 62*(1-2), 107–118. doi:10.1016/S0925-5273(98)00223-0

Ohno, T. (1988). *The Toyota production system: Beyond large-scale production.* Portland, OR: Productivity Press.

Womack, J. P., & Jones, D. T. (1996). *Lean thinking.* New York: Simon & Schuster.

Womack, J. P., Jones, D. T., & Roos, D. (1990). *The machine that changed the world.* New York: Rawson Associates.

Yasuhi, U. (2004). Electronics industry in Asia: The changing supply chain and its effects. In E. Giovannetti, M. Kagami & M. Tsuji (Eds.), *The Internet revolution.* Cambridge University Press.

## ENDNOTES

[1] Accessed from http://seekingalpha.com/article/93357-dell-targets-india on 25/09/2008

[2] Accessed from http://www.pcguide.com/buy/ven/indIndustry-c.html on 25/09/2008

[3] Michael Dell in Direct from Dell

[4] http://www1.ap.dell.com/content/topics/global.aspx/about_dell/company/innovation/cto_product_development?~ck=ln&c=sg&l=en&lnki=0&s=corp

[5] http://www1.ap.dell.com/content/topics/global.aspx/about_dell/company/innovation/cto_product_development?~ck=ln&c=sg&l=en&lnki=0&s=corp

[6] Ibid 4

[7] Accessed from http://www.fastcompany.com/node/51967/print on 17/09/2008

# Chapter 11
# The Business Knowledge and Information Policy Model

**Müjgan Şan**
*The State Planning Organization, Turkey*

## ABSTRACT

*As every technological development, information and communication technology also offers new life patterns to human beings. One of them is related to business and its environment. In this context, the main problem is how to manage knowledge and information and assets related to knowledge and information in business. Therefore, we have constructed the business knowledge and information policy model by using triangulation methodology. The business knowledge and information policy model includes the informative business theory, knowledge and information management (KIM) tools and projects. The first one has six characteristics. KIM tools include nine profiles which are common language, strategy, data-information-concepts, personal and social informatics, ICT infrastructure, measurement, cultural informatics and governance. KIM projects could be designed depending on business conditions and goals.*

## THE CONCEPT OF BUSINESS KNOWLEDGE AND INFORMATION POLICY

Technological advancements in communication and information processing engender the need to design new economic, social and cultural life patterns. Especially in business level, technological development and capabilities canalize business to control communication and organization in electronic environment.[1] Policies offer opportunity to design new life patterns for human-beings. Knowledge policy is a public policy dealing with the production, diffusion, application and effects of knowledge at macroeconomic level (Knowledge 2008). The Knowledge strategy, the other term in the literature used, concerns to produce, share and use knowledge by managing processes and procedures (MacAulay 2000). The subject of information policy is mostly mentioned on the national level in library

DOI: 10.4018/978-1-60566-723-2.ch011

and information science literature. Rowlands (1996:14-15: Cited in: "An Information) divides the national information policy as infrastructural, vertical and horizontal policies. The first one covers national information and communication infrastructure; the second one includes sectoral approaches such as education and tourism; and the third one concerns with legal dimension such as the freedom of information. All terms are used for developing a nation. In the business level, there are various policies for technology, finance, accounting, marketing, etc. in the business literature. Also the term of information policy is mostly mentioned in the technology literature for organizations. Besides this the phenomenon of digital convergence, a dramatic outcome of technological development, has canalized business in order to

control communication and organization. In this context, main problem is how to manage knowledge and information (KI) by using information and communication technology (ICT). Therefore business brings on a holistic thinking for composing all policies in the frame of the **knowledge and information management** (KIM). In addition, it is necessary to be linked to national information and communication infrastructure, national sectoral policies, global sectoral trends, and some juristic issues.

**The Business Knowledge and Information Policy** (The BKIP) provides greater opportunity for business to create new designs to manage **KI and Assets related to KI** (KIAKI) which are business and goals, employees, groups, KI resources, information and communication technology

*Figure 1. Knowledge, information and assets related to knowledge and information*

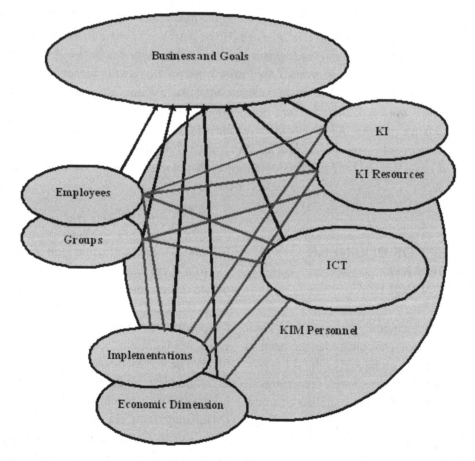

*Figure 2. Knowledge and information management tools*

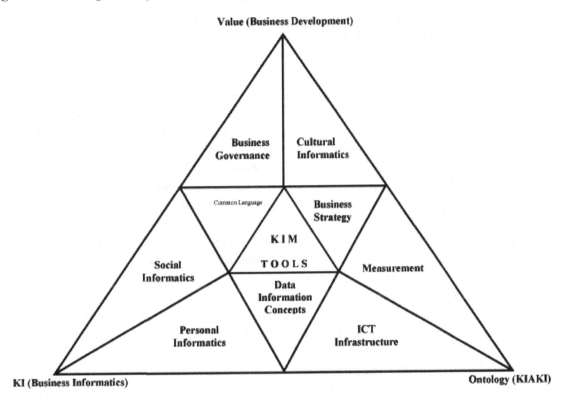

(ICT), implementations, economic dimension of implementations and KIM personnel (Figure 1).

We have constructed The BKIP by using convergent thinking to manage KIAKI for business development (BD).[2] The BKIP provides a holistic approach to all business KIM in an electronic environment. It is possible to operate KIAKI by integrating harmoniously within each other and among them. In the BKIP transitive relations among KIAKI could be defined by using **KIM Tools** (Figure 2). Furthermore with the BKIP, rules and regulations could be improved by adapting equality principles related to KI such as privacy, the right of communication, access to information. With the BKIP meaningful relations could be also constructed with National Information Policy, and Knowledge and Information Society Strategy and international economic order.

## THE BKIP MODEL

The BKIP is a transdisciplinary area involving computer, software, business, library and information science. Therefore we have constructed by using the grounded theory which is one of the qualitative research methods in order to analyze and integrate inside business and its environment. The grounded theory is increasingly being used for research in the field of information systems in the last decades. The triangulation methodology is also adequate for transdisciplinary and multi-faceted studies. All types of convergence can be managed by methodological triangulation. In this study we have used methodological triangulation in order to integrate different knowledge domains as facets.

We have constructed The BKIP with the perspective of the fact that business is an KI integrity. As a term, business covers the whole of activities using KIAKI via KIM Tools. Business is defined as "the buying and selling of goods and services" (Rosenberg 1983:76). Therefore we could define business as "a kind of KI integrity to obtain efficiency and profitability" from the aspects of KIM. And business as a KI integrity could be designed with KI by using ICT. From this perspective, relationships between business and KI are abstracted three aspects which are

- KI are produced in a business,
- KI are tools for business to get organized,
- KI are factors of business development and change.

KI are business products in the frame of information needs, knowing interests and system requirements. Informastion needs in an organization are classified as "new information, elucidate the information held, and confirm the information held" (Weigts 1993: Cited in: Wilson 1997:2). Knowing interests pertaining to human being are technical, practical and emancipatory interests (Habermas 1968-72: Cited in: Trede 2006:31). They come respectively from interaction with the nature, the society and one's own. System requirements are specified according to information needs, knowing interests and types of information systems (IS) such as computing service, information storage and retrieval, and transaction proceesing in the frame of business goals and targets. KI produced by depending on requirements are business models, enterprise architectures, information standards, etc. The other business KI products are decisions, information systems, information resources, etc. as a part of business memory.

Getting organized is realized by **informative action** (IA) covering communication as practical interest of human knowing. Types of communication in organizations are formal, informal (Kreps 1989:169, 201-202), oral, written; internal and external (Özdemirci 1996:94-118). From the other perspectives, types of communication are

classified as obtaining information, evaluational, educational and teaching, persuasive and impressive (Dicle 1974:48). In this context, IAs in business are summarized four titles. First type of IA is the processes of information services realized by information service departments which are information and documentation centers, libraries, archives, public relations department, information processing center and management information centers. Second type of IA is the usage processes of KIAKI such as research and decision making processes. Third type of IA is learning processes related to human development. Last one is the processes of convince and influence of business environment related to business products and services like marketing.

The other aspect of getting organized is to knit business culture. Business culture is weaved by informative actions (IAs) which are KI production, usage, sharing and management. So outcomes of IAs are business memory, rules and mechanism of business operations by employees. Consequently KI are appeared as a tool to get organized.

As a factor, KI are used for business development and change as emancipatory interest of human knowing. Dynamic economic, social, cultural, political and technological conditions canalize business to develop and change. BD covers mostly innovations. Some types of BD are sustainability and electronic business. Business could be changed from behavioral, structural, technological and systematic aspects. For example transformation to electronic business includes not only technological but also behavioral, structural and systematic changing. The other dimension as a factor of KI is the business efficiency and profitability. Especially administrative efficiency needs strategic decisions and activities.

In addition, digital convergence pushes and bears lots of convergence such as data, knowledge, information management convergence. To manage and harmonize the convergence phenomenon we should use a holistic approach. Some examples of holistic approaches are data warehouse and enter-

*Figure 3. The business knowledge and information policy model*

```
                    Value Sphere: Informative

                    ▲ Business Theory
                   ╱ ╲
                  ╱   ╲
                 ╱     ╲
                ╱       ╲
               ╱         ╲
              ╱           ╲
             ╱             ╲
            ╱  THE BUSINESS ╲
           ╱    KNOWLEDGE    ╲
          ╱ AND INFORMATION   ╲
         ╱      POLICY         ╲
        ╱                       ╲
       ╱      (The BKIP)         ╲
      ╱                           ╲
     ╱_____╲

KI Sphere: KIM Projects      Ontology Sphere: KIM Tools
```

prise architectures. However there is no unique structure of data warehouse or enterprise architecture for all business. So we should construct a more flexible frame. This is possible with the BKIP model in order to use for all business.

There are three spheres in the BKIP; value, ontology, and KI (Figure 3). These spheres include **The Informative Business Theory** (The IBT)[3], KIM Tools, KIM Projects.

KIM Project should be realized by operating KIM Tools in the frame of The IBT. They are explained in following sections.

## The Informative Business Theory (The IBT)

The IBT is explained by the structure of IAs among KIAKI for realizing BD in order to create business value via business informatics (BI)[4]. Characteristics of this theory are the following:

- Information is energy,
- Knowledge is operator,
- IA depends on causal relationship,
- IA reduces information gaps (IGs),
- IA is a structure,
- There are some limitations in this theory.

In this theory, information is accepted as the energy. Information, in the KI sphere, is used to minimize business entropy (BE) which is organizational complexity, uncertainty, inconsistency, IGs, lack of consensus among business actors. Business can not be run without information. Business can be operated information entering into system. Information flow is obtained via the language – both technological (technology-readable-understandable) and humanlike (human-understandable).

The language has a hierarchical meaning structure to carry information. So, the BE decreases more and more with IAs in the regularity of the meaning hierarchy belonging to language.

Knowledge is the operator in this theory. Knowledge, in the KI sphere makes business start operating. Business can not be awaked without knowledge. Business can be activated by entering knowledge. Knowledge is born with meaning based on specialties of living conditions; and explicating and internalizing via the language. So in this theory there is an extraction of knowledge, the other saying, there are IAs such as explication and internalization. The regularity of the meaning hierarchy belonging to language carries the knowledge in order to start operating business.

IA depends on causal relationship for BD. The main cause is to decrease BE which is the outcome of IGs among KIAKI. So it can be decreased by managing very well KI with ICT. In other words BE is decreased by creating synergy among KIAKI and business environment. Synergy is occured in the processes of KIM. If convergence is managed successfully, BE is decreased, profitability and efficiency are increased, and BD is also realized successfully. So, IA is the key for all of them. Sources of IGs are information needs, knowing interests, system requirements and communication types.

IA has a function to minimize IGs which are

- among business actors and the existing condition,
- among business actors,
- among goals of business governance actors,
- between the existing condition and the targeted condition,
- between business actors and others, rest of community, society.

First IG aims to describe the existing condition. This is the first step to minimize entropy. The existing condition can be described with statistical, linguistic KI. The more depicting tools are well describe the more existing condition can be depicted as correct and accurate, and, more IGs are decreased, however never disappears.

Description covers three kinds of IA:

- to set of depicting tools,
- to produce correct and adequate data, information, concepts (DIC),
- to describe the original the existing condition.

Depicting tools are DIC for BD. And DIC should be produced appropriate for business goals and targets. First KI direction is from business goals and targets towards existing condition. It is important to produce correct and accurate DIC of existing conditon. Second KI direction is mutual between existing condition and the person producing KI. In other words, it is important to design and operate the architecture of KI and communication infrastructure and business patterns. Third KI direction is from the person producing KI towards business actors. This IG is vertical IG.

Second IG is among business actors (CIO, CKO, executive managers, business developers, employees, researchers, stakeholders, shareholders, etc.). Business actors need to inform interactively each other according to their backgrounds, experiences and recommendations. In this process, expert knowledge in different domain should be integrated for business goals and targets. It is important to harmonize experiences of business actors for business goals and targets. This is horizontal IG. Fourth KI direction is mutual among business actors.

Third IG arises from different goals and targets among business actors. It is related to what business is changed and developed towards. It is an IA to set common target and value. In this process it is important to decrease BE, to reach a consensus. Fifth KI direction is mutual among goals and targets of business actors.

Fourth IG is related to how to realize business goals and targets. The gap is between KI for existing and for targeted condition. It is created KI about what projects should be applied and how to realize projects. Sixth KI direction is mutual among business actors and policy-makers.

Fifth IG is related to informing society about outcomes and activities of business, and socialization of business KI. Seventh KI direction is mutual among business actors and society. Some activities for closing this IG are marketing and creating trust in society.

IA has a structure of the information flow within and among KIAKI. Every KIAKI has potential of KI production, usage, storage, organizing, processing and communicating in the different level of business development and change. So types of IAs are increased in variety in the frame of these potentials, forms of communication (formal, informal, oral, written), types of human knowing interests, types of information needs and the meaning profundity of language depending on business goals and targets. IA can be interactively within each consciousness, database, etc., and, among more than one consciousness, databases, etc. Some types of IAs are monitoring, collecting, internalisation etc. (Table 1). IAs within each KIAKI bring on KIM Tools.

The theory is not explained how to realize IA in the sphere of KI. It is not assumed for the theory to develop and change business very well, business development and change could not be realized. The theory does not answer how to decrease BE, however it offers an outline to realize BD and to define BE, IGs and IAs in a business. The IBT proposes a tool or a method in order to construct the structure of IAs; integrate KI, and to minimize IGs and entropy in a business.

## KIM Tools

In the ontology sphere of the BKIP Model, there are KIM Tools which include BD, BI and KIAKI. They aim to develop business or create the value by managing KIAKI via BI in the frame of the IBT.

Every KIAKI is a node of IA. All KIAKI have functions as KI processor, producer, user, and storage, communication and computing device. Every KIAKI has a management tool. For examples, tool for business and goal is Business Strategy Profile, tool for employees is Personal Informatics Profile, etc. It is possible to manage KIAKI with KIM Tools.

KIM Tools has administrative, discursive, and operational dimensions. Administrative dimension covers BD, discursive dimension absorbs BI, and operational dimension includes KIAKI. BD realized with Business Governance and Cultural Informatics Profiles; BI is fulfilled with Personal Informatics and Social Informatics Profiles; KIAKI mainly includes ICT Infrastructure and Measurement Profiles by harmonizing all of them with Business Strategy, Common Language, and DIC Profiles.

### Common Language Profile (CL)

**The Common Language Profile** (CL) provides understandability among KIM personnel and the other business actors. Integration of knowledge management and information management is

*Table 1. Some types of informative actions*

| As knowledge management activities for exploitation and exploration of knowledge | As knowledge creation process | As collaborative learning mechanism |
|---|---|---|
| Exploitation (externalizing,collecting, disseminating) Exploration (experimenting, monitoring, integrating) (Berends 2007: 320). | SECI process: -Socialization, -externalisation, -combination, -internalisation, (Nonaka, Toyama & Konno 2000:12). | Disagreement, Alternative, Explanation, Internalization, Appropriation, Shared load, Regulation, Synchronicity (Dove 1999:28). |

obtained with CL for processing, usage and retrieval of KI. CL helps to integrate business information systems. CL is a tool for business integration and interoperability (Table 2). CL is a language-oriented integration as a part of KI integrity. Components are concepts, relations and facets.

CL is a kind of thesaurus included business and KIM concepts and terms. Business KIM thesaurus is as a part of the business memory.

## Business Strategy Profile (STR)

**Business Strategy Profile** (STR) is triggered to realize economic, social and cultural goals. STR is used for business efficiency and profitability during realizing goals and targets. Some strategies are sustainable strategy (Ice 174), competitive strategy and electronic business strategy. In one

sense, STR is a goal and target-oriented business integration as a part of KI integrity. STR also ensures the integration of KIAKI. It potentially includes how to integrate and to interoperate KIAKI. In the meanwhile STR includes also the strategy for KIM Tools. Components of STR are goals and targets, needs, interests and requirements, and, solutions such as scenarios, tactics (Table 3).

## The Data Information and Concept Profile (DIC)

**The Data Information and Concepts Profile** (DIC) is the core profile of KIM Tools and an abstraction of business KI. DIC Profile is created appropriate for characteristics of business. It is divided into three dimensions as humanlike, objective and technological (Table 4). Humanlike

*Table 2. Some example concepts for business KIM thesaurus*

| Terms | Explanations |
|---|---|
| Informative principles | Equality principles related to KI. They are rights, freedom, and responsibilities related to KI depending on equality principles:<br>• information access, education,<br>• benefit from services and activities related to KI<br>• participatory governance,<br>• protection and security of individual, organizational and national KI,<br>• limitations of usage of individual, organizational and national KI,<br>• obtaining of retrieval timely to correct KI. |
| Informative action | Producing, processing, using (exchange and sharing) of KI among more than one conscious, KI sources even if, in electronic environment. |
| Technological informative action | All activities among components of electronic environment such as processing of DIC among more than one database, databanks, etc. |
| KIM | Management of KIAKI in the frame of informative principles. |
| Business development epistemology | The vision of the fact that relationships between business and KI are operational dimension in the ontology sphere, discursive dimension in the KI sphere, and administrative dimension in the value sphere. |
| Informative business development | Informative Business Development (IBD) is a kind of BD which benefits from KIAKI in the process of BD. |
| Business actors | Everyone attending activities of KIAKI |
| KIAKI | Knowledge and information, knowledge and information resources, ICT, employees, groups, business and goals, implementations and economic dimension of implementation. |
| KI resources | Objects carrying KI. |
| KIM convergence | It is the convergence of KIM activities, duties and responsibilities related to the integration of KIAKI keeping with their specialties. |

*Table 3. Business strategy*

| Goals and targets | Needs, interests, requirements | Solutions |
|---|---|---|
| [Business development and change] | [Related to KIAKI] | [Business informatics] |
| Sustainable business, Innovative business Business intelligence Knowledge based business | Information needs manegement Knowing interests management System requirement management | Scenarios Tactics Projects etc. |

dimension includes qualitative and quantitative KI including core concepts and indicators. Objective dimension is an ontology for business information resources. Technological dimension concerns data and information standards about storage, computing, representation, etc. DIC is a metadata-oriented integration as a part of KI integrity.

All business DIC could be stored, organized, processed and computed in a knowledge server that covers information about KIM Tools. It is a kind of data warehouse including not only data but also information, concepts, relations and facets. DIC Profile covers also definitions of limitations for security and protection. It is like a map for data warehouse or an integrated business data dictionary; and a guide for business metadata server, business grid and/or middleware structure; and should be located into a business knowledge server as a business DIC repository. It is useful to realized and manage technological IAs such as data mining, search, retrieval, and integration and interoperation of information systems.

## The Personal Informatics Profile (PER)

**The Personal Informatics Profile** (PER) defines the information of employees and the other actors related to KI like stakeholders and suppliers as users. This profile covers qualifications, types of IAs and characteristics of their informative environment (Table 5). Employees use statistical and linguistic KI for monitoring, coordinating, modeling and measurement, etc. Effective working could be obtained by preparing effective informative environment for employees. Business actors want to inform business related to products and services and so the information about business actors should keep in business memory. PER is

*Table 4. DIC profile*

| Humanlike | | Objective | | | | | Technological | | |
|---|---|---|---|---|---|---|---|---|---|
| Qualitative | Quantity | Description standards of information resources | | | | | Data / information standards | | |
| (language) -concepts - ... | -statistics, -indicators | record | documents | publication | Image | Sound | storage | applications (systems, information systems) | Representation (web site) |
| business knowledge map, concepts and their relations, -knowledge objects, | | | | | | -music | -data standards -data models ontologies, data, data models, rules | -Data grid, ---computational ---service -Data architecture | -BPEL* -BPMN** |

\* Business Process Extensible Language. \*\* Business Process Modeling Notation.

*Table 5. Some personal information*

| Qualifications | Personal informative action | Informative environment |
|---|---|---|
| Expert knowledge, Roles and responsibilities Learning stills, research stills, usage stills, Skills, Needs, interests, requirements, Mind maps, knowledge maps backgrounds, research subjects, -behaviour of information usage, etc. | Needs-mapping-information daily usage of computer -calendar, folders, desktop, searchable content, -meetings -face to face conversations, -knowledge sharing, -information processing, -knowledge production, etc. | Personalizations, customization, Subscriptions, Alert and notifications, R&D, knowledge sharing, knowledge production Privacy, security, trust; -information resources, -information processing tools (computing, retrieval, searching), -communication tools (e-mail, e-conference, etc.), -characteristics of personal computer, etc. |

a people-oriented integration as a part of KI integrity. PER should be interoperable with Human Resource Management Systems.

## The Information and Communication Technology Infrastructure Profile (ICTI)

**The Information and Communication Technology Infrastructure Profile** (ICTI) aims to combine business and ICT by managing KI. ICTI should be prepared from business-oriented approach. ICTI covers hardware, software, and, security and protection management (Table 6). Hardware Management includes business hardware architectures, operating hardwares and

monitoring operations. Software Management covers a map of softwares including information systems, software development and its methodology in business. Last one ensures protecting all KIAKI in the frame of informative principles. Some principles of security and protection are privacy, confidentiality, integrity and availability. ICTI is a platform-oriented integration as a part of KI integrity.

All business activities related to KIAKI could be managed, stored and processed with ICTI. So we should know structure of ICT and than we could make ICT plans and strategies, and, we could design architectures, models.

*Table 6. ICT infrastructure profile*

| Hardware management | Software management | Security and protection management | |
|---|---|---|---|
| Operating -input/output management -communication management Monitoring operating -Convergence management, -Capacity planning and management, -Control management, -ICT performance management, Computer/automation management, ICT service continuity, Availability management, Service level management. | Application management, Event management, convergence management, integration management, interoperability management, storage management, job scheduling, service desk, incident management, release management, solution management, component management, software distribution, visualization, software development | Hardware and software -copyrights -licensing -patents -property rights -trade secrets Information security -in operating systems -in computing and information systems (authentication, insurance, invasive software, viruses, etc.) | |

*Table 7. Measurement profile*

| Measurement assets for cost and time of KI and KIA | | Main measurement activities | Measurement outcome |
|---|---|---|---|
| Metrics | Measures | Monitoring, evaluating | [the ratio of] |
| Indicators, indexes etc. | Productivity, innovation, resilient, continuously, competitive, social responsibility, accountability, transparency, etc. | Total quality management Performance management Risk management | BD efficiency, profitability, … |

## Measurement Profile (MEA)

**The Measurement Profile** (MEA) aims to measure the ratio of business development and change, efficiency and profitability. It is necessary to balance among increasing quality and quantity, and decreasing time and cost. The MEA concerns measurement assets, main activities and outcome (Table 7). It is an efficiency and profitability-oriented integration as a part of KI integrity.

The core of measures is assets, outcomes, time and cost as quality and quantity. Basic concepts for MEA are performance, effectiveness, cost effectiveness and cost-benefit, and impact. Metric and measures should be very well defined and designed. Some measurement implementations are total quality management, performance management, risk management, business maturity model, balanced scorecard, and return on investment. For example, the European Foundation for Quality Management (EFQM) has developed business Excellence Model (Ahmed 2002:424), which is concentrated on innovation and learning in business. EFQM Excellence Model includes nine criteria for business enablers and results which are leadership, people, policy and strategy, partnership and resources, processes and results for people, customer, society and key performance (Rusjan 2005:364).

MEA is an important part of monitoring of business activities. It should be interoperable with especially information systems for budget, finance, and risk management.

*Table 8. Social informatics profile*

| Groups | Group informative actions | ICT for groups |
|---|---|---|
| -B2B<br>-B2C<br>-B2G<br>-B2E<br>etc. | -Internalization (internalizes explicit knowledge to create tacit knowledge)<br>-Externalization (turns tacit knowledge into explicit knowledge through documentation, verbalization)<br>-Combination (to create new explicit knowledge via combination of other explicit knowledge)<br>-Socialization (transferring tacit knowledge between individuals).<br>Some types of meetings<br>-presentation and sharing information<br>-exploration and brainstorming<br>-problem solving and decision making<br>-negotiation and resource allocation<br>-morale building and social structuring | Social software<br>-blogs, wikis, tag clouds,<br>-social networks,<br>-podcast<br>-collaborative bookmarking<br>-social tagging podcast<br>--social information processing<br>Group technologies<br>-Call center management<br>-Customer analytics<br>-Sales and marketing<br>-Product management<br>Brand management<br>Customer relationship management<br>Customer services<br>Customer / account management<br>Contact management<br>Partner relationship management<br>Customer feedback |

## Social Informatics Profile (SOC)

**The Social Informatics Profile** (SOC) aims to decrease IG among employees, society and business in order to create awareness in society about business innovations, and to inform society about business activities. SOC includes information about groups, IAs among them and ICT used by groups (Table 8). The SOC is group-oriented integration as a part of KI integrity.

Business social networking and community knowledge map are also shaped in this profile. It helps activities for social responsibility.

## Cultural (Pattern) Informatics Profile (CUL)

**Cultural (Pattern) Informatics Profile** (CUL) comprises business innovation. Business innovations are drawn as business model, enterprise architecture, etc. Innovation covers patterns to obtain balance among higher quality, quantity, and, lower cost and time. Patterns include also processes. They are divided as products, process and life style patterns. They respectively are patterns for KIAKI, information service and business life style. All patterns include their own internal regularity with sub-patterns such as life cycles. CUL is a pattern-oriented integration as a part of KI integrity.

New business life styles are IAs such as familiarity for transparency, accountability, social responsibility and electronic business in context of business transformation. Patterns should be located in a repository. And they show the internal and external regularity of business. A business is an integrated pattern covering trans-faceted sub-patterns and well-designed patterns are reduced IGs. There is no unique pattern for all businesses.

Depending on methodology, to design patterns is operated clockwise or anti-clockwise in the figure of KIM Tools. The other word patterns are designed bottom-up or top-down direction.

*Figure 4. Development Funnel (O'Sullivan 2002:80)*

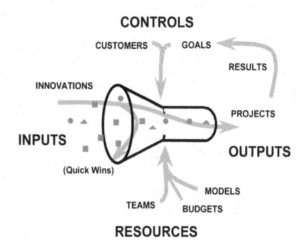

The other way to design patterns is the use of the development funnel (Figure 4) constructed by O'Sullivan (2002:80-81). There are four main flows around the development funnel as controls, input, output, and resources. Constraints occur between inputs and outputs in the context of control and resources and than create the neck of funnel. Seven core processes cover innovations, customers, goals, results, projects, team, budgets and models. However development funnel does not include deployment which shows matching among inputs, controls, resources and outputs.

The Generic Business Pattern (Figure 5) is also used to design patterns. It covers all product, service and business life patterns with interrelated flow in the context of KIM, software development, business management and project management.

## Business Governance Profile (GOV)

**Business Governance Profile** (GOV) is to manage together. It comes from the idea of business justice and ethics (Table 9). It covers organizational structures, KIM personnel, and rules. It is a rule-oriented integration as a part of KI integrity.

Organizational structure should be constructed especially internal regularity of business. It is

*Figure 5. Generic Business Pattern*

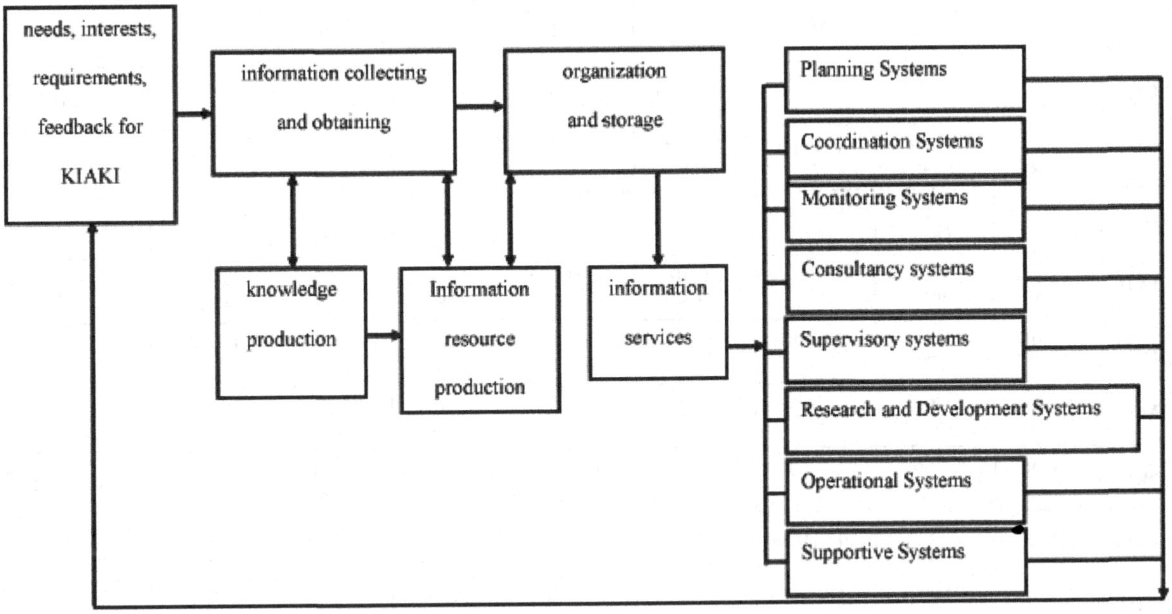

convergence of managerial structure. At the same time governance is a kind of feedback mechanism. Governance structure should be flexible depending on conditions.

KIM personnel is an KI bridge among KIAKI and coordinators of governance activities. It should be described qualification and responsibilities by separating as hardware, software and KI teams supporting each others.

Governance structure helps to set rules and regulations for business activities and KIM Tools. GOV ensures business KI integrity, accountability and transparency. Rules are constructed by clari-

fying and defining informative principles such as (decision) rights, responsibilities, accountability and transparency. Some principles are developed for corporate governance by OECD (Table 10). According to business goals, new governance types, structures and rules could be developed.

## KIM Projects

KIM Projects that take place in the KI sphere depend on a dynamically internal and external development and change of business. O'Sullivan (2002:86) explains the fact that BD needs good

*Table 9 Some governance types*

| Some Governance Types | |
|---|---|
| Corporate governance | Data management governance |
| Enterprise governance | Information management gover- |
| Sustainable governance | nance |
| Data governance | Knowledge management gover- |
| Information governance | nance |
| Knowledge governance | Database management governance |
| Database governance | Enterprise architecture governance |
| | Information security governance |
| | Information technology governance |

*Table 10 OECD Principles of corporate governance*

| OECD Principles of Corporate Governance |
|---|
| I. Ensuring the basis for an effective corporate governance framework |
| II. The rights of shareholders and key ownership functions |
| III. The equitable treatment of shareholders |
| IV. The role of stakeholders in corporate governance |
| V. Disclosure and transparency |
| VI. The responsibilities of the board (OECD Principles 2004: 17-24). |

*Table 11 Projects for creating KIM tools*

| KIM Tools | CL | STR | DIC | PER | ICTI | MEA | SOC | CUL | GOV |
|---|---|---|---|---|---|---|---|---|---|
| **CL** | **Create CL** | STR of CL | DIC of CL | PER of CL | ICTI of CL | MEA of CL | SOC of CL | PAT of CL | GOV of CL |
| **STR** | CL of STR | **Create STR** | DIC of STR | PER of STR | ICTI of STR | MEA of STR | SOC of STR | PAT of STR | GOV of STR |
| **DIC** | CL of DIC | STR of DIC | **Create DIC** | PER of DIC | ICTI of DIC | MEA of DIC | SOC of DIC | PAT of DIC | GOV of DIC |
| **PER** | CL of PER | STR of PER | DIC of PER | **Create PER** | ICTI of PER | MEA of PER | SOC of PER | PAT of PER | GOV of PER |
| **ICTI** | CL of ICTI | STR of ICTI | DIC of ICTI | PER of ICTI | **Create ICTI** | MEA of ICTI | SOC of ICTI | PAT of ICTI | GOV of ICTI |
| **MEA** | CL of MEA | STR of MEA | DIC of MEA | PER of MEA | ICTI of MEA | **Create MEA** | SOC of MEA | PAT of MEA | GOV of MEA |
| **SOC** | CL of SOC | STR of SOC | DIC of SOC | PER of SOC | ICTI of SOC | MEA of SOC | **Create SOC** | PAT of SOC | GOV of SOC |
| **CUL** | CL of PAT | STR of PAT | DIC of PAT | PER of PAT | ICTI of PAT | MEA of PAT | SOC of PAT | **Create PAT** | GOV of PAT |
| **GOV** | CL of GOV | STR of GOV | DIC of GOV | PER of GOV | ICTI of GOV | MEA of GOV | SOC of GOV | PAT of GOV | **Create GOV** |

definition of goals and targets, good alignment of goals to projects, good participation among employees, good idea generation and problem solving, good mapping of change to key processes, good reporting of results, and management of projects. Integration, interoperation and transitive relations among KIM Tools are realized within KIM Projects.

Main projects are for the creation of every KIM Tools (Table 11). For example, the creation of CL Profile and the creation of Strategy Profile. The priority of project implementation is suggested respectively CL, STR, DIC, PER, ICTI, MEA, SOC, CUL and GOV creation. We should remember that CL is a language oriented project, STR is a goal and target oriented project, DIC is a metadata-oriented project, PER is a people-oriented project, ICTI is a platform-oriented project, MEA is an efficiency and profitability-oriented project, SOC is a group-oriented project, CUL is a pattern-oriented project, GOV is a rule-oriented project. All projects are interoperable with each other and integrated depending on some conditions.

Sub-projects depend on transitive relations among KIM Tools. For example, CL Strategy Project and the Project for CL of DIC. Sub-projects of each project are listed from left to right after black cells in the Table 11. Right cells of black cells show the order for preparation of sub-project for each project. Left cells of black cells show the order for implementation of sub-project for each project. For each sub-project are realized in the frame of generic business pattern. Information system maintenance should be also interactively implemented in this order. This implementation order is also obtained cost and time efficiency and quality for all projects.

Every KIM Tool has a different management methodology depending on the nature of every KIAKI and types of integration and interoperability. Processes should be composed from the integrated and interoperated processes of business management, knowledge management, information management, project management and software development management, record management. Each project could be implemented from different software development methods, because nature of every KIAKI is different from each other. Therefore, every project has different transitive methodology for realizing implementations according to business goal and targets, and, characteristics of every KIM Tool.

## CONCLUSION

The BKIP is a key for the resilient, continuous, flexible and operational business. It integrates all business KIAKI via KIM Tools. The BKIP is a kind of lens for business which obtains the alternative ways for absorbing, processing, using, servicing, and diffusing KI in the frame of the IBT. It organizes to harmonizingly operate all of KIAKI in the frame of equality principles. The BKIP makes easier also to prepare and integrate enterprise architectures or business models. The BKIP has a holistic integration for KIM activities. The BKIP is helpful to manage IAs in electronic environment for all business. This policy is useful not only for the transformation of business but also for all types of BD activities depending on characteristics of a business, and its goals and targets.

To prepare the BKIP is like playing an instrument. It gives information how to play an instrument, however the composer may have created a own song. By constructing, using and developing this policy in a business, it is expected that closing IGs among business actors; keeping privacy by respecting the rights of communication, and, decreasing BE and duplications for some activities.

## REFERENCES

Ahmed, A. M. (2002). Virtual integrated performance measurement. *International Journal of Quality and Reliability*, *19*(4), 414–441. doi:10.1108/02656710210421580

Berends, H., Vanhaverbeke, W., & Kirschbaum, R. (2007). Knowledge management challenges in new business development: Case study observations. *Journal of Engineering and Technology Management*, *24*, 314–328. doi:10.1016/j.jengtecman.2007.09.006

Davis, C. H., & Sun, E. (2006). Business development capabilities in information technology SMEs in a regional economy: An exploratory study. *The Journal of Technology Transfer*, *31*, 145–161. doi:10.1007/s10961-005-5027-1

Dicle, Ü. (1974). *Bir yönetim aracı olarak örgütsel haberleşme*. Ankara: Milli Prodüktivite Merkezi.

Dove, R. (1999). Knowledge management, response ability, and the agile enterprise. *Journal of Knowledge Management*, *3*(1), 18–35. doi:10.1108/13673279910259367

Habermas, J. (1967). Zur Logik der sozialwissenschaften. *Philosophische Rundschau*, *14*, 149–176.

Habermas, J. (1971). *Hermeneutik und ideologiekritik*. Frankfurt: Suhrkamp.

Habermas, J. (1972). *Knowledge and human interest* (J. J. Shapiro, Trans.). London: Heinemann. (Original work published 1968).

Habermas, J. (1972). *Towards a rational society* (J. J. Shapiro, Trans.). London: Heinemann. (Original work published 1971).

Habermas, J. (1974). *Theory and practice* (J. Viertel, Trans.). London: Heinemann. (Original work published 1963).

Habermas, J. (1982). A reply to my critics. In J. B. Thompson & D. Held (Eds), *Habermas: Critical debates* (pp. 219-283). London: The Macmillan Press.

Habermas, J. (1984). *The theory of communicative action (volume 1): Reason and the rationalization of society* (T. McCarthy, Trans.). Oxford: Polity Press. (Original work published 1981).

Habermas, J. (1987). *The theory of communicative action (volume 2): The critique of functionalist reason* (T. McCarthy, Trans.). Oxford: Polity Press. (Original work published 1981).

Habermas, J. (1988). *On the logic of the social sciences* (S. W. Nicholson & J. A. Stark, Trans.). Cambridge, MA: The MIT Press. (Original work published 1970).

Habermas, J. (1995). *Moral consciousness and communicative action*. (C. Lenhardt & S. W. Nicholsen, Trans.). Cambridge, MA: The MIT Press. (Original work published 1983).

Hearn, G., & Rooney, D. (Eds.). (2008). *KNOWLEDGE policy: Challenges for the 21st century*. Cheltenham. UK & Northampton, MA: Edward Elgar.

Helfert, M. (2007). Teaching information quality skills in a business informatics programme. *Proceedings of the MIT Information Quality Industry Symposium, Cambridge, Massachusetts,* USA (pp. 908-912). Retrieved on December 24, 2008, from http://mitiq.mit.edu/IQIS/2007/iq_sym_07/Sessions/Session %204C/Session%204C%20-%20Teaching%20Information%20Quality%20Skills%20in%20a%20Business%20Information%20Program%20-%20Markus %20Helfert.pdf

Helfert, M., & Duncan, H. (2005). *Business informatics and information systems–some indications of differences study programmes*. Retrieved on December 24, 2008, from http://www.computing.dcu.ie/~mhelfert/ Research/publication/2005/HelfertDuncan_UKAIS2005.pdf

Helfert, M., & Duncan, H. (2006). Evaluating information systems and business informatics curriculum. *International Conference on Computer Systems and Technologies-CompSysTech'07.* Retrieved on November 24, 2008, from http://ecet.ecs.ru.acad.bg/cst07/Docs/cp/sIV/IV.4.pdf

Ice, J. W. (2007, Winter). Strategic intent: A key to business strategy development and culture change. *Organization Development Journal, 25*(4), 169–175.

James, T. (Ed.). (2001). *An INFORMATION policy handbook for Southern Africa: A knowledge base for decision-makers.* IDRC. Retrieved on December 24, 2008, from http://www.idrc.ca/ev.php?URL_ID=11439&URL_DO= DO_TOPIC

Kind, S., & Knyphausen-Aufseß, D. Z. (2007, April). What is "business development?"–the case of biotechnology. *The Schmalenbach Business Review, 59,* 176–199.

Kreps, G. L. (1989). *Organizational communication: Theory and practice,* 2nd edition. New York: Longman.

MacAulay, A. (2000). *KM strategy.* 31.9.2000. Retrieved on June 12, 2001, from http://kmonline.netfirms.com/Terms/km strategy.htm

Martz, W. B. Jr, & Cata, T. (2007). Business informatics as a research discipline. *International Journal of Teaching and Case Studies, 1*(1/2), 84–96. doi:10.1504/IJTCS.2007.014211

Nonaka, I., Toyama, R., & Konno, N. (2000). SECI, Ba, and leadership: A unified model of dynamic knowledge creation. *Long Range Planning, 33,* 5–34. doi:10.1016/S0024-6301(99)00115-6

O'Sullivan, D. (2002). Framework for managing business development in the networked organisation. *Computers in Industry, 47,* 77–88. doi:10.1016/S0166-3615(01)00135-X

OECD. (2004). *OECD principles of corporate governance.* Paris: OECD. Retrieved on June 21, 2008, from http://www.oecd.org/dataoecd/32/18/31557724.pdf

Özdemirci, F. (1996). *Kurum ve kuruluşlarda belge üretiminin denetlenmesi ve belge yönetimi.* İstanbul: Türk Kütüphaneciler Derneği. İstanbul Şubesi.20.

Pollard, D. (2005, September). CEPA and Pan Pearl River Delta economic integration: A comparative business development perspective. *Global Economic Review, 34*(3), 309–320. doi:10.1080/12265080500292617

Retzer, S., Fisher, J., & Lamp, J. (2003, November 26-28). Information systems and business informatics: An Australian German comparison. *14ᵗʰ Australian Conference on Information Systems,* Perth, Western Australia.

Roithmayr, F., & Kainz, G. A. (1994, April). An emprical-evidence and hypothesis about dissetations in business informatics. *Wirtschaftsinformatik, 36*(2), 174–184.

Rosenberg, J. M. (1983). *Dictionary of business management,* 2ⁿᵈ edition. New York: John-Wiley & Sons.

Rowlands, I. (1996). *Understanding information policy.* London: Bowker-Saur.

Rusjan, B. (2005, May). Usefulness of the EFQM excellence model: Theoretical explanation of some conceptual and methodological issue. *Total Quality Management and Business Excellence, 16*(3), 363–380. doi:10.1080/14783360500053972

Trede, F. V. (2006). *A critical practice model for physiotherapy.* Unpublished doctoral dissetation, School of Physiotherapy, Faculty of Health Sciences, The University of Sydney, Australia. Retrieved on October 6, 2008, from http://ses.library.usyd.edu.au/bitstream/2123/1430/ 2/02whole.pdf

Weigts, W., Widdershoven, G., Kok, G., & Tomlow, P. (1993). Patients' information seeking actions and physicians' responses in gynaecological consultations. *Qualitative Health Research, 3,* 398-429. (Cited in Wilson 1997).

Wilson, T. D. (1997). Information behaviour: An interdisciplinary perspective. *Information Processing & Management, 33*(4), 551–572. doi:10.1016/S0306-4573(97)00028-9

# ENDNOTES

[1] Weller and Bawden (2005:777) have emphasized that railway technology have created crises of communication and organization.

[2] BD is not clearly defined in the literature. Some authors define BD as a business function, (Kind & Knyphausen-Aufseß 2007:185), as a corporate entrepreneurial capability (Davis and Sun 2006:145). Some are mentioned from perspectives of Millennium Development Goals as sustainable BD, of integration global economic order in the context of globalization (Pollard September 2005), and, of new BD transforming to electronic business (e-business). Davis and Sun (2006:145) describe that BD "is a corporate entrepreneurial capability (or competence) that has emerged in the Information Technology industry." All of them and other definitions are explained different aspects of BD depending on business conditions, goals and targets, and global trends. Business could be interested in one or more of them at the same time. In this source BD is to extract and to construct the transitive relations among KIAKI by using KIM Tools in the frame of technological convergence.

[3] The theory is constructed by depending on development philosophy, information theory, communicative planning theory and convergent communication model.

4     The definition of BI is discussed in literature. It is defined as "management-oriented information systems" (Helfert 3); "new aspects for information systems" (Helfert & Duncan 2007); "a research discipline" (Martz & Cata 2007); a unique scientific discipline which still does not have any paradigm (Roithmayr & Kainz:174), synonym of information systems (Helfert & Duncan 2005), "deals with information and communication systems, abbreviated to information systems, in industry and government and increasingly it is also found private households" (Retzer, Fisher & Lamp 2003:3). So there is no consensus on definition of BI as is also controversial nature in the concept of informatics. All definitions cover different aspects of BI. In this paper, BI is a transdisciplinary knowledge and implementation area for business KI integrity among business, computer science, library and information science, information management, records management, software engineering, business engineering, social anthropology, and so on. BI covers all IAs depending on transitive relations among KIAKI in a business.

# Chapter 12
# Information Supply Chains:
## Restructuring Relationships, Chains, and Networks

**Hina Arora**
*Arizona State University, USA*

**T. S. Raghu**
*Arizona State University, USA*

**Ajay Vinze**
*Arizona State University, USA*

## ABSTRACT

*Information supply chains (ISCs) take an information-centric view of supply chains, where information is not only used to support supply chain operations, but also to create value for customers and enable business partners to collectively sense and respond to opportunities in a networked ecosystem. Creating value in the ISC involves gathering, organizing, selecting, synthesizing, and distributing information. In so doing, ISCs should provide secure, confidential, reliable, and real time access to heterogeneous information, while ensuring that the right information is delivered to the intended recipients at the right time. In other words, security, information quality, and information lead-time delays are critical performance determinants in ISCs. Recent disaster events such as Hurricane Katrina have highlighted the need for and value of ISCs by exposing the vulnerability of supply chains to demand surges and supply disruptions. Mitigating supply chain vulnerabilities requires a mechanism that allows for continuously sensing the environment, detecting existing or anticipated vulnerabilities, and responding to these vulnerabilities in real time through information sharing and collaboration. This chapter describes how the autonomic computing paradigm can be used to build resilient information supply chains by restructuring the associated relationships, chains, and networks.*

DOI: 10.4018/978-1-60566-723-2.ch012

## INTRODUCTION

Supply chain vulnerability can be defined as (Rice and Caniato, 2003) *"an exposure to serious disturbance, arising from risks within the supply chain as well as risks external to the supply chain"*. Efficient supply chains should be responsive to demand surges and supply disruptions resulting from internal and external vulnerabilities. Demand surges and supply disruptions are characterized by the probability of their occurrence, the magnitude of the impact, and the ability to cope with them. Firms can respond to these vulnerabilities by either, reallocating and redirecting existing capacity (this involves prioritizing among customers), or, maintaining redundant capacity (this involves an inherent trade off between "just-in-time" lean supply chains and maintaining inventory and capacity slack "just-in-case" (Martha and Subbakrishna, 2002)).

Mitigating supply chain vulnerabilities requires complex coordination mechanisms among a network of entities, systems and organizations. Various points of contact and information hand-offs leave open the possibility of errors. Effective supply chain managers react to such disruptive events by making decisions in real-time (Raghu and Vinze, 2004). This requires high levels of information sharing, real-time responsiveness, and collaboration.

Hurricane Katrina provided evidence of the importance of efficient decision-making, collaboration and information sharing in responding to demand surges and supply disruptions. Wal-Mart was able to move supplies to areas hit by hurricane Katrina because it had an emergency operations center that was staffed around the clock by decision-makers who had access to all of the company's systems (Worthen, 2005). District managers could call in to request supplies, and the decision makers, with the help of the logistics department would decide on how to relocate supplies to the affected area. They also relied on historical point-of-purchase-data from other hurricanes to forecast consumer demand before and after the hurricane, and used this data to stockpile emergency supplies in distribution centers around the affected areas. Wal-Mart therefore mostly relied on reallocating and redirecting existing capacity to meet the demand surge. In contrast, the Federal Government relied on redundant capacity maintained in the Strategic Petroleum Reserve to mitigate the supply disruptions caused by Hurricane Katrina in the Gulf of Mexico (Gross, 2005).

Responding to demand surges and supply disruptions therefore requires efficient redistribution and reallocation of resources based on real-time decision-making through information sharing and collaboration. In other words, there is a need for an information-centric view of supply chains that integrates information gathering, collaboration and decision making in order to support supply chain operations and create value for customers. This gives rise to the notion of Information Supply Chains (ISCs). There are three drivers for ISCs, each with unique perspectives to help with resiliency in the supply chain. The first is an organizational perspective that examines the differences and similarities between traditional supply chains and information supply chains in order to gain a better understanding of information supply chain requirements. The second is a process orientation that considers the unique informational challenges that arise in dynamic decision-making environments such as those caused by supply chain disruptions. The third is a technological perspective that investigates the use of autonomic computing principles in building a resilient information-based supply chain. The next three sections take a closer look at each of these orientations in turn. Section 5 presents an illustrative example of how autonomic computing principles can be used to build an ISC in the context of a healthcare supply chain that has been disrupted by an Influenza pandemic.

# INFORMATION SUPPLY CHAINS

A supply chain is a network of material, information and cash flows between suppliers (who provide raw material), manufacturers (who convert raw material to final products), distributors (who transport and deliver products to customers), and customers. While material flows from suppliers to the customers, information and cash flows in the opposite direction.

Traditional supply chains take an inventory-based approach, where information is treated as a supporting element in the value-adding process, not a source of value itself. The primary focus is on reducing material-flow lead-time delays. However, volatile, unpredictable demand, and complex coordination mechanisms in today's marketplace is driving the need for a high level of information sharing, real-time responsiveness and collaboration. It is therefore becoming increasingly important to take an information-based approach that concentrates on reducing information-flow lead-time delays in addition to material-flow lead-time delays.

ISCs take an information-centric view of supply chains, where information is not only used to support supply chain operations, but also to create value for customers. Creating value in the ISC involves gathering, organizing, selecting, synthesizing and distributing information. In so doing, ISCs should provide secure, confidential, reliable and real-time access to heterogeneous information, while ensuring that the right information is delivered to the intended recipients at the right time. In other words, security, information quality and information lead-time delays are critical performance determinants in ISCs.

We therefore define information supply chains (ISC) as *a collection of information and communication technologies to provide a secure integrated decisional environment that enables business partners to collectively sense and respond to opportunities and challenges in a networked eco-system.*

ISCs differ from traditional supply chains in many respects (based on the concept of virtual value chains, Rayport and Sviolka, 1995). First, ISC shifts away from the traditional supply chain model of a linear sequence of activities with defined points of inputs and outputs, to a matrix of potential inputs and outputs that can be accessed and distributed through a wide variety of channels. Second, ISCs use digital assets that are not used up in their consumption. Hence, companies that create value with digital assets may be able to re-harvest them through a potentially infinite number of transactions. Third, ISCs enable companies to achieve low unit costs of products and services thus redefining economies of scale. Fourth, ISCs can help provide value across many different and disparate markets. Fifth, transaction costs are much lower in ISCs. Finally, ISCs enable companies to be market sensitive (demand-driven rather than forecast-driven). The differences are summarized in Table 1.

These differences not withstanding, ISCs have a lot in common with traditional supply chains. They deal with demand and supply (of information), raw goods (data), finished goods (synthesized information), capacity limitations (hardware and human cognitive limitations), fill-rates, lead-time delays, costs (of searching and synthesizing information), quality of goods, and supply chain disruptions.

Given the above characteristics of ISCs, it can be seen that they would be most relevant in sectors such as Services, Finance, IT and Healthcare. Table 2 compares ISC characteristics across these three domains from the organization, process and technology perspectives. Consider an IT network for instance. The network could be made up of several workstations, servers, routers and printers. Workstation users in this scenario are not only users of information (such as checking the print queue, or looking for an idle machine to run a complex job), but also creators of information (such as a submitted print job). Such an ISC will not only use information to remain functional (say,

*Table 1. Differences between traditional supply chains and information supply chains*

| Traditional Supply Chain | Information Supply Chain |
|---|---|
| Linear sequence of activities with defined points of inputs and outputs. | Network of information sources and sinks. |
| Physical assets used up in consumption. | Digital assets not used up in consumption. |
| Economies of scale reachable only by increasing the number of goods produced. | Small companies can achieve low unit costs of production and services. |
| Companies usually constrained to one market. | Companies can provide value in disparate markets. |
| Characterized by high transaction costs. | Low transaction costs. |
| Forecast driven. | Demand driven. |

by monitoring for attacks), but also produce value for the customers (say, by alerting the user of an update or system shutdown for maintenance). As should be evident from this simple example, in order to create value, the ISC should be capable of gathering information from multiple sources, compiling complex data, and making appropriate recommendations. In the case of IT networks, this was traditionally done by the system administrator. However, due to bounded rationality and cognitive limitations, human administrators can deal with only simple decision making tasks and small amounts of information. In fact, this is true of handling disruptions in other dynamic decision-making environments such as finance and healthcare as well. Concepts across these three varied domains share commonalities in decision-making processes as each of them demonstrate the need for dynamic decision-making.

## EXTENDING ISC THROUGH DYNAMIC DECISION MAKING

As mentioned earlier, responding to demand surges and supply disruptions requires efficient redistribution and reallocation of resources based on real-time decision-making through information sharing and collaboration. This requires solving two types of decision-making problems: the *Situational Analysis Problem* (how to monitor, represent and analyze the various positions, proposals for actions, hypotheses and evidences) and the *Conflict Resolution Problem* (how to enable rapid collaborative decision-making through effective conflict resolution). IT can be a great enabler in enhancing our ability to cope with supply chain disruptions. IT can increase situational awareness among decision-makers and enhance coordination through efficient communication and data sharing (voice, data and chat capabilities). However decision-making support for conflict resolution in such environments is still very limited and not well understood. Decision support can greatly enhance resource mobilization, allocation and coordination efforts, and provide a platform to test various "what-if" scenarios. This can be invaluable in dealing with supply chain disruptions.

Decision-making can be described as a four-step process (Sprague, 1980; Simon, 1960): (a) *intelligence* comprised of searching the environment for problems, (b) *design* involving analysis and development of possible courses of action, (c) *choice* consisting of selecting a particular course of action, and (d) *implementation* of the action. Decision support systems (DSS) provide support for complex decision-making and problem solving tasks (Sprague, 1980; Shim et al, 2002). DSS also include support for communication, coordination and collaboration. A good DSS should improve both the *efficiency* (ratio of result over effort) and the *effectiveness* (goal attainment) of the decision-making process (Shim, 2002; Bots and Lootsma, 2000). While DSS technology has evolved signifi-

*Table 2. ISC characteristics in three domains*

| Characteristic | Domain | | |
|---|---|---|---|
| | IT | Finance | Healthcare |
| Stakeholders | System administrators, users | Stock markets, shareholders | Healthcare providers, patients |
| Information Characteristics | Defined standards, high volume of information, real-time or batch processing | Relatively well defined standards, high volume of information, real-time information processing | Heterogeneous standards or lack of them, high volume of information, real-time information processing |
| Business Objectives | System availability, reliability, application performance, security | Timely transaction execution, real-time information feed and delivery, security, reduce trading cost, maximize returns | System availability, reliability, security, confidentiality, real-time information feed and delivery |
| Constraints | Cognitive limitations of system administrators, limited resources | Information processing, discerning macro economic trends and analyst information | Cognitive limitations of providers, limited resources |
| Resources | CPU availability, memory availability, intrusion monitoring data | Stock prices, options, capital, credits | Beds, medical staff, medicines, vaccinations, epidemic surveillance data |
| Information node characteristic | Peer-to-peer or client-server configuration | Peer-to-peer | Peer-to-peer or client-server configuration |
| Domain specific issues | Gathering and synthesizing requisite information, false positives and false negatives | Trading costs | Gathering and synthesizing requisite information, false positives and false negatives |
| Business Value of Autonomic Approach | Freeing administrators of mundane tasks, facilitating intrusion detection, improved services for users. | Synthesizing and responding to market trends on real-time basis | Enabling collaboration among providers, facilitating epidemic control, improved quality of care for patients. |

cantly in the last three decades (Shim et al, 2002), understanding of dynamic decision-making tasks and decision support for this class of problems remains limited (Gonzalez, 2005).

Dynamic decision making is characterized by the following four properties (Edwards, 1962; Brehmer, 1992): (a) a series of decisions is required to reach the goal, (b) the decisions are interdependent (later decisions are constrained by earlier decisions), (c) the state of the decision problem changes, both autonomously, and as a consequence of the decision maker's actions, and (d) the decisions have to be made in a real-time environment. Dynamic decisions typically arise in military contexts, and extreme events such as natural or technological disasters (Mendonca, 2007). For instance, natural disasters such as Katrina create a demand surge and associated scarcity for food, water, medication and shelter. A series of decisions regarding resource requirements,

allocation, transportation and relative urgency need to be made. The decisions are interdependent in that, the allocation of resources and attention to one population affects the time and resources spent on the remaining population. This in turn determines the extent of human and economic loss associated with the disaster. The state of the decision problem can also change autonomously due to the arrival of a second hurricane or other natural factors. In other words, the state of the decision space at any given moment is dependent both on the characteristics of the natural disaster, and the decisions made by the decision makers. And finally, decisions have to be made in real time in order to be most effective.

These issues resonate with the finance, healthcare and IT domains too. Consider for instance the finance domain, which is characterized by high volumes of financial data. A series of decisions regarding stocks, bonds and options need to be made in order to maximize profits. The decisions are interdependent in that, the allocation of funds from a limited budget to one type of stock or option affects the amount that can be invested in the others. The state of the decision problem can also change autonomously due to external macro-economic trends. In other words, the value of the portfolio is dependent both on the decisions of the investor, and external economic trends not in the investor's control. And finally, decisions have to be made in real time in order to be most effective.

The limitations of bounded rationality are even more pronounced in dynamic decision-making tasks. Decision makers are often unable to comprehend the side effects of their actions thereby causing performance to degrade. As Radner (2000) says, "…in any even semi-realistic decision problem, the DM does not know all of the relevant logical implications of what he knows. This phenomenon is sometimes called the failure of logical omniscience". Feedback delays and poor feedback quality further exacerbate performance. The real-time nature of decisions also introduces an element of stress into dynamic decision-making, and in order to cope with this stress, the decision maker reverts to simpler, more task oriented modes of operation, thereby negatively influencing decision performance (Brehmer, 1992). Situational awareness in a dynamic decision making environment requires two overlapping cognitive activities (Lerch and Harter, 2001) that compete for the decision maker's attentional resources: (a) *monitoring* or tracking of key system variables for information regarding present and expected conditions, and (b) *control* or the generation, evaluation and selection of alternative actions that can change the system. Control can be achieved through feedback (selecting an action based on current system information), or feedforward (selecting actions based on a predicted future state of the system). While feedforward can improve decision quality, decision makers are more likely to use available feedback control

than feedforward, since the former requires less cognitive effort. Monitoring and feedback can be improved through improved collection, processing and delivery of information. Feedforward can be improved through modeling and simulation aids that project future states of the system.

Three different decision support mechanisms are therefore prevalent in the literature for dynamic decision making (Gonzalez, 2005; Huguenard and Ballou, 2006): (a) *outcome feedback*, in which decision makers are provided with feedback on the performance results of their decisions, (b) *cognitive feedback*, in which decision makers are given instructions on how to perform the decision task, and (c) *feedforward*, where decision makers are provided with the models and tools to perform "what-if" analysis of potential decisions. It has been shown that outcome feedback alone is an ineffective form of decision support (Lerch and Harter, 2001; Gonzalez, 2005). However, cognitive feedback and feedforward in combination with outcome feedback resulted in better performance (Sengupta and Abdel-Hamid, 1993).

Outcome feedback requires data gathering and analysis capabilities to provide useful information to the decision makers. Feedforward requires simulation and modeling capabilities to provide optimal solution alternatives. Cognitive feedback requires the ability to learn from experience and come up with rules of thumb or action policies. The effective and efficient functioning of an ISC therefore requires the capability of monitoring large amounts of data (knowledge synthesis), analyzing it (situational analysis), planning a course of action and executing or recommending it (conflict resolution). The ISC should be self-configuring, that is, capable of altering its problem-determination and conflict resolution solutions in the face of changing business policies. And, it should be self-optimizing, that is, capable of providing the optimal solution in the face of changing objectives and constraints.

## AUTONOMIC COMPUTING ENABLEMENT FOR ISCS

It should be clear from the previous section, that building ISCs requires the technology enablement of supply chains. Essentially, there is a need for an information-based view of supply chains with the capability of monitoring large amounts of data, analyzing it, planning a course of action based on stored knowledge and high level policies, and executing or recommending a course of action. As we have seen, these needs play out across domains such as emergency response, IT and finance. The Autonomic Computing paradigm addresses all of these requirements, and can be used to implement ISCs in all of these domains.

Autonomic computing has been suggested as a new paradigm to deal with the ever-increasing complexity in today's systems (Kephart and Chess, 2003). Autonomic systems are composed of self-managed elements. Self-management requires that the system be self-configuring (capable of goal-driven self-assembly with the help of a central registry), self-optimizing (especially with respect to resource allocation), self-healing (the system as a whole should be capable of dealing with the failure of any constituent part) and self-protecting (against undesirable system behavior due to bugs or unanticipated conditions, and against system penetration by attackers). Each autonomic element consists of an autonomic manager and a set of managed components. The autonomic manager continuously monitors the managed components, analyzes the data they generate, plans actions if required, and executes them (the MAPE model) in order to achieve the self-management aspects of the system.

The AM relies on high-level system policies to guide its goals (White et al, 2004). A policy is a representation, in a standard external form, of desired behaviors or constraints on behavior. High-level system policies refer to high-level objectives set by the administrators for the autonomic systems, while leaving the task of how they are achieved

to the autonomic managers. At least three forms of policy have been identified: action policies, goal policies and utility policies (Kephart and Walsh, 2004). Action policies are typically of the form IF (Condition) THEN (Action). Autonomic elements employing these policies must measure and/or synthesize the quantities stated in the condition, and execute the stated actions whenever the condition is satisfied. Goal policies describe the conditions to be attained without specifying how to attain them. Goal policies are more powerful than action policies because they can be specified without requiring detailed knowledge of that element's inner workings. Autonomic elements employing goal policies must possess sufficient modeling and planning capabilities to translate goals into actions. Utility policies specify the relative desirability of alternative states either by assigning a numerical value or a partial or total ordering of the possible states. Utility functions are even more powerful than goal policies because they automatically determine the most valuable goal in any given situation. Autonomic elements employing utility policies must possess sufficient modeling and planning capabilities to translate utilities into actions.

The AM also assumes the existence of a common knowledge base that it continuously uses and modifies according to its experiences and policies (Kephart and Walsh, 2004). For instance, when considering utility policies, the decision problem is essentially one of choosing values of decision variables so as to maximize the utility function. Since the relation between the decision variables and process outcomes is oftentimes dynamic and non-stationary, the agent continuously learns about the process outcomes and updates its knowledge repository.

Autonomic elements can therefore be used to gather data, synthesize information, and distribute it. The elements rely on their knowledge base and high-level policies to decide on what to gather, how to synthesize, and whom to distribute to. Every element can therefore be a consumer and a provider of information in the ISC. While Autonomic Computing has been used in the past to manage resources in the IT context, it can be extended to other domains to manage physical resources as illustrated in the next section in the healthcare context.

## AN ISC CASE STUDY IN PUBLIC HEALTH

This section presents an illustrative example of how autonomic computing principles can be used to build an ISC in the context of a healthcare supply chain that has been disrupted by an Influenza pandemic.

The Healthcare System can be characterized as a collaborative endeavor between physicians, patients, healthcare organizations, insurance companies, laboratories and public health that are intricately connected in a healthcare information supply chain (Figure 1). While the IT ISC deals with IT resources such as memory and CPU usage, the healthcare ISC deals with healthcare resources such as beds, medicines, vaccinations, and hospital staff. Data in the healthcare ISC typically pertains to the patient in terms of health records, medical images etc. The healthcare ISC can create value for the patients by ensuring patient data is available to the right entity at the right time, monitoring for epidemics, and optimizing resource allocation during an epidemic.

A large-scale public health emergency such as an epidemic outbreak can result in an overwhelming number of human casualties. This can result in a demand surge and associated scarcity of healthcare resources such as beds, staffing, supplies and equipment due to demand surges. Surge capacity is a health care system's ability to expand quickly beyond normal services to meet an increased demand. Cooperating through mutual aid at the regional level can help improve surge capacity. This requires real-time collaboration among various entities (such as hospitals and pharmacies) in the Healthcare ISC. However, the complexity of the resource redistribution and allocation problem can quickly overwhelm human decision makers. This is because, resource allocation in this context results in a dynamic decision making environment. A series of decisions regarding vaccination

*Figure 1. A typical Healthcare ISC. Primary data users are in green, secondary data users are in blue, and tertiary data users are in orange*

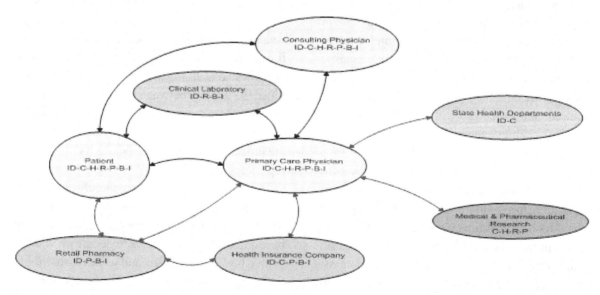

policy, anti-viral allocation and patient priorities need to be made. The decisions are interdependent in that, the allocation of resources and attention to one population affects the time and resources spent on the remaining populations. This in turn determines the extent of the pandemic. The state of the decision problem can also change autonomously due to virus mutations and other natural factors. In other words, the state of the pandemic at any given moment is dependent both on the characteristics of the pandemic, and the decisions made by the decision makers. And finally, decisions have to be made in real time in order to be most effective. Application of self-management and self-optimization concepts can greatly relieve the cognitive challenges faced by decision makers in this context.

A prototype system based on these ideas was built (Arora, Raghu, Vinze, 2006). Autonomic principles of self-optimization and self-configuration were used to address demand surges in the context of healthcare information supply chains that have been disrupted by an epidemic. The system was built using a multi-agent systems platform and the Autonomic Computing Toolkit, to illustrate how an autonomic computing approach can facilitate resource allocation decisions in responding to public health emergencies. The multi-agent toolkit, Repast[1], was used to simulate a Smallpox outbreak. The Autonomic Toolkit was used to implement the Autonomic Manager functionality. Regional healthcare entities communicate their resource requirements (or excesses) to the Autonomic Manager. This information is analyzed for resource shortages and excesses. A utility-based constrained optimization problem, constrained by high-level budget and resource policies, is used to find the optimal resource redistribution solution.

Autonomic computing principles are used to build an ISC in this context as shown in Figure 2. A smallpox outbreak occurs within a population (level 1). Those susceptible to the disease get infected. As the epidemic spreads, casualties start trickling into the care entities (level 2). Timely intervention in the form of immunization (to reduce the number of susceptibles), quarantine (to reduce the number of contacts with the infected) and treatment (to help the infected recover) can help contain the epidemic. However, the exponential nature of the spread of epidemics can cause an overwhelming number of casualties leading to a scarcity of containment resources. Pooling resources at the regional level could help alleviate the scarcity and improve surge capacity. Therefore, on encountering a resource shortage, the healthcare entities contact an Autonomic Manager (level 3) to optimally re-distribute resources between entities at the regional level. The Autonomic Manager uses a "utility policy", to maximize utilities across the various healthcare entities, subject to resource and cost constraints.

The Autonomic Toolkit[2] is used to implement the Autonomic Manager functionality. Each regional healthcare entity communicates its resource requirements (or excesses) to the Autonomic Manager in the form of a Common Base Event (CBE). Effective analysis of event data requires the data to be reported in a consistent manner. Since the data is typically heterogeneous and distributed, the only way to reliably interpret the data, correlate it with events from other diverse sources and respond effectively is to use a common event format with a canonical vocabulary.

*Figure 2. Autonomic resource allocation prototype system*

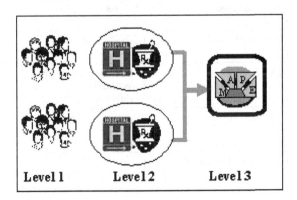

Level 1        Level 2        Level 3

This is accomplished by modeling events using the CBE, which standardizes the format and content of events and provides the foundation for autonomic computing. A CBE describes a situation that has occurred. Table 3 shows an example of some parts of a Common Base Event that could be used to report an epidemic outbreak and associated resource availability.

Custom resource models are defined in order to provide the Autonomic Management Engine (AME) the requisite information to manage healthcare resources. Each regional healthcare

entity communicates its resource requirements (or excesses) to the Autonomic Manager. The Autonomic Manager uses this information to come up with an optimal allocation mechanism. This can be a complex proposition due to a number of reasons. First, resource requirements are often time-bound. For instance, vaccinations are typically effective only in the susceptible stage. Second, resource availability may also be time-bound. For instance, resources such as medicines and vaccinations are consumable, and may also be perishable. Third, resources are often required in

*Table 3. Example of a CBE in the healthcare context*

| Field Name | Example Data | Description |
|---|---|---|
| Version | 1.0.1 | The version of the CBE format that is being used. |
| creationTime | 2005-09-01T01:02:03.456Z | The time that the situation was detected. |
| Severity | 2 | The severity of the event from the point of view of the entity that is reporting it. |
| globalInstanceId | C1F2ACFE... | A unique value that identifies the event instance such as a GUID (Globally Unique Identifier). |
| sourceComponentId | [source identifier] | Identifies who was affected by the situation. |
| Location | [source location] | Identifies the location of the source. |
| locationType | [source location type] | The type of location. |
| reporterComponentId | [reporter identifier] | Indicates who reported the event (e.g. unique identifier for a hospital, doctor, etc.). |
| Location | [reporter location] | Identifies the location of the reporter (e.g. location of hospital). |
| locationType | [reporter location type] | The type of location (e.g. hospital). |
| Situation | ---- | The situation that has occurred (contains information in the next three rows). |
| categoryName | ReportSituation | Category of the type of situation that is being reported. |
| situationType | STATUS | Provides additional information associated with each situation category. |
| ResoningScope | EXTERNAL | Defines whether the impact of the situation is internal or external to the source. |
| ExtensionName | ReportableDisease | Extensions are used to provide information that is specific to a situation. There must be a canonical definition for this data. |
| ExtendedDataElement[0] | name='DiseaseCategory' type='string' values='A' | The first entry in this extension. |
| ExtendedDataElement[1] | name='DiseaseName' type='string' values='Smallpox' | The second entry in this extension. |
| ExtendedDataElement[..] | ... | Additional extended data elements could be used. |

bundles. For instance, transferring medicines from one region to another requires trucks and drivers, just as administering vaccinations requires nurses. These additional constraints result in analytically intractable problems, making it difficult to come up with perfectly optimal solutions under all possible objectives and constraints. Model execution is therefore done in two phases – training and refinement. During the training phase, agents make random decision choices and observe process outcomes. This builds a repository of information (knowledge base) over time and forms the basis for the agents' informed decisions during the refinement phase. Then, given the repository, agents systematically relate the decision choices and the process outcomes (or their utility values). Models of the environment further enhance learning. This two-phase mechanism allows the system to learn and explore in a protected environment and exploit the learning in real situations. Feedback gained from real situations is used to update learning patterns.

Initial feedback from this implementation suggests that both process and procedural efficiencies can be gained by using an autonomic approach to building healthcare information supply chains. This approach facilitates data monitoring and decision making capabilities, and ensures that the right information reaches the right entity at the right time. Preliminary results suggest policy implications for public health in terms of the organizational, process and technology changes that will have to be incurred in order to make the healthcare supply chain more resilient (Arora, Raghu, Vinze, Submitted; Arora, Raghu, Vinze, 2007).

## CONCLUSION

An ISC is a collection of information and communication technologies to provide a *secure integrated decisional environment* that enables business partners to *collectively sense and respond* to opportunities and challenges in a networked eco-system. Such an information-centric view can be instrumental in making supply chains more responsive to demand surges and supply disruptions. It can enhance the ability of decision makers to cope with supply chain disruptions by increasing situational awareness, enhancing co-ordination, and presenting feasible alternatives in an otherwise complex solution space. Autonomic computing presents a promising environment to implement ISCs, by providing a framework for information gathering, analysis, learning, and decision-making.

## REFERENCES

Arora, H., Raghu, T. S., & Vinze, A. (2007, January). Optimizing regional aid during public health emergencies: An autonomic resource allocation approach. *40th Hawaii International Conference on System Sciences (HICSS)*, HI.

Arora, H., Raghu, T. S., & Vinze, A. (Manuscript submitted for publication). Optimizing antiviral allocation policy through regional aid during an Influenza pandemic. *Journal of Decision Sciences Special Issue on Decision Making in the Health-Sector Supply Chain*.

Arora, H., Raghu, T. S., Vinze, A., & Brittenham, P. (2006). Collaborative self-configuration and learning in autonomic computing systems: Applications to supply chain. *Poster, 3rd IEEE International Conference on Autonomic Computing (ICAC)*, Dublin, Ireland.

Bots, P. W. G., & Lootsma, F. A. (2000). Decision support in the public sector. *Journal of Multi-Criteria Decision Analysis, 9*(1-3), 1–6. doi:10.1002/1099-1360(200001/05)9:1/3<1::AID-MCDA262>3.0.CO;2-D

Brehmer, B. (1992). Dynamic decision making: Human control of complex systems. *Acta Psychologica, 81*(3), 211–241. doi:10.1016/0001-6918(92)90019-A

Edwards, W. (1962). Dynamic decision theory and probabilistic information processing. *Human Factors, 4*, 59–73.

Gonzalez, C. (2005). Decision support for real-time, dynamic decision-making tasks. *Organizational Behavior and Human Decision Processes, 96*, 142–154. doi:10.1016/j.obhdp.2004.11.002

Gross, D. A. (2005, September 23). What FEMA could learn from Wal-Mart-less than you think. *Slate*. Retrieved from http://www.slate.com/id/2126832

Huguenard, B. R., & Ballou, D. J. (2006). Dispatcher: A theory-based design for study of real-time dynamic decision-making. *Proceedings of the 2006 Southern Association for Information Systems Conference* (pp. 117-122).

Kephart, J. O., & Chess, D. M. (2003). The vision of autonomic computing. *IEEE Computer, 36*(1), 41–50.

Kephart, J. O., & Walsh, W. E. (2004). An artificial intelligence perspective on autonomic computing policies. *Fifth IEEE International Workshop on Policies for Distributed Systems and Networks* (pp. 3-12).

Lerch, F. J., & Harter, D. E. (2001). Cognitive support for real-time dynamic decision making. *Information Systems Research, 12*(1), 63–82. doi:10.1287/isre.12.1.63.9717

Martha, J., & Subbakrishna, J. S. (2002, September/October). Targeting a just-in-case supply chain for the inevitable next disaster. *Supply Chain Management Review* (pp. 18-23).

Mendonca, D. (2007). Decision support for improvisation in response to extreme events: Learning from the response to the 2001 World Trade Center attack. *Decision Support Systems, 43*, 952–967. doi:10.1016/j.dss.2005.05.025

Radner, R. (2000). Costly and bounded rationality in individual and team decision-making. *Industrial and Corporate Change, 9*(4), 623–658. doi:10.1093/icc/9.4.623

Raghu, T. S., & Vinze, A. (2004, September). Collaborative self-configuration and learning in autonomic computing systems. IBM Proposal.

Rayport, J. F., & Sviokla, J. J. (1995). Exploiting the virtual value chain. *Harvard Business Review*.

Rice, J. B., & Caniato, F. (2003, September/October). Building a secure and resilient supply network. *Supply Chain Management Review*, 22–30.

Sengupta, K., & Abdel-Hamid, T. K. (1993). Alternative conceptions of feedback in dynamic decision environments: An experimental investigation. *Management Science, 39*(4), 411–428. doi:10.1287/mnsc.39.4.411

Shim, J. P., Warkentin, M., Courtney, J. F., Power, D. J., Sharda, R., & Carlsson, C. (2002). Past, present, and future of decision support technology. *Decision Support Systems, 33*(2), 111–126. doi:10.1016/S0167-9236(01)00139-7

Simon, H. (1960). *The new science of management decision*. New York: Harper and Row.

Sprague, R. H. (1980). A framework for the development of decision support systems. *MIS Quarterly, 4*(4), 1–26. doi:10.2307/248957

White, S. R., Hanson, J. E., Whalley, I., Chess, D. M., & Kephart, J. O. (2004). An architectural approach to autonomic computing. *IEEE Proceedings of the International Conference On Autonomic Computing*.

Worthen, B. (2005). How Wal-Mart beat feds to New Orleans. *CIO Magazine*. Retrieved on November 1, 2005, from http://www.cio.com/archive/110105/tl_katrina.html?CID=13532

## ENDNOTES

[1]  http://repast.sourceforge.net/

[2]  http://www-128.ibm.com/developerworks/autonomic/overview.html

# Chapter 13
# Sustaining the Green Information Technology Movement

**Miti Garg**
*The Logistics Institute – Asia Pacific, Singapore*

**Sumeet Gupta**
*Shri Shankaracharya College of Engineering and Technology, India*

**Mark Goh**
*The Logistics Institute – Asia Pacific, Singapore*

**Robert Desouza**
*The Logistics Institute – Asia Pacific, Singapore*

**Balan Sundarkarni**
*The Logistics Institute – Asia Pacific, Singapore*

**Ridwan Kuswoyo Bong**
*The Logistics Institute – Asia Pacific, Singapore*

## ABSTRACT

*Green computing paradigm is a term used to describe a movement in the field of information technology whereby users and information technology professionals are adopting 'less environmentally destructive' practices to mitigate the detrimental effects of excessive computing to the environment. Environment friendly practices such as virtualization, cloud computing, greening of data centres, recycling, tele-commuting, and teleworking are discussed in this chapter. A summary of the initiatives undertaken by government agencies in various countries is also provided.*

DOI: 10.4018/978-1-60566-723-2.ch013

## INTRODUCTION

The word 'green' has attained a new meaning in our vocabulary today. 'Green' connotes 'less environmentally destructive' practises that minimize the damage to the environment and decrease the side- effects of excessive computing. The excessive use of modern day appliances such as laptops and personal computers have contributed to environmental pollutants that are damaging the environment slowly but steadily. Carbon laden fumes emitted from countless automobiles and modern day factories have been polluting our environment making the air unbreathable in several cosmopolitan cities of the world. The extent of the damage from carbon emissions can be gauged from the subtle climate changes that are being experienced in recent years. *"Just days after experts warned the Arctic ice cap is melting faster than ever, a huge 30-sq-km sheet of ice has broken free near Canada"* (Noronha, 2008).

So what is the cause of these climatic changes? The answer lies right before our eyes in the form of the desktop personal computers, cars and buses we use to commute to our workplace and in fact modern day gizmo that consumes energy. The real culprit behind the use of this equipment is the carbon laden fumes that are being generated during the manufacture of these machines and the fumes emitted in the production of electricity that runs this equipment. Another source of environmental damage is the improper disposal of tonnes of non-degradable plastic used to manufacture these appliances.

Technology has overtaken our lives at breakneck speed. At home, labour saving devices such as washing machines, dishwashers, and microwave ovens are making processes more efficient replacing human effort. Computers and other machines are rapidly reducing the human interface within offices and institutional environments. In the place of a well-groomed receptionist answering queries, a sophisticated information kiosk with touch screen facilities provides information in the modern day office environment. LCD monitors, personal computers, laptops, hand held devices like PDAs and digital assistants, have become the norm in the business world today. Information is being stored in large data centres and servers. Entire operations depend on machines which serve as the backbone of the modern day organization.

In fact the information technology hardware and software expenditure of companies forms a major chunk of the total budget. Computers have overtaken the workspace, with at least one PC per worker. Laptops and personal digital assistants, other presentation hardware, storage devices such as data centres dominate the work place. Desktop computing has replaced the reams of paperwork and files that once characterized the workplace. While making office work more efficient and less labour intensive, personal computers contribute to the carbon footprint in several ways.

A carbon footprint is the impact on the environment of all the green house gases which are produced by the usage of energy consuming equipment in our day-to-day lives. A carbon footprint consists of a primary footprint and a secondary footprint. A primary footprint measures the direct emission of fuel gases produced by domestic consumption and transportation. Secondary footprint consists of emissions from the whole lifecycle of the products which we use- from the design of the product to its disposal (What is a Carbon Footprint? 2008). The manufacture of computers involves hundreds of raw materials like - plastics, semi conductor chips, batteries the manufacture, delivery and recycling of which consume energy and emits green house gases. For instance, semi-conductor chips used as computer memory involve the use of large quantities of potable water and toxic substances which may jeopardize the health of workers. The manufacturing of personal computers, semi conductors, batteries and micro electronics also generate toxic waste, effective disposal of which is rarely undertaken.

*Figure 1. Components of green organization management*

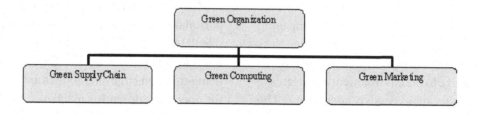

## HP Posts Supply Chain Emissions Data, Urges IT Co.'s to Do More

Hewlett-Packard became the first company to post data on carbon emissions from its first-tier manufacturing supply chain which equaled about 3.5 million tons of CO2 equivalents in 2007, and in doing so became the first IT Company to release that level of information about its supply chain. The data represents emissions from more than 80 percent of the company's overall operations, and HP will use the data it collected to explore ways to bring energy efficiency to its suppliers and further lower its total carbon footprint (Green Computing Staff, 2008).

## DEFINITION OF GREEN COMPUTING

In such a scenario, it has been found necessary to mitigate the long term disadvantages of excessive computing to human beings and the environment. A new area of research known as 'green computing' or 'green IT' has emerged. Green computing is defined as the use of computers in an environmentally responsible way (Search Data Center, 2007). The objective of green computing is to reduce or offset the secondary carbon footprint created by the usage of computing devices such as personal computers (PCs), data centres and laptops and also by employing green computing techniques such as virtualization and cloud computing. These and some other aspects of are green computing paradigm are discussed in this chapter.

## ORGANIZATION OF THE CHAPTER

The green paradigm is part of the complete attempt to make an organization green. There are three aspects of a green organization: green supply chain management, green workplace (includes green Information Technology) and green marketing. We shall cover green Information Technology in this chapter. (see Figure 1)

In this chapter we shall discuss the different aspects of the green information technology. We also examine the recent advances in green computing research such as virtualization, cloud computing, greening of data centres and government initiatives to promote green computing.

## PERSONAL COMPUTERS

Computers, laptops and PDAs run on electricity manufactured by burning fossil fuels. In addition to the cost of running equipment, cooling IT equipment consumes energy. There is no way to power the world's computers without adding significantly to the world's pollution problems (Anzovin, 1993). Energy is an expensive commodity, for every dollar spent on IT hardware, 50 cents goes to energy. By 2010, 70 cents would go to running and cooling these devices (Buttner, Geuder & Hittner, 2007). Therefore in order to reduce costs and mitigate the damage to the environment, energy must be saved. Using greener and renewable sources of energy is an option to decrease the environmental damage.

Carrying out an energy audit is the first step in saving power. Emphasis should be laid down on switching off personal computers when not in use, saving electricity through power saving devices etc. Peripherals and CPUs must be powered down during extended periods of inactivity. Manufacturers have large safety margins when it comes to the voltage they feed their products. This means that you can feed your CPU less energy while still have it running at 100%. This is called undervolting. Undervolting a computer or a notebook will help to save energy and also prolong the life of the battery. Computing peripherals such as laser printers should be powered-up or powered-down as per need. Power management tools should be used to turn of the computer after periods of inactivity. Alternate energy sources should be employed for computing workstations, servers, networks and datacenters.

## DISPOSAL OF COMPUTERS (E-WASTE)

According to US Environmental Protection Agency (EPA), Americans throw out more than 2 million tons of consumer electronics annually, making electronic waste (E-Waste) one of the fastest growing components of the municipal waste stream (Velte, Velte and Elsenpeter, 2008). Improper disposal of personal computers, computer monitors (which consists of 6% of lead by weight), laptops and batteries result in the accumulation of non-biodegradable plastics, toxic and carcinogenic elements such as lead, mercury, cadmium and Polychlorinated biphenyls (PCBs) in the environment, harming those who handle these materials during the recycling process and eventually contaminating the air and water thus affecting everybody.

The first step in the disposal of e-waste is to separate e-waste from regular waste. The next step is to adopt the three pronged strategy of "recycle, reuse and reduce".

## MATERIALS RECYCLING

The 'Recycle, Reuse and Reduce' strategy has been adopted by several companies to get rid of non-biodegradable materials such as PCs and laptops which can no longer be used. Recycled paper is also being used in offices to reduce the paper consumption. Dell offers to collect and recycle desktops and laptops it manufactures from its customers after the product life is over. One in two computers sold by Dell is recycled by the company.

### Recycle

E-waste is disposed off either within developed countries or shipped off to developing nations such as China, India and Africa since recycling in the US costs 35 USD per hour while it costs 25 cents per hour in developing countries (Velte, Velte and Elsenpeter, 2008). There is no standard procedure for the disposal of e-waste in developed countries and government regulation varies from district to district. Most of the waste ends in landfills, or is disposed of by sophisticated machines. America ships off most of its e-waste to China where it is processed and recycled to yield precious metals. While recycling yields precious metals and helps to dispose of waste protect the environment, the process of extracting these materials may harm those handling this waste.

Refurbishment is a viable alternative to the e-waste problem. In refurbishment, usable parts of a machine are removed, repaired and reused. Several companies such as Dell, HP and IBM and non-government bodies collect e-waste and refurbish the equipment, and sell it at a lower price.

### Reuse

Reusing old equipment helps to decrease demand for new products, which in turn decreases costs and environmental damage by decreasing electronic waste. Used computers can be sold at lower prices or redeployed within organizations, depending on the requirement of a particular department or individual.

## Reduce

Another option to reducing e-waste is to decrease the IT hardware that is purchased by an organization. One of the things to keep in mind while procuring is to purchase only enough hardware and software to support the current needs of the organization.

Personal computers also have a direct effect on the user since the human beings adapt to long hours of computer usage instead of vice versa. Scientists have proven that there are several health hazards of excessive computing. Personal computers fuel the carbon emissions indirectly and pollute the environment, affect health and increase the carbon footprint.

Other personal computing consumables such as paper, printer cartridges and other equipment contribute to the environmental destruction. Paper- one of the largest consumable of a computer is manufactured by cutting down trees. Paper manufacturing is one of the most wasteful and polluting of industries (Anzovin, 1993). Deforestation compounds the problem of pollution since forests are the lungs of our world rejuvenating the environment with life sustaining oxygen.

Going paperless is an organizational decision that can help to reduce the damage to the environment as well as reduce costs. Handling paper can account for 30% of your organization's overhead (Velte, Velte and Elsenpeter, 2008). Gartner, 1997 reports that an average document is copied 9-11 times at cost of US$ 32. To file a document it costs US$ 25 and to retrieve a misfiled document is US$ 153. Scanning and storing documents as PDF files, using electronic billing, electronic data interchange (EDI) and intranets can reduce costs in the long run, save storage space, improve efficiency and decrease damage to the environment

by reducing the number of trees that are cut to produce paper.

Green Computing includes the deployment of energy efficient servers, peripherals and central processing units with reduced resource utilization. This equipment should be manufactured through a green manufacturing supply chain management process and should be disposed off in a proper manner. There are several steps to promoting green computing practises in the workplace-

## Procurement

The procurement of hardware and software which has been manufactured through a green supply chain management process is the first step of green computing. Several certification programs such as Electronic Product Environmental Assessment Tool (EPEAT) evaluate electronic products according to three tiers of environmental performance: bronze, silver and gold. RoHS (Restriction of Hazardous Substances) laws ensure that products are manufactured by environmentally responsible processes. The first government initiative towards enforcing green computing law was in the US in 1992 when they pioneered a program called the Energy Star. It was started by the Environment Protection Agency (EPA) to promote energy efficiency in all hardware such as printers, laptops and personal computers. Energy star computers can automatically power down when not in use which reduces their energy usage by 60-70% and this could eventually save enough energy to power a whole town and reduce emissions of 5 million cars. Energy Star is the most well known program for certifying energy efficient products in the US. Energy Star exists for computers, monitors, printers, scanners and all-in-ones. Understanding energy certifications before purchasing equipment is an important step in the green procurement process.

Thin clients use the server for processing activities and are mainly used for input and output between the server. Fat clients do most of the processing and then transfer the results to the server. Using thin clients helps to improve the business process continuity since there is lower chance of hardware failure, and lower chances of virus infection or malware infection. Other benefits include lower hardware costs, increased efficiency, lower energy consumption, easier hardware failure management, operability in hostile environments and ease of upgrade, less noise and less disposed off equipment.

Using blade servers is another environmentally friendly decision. Blade servers occupy 35-45% of space less than ordinary servers, consume less energy, lower management costs and use simplified cabling which allows for easier cooling (Velte, Velte and Elsenpeter, 2008).

## Economical Usage of Power in the Work Place

According to Gartner, 2007 information and communications technology accounts for 2% of global carbon dioxide emissions, which is roughly equivalent of what the airline industry produces.

US businesses spent 4-10% of their IT budgets on energy. Gartner predicts that this will rise fourfold in the next 5 years (Velte, Velte and Elsenpeter, 2008). The first step of economical power usage is to study the power usage patterns using power monitoring software such as IBM PowerExecutive for data centers which provides tools to manage and monitor power consumption accurately. Backing up data excessively (known as Data De-duplication) can also be wasteful. Virtualization reduces the number of servers that are used and hence helps to reduce power consumption. Low power consuming computers, equipment such as monitors, printers etc. which can be used on low energy settings are a boon to the environment.

## Work Practices

Work should be grouped in hard blocks of time which leaves hardware free at times. The use of paper should be minimized and recycled paper must be used. Use of Notebook computers should be encouraged instead of desktop computers as often as possible. LCD monitors should be used instead of cathode ray monitors.

Other than carbon neutrality and recycling programs, Dell is looking to include more green products. Having created the world's first fully recyclable PC in 1992, Dell continues with this trend as they have decided to do away with mercury-containing LCD laptop displays. Instead, they are creating LED screens, requiring less power and containing no harmful mercury. With a large percentage of Dell sales coming from corporations, this initiative resonates well as companies are looking to adopt green technologies (Techweb, 2008). Furthermore, these screens are lighter, reducing transportation costs as the product is shipped to the consumer (Hachman, 2008). Creating stronger relations with government officials has aided them in decreasing costs and has the potential to take advantage of potential "green" incentives, such as tax breaks, that many governments are creating. Furthermore, moving manufacturing to 3PL providers will allow Dell to choose providers that are more environmentally-conscious and have created or adopted green supply chain initiatives.

Several universities such as that of Buffalo, New York initiated several green computing practises at their campuses to save energy and ultimately the costs of computing (Simpson, 1994).

## DATA CENTRES

Data Centres are facilities to store data, telecommunication systems and associated systems. Data

Centres have their origin in the huge computer systems of the past. Since housing so much infrastructure at one place leads to the generation of significant amounts of heat, data centres have to be kept cool at all times. This contributes significantly to the power bills of the corporation. Earlier electricity was treated as an overhead expense however with the rising cost of power electricity requires its own specific strategy (Ohara, 2008). According to the US Environmental Protection Agency (EPA), data centre energy efficiency report, in 2006, the total amount of power used by data centres represented approximately 1.5% of total US electricity consumption. Ohara, (2008) recommends a series of steps required to establish green data centres. The first step is to study the current electricity usage pattern and determine which equipment consumes the maximum amount of energy. Unfortunately there is no clear break up of energy consumption patterns in the monthly bill. A data centre consumes 10 times the power of an ordinary work place and therefore even minor improvements result in significant savings in the power bill. Electricity consumption monitoring equipment though expensive can help to save electricity in the long run. Settings on the server equipment can be adjusted to run them on the optimum power configuration.

The second step is to garner executive support to establish a green data centre. This too unfortunately is not always available. However certain norms are available for energy consumption at data centres which one should follow. One of the practises followed by the risk averse industry is to buy excessive computing hardware which contributes to waste. Executives should calculate the 'watts per performance unit' to get a clear measure of the energy consumed. It is best to have a team which will be responsible for implementing green norms in the organization.

Even the location of data centres matters. Racks should not have one side facing north-south and the other facing south-north. So air that cools one side cannot cool the other side effectively

(Ohara, 2008). Outside air can be used to cool datacenters.

Green data centres are the buzzword today. Green data centres should have lower power consumption and heat output, configured to reduce cooling requirements in data centres, meet government directives regarding construction and recycling, are manufactured by suppliers that have a green supply chain and come from socially responsible suppliers.

## VIRTUALIZATION

Virtualization is defined as the process of running multiple virtual operating systems on one set of the physical hardware. By consolidating multiple servers into virtualized servers, a great deal of energy required to run the server can be saved. In addition, energy consumption required to cool the servers is also reduced.

Virtualization helps to save costs by reducing hardware. By consolidating servers, reducing downtime and improving application performance and freeing up critical resources, virtualization helps to save up to 80% of running costs.

There are several other advantages of server virtualization. Users can work remotely using a WAN link. Server virtualization can also help to provide standard enterprise environment across the organizations desktops. Virtual servers combine deployment software with preconfigured deployment making it easier to introduce new services and applications faster and easier than if they are rolled out conventionally. It is possible to move legacy systems from an old server to a new server, which will consume less energy and help to save costs.

While ideally it seems that having one virtualized server will reduce both energy and hardware costs, one should be cautious in consolidating servers since it may run the risk of having an extended outrage or losing everything in case the server fails.

Several virtualization softwares are offered by VMWare. VMWare Infrastructure 3 comes in three editions such as Starter, Standard and Enterprise.

Microsoft offers Windows Server 2008 operating system with Hyper-V technology. Using Hyper-V, companies can to reduce its centralized physical server holdings by 60 percent. Fewer servers will reduce the server management workload. To attain further efficiencies, the IT staff Microsoft System Center Virtual Machine Manager 2008 applications are also available (Microsoft Website, 2008).

## CLOUD COMPUTING

Cloud computing is a cutting-edge technology which involves using the internet (cloud) to allow users to access technology enabled services. A cloud is a pool of virtualized computer resources. In order to access a cloud one only needs an internet connection and a computer (Boss, Malladi, Quan, Legregni & Hall, 2007).

Cloud computing is a way of increasing capacity or add capabilities without investing in new infrastructure, training new staff or licensing new softwares. Cloud computing involves subscription based or pay-per-use service that in real time over the internet, extends Information Technologies's existing capabilities (Gruman & Knorr, 2008). "It is a paradigm in which information is permanently stored in servers on the Internet and cached temporarily on clients that include desktops, entertainment centers, table computers, notebooks, wall computers, handhelds, etc." (Hewitt, 2008). Cloud computing helps to save both hardware and software costs. By pooling resources into large clouds, companies can drives down costs and increases utilization by delivering resources only for as long as those resources are needed. Cloud computing allows individuals, teams, and organizations to streamline procurement processes and eliminate the need to duplicate certain computer

administrative skills related to setup, configuration, and support.

Since cloud computing is an emerging technology, it is yet to gain the popularity that other applications such as the internet have achieved. Several companies such as Amazon and IBM are at the fore front of implementing this technology. IBM has opened thirteen cloud computing centers in emerging economies in addition to its existing nine centers (ComputerWire Staff, 2008).

## TELECOMMUTING AND TELEWORKING

Telecommuting i.e. working from home or a location instead of an office on certain days of the year has become a global trend, increasingly practised by leading organizations in the world. Telecommuting allows regular employees to work from home on certain days or for certain hours. Hewitt Associates, a human resource consulting firm, conducted a survey of 936 large companies and found that 32% of these companies offered telecommuting opportunities in 2004 (Velte, Velte and Elsenpeter, 2008). It helps to reduce green house emissions related to travel, saves real estate costs, electricity costs, improves overall productivity and increases employee satisfaction levels. Telecommuting is suited to certain types of tasks and requires a certain method of monitoring workers. Sun Microsystems saved US $ 255 million over 4 years by telecommuting (Velte, Velte and Elsenpeter, 2008). Telecommuting practises help to improve the work-life balance of employees and has been adopted by several companies such as IBM and Citibank. According to a study telecommuting has become a trend in USA. Research organization IDC stated that 8.9 million Americans worked at home at least 3 days a month in 2004 (Velte, Velte and Elsenpeter, 2008).

Teleworking is a phenomenon whereby the employee does not have a permanent physical position of work. He may be working at a location but however only owns a locker. Knowledge or technology based jobs are suited for teleworking. Certain jobs such as medical transcriptions, web designing, software development and accounting are suited for this phenomenon. A requirement of this form of work is that the person undertaking the job should be capable of working with less or no supervision. The advent of technology such as video conferencing, virtual private networks and broadband access has provided impetus to this phenomenon. Teleworking has become popular in several countries, due to its obvious advantages of flexible hours which can be used to engage in other business activities, manage the family especially small children and the elderly and other perks such as a stress free work environment. For the company hiring tele-workers the most obvious advantage is the savings on rentals, costs of running operations and supporting a large staff. There is flexibility in terms of the number of people on role since teleworkers often engage in ad hoc projects when manpower is required urgently. However there are adjustments issues in teleworking and agencies observe that self starters, with good knowledge of the job and good communicators are most successful at this kind of a job.

Telecommuting and teleworking help in cutting down the costs in running an operation. They also help to reduce the number of people who commute to a certain destination for work, decreasing the carbon emissions from travelling. While these savings seem paltry, when adopted on a large scale, the savings add up.

## GREEN ENERGY

Energy produced from renewable sources such as the sun, wind and water is known as green energy. Companies must endeavour to run their operations from producing and consuming green energy. Wal-Mart is an example of a company that has started running its operations on renewable energy.

## GREEN ORGANIZATION

In February 2008, Computerworld conducted a survey to study the adoption of green practises in the organization. The main ideas tested in the survey can be summarized as follows-

1. Explicit, vigorous commitment to energy efficiency by top executives (e.g., the CEO)
2. Purchasing practices that favor energy-efficient products
3. A program to recycle unused/discarded high-tech equipment (e.g., old PCs and monitors)
4. Encouragement of telecommuting and provide the necessary equipment & support
5. Installation of energy-efficient HVAC and building automation controls in the past 12 months
6. Reduction of IT equipment energy consumption by at least 5% in the past 12 months
7. Improvement of IT equipment energy efficiency by at least 5% in the past 12 months
8. Implementation of server virtualization to reduce the number of servers needed
9. Revision of its data center layout (or design) to reduce power demand
10. Usage of alternative energy supplies (e.g. solar, wind) to provide power to IT facilities or systems

Several IT companies such as IBM, Dell and non-IT companies such as Wal-Mart have adopted the green computing paradigm. What remains to be seen is whether the green computing paradigm emerges from the haloed heights to adoption by small and medium enterprises. There are several examples of environment friendly practises adopted by big businesses which can be emulated by small and medium sized enterprises. The government can support the green information technology movement by providing grants, consultancy support and advice to businesses.

## COSTS AND BENEFITS OF GREEN COMPUTING AND GREEN PRODUCT DESIGN

Every business innovation or improvement in a process or a function is accompanied by a cost which can prove to be a big deterrent in its adoption. The costs and benefits of adopting green information technology are varied in number. Unlike other environment friendly practises, green computing results in providing a financial incentive to its adopters. As discussed earlier, the cost of cooling data centres is exorbitant. Designing energy efficient data centres not only decreases the cost of cooling the hardware but also leads to savings in running the data centre. Leading companies such as IBM and HP which offer consultancy in these fields provide evidence of the financial success of green data centres. Company X, a manufacturer of scuba diving equipment is interested in saving energy by decreasing the amount used to cool its datacenters. Working with large consultancies has helped it to decrease costs significantly.

The financial benefits of telecommuting and tele-working are also evident directly. Telecommuting creates a win-win situation for the employee as well as the employer. It helps the employee to maintain a work-life balance, while helping the environment by saving fuel required for the commute. Teleworking allows the employee to work under flexible conditions. Not only are the hiring companies able to save on energy costs they can also maintain flexibility in their work force by hiring people on a tele-working arrangement.

Green computing practices in the work place are simple to follow and enforce. By actively engaging employees and enforcing simple rules such as use of recycled paper, regulations for use of personal computers, laptops and other hardware, companies can drive across the message of environment friendliness. Though the savings seem paltry as compared to the budget of a large office, the message of environment friendliness permeates the organization and helps the employees to

be engaged in a common agenda.

Virtualization is gaining popularity nowadays. Though the costs of engaging expertise to perform virtualization and investing in the required software and hardware are present, nevertheless the benefits accrued from savings in hardware and power savings are significant.

Cloud computing is a new technology which is being implemented by a few companies. However mass proliferation of this technology is yet to occur. By reducing the amount of hardware required, cloud computing indirectly helps to reduce the environmental destruction.

The cost of recycling materials is borne by large corporations who indirectly gain from the publicity of being environment friendly. While the cost of collecting used laptops may be borne by Dell, this practise helps Dell to prove to its customers that it is an environment friendly company and in turn may help to increase brand loyalty amongst its followers. Recycling of used cartridges collected from offices by HP is another example of green management. Using green energy in its supply chain, is another example of a green practise that has won hearts for Wal-Mart amongst its customers. While several such examples can be found in our daily lives, green computing requires the support of both government and non-government organizations in order to attain success.

## GOVERNMENT INITIATIVES TO PROMOTE GREEN COMPUTING

Several world organizations such as UN have formulated policies and legislation to solve the E-Waste problem through a program known as StEP (Solving the E-Waste Problem). The Basel Action Network (BAN) located in Seattle, Washington operates globally to reduce the impact of e-waste and promote green, toxic-free design for consumer products. EU has initiated the Waste Electrical and Electronic Equipment (WEEE) Directive. Restriction of Hazardous Substance Directive

(RoHS) adopted in February 2003 by the European Union aims at restricts the use of lead, mercury, cadmium, Hexavalent chromium, Polybrominated biphenyls (PBBs) and Polybrominated diphenyl ether (PBDE) in the manufacture of certain types of electronic equipments. In addition to this the individual EU countries have passed their own environmental legislation.

Environmental legislation is also implemented by individual countries such as the United States. EPEAT, National Computer Recycling Act have been instituted at the country level. The states have implemented their individual environmental legislation. Different provinces of Canada have adopted different e-waste laws.

Japan has implemented its own WEEE standards and views the products end-of-life as another step in its lifecycle and reuses old parts into new machines. Recycling is undertaken by two large recycling companies run by electronics manufacturers. China has also initiated its own RoHS program known as the China RoHS. Korea adopted the Korea RoHS in 2007 which requires restrictions on the use of hazardous materials, design for efficient recycling, collection and recycling of WEEE and recycling of vehicles at the end-of-life.

## IMPLICATIONS OF GREEN INFORMATION TECHNOLOGY

It is the irony of our times that the technologies that enabled human beings to advance rapidly may also become the cause of our annihilation. The invention of the nuclear bomb, sophisticated weaponery, submarines and machine guns may kill millions and even lead to the end of mankind. However another and equally threatening cause of extinction of the human race is the proliferation of technology. Technology that has been the vehicle of growth has also lead to increasing consumption of fossil fuels and other natural resources.

Disposal of tons of non-bio degradable materials has been polluting our rivers, seas and converting arable land into wastage dumps. Human beings are using up natural resources such as forests and fuels faster than they can be replinished. In other words we have run into an 'ecological debt' (Press Assoc., 2008). As consumption rises, the risks of environmental destruction become more real.

In this scenario, large corporations and individuals alike must respond by becoming more environmentally concious. Several measures can be adopted to provide a sustainable and green computing environment by adopting and implementing old and new ideas. While virtualization, cloud computing are cutting edge technology, telecommuting, teleworking, recycling have been accepted by organizations all over the world. Governments must work with organizations to chart the right course of action to decrease the carbon footprint. New ideas such as carbon credits traded by companies in international markets can be used to control and regulate the market. Through successful implementation of the green computing paradigm firms can successfully decrease their carbon footprint and contribute to decreasing the harm wrought to the environment.

## REFERENCES

Anzovin, S. (1993). *The green PC: Making choices that make a difference.* Windcrest/McGraw-Hill.

Boss, G., Malladi, P., Quan, D., Legregni, L., & Hall, H. (2007). *Cloud computing.* Retrieved from download.boulder.ibm.com/.../hipods/Cloud_computing_wp_final_8Oct.pdf

Butner, K., Geuder, D., & Hittner, J. (2008). *Mastering carbon management-balancing trade-offs to optimize supply chain efficiencies.* IBM Institute for Business Value.

ComputerWire Staff. (2008). *IBM opens four cloud computing centers.* Retrieved from rshttp://uk.news.yahoo.com/cwire/20080929/ttc-ibm-opens-four-cloud-computing-cente-78e70a2.html

Gartner Hype Cycle. (2008). Retrieved from http://www.techcrunch.com/wp-content/uploads/2008/08/gartner-hype-cycle1.jpg

Green Computing Staff. (2008). Retrieved from http://www.greenercomputing.com/news/2008/09/24/hp-posts-supply-chain-emissions-data-urges-it-cos-do-more

*Greener, leaner IT lowers costs, boosts efficiency.* Retrieved from http://www-304.ibm.com/jct03004c/businesscenter/smb/us/en/newsletterarticle/gcl_xmlid/131487?&ca=smbGreen031108&tactic=html&me=W&met=inli&re=smbNewsArticle1

Gruman, G., & Knorr, E. (2008). *What cloud computing really means.* Retrieved from http://www.infoworld.com/article/08/04/07/15FE-cloud-computing-reality_1.html

Hachman, M. (2008). *Dell shifting all laptops to LED backlights.* Retrieved from Extremetech.com

Hewitt, C. (2008). ORGs for scalable, robust, privacy-friendly client cloud computing. *IEEE Internet Computing, 12*(5), 96–99. doi:10.1109/MIC.2008.107

Hu, J. (2006, June). Balance of product greening cost and benefit proceedings of service operations and logistics, and informatics. *SOLI '06, IEEE International Conference* (pp. 1146-1150).

Khiewnavawongsa, S. (2007). *Green power to the supply chain.* Retrieved from http://www.tech.purdue.edu/it/GreenSupplyChainManagement.cfm

Microsoft Website. (2008). Retrieved from http://www.microsoft.com/virtualization/casestudy-kentuckydoe.mspx

Noronha, C. (2008). *19-square-mile ice sheet breaks loose in Canada.* Retrieved from http://sg.news.yahoo.com/ap/20080904/twl-arctic-ice-shelf-1be00ca.html

Ohara, D. (2007). *Green computing-build a green data centre by green computing.* Retrieved from http://www.osisoft.com/Resources/Articles/Green+Computing++Build+a+Green+Datacenter.htm

Plambeck, E. L. (2007). *The greening of Wal-Mart's supply chain.* Retrieved from http://www.scmr.com/article/CA6457969.html

Press Assoc. (2008). *Nature's budget has run out.* Retrieved from http://uk.news.yahoo.com/pressass/20080923/tuk-nature-s-budget-has-run-out-6323e80.html

Search Data Center. (2007). *What is green computing?* Retrieved from http://searchdatacenter.techtarget.com/sDefinition/0,sid80_gci1246959,00.html

Simpson, W. (1994). *Guide to green computing.* Retrieved from http://wings.buffalo.edu/ubgreen/content/programs/energyconservation/guide_computing.html#sec04

Srivastara, S. K. (2007). Green supply-chain management: A state-of-the-art literature review. *International Journal of Management Reviews, 9*(1), 53–80. doi:10.1111/j.1468-2370.2007.00202.x

Stonebraker, P. W., & Liao, J. (2006). Supply chain integration: Exploring product and environmental coningencies. *Supply Chain Management, 11*(1), 34–43. doi:10.1108/13598540610642457

Sushil. (1997). Flexible systems management: An evolving paradigm. *Systems Research and Behavioural Science, 14*(4), 259-275.

Techweb. (2008, September 24). *Dell to move to greener notebook displays*. Techweb.

Udomleartprasert, P. (2004). Roadmap to green supply chain electronics: Design for manufacturing implementation and management. *Asian Green Electronics, International IEEE Conference* (pp. 169-173).

Velte, T., Velte, A., & Elsenpeter, R. C. (2008). *Green IT: Reduce your information system's environmental impact while adding to the bottom line*. McGraw-Hill.

What is a Carbon Footprint? Retrieved from http://www.carbonfootprint.com/carbonfootprint.html

What is Green Computing? Retrieved from http://www.tech-faq.com/green-computing.shtml Wikipedia-Data Center. (2008). *Data center*. Retrieved from http://en.wikipedia.org/wiki/Data_center

Wikipedia-Carbon Footprint. (2008). Retrieved from http://en.wikipedia.org/wiki/Carbon_footprint

Wikipedia-Telecommuting. (2008). *Telecommuting*. Retrieved from http://en.wikipedia.org/wiki/Telecommuting

Wikipedia-Virtualization. (2008). Retrieved from http://en.wikipedia.org/wiki/Virtualization

# Chapter 14
# Swift Trust and Self–Organizing Virtual Communities

**Stephane Ngo Mai**
*University of Nice Sophia Antipolis, France*

**Alain Raybaut**
*University of Nice Sophia Antipolis, France*

## ABSTRACT

*Numerous communities of experts supported by firms tend nowadays to form an important part of corporate social capital. Composed of free will agents, those communities aim at creating knowledge through cognitive interactions and heavily rely on ICTs to free themselves from many constraints. Previous studies of such virtual groupings pointed out that their organization features were not similar to market nor hierarchy. Consequently, neither price nor contract or authority are used in such communities which rather seem to self-organize. Instead of traditional economic concepts, notions such as trust and leadership are advanced to explain the functioning of these virtual assemblies. This contribution proposed a tentative model which attempts to grasp some of the empirical aspects of these communities. More precisely, we were interested in the relation between trust, performance, and organizational feature within a given virtual group. Simulations of the model with different functions of swift trust display various organizational structures similar to those described by stylized facts. The organizational attributes range from pure collaborative communities to pure competitive ones. Intermediate cases also emerge with the appearance of leader(s).*

## INTRODUCTION

In knowledge-based economies organizations may exist because the conduct of any complex projects necessitate to coordinate *distributed* knowledge and competencies. This 'Simonian' justification of the firm has been recently confirmed by numerous empirical studies stating that most technological and organizational knowledge is created by combination of pre-existent knowledge. Since knowledge is basically held by agents with limited cognitive capacities the conduct of complex project is, at first, a process of searching and coordinating the adequate competencies. One consequence of such

DOI: 10.4018/978-1-60566-723-2.ch014

'production of knowledge by means of knowledge' is the apparition of codified modules of competencies to be exchanged across firms and sectors. Indeed firms do not necessarily possess all knowledge and competencies to manage new projects. Competencies maps, knowledge management platforms, electronic cooperative tools as well as the increase of R&D inter firms cooperation agreements during the past decades are in line with such a perspective. The diffusion of ICTs to that respect facilitates the creation and activation of networks of experts but in return might impose new constraints to the evolution of organizations.

Among those networks, virtual communities involving several potential electronically interacting free will agents represent an important case (cf.e.g. Pantelli N., Chiasson M. (eds) (2008)). Acting as technological watch, learning areas as well as coordinating devices those communities have been identified as strategic assets in promoting creation and diffusion processes. It is worth noticing that numerous communities composed of experts supported by firms tend to form nowadays an important part of their social capital. From the economic point of view it is not quite clear if such communities are reducible to standard form of allocating and coordinating resources devices such as traditional markets and organizations distinction. If they seem to perform similar tasks - although on a lower scale - they do not heavily rely on neither price or contracts nor pure hierarchical mechanisms. Notions such as trust, beliefs, imitation and leadership have been suggested to explain some specific coordination processes (cf e.g. Cohendet, Diani 2003). Much more empirical and theoretical studies have probably to be devoted to this issue in order to have better understanding of the exact nature and role of such communities This chapter is dedicated to a further understanding of the dynamics of a virtual community of knowledge and competencies sharing. We do not here directly address the important issue of individual strategic interest in

participating to such communities nor the incentive scheme or economic consequences of such networks (cf. e.g. Cowan, Jonard, Zimmermann 2003). We rather try to concentrate some attention to the evolution of bilateral interactions in line with knowledge sharing performance within a virtual community in relation with the trust issue. We are then interested in the nature of relationships within the internal community organization, be they hierarchical, reciprocal or competitive, which eventually result from peculiar conditions on the interaction of trust and cognitive distance. Indeed the development of ICTs tools, thanks for geographical constraints freeing, allows for virtual communities to emerge with a large potential spectrum in regard of competencies to be included in the groupings (enhancement of either horizontal or vertical cognitive division of labor) but this neighborhood release has also been identified as an important factor in trust determination. Since different aspects of trust has been recognized to play an important role in the establishment and permanence of bilateral interactions, the result of the overall internal dynamics of a virtual community is still unclear. In order to try to cope with this issue we will first present some stylized facts about virtual communities in line with our questioning and then present a heuristic model and the tentative implied results.

## VIRTUAL COMMUNITIES, PATTERNS AND TRUST: SOME STYLIZED FACTS

Recent empirical studies in the field of economic and management sciences seem now to converge to the idea that contrarily to what was previously thought in the 90's virtual communities are not similar to 'market mechanism that allocates people and resources to problems and projects in a decentralized manner' (cf.e.g. Baker 1992). Indeed, as noticed by Ahuja and Carley (1999) premature research suggested that virtual communities tended to be non hierarchical and decentralized due to intensive ICTs utilization and promptly concluded that such communities where mainly important devices in information management. More thorough attention devoted to the real functioning of such groupings has shown the possibility to establish a typology of communities in accordance with their objectives; information management appears then to be a quite small sub case while knowledge creation and diffusion seems to be the general feature. Beyond categories such as communities of practices, epistemic communities and virtual communities some common features have been stressed (cf.e.g. Pantelli N. and Chiasson M. (eds) (2008), Gensollen M. (2003). Quite important are (i) the autonomy of volunteer participating agents, (ii) the bilateral communication mode, (iii) the nature of the virtual collective object, (iv) the role of trust. Third, the internal organizations of virtual communities seem to have some relationships with the previous features and in particular with the bilateral communication mode and form of trust. This paper is intended to precisely concentrate on such a point.

One important characteristic of virtual communities is to heavily rely on informal communication since global formal rules are not fully defined. Contrarily to formal communication, informal ones are peer oriented, strongly interactive and potentially characterized by a self-organizating process of the internal architecture of relationships. Evidence of both centralization and hierarchy as well as decentralization and pure reciprocity or intermediate cases have been found in virtual communities. The important point is to stress the emergent propriety of such architectures which strongly differentiate virtual groupings from traditional organizations in which hierarchy for instance is included in a given authority structure based on status differences. As stated by Ahuja and Carley (1999), 'we found no evidence that the formal and informal structures in the virtual organization were indistinguishable. Rather this work suggests that in virtual organizations the

decoupling of the authority structure from the communication structures results in a decoupling of power from information'.

Since the concept of community here at sketch relies on volunteers, the commitment of members of such groupings has been largely acknowledged. This in turn links with some trust notion which can be defined following Gambetta (1988) as a particular level of the subjective probability with which an agent or group of agents assesses that another agent or group of agents will perform a particular action, both before he (they) can monitor such action and in a context in which *it affects his (their) own action*. Trust then conveys a certain idea of reciprocity. Two important remarks should be here formulated.

First, trust is a form of beliefs and as such it is difficult for agents to observe signals from others. This is why much literature on trust building stresses the importance of history and small steps learning processes. One can doubt that this kind of 'trust need touch' definition could be applied to all virtual communities since many of them are characterized by no common history in bilateral relationships, strong uncertainty about long term viability, weak involvement, free entry and exist, no frequent face to face etc.. In order to overcome this problem some authors proposed on empirical basis some notion of 'swift trust' (cf.e.g. Meyerson, Weick, Kramer (1996), Javerpaa, Leidner (1999)). Swift trust theory is mainly concerned by how trust is maintained via electronic communication in a priori finite life span virtual organizations. The main idea is whereas traditional conceptualizations of trust are based on interpersonal relationships, swift trust substitutes to interpersonal dimensions broad categorical social structures and action. In other words such a notion takes into account that virtual communities involving agents with no necessary common past or future, with cultural, geographical and skill differences can not rely on traditional trust building. They rather depend on a special form of trust which strongly builds on pre-existent stereotypes and most interesting for us on current action of the community. This swift trust appears to be very fragile and temporal. An empirical analysis performed on 29 cases showed that one third of the sample experimented transitions from high trust to low trust or conversely.

Secondly, the notion of reciprocity involved in the generic definition of trust does not necessarily stands for symmetric positive influence. Intensity of incidence can vary as well as benefits As soon as pure hierarchies have been empirically identified within virtual communities one must take into account that bilateral reciprocity involved in some notion of trust is blurred and also depends on global individual objectives. One can think of situations such as the acceptance by some agents or groups of agents of a hierarchy with some leaders having a quite negative or positive impact on everybody else in terms of opportunity costs for instance. In that case the negative effects must be balanced by some interest produced by counterparts. Reputation effects as 'being known as a member of an esteemed community' might illustrate such counterparts. That is to say that so-called reciprocity in trust should include many dimensions in order to explain why agents do accept say hierarchy and centralization in virtual communities primarily defined as groupings of autonomous and volunteers agents.

## NETWORK CONNECTIVITY, SWIFT TRUST AND HIERARCHY IN VIRTUAL COMMUNITIES: AN ILLUSTRATIVE MODEL

From a modeling point of view, virtual communities have been acknowledged to belong to complex systems which share the common feature of organizing themselves in networks. The architecture of connectivity is a convenient way to classify such systems. While scale free and small worlds systems have been sometimes utilized to characterize virtual communities, we are rather here interested in

hierarchical systems. Since virtual organizations have often be considered as evolutionary systems we chose a standard replicator system to model the dynamics of such a grouping of electronically interacting autonomous and volunteer agents. That is to say that the overall evolution of participation of a given number of experts to a specific community is driven by some reference to the average growth rate of participation. We are then specifically interested in the dynamics of the interaction matrix which represents the evolution of influences between agents. Those bilateral influences are then not supposed given once for all but depends on the current activity of the community. More precisely we design two complementary procedures to define the interaction matrix. The first one intends to describe the matching process between agents and consists for an agent to maintain a link with an other in the community if he (she) gets a benefit in doing so, taking into account a network effect and a cost of participation. The second procedure aims at introducing the idea of swift trust functions which depends on current actions. This determines the nature and intensity of the links between agents and heavily rely on the relative rate of participation of agents. The overall performance of the community is then associated with the characteristics of both the swift trust functions and the resulting interaction matrix. (See Figure 1)

Let us consider a set $N$ of $n$ agents $i$, endowed with different kinds of knowledge or competencies $i = 1, \ldots n$ located on a one-dimensional lattice. Define by $x_i(t)$ the level of activation or participation of $i$ at time $t$ in the virtual team, where $\forall t$, $\sum_{i=1}^{n} x_i(t) = 1$. We suppose that a potential virtual community exists and composed of $n$ agents.

The level of production achieved by this virtual network is given by:

$$Q(t) = \sum_{i=1}^{n} \left( \frac{1}{\phi} [X_i(t)]^{\phi} \right) \tag{1}$$

*Figure 1.*

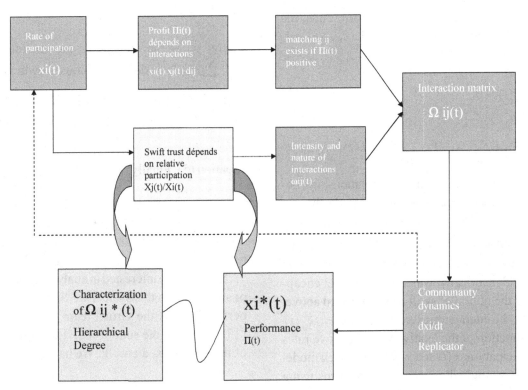

with, $0 < \varphi < 1$. Define, for $i = 1, \ldots n$ $X_i(t)$ by:

$$X_i(t) = \sum_{j \neq i} x_i(t) x_j(t) d_{ij} + x_i(t) \qquad (2)$$

where, $d_{ij}$ stands for a distance between $i$ and $j$[1]

This captures the fact that each agents creates knowledge according to his own participation rate to the virtual team $x_i(t)$, and in relation with his interactions with other agents, $\sum_{j \neq i} x_i(t) x_j(t) d_{ij}$ We consider that $d_{ij}$ stands for some cognitive distance between the different kinds of knowledge owned by the agents. We assume that distance plays a positive role in the process of knowledge creation, but is also costly.

Consequently, fixed and variable costs are necessary to implement this network and to ensure its smooth running. This cost function is the following:

$$\Upsilon(t) = \sum_{i=1}^{n} \left( \frac{1}{\theta} L(t) \left[ X_i(t) \right]^{\theta} \right) + \Psi \qquad (3)$$

where, $\theta > 1$ and $\Psi \geq 0$ stands for a fixed cost; $L(t)$ is a decreasing function in $t$ which captures the fact that the cost of collaboration with different distributed competencies decreases over time due to a learning process. In the rest of the paper, we suppose that:

$$L(t) = \varsigma + \xi Exp[-vt] \qquad (4)$$

where, $v, \varsigma, \xi$ are positive parameters.

We suppose that the matrix $C = \left\{ c_{ij} \right\}_{n \times n}$ encodes the connection topology: $c_{ij} = c_{ji} = 1$ if $j$ and $i$ are connected, otherwise $c_{ij} = c_{ji} = 0$, and $c_{ii} = 0$ for all $i$. We consider that this connection topology is determined, for each agent $i = 1, \ldots n$, by the value $\prod_{j=1,\ldots n}^{i}(t)$ created by its participation to the virtual team. Accordingly, we simply suppose that the connection-set should ensure to each agent a strictly positive profit. Thus, the structure of connections of $i$, $i = 1, \ldots n$ to $j = 1, \ldots n$, with $i \neq j$ satisfies:

$$\Pi^i_{\Sigma j \neq i}(t) > 0 \qquad (5)$$

where, $\Pi^i_{\Sigma j \neq i}(t) = \frac{1}{\phi}[X_i(t)]^\phi - \frac{L(t)}{\theta}[X_i(t)]^\theta$.

The nature and intensity of relationships between connected agents are determined by the matrix $\Omega_t = \{\omega_{ij}(t)\}_{n \times n}$. In line with Yokozawa and Hara (1999) and Sakaguchi (2003) we consider that these interaction strengths are non symmetric and change dynamically, which in our model encapsulates the notion of swift trust discussed above. Indeed, the interaction exercised by $j$ over $i$, $\omega_{ij}(t)$, is a function of the relative size of the two rates of participation, $x_j(t)$ and $x_i(t)$. While such model have been studied for ecological systems using piecewise linear function of the ratio $x_j(t)$ to $x_i(t)$, we adopt here the same perspective but consider a nonlinear continuous differentiable 'swift-trust function' of this ratio $r_{ij}(t) = \frac{x_j(t)}{x_i(t)}$. Disregarding the time symbol "$t$", we suppose that:

$$\omega_{ij} = c_{ij} f(r_{ij}) \qquad (6)$$

where, $f$: $R^+ \rightarrow R$, is a continuous differentiable function. We study below the influence of different 'swift-trust functions' on the dynamics of the rates of participation $x_i$.

The dynamics of the $x_i$ obeys the following replicator equations (0.8), for $i = 1, \ldots n$. Indeed, such dynamical systems have been applied to many complex evolutionary phenomena (see e.g. Kaufman 1969, Bak and Sneppin 1993, Shapovalov A.V. and Evdokimov E.V. 1998, Yokozawa and Hara 1999, Jasen V.A.A and de Ross A.M. 2000, Sakaguchi 2003).

$$\frac{dx_i}{dt} = x_i \left( g_{io} + h_i - \bar{h}_i \right) \qquad (7)$$

where, $g_{i0}$ is the exogenous growth rate of $i$, $h_i = \sum_j \omega_{ij} x_j$ is the endogenous growth rate of $i$ determined by the structure of interactions. Notice that the sum $j$ is taken only for the range satisfying equation (5). Finally, $\bar{h}_i = \frac{\sum_{i=1}^{n}(g_{io} + h_i)x_i}{\sum_{i=1}^{n} x_i}$ refers to the average growth rate of $i$. In addition, we suppose that $g_{i0} = g_0$, for $i = 1, \ldots n$, thus all characteristics are *a priori* equivalent in the dynamics.

Since we are interested in analyzing the impact of swift trust on this system we finally define the performance of the virtual team by total profits $\Pi^T(t)$ given by the sum of individual profits, net of the global fixed cost $\Psi$. We have:

$$\Pi^T(t) = \sum_{i=1}^{n} \Pi^i_{\Sigma j \neq i}(t) - \Psi \qquad (8)$$

In the remainder of this paper, we perform numerical simulations of equation (7).(see Sakaguchi 2003 for some hints of stability analysis with a piecewize linear function and a different network topology). The $n$ initial conditions are randomly picked-out in a neighborhood $\{-0.1, +0.1\}$ of the stationary solution $\frac{1}{n}$.

We are interested in the stationary distribution of participation rates and its related performance, in relation with the knowledge sharing network. We infer that the structure of reciprocal positive edges fits more closely with the notion of a sustained collaborative community in which trust relationships and loyalty play a key role. We consider, that the higher the number of positive reciprocal links, the less hierarchical the community. In this perspective, we compute in $t = 0$ and $t = T$, a quite standard indicator of hierarchy in organizations to measure the relative weight of mutual positive links in the graph structures (see. e.g. Ahuja M.K., Carley K.M. 1999). We have:

$$H_t = 1 - \frac{\text{Number of positive reciprocal links}}{\text{Total number of links}}$$

(9)

To complete the characterization of the community we compute a second indicator which gives the relative number of all positive links. This captures the relative degree of collaboration in the network. We define:

$$C_t = \frac{\text{Number of positive links}}{\text{Total number of links}}$$ (10)

The following results obtain, in different swift-trust settings, with the parameters shown in Table 1.

All simulations have been performed with a complete graph at the initial stage (t=0) to capture

*Table 1.*

| $n$ | $\theta$ | $\varphi$ | $\Psi$ | $v$ | $\varsigma$ | $\xi$ |
|---|---|---|---|---|---|---|
| 9 | 2 | 3/4 | 0.2 | 0.01 | 0.5 | 1 |

*Figure 2. Complete graph with positive and negative links in t = 0*

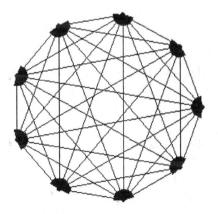

*Figure 3. Structure of $x_i$ in t=0*

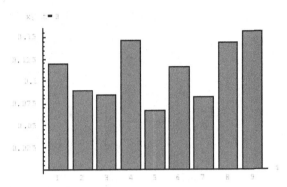

the idea of an initial existing community composed of n agents with an almost identical rate of participation $\frac{1}{n}$. Initial conditions generate then for all simulations the following graph at t = 0, although the different cases vary in the relative number of positive links. (see Figure 2)

The initial distribution of the rates of participation $x_i(t)$, $i = 1, \ldots n$, $t = 0$, for all simulations is shown in Figure 3.

## Case 1: A Collaborative and Reliable Opening Community

We are first interested in the case where most, if not all, agents are confident in the starting network. Many positive reciprocal links are then generated at the initial stage stating that the community opens on a quite collaborative basis. Moreover agents are reliable in the sense that a small increase of activity of agent j has a positive influence on the participation of agent i. Swift trust encapsulates however the idea that a switching point exists: when the rate of participation of agent j exceeds too much the rate of participation of agent i the intensity of influence of j upon i decreases to reach zero. Figure 4 depicts such a case of swift trust.

In such a setting the dynamics of the rate of participation reach a stationary state where all

*Figure 4. Swift trust*

| $\Psi(r) = Exp[-\beta r^2](\beta r^3 + \gamma r^2 + \delta r)$ | | |
|---|---|---|
| β | γ | δ |
| 0.75 | -0.35 | -0.5 |

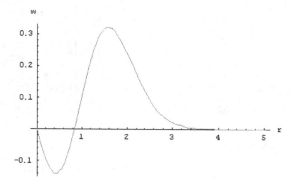

*Figure 5. Dynamics of $x_i$*

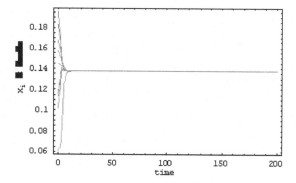

agents equally participate to the community as shown in Figure 5 and Figure 6.

Since we are also interested in the structure of interactions we show in Figure 7 and Figure 8 the graphs of links associated with the interaction matrix.

*Figure 6. Structure of $x_i$ in t = 200000*

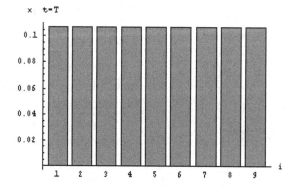

*Figure 7. The left-hand side figure display the graph structures of positive links, and the right-hand side one the graph of the negative ones, t = 0*

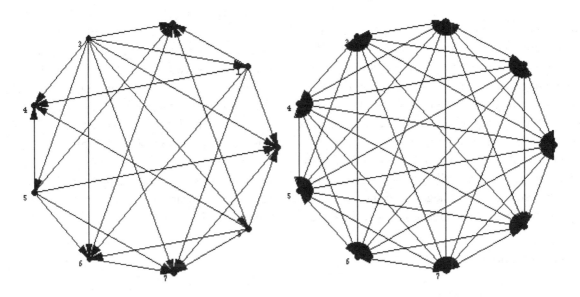

The computation of our indexes of hierarchy and collaboration shows that this case of swift trust leads to a strong decrease of hierarchy which goes from H0 = 0.72 to HF = 0 and to an increase of collaboration which goes from C0 = 0.64 to CF = 1

Meanwhile total profits generated by the community increased as shown in Figure 9.

As we will note below and in line with intuition this case of collaborative and reliable opening community leads to the best performance index.

*Figure 8. The left-hand side figure display the graph structures of positive links, and the right-hand side one the graph of the negative ones, t = 200000*

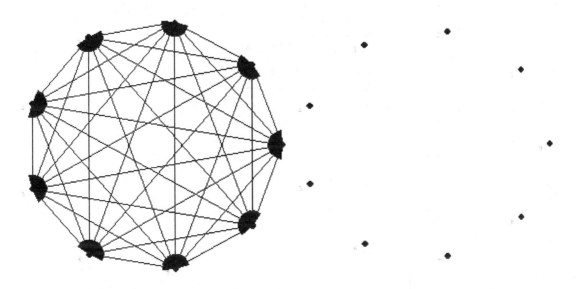

## Case 2: A Collaborative and Mistrust Opening Community

We depict here the case where most, if not all, agents are confident in the starting network. As the situation above, many positive reciprocal links are generated at the initial stage stating that the community begins with a quite collaborative basis. But on the contrary of the reliable agents conjecture we suppose here that agents are suspicious of others in the sense that a small increase of activity of agent j leads to a smaller influence on agent i which even ends up to a negative influence. Here again the idea of switching point is maintained to qualify the swift trust. Figure 10 depicts such a case of swift trust.

In such a case the dynamics of the xi reach a stationary state where only one agent still participate to the community. This means of course that the dynamics led to the failure of the collaborative network even though the opening stage was characterized by the presence of numerous positive reciprocal links. The diagrams and indexes (Figures 11, 12, 13, 14, and Table 2) describe such a situation.

Not surprisingly such a case leads to the worst situation in terms of community performance. (see Figure 15)

*Figure 9. Total profits*

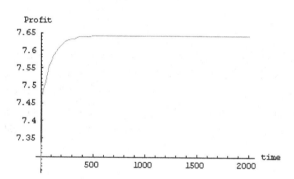

*Figure 10. Swift Trust*

| $\Psi(r) = Exp[-\beta r^2](\beta r^3 + \gamma r^2 + \delta r)$ | | |
|---|---|---|
| β | γ | δ |
| 0.75 | 075 | 0.5 |

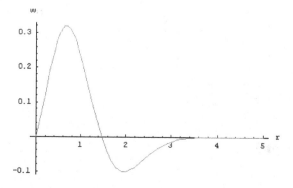

*Figure 11. Dynamics of $x_i$*

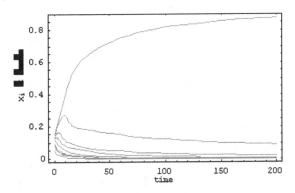

*Figure 12. Structure of $x_i$ in t = 200000*

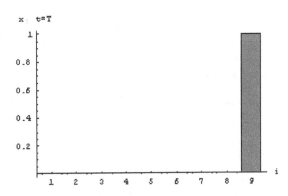

*Figure 13. The left-hand side figure display the graph structures of positive links, and the right-hand side one the graph of the negative ones, t =0*

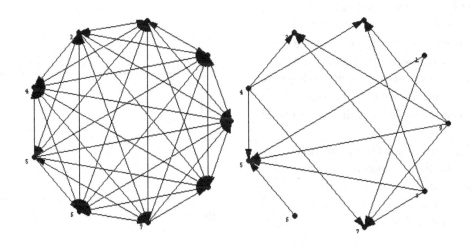

*Figure 14. The left-hand side figure display the graph structures of positive links, and the right-hand side one the graph of the negative ones, t = 200000*

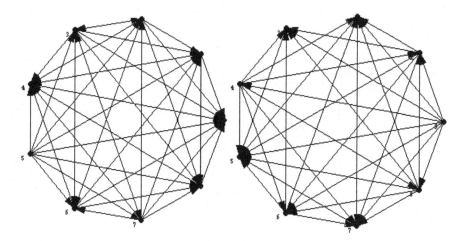

*Table 2.*

|  | t = 0 | T = Final (200000) |
|---|---|---|
| Ht | 0.41 | 1 |
| Ct | 0.79 | 0.53 |

*Figure 15. Profits*

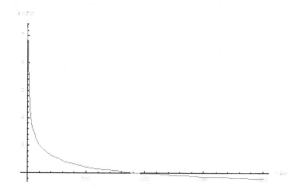

## Case 3: A Collaborative and Mistrust Opening Community with Cyclical Swift Trust

We describe here a case where hierarchy at the starting stage is near to zero associated with the idea that the highest level of trust is reached at the beginning. Moreover we suppose that the intensity of influence do not vanish with an increasing ratio of participation but rather shows some cyclical features. Figure 16 stands for such a case of swift trust.[2]

Interestingly this case leads to a situation where all agents are still participating to the network but some leaders clearly appear. The dynamics leads to a pure collaborative network with the removal of all negative links showing some intermediate

*Figure 16. Swift-Trust*

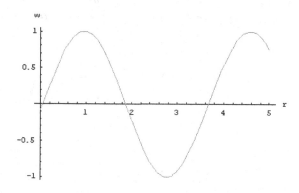

performance. The Figures 17, 18, 19, 20, 21, and Table 3 illustrate the case.

## Case 4: Non Collaborative and Reliable Opening Community with Cyclical Swift Trust

This case is quite the opposite of the previous one since we conjecture here a community starting with the lowest level of trust. Many negative reciprocal links characterize bilateral relationships between agents and Hierarchy index is maximum. We have[3]: (see Figure 22)

Here again the dynamics leads to an all participating agents community but with the emergence of one leader. The graph structure obtained at final stage shows the preponderance of negative relationships between agents although the leader

positively influence other participants. Hierarchical and collaborative indexes did not change through the dynamics of the system with high hierarchy and low collaboration. The overall performance of such a community seems quite high although less compared to our collaborative and reliable case. The Figures 23, 24, 25, 26, Table 4, and Figure 27 characterize this fourth case.

## Case 5: Non Collaborative and Mistrust Opening Community

We turn now to a case characterizing a starting community with a strong non collaborative background and then a high degree of hierarchy.

*Figure 17. Dynamics of $x_i$*

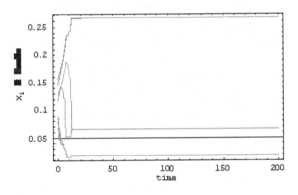

*Figure 18. Structure of $x_i$ in t= 200000*

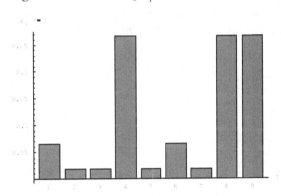

*Figure 19. The left-hand side figure display the graph structures of positive links, and the right-hand side one the graph of the negative ones, t = 0*

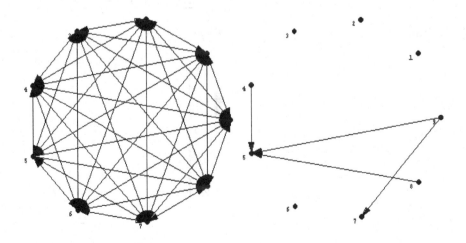

*Figure 20. The left-hand side figure display the graph structures of positive links, and the right-hand side one the graph of the negative ones, t = 200000*

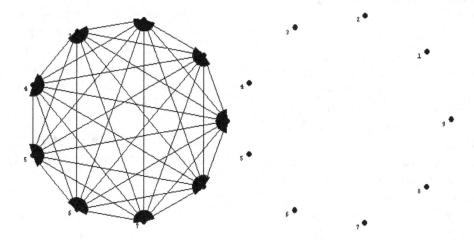

Mutual influences are negative and moreover agents are suspicious in the sense that a relative increase of activity of agent *j* raises the negative influence on agent *i*. Simulations show the emergence of several leaders with positive influences on others agents with differentiated activity rates and negative pressure on each others. The overall performance of the group is relatively low. Hierarchy remains high and collaborative index increases a bit due to the positive influence of leaders on others. The Figures 28, 29, 30, 31, 32, 33, and Table 5 depict this result.

*Figure 21. Profit*

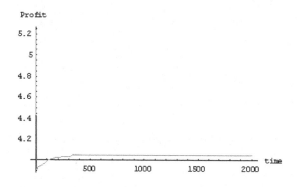

*Table 3.*

|  | t = 0 | T = Final (200000) |
|---|---|---|
| Ht | 0.06 | 0 |
| Ct | 0.94 | 1 |

*Figure 22. Swift Trust*

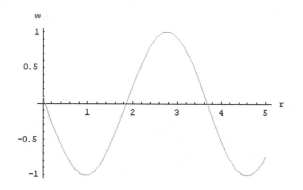

*Figure 23. Dynamics of $x_i$*

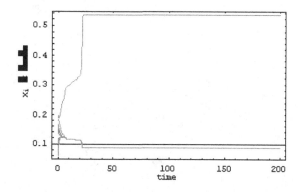

*Figure 24. Structure of x$_i$ in t= 200000*

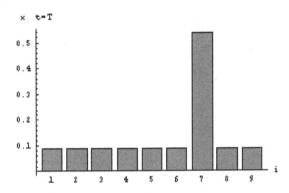

*Figure 25. The left-hand side figure display the graph structures of positive links, and the right-hand side one the graph of the negative ones, t = 0*

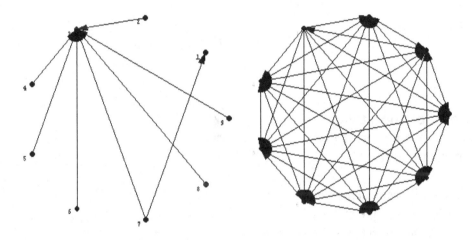

*Figure 26. The left-hand side figure display the graph structures of positive links, and the right-hand side one the graph of the negative ones, t = 200000*

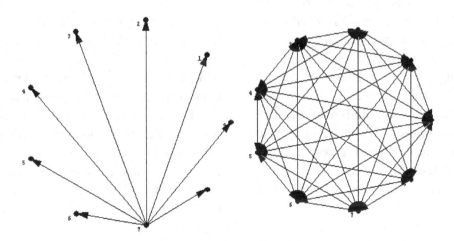

*Table 4.*

|  | t = 0 | T = Final (200000) |
|---|---|---|
| Ht | 1 | 1 |
| Ct | 0.11 | 0.11 |

*Figure 27. Profits*

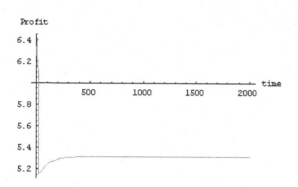

*Figure 28. Swift trust*

| $\Psi(r) = Exp[-\beta r^2](\beta r^3 + \gamma r^2 + \delta r)$ | | |
|---|---|---|
| β | γ | δ |
| 0.155 | -0.35 | 0.55 |

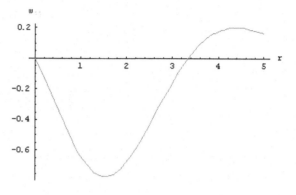

*Figure 29. Dynamics of $x_i$*

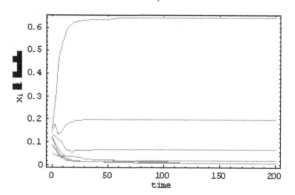

## Case 6: Non Collaborative, Reliable Opening Community with Switching Point

Finally we simulated a case where the community begins with a rather non collaborative background but contrarily to the previous case is characterized by confident agents in the sense that a relative increase of activity of agent j reduces the intensity of negative influence on agent i and even rapidly becomes a positive influence until a switching point appears. This situation results in our dynamics to the emergence of equal participation of all agents but contrarily to our first case the hierarchical degree is high and the collaborative index low. Only negative bilateral influences characterize the community. The total profit is relatively high although less than in the collaborative and reliable opening community case. (see Figures 34, 35, 36, 37, 38, 39, and Table 6)

Finally we can summarize our main results in Figure 40.

## CONCLUSION

Numerous communities of experts supported by firms tend nowadays to form an important part of corporate social capital. Composed of free will agents, those communities aim at creating knowledge through cognitive interactions and heavily rely on ICT's to free themselves from many constraints. Previous studies of such virtual groupings pointed out that their organization features were not similar to market nor hierarchy. Consequently neither price nor contract or authority are used in such communities which rather seem

*Figure 30. The left-hand side figure display the graph structures of positive links, and the right-hand side one the graph of the negative ones, t = 0*

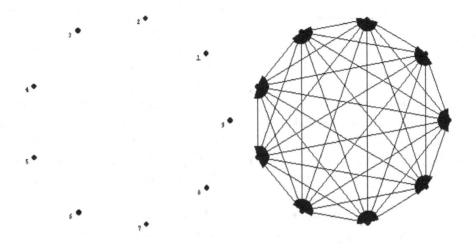

*Figure 31. The left-hand side figure display the graph structures of positive links, and the right-hand side one the graph of the negative ones, t = 200000*

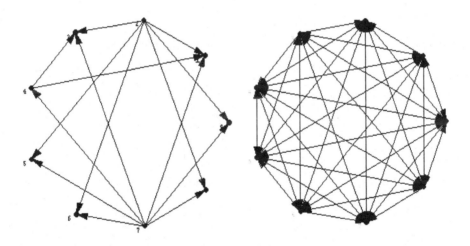

*Figure 32. Structure of $x_i$ in t = 200000*

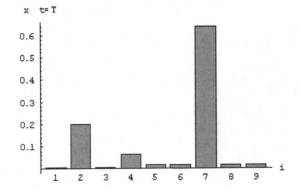

*Figure 33. Profits*

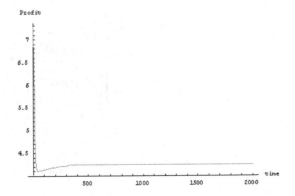

*Table 5.*

| | t = 0 | T = Final (200000) |
|---|---|---|
| Ht | 1 | 1 |
| Ct | 0 | 0.21 |

to self-organize. Instead of traditional economic concepts, notions such as trust and leadership are advanced to explain the functioning of these virtual assemblies. This contribution proposed a tentative model which attempts to grasp some of the empirical aspects of these communities. More precisely we were interested in the relation between trust, performance and organizational feature within a given virtual group.

Trust takes here the particular form of so-called 'swift trust'. Contrarily to the traditional

'trust need touch' concepts based on small steps learning and long history, swift trust basically relies on pre existent stereotypes at the beginning of collaboration and afterward on current action of others agents. It is then well suited to virtual communities characterized by (i) no common history in bilateral relationships and scarce face to face (ii) uncertainty about viability, (iii) possible weak involvement. Swift trust demonstrates to be very fragile and on occasion cyclical. Our model proposed different functions of swift trust which tried to capture both the average pre existent stereotypes in a given opening community and the fragile and cyclical movement of influences depending on relative action during the group lifespan. The performance or profit index both at individual and community level has been built in such a way as to encapsulate the idea

*Figure 34. Swift Trust*

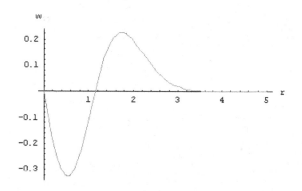

*Figure 35. Dynamics of $x_i$*

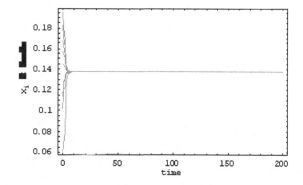

*Figure 36. Structure of $x_i$, t=200000*

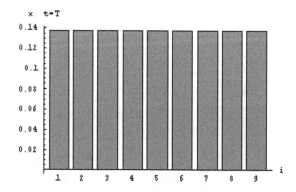

*Figure 37. The left-hand side figure display the graph structures of positive links, and the right-hand side one the graph of the negative ones, t = 0*

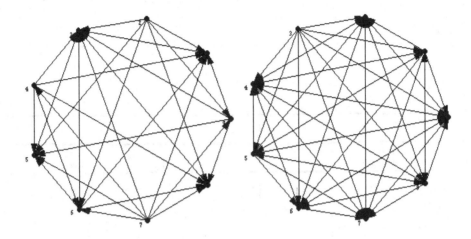

*Figure 38. The left-hand side figure display the graph structures of positive links, and the right-hand side one the graph of the negative ones, t = 200000*

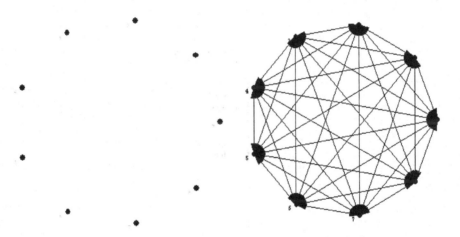

*Figure 39. Profits*

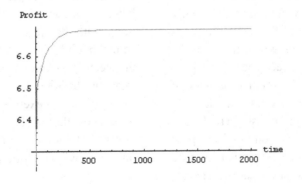

*Table 6.*

|  | t = 0 | T = Final (200000) |
|---|---|---|
| Ht | 1 | 1 |
| Ct | 0.26 | 0 |

*Figure 40.*

| initial t = 0 F | | | inal t = T | | | |
|---|---|---|---|---|---|---|
| Swift Trust | Hierarchical degree | Collaborative degree | Xi* | Performance relative | Hierarchial degree | Collaborative degree |
| Collaborative and reliable with switching point | 0.72 | 0.64 | All agents with identical particpation | ***** | 0 | 1 |
| Collaborative and mistrust with switching point | 0.41 | 0.79 | Only one agent | * | 1 | 0.53 |
| Collaborative, mistrust and cyclical trust | 0.06 | 0.94 | All agents with different activities and several leaders | ** | 0 | 1 |
| Non collaborative, reliablewith cyclical trust | 1 | 0.11 | All agents and emergence of one leader | *** | 1 | 0.11 |
| Non collaborative, mistrust and switching point | 1 | 0 | All agents with different activities and several leaders | ** | 1 | 0.21 |
| Non collaborative, reliable and switching point | 1 | 0.26 | All agents with identical particpation | **** | 1 | 0 |

of knowledge creation as a function of bilateral interaction within a network and of the cognitive distance between individuals. A cost function with a learning effect has also been introduced. Finally the organizational feature of the community has been seized by two indexes which measure the relative number of positive reciprocal influences between individuals and the relative number of positive influence. Simulations of the model with our different swift trust functions using a replicator equation for the dynamics of the community display various organizational structures similar to those described by stylized facts. The organizational at-

tributes range from pure collaborative communities to pure competitive ones. Intermediates cases also emerge with the appearance of leader(s). Those latter cases could be linked, among other conditions, with the presence of cyclical swift trust. A somewhat interesting result of our simulations is the fact that community performance could be less explained by initial condition about average a priori stereotypes – to exert positive or negative initial influences - than by the initial 'marginal' reliability or mistrust with regard to a change in the relative rate of individual participation.

# REFERENCES

Ahuja, M. K., & Carley, K. M. (1999). Network structure in virtual organizations. *Organization Science, 10*(6), 741-757. doi:10.1287/orsc.10.6.741

Arena, R. (2003). Relations interentreprises et communautés médiatées. *Revue d'Economie Politique*, Marchés en ligne et communautés d'agents, M. Gensollen (Ed.).

Cohendet, P., & Diani, M. (2003). L'organisation comme une communauté de communautés: Croyances collectives et culture d'entreprise. *Revue d'Economie Politique*.

Copelli, M., Zorzenon dos Santos, R. M., & Sa Martin, J. S. (2001). Emergence of hierarchy on a network of complementary agents. *arXiv:cond-mat/0110350v1*

Cowan, R., Jonard, N., & Zimmermann, J. B. (2003). Complementarités cognitives et production de connaissances nouvelles. *Revue d'Economie Industrielle* N° 103.

Jarvenpaa, S. L., & Leidner, D. (1999, Winter). Communication and trust in global virtual teams. *Organization Science*.

Jasen, V. A. A., & de Ross, A. M. (2000). The role of space in reducing predator-prey cycles. In U. Dieckmann, R. Law & J. A. J. Metz (Eds.), *The geometry of ecological interactions: Simplifying spatial complexity* (pp. 183-201). Cambridge University Press.

Li, C., & Chen, G. (2004). Phase synchronization in small-world networks of chaotic oscillators. *Physica A, 341*, 73–79. doi:10.1016/j.physa.2004.04.112

Meyerson, D., Weick, K., & Kramer, R. (1996). Swift trust and temporary groups. In *Trust in organizations: Frontiers of theory and research*. Thousands Oaks: Sage Publications.

Muller, P. (2003). *On reputation, leadership, and communities of practice.*

Pantelli, N., & Chiasson, M. (Eds.). (2008). *Exploring virtuality within and beyond organizations*. Palgrave Macmillan.

Pelillo, M., Siddiqi, K., & Zucker, S. (2001, November). Matching hierarchical structures using association graphs. *IEEE Transactions on Patterns Analysis and Machine Intelligence, 21*(11).

Pemmaraju, S., & Skiena, S. (2003). *Computational discrete mathematics*. Cambridge University Press.

Sakaguchi, H. (2003). *Self-organization and hierarchical structures in nonlocally coupled replicator models. arXiv: nlin.*AO/0305003 v1.

Shapovalov, A. V., & Evdokimov, E. V. (1998). *The geometry of the Fisher selection dynamics. arXiv:physics*/9805006 v1.

Steinmueller, E. (2002). Virtual communities and the new economy. In Mansell (Ed.), *Inside the communication revolution*. OUP.

# ENDNOTES

[1]   In the rest of the paper we simply assume that $d_{ij} = |i - j|$

[2]   We have: $\Psi(r) = MathieuS[a, q, r]$, with $a = 3$ and $q = 0.05$, where the Mathieu function is solution of the equation $z'' - (a - qCos[2r]) z = 0$

[3]   Accordingly, $\Psi'r) = MathieuS[a, q, r]$, with $a = 3$ and $q = 0.05$

# Chapter 15
# Authority and Its Implementation in Enterprise Information Systems

**Alexei Sharpanskykh**
*Vrije Universiteit Amsterdam, The Netherlands*

## ABSTRACT

*The concept of power is inherent in human organizations of any type. As power relations have important consequences for organizational viability and productivity, they should be explicitly represented in enterprise information systems (EISs). Although organization theory provides a rich and very diverse theoretical basis on organizational power, still most of the definitions for power-related concepts are too abstract, often vague and ambiguous to be directly implemented in EISs. To create a bridge between informal organization theories and automated EISs, this article proposes a formal logic-based specification language for representing power (in particular authority) relations. The use of the language is illustrated by considering authority structures of organizations of different types. Moreover, the article demonstrates how the formalized authority relations can be integrated into an EIS.*

## INTRODUCTION

The concept of *power* is inherent in human organizations of any type. Power relations that exist in an organization have a significant impact on its viability and productivity. Although the notion of power is often discussed in the literature in social studies (Gulick &Urwick, 1937; Parsons, 1947; Friedrich, 1958; Blau& Scott, 1962; Peabody, 1964;

Hickson et al., 1971; Bacharach & Aiken, 1977; Clegg, 1989), it is only rarely defined precisely. In particular, power-related terms (e.g., control, authority, influence) are often used interchangeably in this literature. Furthermore, the treatment of power in different streams of sociology differs significantly. One of the first definitions for power in the modern sociology was given by Max Weber (1958): *Power is the probability that a person can carry out his or her own will despite resistance.* Weber and his followers (Dahl, Polsby) considered power as an inherently coercive force that implied involuntary submission and ignored the relational aspect of power. Other sociologists (Bierstedt, Blau) considered power as a force or the ability to apply sanctions (Blau & Scott, 1962). Such view was also criticized as restrictive, as it did not pay attention to indirect sources and implications of power (e.g., informal influence in decision making) and subordinate's acceptance of power. Parsons (1947) considered power as *"a specific mechanism to bring about changes in the action of organizational actors in the process of social interaction."*

Most contemporary organization theories explore both formal (normative, prescribed) and informal (subjective, human-oriented) aspects of power (Peabody, 1964; Clegg, 1989; Scott, 2001). Formal power relations are documented in many modern organizations and, therefore, can be explicitly represented in models on which enterprise information systems (EISs) are based. The representation of formal power in EISs has a number of advantages. First, it allows a clear definition of rights and responsibilities for organizational roles (actors) and a power structure. Second, based on the role specifications, corresponding permissions for information, resources and actions can be specified for each role. Third, explicitly defined rules on power enable the identification of violations of organizational policies and regulations. Fourth, data about power-related actions (e.g., empowerment, authorization) can be stored in an EIS for the subsequent analysis.

For modeling of power relations, the rich theoretical basis from social science can be used. Notably, many modern EISs implement no or very simplified representations of power relations and mechanisms. In particular, the architecture ARIS (Scheer & Nuettgens, 2000) used for development of EISs identifies responsibility and managerial authority relations on organizational roles, however, does not provide general mechanisms for representing such relations and does not address

change of these relations over time. The enterprise architecture CIMOSA (1993) distinguishes responsibilities and authorities on enterprise objects, agents, and processes/activities. However, no precise meaning (semantics) is attached to these concepts, which may be interpreted differently in different applications. Also, different aspects of authorities are not distinguished both in ARIS and in CIMOSA (e.g., authority for execution, authority for supervision, authority for monitoring).

Often EISs realize extensive access schemata that determine allowed actions for roles and modes of access of roles to information (Bernus, Nemes, & Schmidt, 2003). Normally, such schemata are based on power relations established in organizations. Thus, to ensure consistency, unambiguousness and completeness of EISs' access schemata, organizational power relations should be precisely identified and specified using some (formal) language. To this end, theoretical findings on organization power from social science are useful to consider. However, there is an obstacle to the direct implementation of this knowledge in EISs—the absence of operational definitions of power-related concepts in social theories.

The first step to make the concept of power operational is to provide a clear and unambiguous meaning for it (or for its specific aspects). In this article, this is done by identifying the most essential characteristics and mechanisms of power described in different approaches and by integrating them into two broad categories: formal power (or authority) and informal power (or influence), which are described in the Power, Authority and Influence section. Further, this article focuses on the formal representation of authority, for which a formal language is described in the Authority: A Formal Approach section. Moreover, this section illustrates how the introduced formal language can be used to model authority systems of different types of organizations. The next section discusses the integration of formal authority relations into an automated EIS. Finally, the article concludes with a Discussion section.

## POWER, AUTHORITY AND INFLUENCE

As in many contemporary social theories (Peabody, 1964; Clegg, 1989), we assume that power can be practiced in an organization either through (formal) *authority* or through (informal) *influence relations*. Authority represents formal, legitimate organizational power by means of which a regulated normative relationship between a superior and a subordinate is established. Usually, authority is attached to positions in organizations. For example, authority of some managerial positions provides power to hire or to fire; to promote or to demote; to grant incentive rewards or to impose sanctions. In many approaches, it is assumed that authority implies involuntary obedience from subordinates. Indeed, as authority has a normative basis that comprises formal, explicitly documented rules, it is expected that subordinates, hired by the organization, should be aware of and respect these rules, which implies the voluntary acceptance of authority.

All manifestations of power that cannot be explained from the position of authority fall into the category of influence. In contrast to authority, influence does not have a formal basis. It is often persuasive and implies voluntary submission. Some of the bases of influence are technical knowledge, skills, competences and other characteristics of particular individuals. Influence is often exercised through mechanisms of leadership; however, possession of certain knowledge or access to some resources, as well as different types of manipulation may also create influence. Influence may be realized in efforts to affect organizational decisions indirectly.

Although authority and influence often stem from different sources, they are often interrelated in organizations. For example, the probability of the successful satisfaction of organizational goals increases, when a strong leader (meaning a leader that has a great value of influence) occupies a superior position of authority. Furthermore, sometimes patterns of influence that frequently occur in an organization may become institutionalized (i.e., may become authority relations).

Modeling methods for authority and influence are essentially different. While authority relations are often prescriptive and explicitly defined, influence relations are not strictly specified and may vary to a great extent. Therefore, whereas authority relations can be generally represented in EISs, the specification of influence relations is dependant on particular (cognitive) models of agents that represent organizational actors. Relations between authority and influence can be studied by performing simulation with different types of agents situated in different organizational environments. The focus of this article is on modeling of formal authority relations. Influence relations and relations between authority and influence will be considered elsewhere.

## AUTHORITY: A FORMAL APPROACH

First, a formal language for specifying authority-related concepts and relations is introduced. The next section discusses how the introduced language can be used for representing authority structures of organizations of different types.

### A Formal Language

Simon (1957) describes three contributions of authority for an organization: (1) the enforcement of responsibility, (2) the specialization of decision making, and (3) the coordination of activity. Based on this and other theoretical findings that describe power, duties and responsibilities of organizational positions (Mintzberg, 1979), a number of relations for the specification of formal authority can be identified. These relations are defined on positions (or roles), without considering particular agents (individuals). The relations are formalized using the order sorted-predicate language (Manzano,

1996) and are presented graphically in Figure 1.

We represent all activities of an organization (including decision making and personnel-related activities) by processes. Each organizational role is associated with one or more process. Roles may have different rights and responsibilities with respect to different aspects of the process execution. Furthermore, often several roles may potentially execute or manage certain processes. This is represented by the relation

*is_authorized_for:* r: ROLE x aspect: ASPECT
x a: PROCESS,

where aspect has one of the values {execution, monitoring, consulting, tech_des (making technological decisions), manage_des (making managerial decisions), user_defined_aspect}.

All types of decisions with respect to a particular process can be divided into two broad groups: *technological* and *managerial decisions* (inspired by Bacharach and Aiken [1977]). Technological decisions concern technical questions related to the process content and are usually made by

technical professionals. Managerial decisions concern general organizational issues related to the process (e.g., the allocation of employees, process scheduling, the establishment of performance standards, provision of resources, presenting incentives and sanctions). Managers of different levels (i.e., from the lowest level line managers to strategic apex [top] managers) may be authorized for making different types of managerial decisions varying from in scope, significance and detail. A particular decision type is specified as an aspect in the is_authorized_for relation. The same holds for technological decisions. Whereas *consulting* has a form of recommendation and implies voluntary acceptance of advices, decisions imposed on a role(s) that execute(s) the process are considered as imperatives with corresponding implications.

Authorization for *execution* implies that a role is allowed to execute the process according to existing standards and guidelines. Whenever a problem, a question or a deviation from the standard procedures occurs, the role must report about it to the role(s) authorized for making tech-

*Figure 1. Graphical representation of the concepts and relations of the language used for specifying formal authority relations*

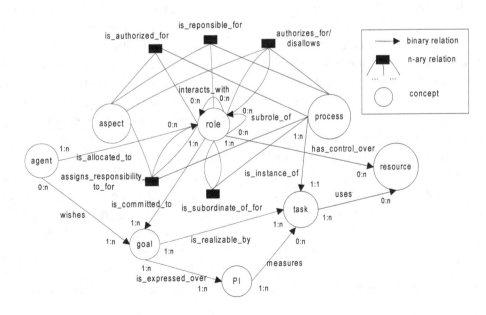

nological/managerial (depending on the problem type) decisions and must execute the decision(s) that will follow.

*Monitoring* implies passive observation of (certain aspects of) process execution, without intervention.

Notice that other aspects of process execution described in the managerial literature (e.g., control, supervision) can be represented as a combination of already introduced aspects. In particular, control can be seen as the conjunction of monitoring and making technological and/or managerial decisions aspects; supervision can be defined as the combination of consulting and control. Furthermore, the designer is given the possibility to define his/her own aspects and to provide an interpretation to them.

Although several roles in an organization may be authorized for a certain aspect related to some process, only one (or some) of them will be eventually (or are) responsible for this aspect. For example, the responsibility of a certain role with respect to the process execution means that the role is actually the one who will be performing the process and who holds accountability of the process execution. Furthermore, responsibility for the process execution implies allowance to use resources required for the process performance. The responsibility relation is specified as:

*is_responsible_for:* r:ROLE x aspect:ASPECT x a: PROCESS: process a is under responsibility of role r with respect to aspect (defined as for authorized_for).

Some roles are authorized to make managerial decisions for authorizing/disallowing other roles for certain aspects with respect to process execution. The authorization/disallowance actions are specified by the following relations:

*authorizes_for:* r1: ROLE x r2: ROLE x aspect: ASPECT x a:PROCESS: role r1 gives the authority for aspect of process a to role r2

disallows: r1:ROLE x r2:ROLE x aspect: ASPECT x a: PROCESS: role r1 denies the authority for aspect of process a for role r2.

However, to make a role actually responsible for a certain aspect of the process, another role besides the authority to make managerial decisions should also be the superior of the role with respect to the process. Superior-subordinate relations with respect to organizational processes are specified by: is_subordinate_of_for: r1: ROLE x r2: ROLE x a: PROCESS. Then, responsibility is assigned/retracted using the following relations:

*assigns_responsibility_to_for:* r1: ROLE x r2: ROLE x aspect: ASPECT x a: PROCESS: role r1 assigns the responsibility for aspect of process a to role r2.

retracts_responsibility_from_for: r1:ROLE x r2: ROLE x aspect: ASPECT x a: PROCESS: role r1 retracts responsibility from role r2 for aspect of process a.

Using these relations, superiors may delegate/retract (their) responsibilities for certain aspects of processes execution to/from their subordinates, and may restrict themselves only to control and making decisions in exceptional situations.

In Hickson et al. (1971), control over resources is identified as an important source of power. Therefore, it is useful to identify explicitly which roles control resources by means of the relation has_control_over: r1: ROLE x res: RESOURCE. In the proposed modeling framework, the notion of resource includes both tangible (e.g., materials, tools, products) and abstract (information, data) entities.

Our treatment of authority is different from both formal approaches that consider authority as an attribute or a property inherent in an organization (Gulick & Urwick, 1937; Weber, 1958) and from the human-relation view that recognizes authority as an informal, non-rational and subjective relation (e.g., Follett, Mayo, cf. [Clegg,

1989]). As many representatives of converging approaches (e.g., C.I. Barnard, Simon [1957]), we distinguish between the formal authority prescribed by organizational policies and actual authority established between a superior and his/her subordinate in the course of social interactions. In the latter case, a special accent lies on the acceptance of authority by a subordinate. In Clegg (1989), different cases of the authority acceptance are discussed: orders anticipated and carried out (anticipation); acceptance of orders without critical review; conscious questioning but compliance (acceptance of authority); discusses but works for changes; ignores, evades, modifies orders (modification and evasion); rejection of authority (appeals to co-workers or higher rank for support). Depending on the organizational type, varying administrative sanction may be applied in case an employee does not accept an authoritative communication, when he/she: (a) correctly understands/interprets this communication; (b) realizes that this communication complies with formal organizational documents and/or is in line with organizational goals; (c) is mentally and physically able to perform the required actions. In many modern organizations, rewards and sanctions form a part of authority relation, thus, explicitly defined:

*grants_reward_to_for: r1:* ROLE x r: REWARD x r2: ROLE x reason: STRING: role r1 grants reward r to role r2 for reason

imposes_saction_on_for: r1: ROLE x s: SANCTION x r2: ROLE x reason: STRING: role r1 imposes sanction s to role r2 for reason.

Sometimes authority relations may be defined with respect to particular time points or intervals (e.g., responsibility for some aspect of a process may be provided for some time interval). To express temporal aspects of authority relations, the temporal trace language (TTL) (Jonker & Treur, 2003) is used.

TTL allows specifying a temporal development of an organization by a trace. A trace is defined as a temporally ordered sequence of states. Each state corresponds to a particular time point and is characterized by a set of state properties that hold in this state. State properties are formalized in a standard predicate logic way (Manzano, 1996) using state ontologies. A state ontology defines a set of sorts or types (e.g., ROLE, RESOURCE), sorted constants, functions and predicates.

States are related to state properties via the formally defined satisfaction relation $|=$: state$(\gamma, t) |= p$, which denotes that state property p holds in trace $\gamma$ at time t. For example, state$(\gamma1, t1) |=$ is_responsible_for(employee_A, execution, p1) denotes that in trace $\gamma1$ at time point t1 the employee_A is responsible for the execution of process p1.

Dynamic properties are specified in TTL by relations between state properties. For example, the following property expresses the rule of a company's policy that an employee is made responsible for making technological decisions with respect to process p1 after s/he have been executing this process for two years (730 days):

$\forall\gamma$: *TRACE* $\forall t1$: *TIME* $\forall empl$: EMPLOYEE
state$(\gamma, t1) |=$ is_responsible_for(empl, execution, p1) & $\exists t2$: TIME state$(\gamma, t2) |=$ assigns_responsibility_to_for(management, empl, execution, p1) & t1-t2 = 730
$\Rightarrow$ state$(\gamma, t1) |=$ assigns_responsibility_to_for(management, empl, tech_des, p1).

Other specific conditions (e.g., temporal, situational) under which authority relations may be created/maintained/dissolved are defined by executable rules expressed by logical formulae. The specification of these rules will be discussed in the Integration of Autority Relations Into an EIS section.

## Modeling Authority Relations in Different Types of Organizations

Authority is enforced through the organizational structure and norms (or rules) that govern the organizational behavior. In general, no single authority system can be equally effective for all types of organizations in all times. An organizational authority system is contingent upon many organizational factors, among which organizational goals; the level of cohesiveness between different parts of an organization, the levels of complexity and of specialization of jobs, the level of formalization of organizational behavior, management style (a reward system, decision making and coordination mechanisms), the size of an organization and its units. Furthermore, the environment type (its uncertainty and dynamism; the amount of competitors), as well as the frequency and the type of interactions between an organization and the environment exert a significant influence upon an organizational authority structure.

In the following it will be discussed how authority is realized in some types of (mostly industrial) organizations and how it can be modeled using relations introduced in the previous section.

Authority in small firms of the early industrial era was completely exercised by their owners through mechanisms of direct personal control. Firm owners were managers and technical professionals at the same time, and, therefore, had authority and responsibility for all aspects related to processes, except for their execution, responsibility for which was assigned to hired workers. This can be expressed using the introduced formal language as follows:

$\forall p$: *PROCESS* $\forall t$: *TIME* $\forall \gamma$: *TRACE* $\exists empl$: HIRED_EMPLOYEE state($\gamma$, t) |= [ is_responsible_for(firm_owner, control, p) & is_responsible_for(firm_owner, supervision, p) & is_responsible_for(empl, execution, p) ].

The owners controlled all resources ($\forall r$: RESOURCE $\forall t$: TIME $\forall \gamma$: TRACE state($\gamma$, t) |= has_control_over(firm_owner, r)). Currently, similar types of organizations can be found in family business and small firms.

With the growth of industry, which caused joining of small firms into larger enterprises, owners were forced to hire subcontractors, who took over some of their managerial functions. This can be modeled using the introduced language as assigning responsibility to subcontractors by the owner for some managerial and technological decisions, as well as monitoring and consulting of workers with respect to some processes execution. For example, the responsibility assignment to role subcontractor_A for making managerial and technological decisions related to the process p1 is expressed as:

$\forall \gamma$: TRACE $\exists t$: TIME state($\gamma$, t) |=
[ assigns_responsibility_to_for(firm_owner, subcontractor_A, tech_des, p1) $\wedge$ assigns_responsibility_to_for(firm_owner, subcontractor_A, manage_des, p1) ].

The owner reserved often the right to control for himself, which included granting rewards and imposing sanctions to/on subcontractors and workers, realized through superior-subordinate relations. For example, the following rule describes the superior-subordinate relations between the firm owner and subcontractor_A, responsible for making technological decisions related to process p1 and employee_A responsible for execution of process p1:

$\forall \gamma$: *TRACE* $\forall t$: *TIME* state($\gamma$, t) |= is_subordinate_of_for(subcontractor_A, firm_owner, p1) & is_subordinate_of_for(employee_B, firm_owner, p1).

Organizational resources were usually controlled by the owner.

Large industrial enterprises of the 20th century are characterized by further increase in number of managerial positions structured hierarchically by superior-subordinate relations. Such organizations are often defined as mechanistic (Scott, 2001) and have the following typical characteristics: strong functional specialization, a high level of processes formalization, a hierarchical structure reinforced by a flow of information to the top of the hierarchy and by a flow of decisions/orders from the top. Responsibilities were clearly defined for every position in a hierarchy. In most organizations of this type, responsibility for execution was separated from responsibilities to make decisions. Managerial positions differed in power to make decisions depending on the level in the hierarchy. Often, technological decisions were made by managers of lower levels (or even by dedicated positions to which also execution responsibilities were assigned), whereas managerial decisions were made by managers at the apex. For example, the following formal expression identifies one of the upper managers responsible for making strategic decisions related to process p, one of the middle level managers responsible for making tactical decisions related to p and one of the first level managers responsible to making technological decisions related to p:

∃*manager1: UPPER_MANAGER* ∃*manager2:* MIDDLE_LEVEL_MANAGER ∃manager3: FIRST_LEVEL_MANAGER ∀γ: TRACE ∀t: TIME state(γ, t) |= [ is_responsible_for(manager1, making_strategic_decisions, p) ∧ is_responsible_for(manager2, making_tactical_decisions, p) ∧ is_responsible_for(manager3, tech_des, p) ].

In many of such organizations, managers at the apex shared responsibility for making (some) decisions with lower-level managers. Therefore, decisions that were usually proposed by lower level managers had to be approved by the apex managers. In connection to the previous example,

the following superior-subordinate relations can be identified: is_subordinate_of_for(manager2, manager1, p) & is_subordinate_of_for(manager3, manager2, p).

Initially, such enterprises operated in relatively stable (however, sometimes complex) environmental conditions that reinforced their structure. However, later in the second half of the 20th century, to survive and to achieve goals in the changed environmental conditions (e.g., a decreased amount of external resources; increased competition; diversification of markets), enterprises and firms were forced to change their organizational structure and behavior. In response to the increased diversity of markets, within some enterprises specialized, market-oriented departments were formed. Such departments had much of autonomy within organizations. It was achieved by assigning to them the responsibility for most aspects related to processes, which created products/services demanded by the market. Although department heads still were subordinates of (apex) manager(s) of the organization, in most cases the latter one(s) were restricted only to general performance control over departments. Often departments controlled organizational resources necessary for the production and had the structure of hierarchical mechanistic type.

Although a hierarchical structure proved to be useful for coordination of activities of organizations situated in stable environments, it could cause significant inefficiencies and delays in organizations situated in dynamic, unpredictable environmental conditions. Furthermore, the formalization and excessive control over some (e.g., creative and innovative) organizational activities often can have negative effects on productivity. Nowadays, large enterprises often create project teams or task forces that are given complex, usually innovative and creative tasks without detailed descriptions/prescriptions. As in the case with departments, teams are often assigned the responsibility to make technological and (some) managerial decisions and are given necessary resources to perform their tasks. For example, the following formal expression represents the responsibility assignment to the team_A for making technological and strategic managerial decisions related to the process of development of a design for a new product:

$\forall \gamma$: TRACE $\exists t$: TIME state($\gamma$, t) |=
[ assigns_responsibility_to_for(management, team_A, tech_des, develop_design_new_product_A) $\land$ assigns_responsibility_to_for (management, team_A, strategic_managerial_des, develop_design_new_product_A) ].

Usually teams have highly cohesive plain structures with participants selected from different organizational departments based on knowledge, skills and experience required for the processes assigned to these teams. Although many teams implement informal communication and participative decision making principles (Lansley, Sadler, & Webb, 1975), also formal authority relations can be found in teams. In particular, in some project teams superior-subordinate relations exist between the team manager and team members. In this case, whereas responsibility for making technological decisions is given to team members, the responsibility for most managerial decisions is assigned to the team manager. Then, the members of such teams, being also members of some functional departments or groups, have at least two superiors. In other teams the team manager plays the integrator role and does not have formal authority over team members. In this case, the responsibility for decisions made by a team lies on all members of the team. Sometimes to strengthen the position of a team manager, s/he is given control over some resources (e.g., budgets) that can be used, for example, to provide material incentives to the team members.

The principles on which teams are built come close to the characteristics of the organic organizational form (Scott, 2001). Some of such organiza-

tions do not have any formal authority structure, other allow much flexibility in defining authority relations between roles. In the former case formal authority is replaced by socially created informal rules. In the latter case, authority may be temporally provided to the role that has the most relevant knowledge and experience for current organizational tasks. In many organic organizations formal control and monitoring are replaced by informal mutual control and audit. For the investigation of dynamics of organic organization, informal aspects such as influence, leaderships, mental models of employees are highly relevant, which will be discussed elsewhere. Often interactions between organic organizations (e.g., of network type) are regulated by contracts. Usually, contracts specify legal relationships between parties that explicitly define their rights and responsibilities with respect to some processes (e.g., production, supply services). Several organizations may be involved in the process execution (e.g., supply chains for product delivery); therefore, it is needed to identify particular aspects of responsibility in contracts for such processes. The introduced language may be used for specifying such responsibilities and their legal consequences through reward/sanctions mechanisms.

## INTEGRATION OF AUTHORITY RELATIONS INTO AN EIS

In our previous work, a general framework for formal organizational modeling and analysis is introduced (Popova & Sharpanskykh, 2007c). It comprises several perspectives (or views) on organizations, similar to the ones defined in the Generalized Enterprise Reference Architecture and Methodology (GERAM) (Bernus, Nemes, & Schmidt, 2003), which forms a basis for comparison of the existing architectures and serves as a template for the development of new architectures. In particular, *the performance-oriented view* (Popova & Sharpanskykh, 2007b) describes organizational goal structures, performance indicators structures, and relations between them. *The process-oriented view* (Popova & Sharpanskykh, 2007a) describes task and resource structures, and dynamic flows of control. In *the agent-oriented view* different types of agents with their capabilities are identified and principles for allocating agents to roles are formulated. Concepts and relations within every view are formally described using dedicated formal predicate-based languages. The views are related to each other by means of sets of common concepts. The developed framework constitutes a formal basis for an automated EIS.

To incorporate the authority relations introduced in this article into this framework, both syntactic and semantic integration should be performed. The syntactic integration is straightforward as the authority relations are expressed using the same formal basis (sorted predicate logic) as the framework. Furthermore, the authority relations are specified on the concepts defined in the framework (e.g., tasks, processes, resources, performance indicators). For the semantic integration rules (or axioms) that attach meaning, define integrity and other types of organization constraints on the authority relations should be specified. A language for these rules is required to be (1) based on the sorted predicate logic; (2) expressive enough to represent all aspects of the authority relations; (3) executable, to make constraints (axioms) operational. Furthermore, as authority relations are closely related to dynamic flows of control that describe a temporal ordering of processes, a temporal allocation of resources, and so forth, a language should be temporally expressive. A language that satisfies all these requirements is the temporal trace language (TTL). In Sharpanskykh and Treur (2006), it is shown that any TTL formula can be automatically translated into executable format that can be implemented in most commonly used programming languages.

In the following, the semantic integration rules and several examples of constraints defined for particular organizations are considered.

The first axiom on the authority relations expresses that roles that are responsible for a certain aspect related to some process should be necessarily authorized for this:

**Ax1**: ∀r ROLE ∀a: PROCESS ∀aspect: ASPECT ∀γ: TRACE ∀t: TIME state(γ, t) |= [ responsible_for(r, aspect, a) ⇒ authorized_for(r, aspect, a) ].

Another axiom expresses the transitivity of the is_subordinate_of_for relation: r1: ROLE x r2: ROLE x a: PROCESS:

**Ax2**: ∀r1, r2, r3: ROLE ∀a: PROCESS ∀γ, t state(γ, t) |= [ is_subordinate_of_for(r2, r1, a) ∧ is_subordinate_of_for(r3, r2, a)] ⇒ is_subordinate_of_for(r3, r1, a)]

One more axiom (**Ax3**) that relates the interaction (communication) structure of an organization with its authority structure based on superior-subordinate relations expresses that there should be specified a communication path between each superior role and his/her subordinate(s). Such a path may include intermediate roles from the authority hierarchy and may consist of both interaction and inter-level links.

The following axiom expresses that only roles that have the responsibility to make managerial decision with respect to some process are allowed to authorize other roles for some aspect of this process:

**Ax4**: ∀r1,r2:ROLE ∀a: PROCESS ∀asp: ASPECT ∀γ, t state(γ, t) |= [ authorizes_for(r1, r2, asp, a) ⇒ is_responsible_for(r1, manage_des, a) ].

In general, rules that describe processes of authorization, assigning/retracting of responsibilities may have many specific conditions. However, to assign responsibility for some aspect of a process a role should necessarily have at least the responsibility to make managerial decisions and be the superior (with respect to this process) of a role, to which the responsibility is assigned. All other conditions may be optionally specified by the designer. Responsibility may be assigned on a temporal basis. To specify that a responsibility relation holds in all states that correspond to time points in the time interval limit, a responsibility persistency rule should be defined:

**C1**: $\forall$asp: ASPECT $\forall$r1,r2:ROLE $\forall$a: PROCESS $\forall\gamma$, $\forall$t1, t2:TIME state($\gamma$, t1) |= is_responsible_for(r1, asp, a) & state($\gamma$, t2) |= assigns_responsibility_to_for(r1, r2, asp, a) & (t1-t2) < limit
$\Rightarrow$ state($\gamma$, t1+1) |= is_responsible_for(r1, asp, a).

Using concepts and relations from other organizational views, more complex constraints related to formal authority can be described. For example, "the total amount of working hours for role r1 should be less than a certain limit":

**C2**: sum([a: PROCESS], case($\exists$t1 state($\gamma$, t1)|= is_responsible_for(r1, execution, a), a.max_duration, 0)) < limit.

This property can be automatically verified every time when roles are assigned additional responsibilities for some processes. This is particularly useful in matrix organizations (Scott, 2001), in which roles often combine functions related to different organizational formations (departments, teams), and, as a result, their actual workload may not be directly visible.

Another constraint expresses that when the execution of a process begins, for each of the basic aspects for this process (execution, tech_des, and manage_des) a responsible role should be assigned:

**C3:** $\forall$a: PROCESS $\forall\gamma$, t  state($\gamma$, t) |= process_started(a)
$\Rightarrow \exists$r1,r2,r3: ROLE state($\gamma$, t) |= [ is_responsible_

for(r1, manage_des, a) $\wedge$ is_responsible_for(r2, tech_des, a) $\wedge$ is_responsible_for(r3, execution, a) ].

Another example is related to rewards/sanctions imposed on a role depending on the process execution results. As shown in Popova and Sharpanskykh (2007b), performance indicators (PIs) may be associated with organizational processes that represent performance measures of some aspects of the tasks execution. Depending on the PIs values, a company may have regulations to provide/impose some rewards/sanctions for roles (agents) responsible for the corresponding processes. Although such rules are rarely completely automated, still an EIS may signal to managers about situations, in which some rewards/sanctions can be applied. For example, the system may detect and propose a reward granting action to the manager, when a role has been keeping the values of some PI(s) related to its process above a certain threshold for some time period [period_start, period_end]. In TTL:

**C4**: $\forall\gamma$, t1 t1 $\geq$ perod_start & t1 $\leq$ perod_end & state($\gamma$, t1) |=       [ is_responsible_for(r2, execution, a1) $\wedge$ measures(PI1, a1) $\wedge$ is_subordinate_of_for(r2, r1, a1) $\wedge$ PI1.value > limit ]
$\Rightarrow$ state($\gamma$, period_end+1) |= grants_reward_to_for(r1, bonus_5_procent, r2, excellent_performance_of_a1).

The axioms Ax1-Ax4 can be checked on a specification of organizational formal authority relations. To this end, simple verification algorithms have been implemented. Whereas the constraints C1-C4 and similar to them need to be checked on actual executions of organizational scenarios (e.g., traces obtained from an EIS). An automated method that enables such types of analysis is described in (Popova & Sharpanskykh, 2007a).

Furthermore, the identified rules can be used to determine for each user of an EIS relevant to him/her information and a set of allowed actions that are in line with his/her (current) responsibilities defined in the system. Moreover, (possible) outcomes of each action of the user can be evaluated on a set of (interdependent) authority-related and other organizational constraints, and based on this evaluation the action is either allowed or prohibited.

## DISCUSSION

This article makes the first step towards defining the formal operational semantics for power-related concepts (such as authority, influence, control), which are usually vaguely described in organization theory. In particular, this article addresses formal authority, different aspects of which are made operational by defining a dedicated predicate logic-based language. It is illustrated how the introduced relations can be used for representing authority structures of organizations of different types.

Modern enterprises can be described along different dimensions/views, that is, human-oriented, process-oriented and technology-oriented. However, most of the existing EISs focus particularly on the process-oriented view. An extension of the models on which EISs are built with concepts and relations defined within the human-oriented view allows conceptualizing more static and dynamic aspects of organizational reality, thus, resulting in more feasible enterprise models. Among the relations between human actors, authority deserves special attention, as it is formally regulated and may exert a (significant) influence on the execution of enterprise processes. This article illustrates how the concepts and relations of authority can be formally related to other organizational views, thus resulting into an expressive and versatile enterprise model. The introduced authority relations may be also incorporated into other existing enterprise architectures that comply with the requirements of the GERAM (e.g., CIMOSA) based on which modern EISs are built. However, to enable semantic integration of the authority concepts, an EIS is required to have formal foundations, which are missing in many existing enterprise architectures and systems.

In the future it will be investigated how the proposed authority modeling framework can be applied for the development of automated support for a separation task (i.e., maintaining a safe distance between aircrafts in flight) in the area of air traffic control. Originally this task was managed by land controllers, who provided separation instructions for pilots. With the increase of air traffic, the workload of controllers rose also. To facilitate the controllers' work, it was proposed to (partially) delegate the separation task to pilots. This proposal found supporters and opponents both among controllers and pilots. The resistance to a large extent was (is) caused by ambiguity and vagueness of issues related to power mechanisms. Such questions as "whom to blame when an incident/accident occurs?", "which part of the task may be delegated?", "under which environmental conditions the task can be delegated?" still remain open. By applying the framework proposed in this article, one can precisely define responsibilities of both controllers and pilots and conditions under which the responsibility can be assigned/retracted. Notice that these conditions may include relations from different views on organizations (e.g., "current workload is less than x," "has ability a"), which allows a great expressive power in defining constraints.

## REFERENCES

Bacharach, S., & Aiken, M. (1977). Communication in administrative bureaucracies. *Academy of Management Journal, 18,* 365-377.

Bernus, P., Nemes, L., & Schmidt, G. (2003). *Handbook on enterprise architecture.* Berlin: Springer-Verlag.

Blau, P., & Scott, W. (1962). *Formal organizations.* Chandler Publishing.

CIMOSA. (1993). *CIMOSA—open system architecture for CIM. ESPRIT consortium AMICE.* Berlin: Springer-Verlag.

Clegg, S. (1989). *Frameworks of power.* London: Sage.

Friedrich, C. (Ed.). (1958). *Authority.* Cambridge, MA: Harvard University Press.

Gulick, L., & Urwick, L. (Eds.). (1937). *Papers on the science of administration.* New York, NY: Institute of Public Administration.

Hickson, D., Hinings, C., Lee, C., Schneck, R., & Pennings, J. (1971). A strategic contingency theory of intra-organizational power. *Administrative Science Quarterly, 16,* 216-229.

Jonker, C., & Treur, J. (2003). A temporal-interactivist perspective on the dynamics of mental states. *Cognitive Systems Research Journal, 4,* 137-155.

Lansley, P., Sadler, P., & Webb, T. (1975). *Organization structure, management style and company performance.* London: Omega.

Manzano, M. (1996). Extensions of first order logic. Cambridge, UK: Cambridge University Press.

Mintzberg, H. (1979). *The structuring of organizations.* Englewood Cliffs. NJ: Prentice Hall.

Parsons, T. (1947). The institutionalization of authority. In: M. Weber, *The theory of social and economic organization.* New York, NY: Oxford University Press.

Peabody, R. (1964). *Organizational authority: Superior-subordinate relationships in three public service organizations.* New York, NY: Atherton Press.

Popova, V., & Sharpanskykh, A. (2007a). Process-oriented organization modeling and analysis. In: J. Augusto, J. Barjis, U. Ultes-Nitsche (Eds.), *Proceedings of the 5th International Workshop on Modelling, Simulation, Verification and Validation of Enterprise Information Systems (MSVVEIS 2007)* (pp. 114-126). INSTICC Press.

Popova, V., & Sharpanskykh, A. (2007b). Modelling organizational performance indicators. In: F. Barros, et al. (Eds.), *Proceedings of the International Modeling and Simulation Multi-conference IMSM'07* (pp. 165-170). SCS Press.

Popova, V., & Sharpanskykh, A. (2007c). A formal framework for modeling and analysis of organizations. In: J. Ralyte, S. Brinkkemper, B. Henderson-Sellers (Eds.), *Proceedings of the Situational Method Engineering Conference, ME'07* (pp. 343-359). Berlin: Springer-Verlag.

Scheer, A.-W., & Nuettgens. M. (2000). ARIS architecture and reference models for business process management. In: W. van der Aalst, et al. (Eds.), LNCS 1806, Berlin, 366-389

Scott, W. (2001). *Institutions and organizations.* Thousand Oaks, CA: Sage Publications.

Sharpanskykh, A., & Treur, J. (2006) Verifying inter-level relations within multi-agent systems. *Proceedings of the 17th European Conference on AI, ECAI'06* (pp. 290-294). IOS Press.

Simon, H. (1957). *Administrative behavior* (2nd ed.). New York, NY: Macmillan Co.

Weber, M. (1958). From Max Weber: Essays in sociology. In: H. Gerth, & C. Mills (Eds.). New York, NY: Oxford University Press.

*This work was previously published in International Journal of Enterprise Information Systems, Vol. 4, Issue 3, edited by A. Gunasekaran, pp. 66-78, copyright 2008 by IGI Publishing (an imprint of IGI Global).*

# Chapter 16
# A Procedure Model for a SOA–Based Integration of Enterprise Systems

**Anne Lämmer**
*sd&m AG, Germany*

**Sandy Eggert**
*University of Potsdam, Germany*

**Norbert Gronau**
*University of Potsdam, Germany*

## ABSTRACT

*Enterprise systems are being transferred into a service-oriented architecture. In this article we present a procedure for the integration of enterprise systems. The procedure model starts with decomposition into Web services. This is followed by mapping redundant functions and assigning of the original source code to the Web services, which are orchestrated in the final step. Finally an example is given how to integrate an Enterprise Resource Planning System and an Enterprise Content Management System using the proposed procedure model.*

## INTRODUCTION

Enterprise resource planning systems (ERP systems) are enterprise information systems designed to support business processes. They partially or completely include functions such as order processing, purchasing, production scheduling, dispatching, financial accounting and controlling (Stahlknecht & Hasenkamp, 2002). ERP systems are the backbone of information management in many industrial and commercial enterprises and

focus on the management of master and transaction data (Kalakota & Robinson, 2001). Besides ERP systems, enterprise content management systems (ECM systems) have also developed into companywide application systems over the last few years. ECM solutions focus on indexing all information within an enterprise (Müller, 2003). They cover the processes of enterprise-wide content collection, creation, editing, managing, dispensing and use, in order to improve enterprise and cooperation processes (Koop, Jäckel, & van

Offern, 2001; Kutsch, 2005). In order to manage information independently, ECM combines technologies such as document management, digital archiving, content management, workflow management and so forth. The use of ECM systems is constantly on the rise (Zöller, 2005). This leads to an increasing motivation for enterprises to integrate the ECM systems within the existing ERP systems, especially when considering growing international competition. The need for integration is also eminently based on economical aspects, such as the expense factor in system run time (Schönherr, 2005). For a cross-system improvement of business processes, enterprise systems have to be integrated.

## RELATED WORK

### Service Oriented Architecture as an Integration Approach

A number of integration approaches and concepts already exist. They can be differentiated by integration level (for example data, functions or process integration) and integration architecture (for example point-to-point, hub & spoke, SOA) (Schönherr, 2005). This article presents an approach to integrating enterprise systems by way of building up service-oriented architectures. This integration approach is of special interest and will be described in more detail.

The concept of service orientation is currently being intensively discussed. It can be differentiated from component orientation by its composition and index service (repository). Additionally, SOA is suitable for a process oriented, distributed integration (Schönherr, 2005). However, the addressed goals of component orientation and SOA are similar: different enterprise systems are connected through one interface, and a cross-system data transfer and the reusage of objects or components is enabled. Thereby a service represents

a well-defined function which is generated in reaction to an electronic request (Burbeck, 2000). The SOA approach offers a relatively easy way to connect, add and exchange single services, which highly simplifies the integration of similar systems (e.g., enterprise take-over). Moreover, SOA offers a high degree of interoperability and modularity (Behrmann & Benz, 2005), which increases the adaptability of enterprise systems (Gronau et al., 2006).

The SOA approach is based on the concept of service. The sender wants to use a service and in doing so the sender wants to achieve a specific result. Thereby the sender is not interested in how the request is processed or which further requests are necessary. This is the idea of SOA, where services are defined in a specific language and referenced in a service index. Service request and data exchange occur via use of predefined protocols (Dostal, Jeckle, Melzer, & Zengler, 2005; Küster, 2003).

This service orientation can be used on different levels of architecture. The grid architecture is a common example of infrastructure level (Bermann, Fox, & Hey, 2003; Bry, Nagel, & Schroeder, 2004). On the application level an implementation usually takes place in terms of Web services.

The use of Web services offers the possibility of reusing raw source code, which is merely transferred to another environment (Sneed, 2006). The benefit of this transfer is the re-usage of perfected (old) algorithms. The main disadvantage is the necessity of revising the raw source code in order to find possible dependencies (Sneed, 2006). This is also true for enterprise systems. It is not efficient to reuse the entire old system, but rather only significant parts of it. To accomplish this it is necessary to deconstruct the old enterprise system and to locate the source code parts which can effectively be reused. Our approach uses self-diagnosis for finding these source code locations. This analysis will be considered in the third integration step.

## Self-Diagnosis

As just described, our approach uses self-diagnosis for location of useful source code. For this, the method of self-diagnosis will be presented and the differences to other approaches will be shown.

Some approaches for transformation of legacy-systems into a SOA exist already. However, these approaches see the whole system as one service. The system gets a service description for using this service in a SOA. Our approach differs in that it deconstructs the system for a tailored need. For this, the method of self-diagnosis is used.

Self-diagnosis can be defined as a system's capacity to assign a specific diagnosis to a detected symptom. The detection of symptoms and assignment are performed by the system itself without any outside influence (Latif-Shabgahi, Bass, & Bennett, 1999). The mechanism of self-diagnosis has been detected surveying natural systems; it can partly be applied to artificial systems as well.

The first step of self-diagnosis is the detection of symptoms. Usually the detection of one existing symptom is not sufficient to make an indisputable diagnosis. In this case, more information and data have to be gathered. This can be described as symptom collection. In a second step the symptoms are assigned to a specific diagnosis. Depending on the diagnosis, corresponding measures can be taken (Horling, Benyo, & Lesser, 2001).

Symptoms are a very abstract part of self-diagnosis. These symptoms can be a high network load in distributed systems, missing signals, or buffer overload of the hardware layer. For enterprise systems the symptoms can be the frequency of usage of user interface elements by the user or dependencies of code parts or components. Other types of symptoms are possible. In general, the answer to questions concerning the measure of interesting items provides hints for possible symptoms.

Self-diagnosis can be categorized by the symptom acquisition method. Active and passive self-diagnosis must also be distinguished. In this context, the program or source code is the crucial factor for a division between active and passive self-diagnosis. A fundamental basis for either alternative is an observer or monitor.

Using passive self-diagnosis, the monitor detects and collects symptoms and information. It can either be activated automatically or manually (Gronau et al., 2006). If you know which items need to be observed and the point where this information can be gathered, you only have to monitor this point. This is what passive self-diagnosis does. For example: if you want to know how often a button is pressed, you have to find where the button-event is implemented in the code and observe this button-event.

In active self-diagnosis, the program's function or modules are the active elements. They send defined information to the monitor and act independently if necessary. The monitor is used as receiver and interprets the gathered information and symptoms. The main advantage of active self-diagnosis is the possibility of detecting new symptoms, even if no clear diagnosis can be made before the problems become acute and are forwarded to other systems. In contrast, using passive self-diagnosis, the monitor can only inquire about specific data. In this case, a response or further examination is only possible if the problem is already known. For example: if you do not know the location of all the buttons and or the code component for the button-event, you will have to recognize all events with their initial point and filter them with the monitor. The monitor does not have to know how many buttons exist or where their code is located, but the buttons have to "know" to register with the monitor. These are the requirements of active self-diagnosis.

The assembly of diagnosis points depends on the application context and the software system. The required time and effort cannot be specified; it depends on the design and implementation of the software system.

Self-diagnosis can also be employed for the examination of source-code usage and interdependences. Depending on the desired information, different points of diagnosis have to be integrated into the source-code.

Different points of diagnosis have to be determined in order to allow for the allocation of code parts to various fields and functions. Therefore context, programming language, and software system architecture must be considered.

Our approach uses this method to locate code parts that can be collected into components. As we will demonstrate later in this article, we need to locate functions and enterprise systems business objects.

This method can be used for the detection of code parts which are possible services. Diagnosis points must thereby be integrated into the system source code, and software dependencies analyzed.

As we discussed earlier in this article, the main challenges in integration of legacy enterprise systems like ERP and ECM are, first, the deconstruction and second, the allocation of code. To address these challenges, we have developed a procedure model which will be described next.

## PROCEDURE MODEL

In the following, a procedure model that integrates general application systems within a company is presented. The procedure model begins with the deconstruction of systems into Web services. This is followed by a mapping of redundant functions and the assignment of original source code to Web services, which is orchestrated in the last step.

The process includes taking the old ERP system; deconstructing it into different abstraction levels such as functional entities or business objects, searching for redundant entities, allocating the code fragments dependent on these functional entities and encapsulating them. This results in many independent functional entities, which can be described as a service. They have different abstraction levels and have to compose

and orchestrate with, for example BPEL-WS. This composition and orchestration is the way of integration.

## Deconstruction of Systems

First, the systems which are to be integrated are deconstructed into services. The challenge of this step depends on the number of particular services, which could span the range from one single service per system, up to a definition of every single method or function within a system as a service. In the case of a very broad definition, the advantages, such as easy maintenance and reuse and so forth, will be lost. In case of a very narrow definition, disadvantages concerning performance and orchestration develop; the configuration and interdependencies of the services become too complex.

This article proposes a hierarchical approach which describes services of different granular qualities on three hierarchical levels. *Areas of function* of a system are described as the first of these levels (Figure 1, Part 1). For example, an area of functions could include purchase or sales in the case of an ERP system or, in the case of ECM systems, archiving or content management. An area of function can be determined on the abstract level by posing questions about the general "assigned task" of the system. The differences between the three hierarchical levels can be discovered by answering the following questions:

1.  **Question:** What are the tasks of the particular system? The answers resulting from this step correspond to services on the first level, which constitute the general task—for example sales, purchasing, inventory management or workflow management, archiving or content management. These tasks are abstract and describe main functionalities. They consist of many other functions which are the objects of the next level.

*Figure 1. Procedure model for the integration of application systems*

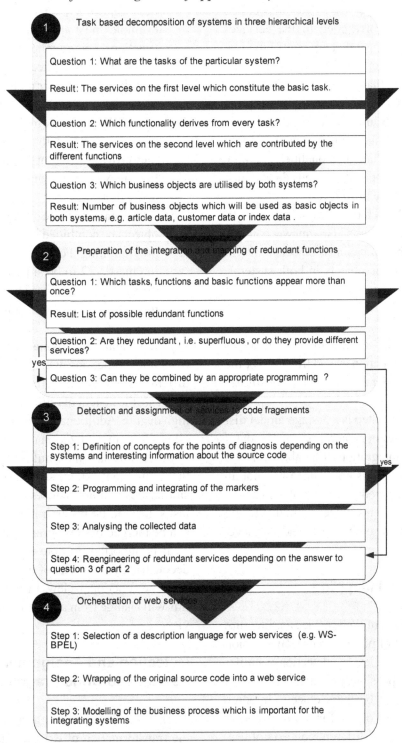

2. **Question:** Which functionality derives from every single task? The answers to this question correspond to the services on the second level that are contributed by the various functions. These functions are more detailed than the general tasks. They describe what the tasks consist of and what they do—for example, calculate the delivery time, identify a major customer, or constitute check-in and e-mail functionalities. For these functions the application needs data, which can found in the third level.

3. **Question:** Which business objects are utilized by both systems? This answer consists of the number of business objects that will be used as basic objects in both systems, for example article data, customer data or index data.

In this procedure model, all possible levels of service deconstruction are addressed; yet the realization on all hierarchical levels constitutes an individual task.

The result of this step is a 3-stage model displaying the services of an application. The data-level, that is the integration of databases, is not further examined at this point since it is not an integral part of our model, the aim of which is to wrap functions as Web services without altering them or the original source code. The data level is not touched by this process.

## Preparation and Mapping

The main advantage of Web service architecture is the high degree of possible reuse. By division into three hierarchical levels, a detection of similar functions is made possible, especially on the level of functionality and business objects. In some cases an adjustment of the functions is necessary in order to serve different contexts of use. Therefore, the next step consists of integration on different levels and the mapping of identical functions (Figure 1, Part 2). This step poses the following questions:

1. **Question:** Which tasks, functions and business objects appear more than once? For example, most applications contain search functions. Some applications have functions for check in and check out. ERP systems calculate the time for many things with the same algorithm under different names.

2. **Question:** Are these multiple functions and objects-redundant, that is superfluous, or do they provide different services? Some functions may have the same name but perform different tasks.

3. **Question:** Can these multiple functions and objects be combined by way of appropriate programming? For the functions ascertained in Question 2 to be similar functions with different names the possibility of integrating them into one has to be analyzed.

The advantage of this mapping is the detection of identical functions, which may by only named differently while completing the same task. In doing so, the benefit of reuse can be exploited to a high degree. Additionally, this part of the survey allows for a minimization of programming, due to the encapsulation of multiple functions. Only those functions which share a high number of similarities, but nevertheless complete different tasks, have to be programmed differently; they can be merged by reprogramming.

It is important to note that for this part the deconstruction consists of an abstract level and is in the functional view. In the following step, this will change from a functional view to a code view.

## Detection and Assignment of Services to Code Fragments

The next step brings the biggest challenge, namely the transformation of existing applications into service oriented architecture. Until now, services have been identified by their tasks, but the correlation to existing source code still needs to be done. This is going to be accomplished in the next step (Figure 1, Part 3).

Self-diagnosis is used at this point to integrate earlier defined points of diagnosis into the source code. These points of diagnosis actively collect usage data and facilitate conclusions concerning the fields and functions via their structure. The structure of the points of diagnosis depends on the context of their application and on the software system. It is not possible to describe the complexity of the process, which also depends on the structure and programming of the software systems.

As we discussed earlier in Section 2.2, the points of diagnosis depend on what needs to be observed. Here we want to know which code fragments share correspondences and execute the identified functions in the functional view. From this follows the necessity of a monitor. For example, the points can be every method call in the source code of an ERP system. If the user calls a function, the points of diagnosis have to inform the monitor that they were called. The monitor has to recognize and to analyze which method calls belong together.

Now the code fragments are analyzed and assigned to the functions identified in Part 1, and the wrapping of code fragments into Web services can be started. This step necessitates the usage of the existing source code and the description of relevant parts with a Web service description language, making possible the reuse of source code in service oriented architecture.

If redundant services have been detected in Part 2, which need to be reengineered, then the reengineering happens now.

## Orchestration of Web Services

The results of stage 3 are the described Web services. These have to be connected with each other depending on the business process. This orchestration takes place in several steps (Figure 1, Part 4).

First, the context must be defined; second, the service description language has to be selected; and third, the Web services need to be combined.

A four-stage procedure model for a service-oriented integration of application systems has just been described. This process holds the advantages of a step-by-step transformation. The amount of time needed for this realization is considerably higher than in a "big bang" transformation, however, a "big bang" transformation holds a higher risk and therefore requires high-quality preparation measures. For this reason, a "big bang" transformation is dismissed in favor of a step-by-step transformation.

There is yet another important advantage in the integration or deconstruction of application systems into services when carried out in several steps. First, a basic structure is built (construction of a repository, etc.). Next, a granular decomposition into Web services occurs on the first level, thereby realizing a basic transformation of a service oriented concept. Following this, Web services of the second and third hierarchical level can be integrated step-by-step. This reduction into services provides high quality integration.

The procedure model we just presented is very abstract. Therefore, a practical example for two enterprise systems, ERP and ECM, will be given in Part 4.

## EXAMPLE OF APPLYING THE PROCEDURE MODEL

It is necessary to develop a general usage approach and to test it on ERP and ECM systems since no concrete scenario of these technologies in regard to praxis as of yet exists (Issing, 2003). The aim of this example of use is to describe the integration of both company-wide systems, ERP and ECM, using our presented approach.

In what follows, we present a case study of a situation of integration of two systems: an ERP and an ECM system. A German manufacturer of engines and devices administer a complex IT landscape. This IT landscape includes, among others, two big enterprise systems. One of them is the ERP system "Microsoft Dynamics NAV" and the other is the ECM system "OS.5|ECM" of Optimal Systems. The ERP System includes modules such as purchasing, sales and inventory management. The ECM system consists of modules such as document management, archiving and workflow management. In the current situation a bidirectional interface between both systems exists. One example of a business process in which both systems are used is the processing of incoming mails and documents. In order to scan and save the incoming invoices of suppliers, the module of the ECM System "document management" is used. The access to the invoice is made possible through the ERP system.

In the future, a SOA-based integration of both enterprise systems can be reasonably expected under the aspect of business process improvement. Referring to the example mentioned above, the "portal management" component could be used to access, search, and check-in all incoming documents. What follows is a description, in four parts, of the integration based on the procedure model we presented in Part 3.

Part 1: Segmentation of ERP and ECM Systems into Services

According to the procedure model (Figure 1), the individual systems will be separated into independent software objects, which in each case complete specified functions or constitute business objects. The segmentation is structured in three bottom-up steps (Figure 2).

Identification is based on the answers to questions concerning main tasks of specific systems. The basic functions of an ERP system are purchasing, sales, master data management, inventory management und repository management. Document management, content management, records management, workflow management and portal management are basic functions of ECM systems. Subsequently, the areas of functions are disaggregated into separate tasks. Business objects are classified such as the business object "article" or "customer". Thus, segmentation in areas of functions, tasks of functions and business objects is achieved and a basis for the reusage of services is created.

*Figure 2. Segmentation of services*

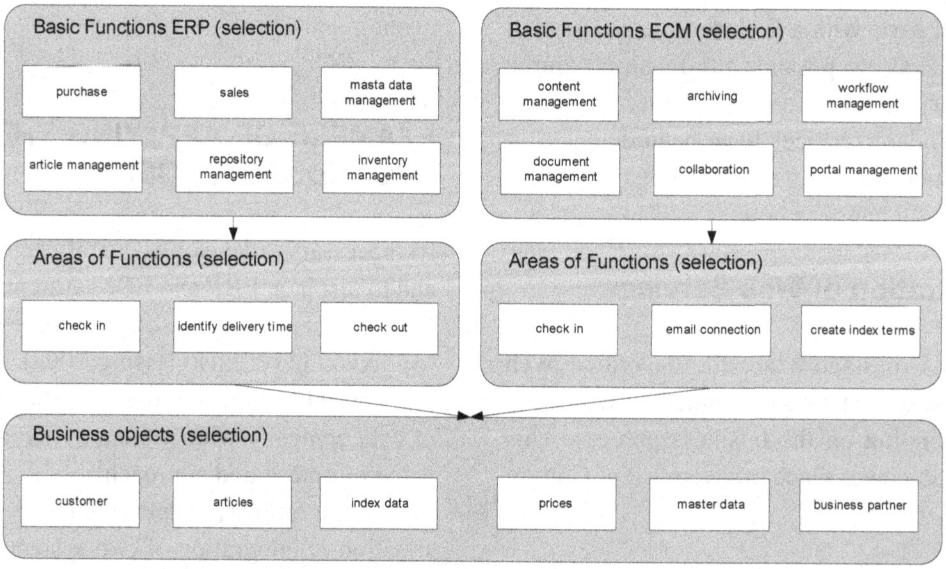

Part 2: Preparation of Integration/Mapping

The results of the first step of the segmentation are separation of services of differentiated granularity per system. According to the procedure model, the mapping on the different areas will be arranged in the second step. For that purpose, the potential services described will be examined for similarities. On every level of hierarchy, the functional descriptions (answers to questions in Part 1) of services are checked and compared with each other. If functions or tasks are similar, they will have to be checked for possibility of combination and be slotted for later reprogramming. One example of such similarity between functions is "create index terms". Most enterprise systems include the function "create index terms" for documents such as invoices or new articles. The estimation of analogy of different functions, particularly in enterprise systems where implementation is different, lies in the expertise of the developer. Another example is the service "check in/check out". This service is a basic function of both ERP and ECM systems and is now to be examined for possible redundancy. After determining that the services "check in" or "check out" are equal, the service will be registered as a basic function only once. Services which are not equal but related will be checked in another step and either unified with suitable programming or, if possible, spilt into different services. The results

of this step are the classification of services from ERP and ECM systems into similar areas and the separation of redundant services. The following table shows examples of separated services.

By this separation of both enterprise systems, a higher degree of re-usage and improved complexity handling of these systems is achieved. For the application of services, a service-oriented architecture (SOA) which defines the different roles of participants is now required (Burbeck, 2000).

Part 3: Detection and Assignment of Services to Code Fragments

As already described in the general introduction, the identification of functions to be segmented in the source code constitutes one of the biggest challenges in a transfer to service-oriented architecture. As part of this approach, the method of self-diagnosis is suggested. Appropriate points of diagnosis will be linked to the source code in order to draw conclusions from used functions to associated class, method or function in the original source code. Through the use of aspect oriented programming, aspects can be programmed and linked to the classes and methods of the application system. Necessary data, such as the name of the accessed method, can be collected by accessing the respective classes and methods (Vanderperren, Suvée, Verheecke, Cibrán, & Jonckers, 2005).

*Table 1. Examples of separate services of ERP and ECM systems*

| Separate services | ERP | ECM |
|---|---|---|
| Basic Functions | Purchase | Content management |
| | Sales | Archiving |
| | Article management | Document management |
| | Repository management | Workflow management |
| Areas of Functions | Check in | E-mail connection |
| | Identify delivery time | Save document |
| | Check out | Create index terms |

Based on a defined service, "order transaction", all the names of methods which are necessary for the execution of "order transaction" must be identified. To wrap the service "order transaction", for example to combine it with a Web service description language, the original methods need be searched for and encapsulated. Additionally, the reprogramming of redundant functions is part of the phase of identification and isolation of services. This, as well, is only possible if the original methods are identified.

Part 4: Orchestration of Web Services

The last integration phase is used to compile Web services. The previous steps had to be completed in preparation for the procedure model. The Web services now are completely described and have a URI to be accessed. Now, only the composition and the chronology of requests of the specific Web services are missing. For the orchestration the Web service business process execution language (WS-BPEL) is recommended. The WS-BPEL was developed by the OASIS-Group and is currently in the process of standardization (Cover, 2005). If the Web services present a function with a business process, the WS-BPEL is particularly suitable for orchestration of Web services (Lübke, Lüecke, Schneider, & Gómez, 2006). Essentially, BPEL is a language to compose (Leymann & Roller, 2000) new Web services from existing Web services with help of workflow technologies (Leymann, 2003). In BPEL, a process is defined which is started by a workflow system in order to start a business process.

Web services are addressed via a graphical representation with a modelling imagery of WS-BPEL. The business process is modelled independently from the original enterprise systems. Since in the first integration step, the systems were separated by their tasks and functions, now all of the functions are available for the business process as well.

## CONCLUSION

The procedure model for the integration of application systems as it has been presented in this paper is an approach that has been successfully deployed in one case. Currently the assignment ability and the universality are being tested. The self-diagnosis, that is the assignment of source code to services via aspect oriented programming, constitutes a bigger challenge.

A verification of costs and benefits cannot be given sufficiently; however, several examples show convincing results and suggest a general transferability. The complexity in such a realization cannot be specified. Particularly for bigger and complex systems, the cost-to-benefit ratio has to be verified. Despite this, it must be recognized that the assignment of code fragments to functions is not an easy task. If one observes every method call a high number of calls must be analyzed. Visualization can be helpful for analyzing, since method calls belonging together will build a cluster in the emerging network. The observation of method calls is possibly not the most optimal way for very complex systems. If the functional view of services in Part 1 is not part of the business object layer, but only of the general task layer, one can reduce the numbers of diagnosis points. The possibilities depend on the programming language and their constructs.

Finally, the approach presented above describes a procedure model for service-oriented integration of different application systems. The integration proceeds using Web services which thereby improve the integration ability, interoperability, flexibility and sustainability. The reusable Web services facilitate the extraction of several functions and combination of these into a new service. This allows for reuse of several software components.

Altogether, Web services improve the adaptability of software systems to the business processes and increase efficiency (Hofman, 2003). To give an example of the realization of the procedure model, an integration of an ERP- and ECM-system was chosen. The reasons for this choice consist in targeted improvement of business aspects and increasing complexity of both application systems. Dealing with this complexity makes integration necessary. Through mapping, redundant functions can be detected and as a consequence, a reduction of the complexity is made possible. Regarding the adaptability and flexibility of affected application systems, Web services are a suitable approach for integration. In particular, it is the reuse of services and an adaptable infrastructure which facilitate the integration.

In addition to all of this, we expect to discover additional advantages concerning maintenance and administration of affected application systems.

# REFERENCES

Behrmann, T., & Benz, T. (2005). Service-oriented-architecture-ERP. In T. Benz (Ed.), Forschungsbericht 2005 Interdisziplinäres Institut für intelligente Geschäftsprozesse.

Berman, F., Fox, G., & Hey, T. (2003). Grid computing. *Making the global infrastrucure a reality*. Wiley.

Bry, F., Nagel, W., & Schroeder, M. (2004). Grid computing. *Informatik Spektrum, 27*(6), 542-545.

Burbeck, S., (2000). *The Tao of e-business services*. IBM Corporation. Retrieved January 12, 2008, from http://www.ibm.com/software/developer/library/ws-tao/index.html

Cover, R. (2004). *Web standards for business process modelling, collaboration, and choreography*. Retrieved January 12, 2008, from http://xml.coverpages.org/bpm.html

Dostal, W., Jeckle, M., Melzer, I., & Zengler, B. (2005). *Service-orientierte architekturen mit Web services* [Service oriented architectures with web services]. Spektrum Akademischer Verlag.

Gronau, N., Lämmer, A., & Andresen, K. (2006). Entwicklung wandlungsfähiger auftragsabwicklungssysteme [Development of adaptable enterprise systems]. In N. Gronau, A. Lämmer (Eds.), *Wandlungsfähige ERP-Systeme* (37-56). Gito Verlag.

Gronau, N., Lämmer, A., & Müller, C. (2006). Selbstorganisierte dienstleistungsnetzwerke im maschinen- und anlagenbau [Self organized service networks at engineering]. *Industrie-Management, 2*, 9-12.

Hofmann, O. (2003). Web-services in serviceorientierten IT-Architekturkonzepten [Web services in service oriented concepts of IT architecture]. In H.-P. Fröschle (Ed.), *Web-services*. Praxis der Wirtschaftinformatik, HMD 234, dpunkt Verlag, Wiesbaden 2003, S.27-33.

Horling, B., Benyo, B., & Lesser, V. (2001) *Using self-diagnosis to adapt organizational structures*. Computer Science Technical Report TR-99-64, University of Massachusetts.

Issing, F. (2003). Die softwarestrategie für web-services und unternehmensinfrastrukturen der firma Sun Microsystems [Software strategy for web services and enterprise infrastructures of Sun Microsystems]. In H.-P. Fröschle (Ed.), *Web-Services* (pp. 17-26). Praxis der Wirtschaftinformatik, HMD 234, dpunkt Verlag.

Kalakota, R., & Robinson, M. (2002). Praxishandbuch des e-business [Practice e-business]. *Book of practice financial times*. Prentice Hall, 317ff.

Koop, H. J., Jäckel, K. K., & van Offern, A. L. (2001). Erfolgsfaktor content management—Vom Web-content bis zum knowledge management [Success factor enterprise content management—from web-content to knowledge management]. Vieweg:Verlag.

Küster, M. W. (2003). Web-services—Versprechen und realität [Web services—promises and reality]. In H.-P. Fröschle (Ed.), *Web-services* (pp. 5-15). Praxis der Wirtschaftinformatik, HMD 234, dpunkt Verlag.

Kutsch, O. (2005). *Enterprise-content-management bei finanzdienstleistern—Integration in strategien, prozesse und systeme* [Enterprise content management at financial service provider—Integration at strategies, processes and systems]. Deutscher Universitäts: Verlag.

Kuropka, D., Bog, A., & Weske, M. (2006). Semantic enterprise services platform: Motivation, potential, functionality and application scenarios. In *Proceedings of the 10th IEEE International EDOC Enterprise Computing Conference* (pp. 253-261). Hong Kong.

Leymann, F., & Roller, D. (2000). *Production workflow—Concepts and techniques*. Prentice Hall International.

Leymann, F. (2003). Choreography: Geschäftsprozesses mit web services [Choreography: Business processes with web services]. *OBJECTspektrum, 6*, 52-59.

Latif-Shabgahi, G., Bass, J. M., & Bennett, S. (1999). Integrating selected fault masking and self-diagnosis mechanisms. In *Proceedings of the 7th Euromicro Workshop on Parallel and Distributed Processing*m, *PDP'99 IEEE Computer Society* (pp. 97-104).

Lübke, D., Lüecke, T., Schneider, K., & Gómez, J. M. (2006). Using event-driven process chains of model-driven development of business applications. In F. Lehner, H. Nösekabel, & P. Kleinschmidt (Eds.), *Multikonferenz wirtschaftsinformatik 2006* (pp. 265-279). GITO-Verlag.

Müller, D. (2003). *Was ist enterprise-content-management?* [What is enterprise content management?] Retrieved January 14, 2008, from http://www.zdnet.de/ itmanager/strategie/0,39023331,2138476,00.htm

Schönherr, M. (2005). Enterprise applikation integration (EAI) und middleware, grundlagen, architekturen und auswahlkriterien [Enterprise application integration (EAI) and middleware, fundamentals, architectures and criteria of choice]. *ERP Management, 1*, 25-29.

Scheckenbach, R. (1997). *Semantische geschäftsprozessintegration* [Semantic integration of business processes]. Deutscher Universitäts:Verlag.

Stahlknecht, P., & Hasenkamp, U. (2002). Einführung in die wirtschaftsinformatik [Introduction to business computing] (10th ed). Springer Verlag.

Sneed, H. M. (2006). Reengineering von legacy programmen für die wiederverwendung als web services [Reengineering of legacy software for reuse as web services]. In *Proceedings zum Workshop Software-Reengineering und Services der Multikonferenz Wirtschaftsinformatik.*

Vanderperren, W., Suvée, D., Verheecke, B., Cibrán, M. A., & Jonckers, V. (2005). Adaptive programming in JAsCo. In *Proceedings of the 4th International Conference on Aspect-Oriented Software Development.* ACM Press.

Zöller, B. (2005). Vom archiv zum enterprise content management [From archive to enterprise content Management]. *ERP Management, 4*, 38-40.

*This work was previously published in International Journal of Enterprise Information Systems, Vol. 4, Issue 2, edited by A. Gunasekaran, pp. 1-12, copyright 2008 by IGI Publishing (an imprint of IGI Global).*

# Chapter 17
# An Adaptive E–Commerce Architecture for Enterprise Information Exchange

**Youcef Aklouf**
*University of Science and Technology, Algeria*

**Habiba Drias**
*University of Science and Technology, Algeria*

## ABSTRACT

*This article contributes to the design of a generic framework for providing a new way to exchange information between enterprises. This concept is a well addressed in the context of B2B standards. Many organizations are increasingly searching for adopting these standards to automate data exchange. But the limit of such models resides in the fact that the content of exchange is defined in several formats which make their use difficult. To overcome this difficulty, we have explored the possibility to integrate new models for describing content involved in B2B transaction which represent a key issue. Our finding establishes the feasibility of integrating product models described by ontology with e-commerce standards especially at the business process level. This article presents a descriptive model allowing partners to exchange information with other organisations without modifying their Information System. The case study also indicates that our system is developed as a Service Oriented Architecture.*

## INTRODUCTION

Over the last 20 years, e-commerce (EC) has been recognized as an efficient tool to handle complex exchange and transactions between companies. EC is becoming ever more important in developing new activities and new models especially for business-to-business (B2B) interactions.

B2B is concerned with all activities involved in obtaining information about products and services and managing these information flows between organisations (Peat & Webber, 1997). The B2B architectures are difficult to conceptualize because they handle several scenarios as a Business Process (BP) and several contents with different formats as product catalogs defined separately by different organisations.

EC systems are well-conceived to address these different issues, even when the multiples sources of information will cause heterogeneity of exchange (Tellmann & Meadche, 2003). To ensure and exchange competitively between partners it will be necessary to have a new view about how we describe all concepts involved in such interactions.

The main concepts related to EC models are a BP concept and a content (payload or useful data) concept. These two pieces of information are defined separately by each standard in a specific format. This article proposes an adaptive architecture that gathers product catalogues standards with EC standards in order to automate exchange and purchasing operation.

A number of standards try to define a global and a generic architecture to consider large industry sectors and areas. The old one is the UN initiative: Electronic Data Interchange for Administration, Commerce, and Transport (EDIFACT) (United Nations, 1999). The shortcoming of this generation of approaches like EDIFACT is in the fact that they require a significant programming effort from organizations to be able to use these standards. Thus, the cost will is higher for this reason. EDIFACT has just been used by small number of companies and was not allowed for small organizations. To overcome this limitation and to close this gap in order to reduce cost and to improve quality of interaction and communication between partners, new standards have appeared in the same time with the development of the Internet infrastructure. For example, there are some e-commerce portals for online purchasing and ordering product from online catalogues—harbinger.net, mysap.com, verticalNet.com—in which transaction content specifications can be rendered easily by standard browsers. In addition to XML and EDI initiatives (Westarp, Weitzel, Buxmann, & König, 1999), a proprietary standard (de facto) exists like RosettaNet which is a B2B architecture used for IT and semi-conductors content. The BP model of RosettaNet named PIP (Partner Interface Process, RosettaNet, 2001c) can be used with other catalogues. ebXML (ebXML, 2001a) is a horizontal model defined without any relation to any product catalogues, it just describes some specifications for BP, core component, registry, and all pieces required to implement a global B2B system.

As a result, a B2B system is built using the existing standards cited above by overcoming their limits and sharing their different advantages. Also, the system will ensure interoperability, which is a key issue in order to share several product catalogs with the same architecture. This is the main reason why we propose in this article to use product ontology[1] for characterizing product catalogs and trying to define BP ontology for managing any kind of transactions. Shared ontologies play a crucial role for supporting an adaptive architecture to save time and money and to increase its efficiency through B2B transactions.

This work aims to define an adaptive infrastructure using ontologies for the electronic commerce, especially in the B2B framework. The exchange of data, information, and knowledge are the key issues. Two kinds of ontologies can be used to improve exchange in such architecture. One addresses products and services characterization, whereas the other addresses business processes. We demonstrate the capability of integration of these two kinds of ontologies in a unique and global B2B-layered architecture. The idea is to use several business process ontologies conjointly with several products ontology in order to ensure reliability and feasibility of such exchange in different ways.

In the first part of this article, we argue that ontology for both BP and product is needed to automate B2B exchange. In the second part, the proposed architecture and its three parts are presented. The third part describes the different components of the system with an overview of objectives and functionalities for each part. Finally, the last part shows a case study of the developed platform using PLIB ontology and the Web services paradigm.

## ONTOLOGIES FOR E-COMMERCE ARCHITECTURES

In spite of the promise that e-commerce holds, most implementing organisations have not received the full benefits from their B2B investments. This is because they use their proprietary solutions (backend systems) for modelling BP and for describing product catalogs. In addition, this information doesn't provide an agreement among all participants. For this reason, a B2B e-commerce exchange requires some consensual decisions about all data shared and all services used in transactions. As suggested by several authors (BIC, 2001; Trastour, Preist, & Colemann, 2003), it is necessary to have a meta-model that states the high-level architectural elements without getting into details of their implementations. Such a model will remain relatively stable over time, even if technologies, standards, and implementation details evolve. It also was allowed to split the work and to select a best-in-class solution for each facet of the global system in order to be adaptive, to ensure scalability and to provide a highly integrated organization. Ontology is being used to define this global view as an abstraction level sharing product catalogs and BP descriptions. Thus, product data and BP will be shared and have a same description for all participants in order to promote exchange between them. Ontology deals with interoperability of business contents and of message exchanges among business systems of different enterprises.

If it is clear that ontologies are necessary to be integrated in e-commerce architectures (McGuinness, 1999; Jasper, & Uschold, 1999), many issues and challenges have to be addressed very carefully. The implementation of such system technology is also a key management issue. It is a high operation, a cost project and it is a complex process. According to this, different organizations and industries leaders must work conjointly in order to drive B2B standards, to define both content ontology and collaboration in its different implementations steps in order to reach an agreement about the shared ontologies.

Therefore, on top of the structure of the exchanged message, two kinds of knowledge need to be modeled and shared across all the partners involved in B2B transactions: business process knowledge and product and service knowledge. Such shared conceptualizations are usually called ontologies. Thus, two kinds of standard ontologies have to be developed: ontology of products and services on one hand, and ontologies of business processes on the other hand.

With this motivation in mind, our objective is to define a generic architecture allowing the use of any BP interfacing it with any product catalogs content. This model could be applied in several areas.

## THE PROPOSED ARCHITECTURE

This section proposes an exchange model represented by a layered architecture (Aklouf, Pierra, Ait Ameur, & Drias, 2005) gathering the various classes of information necessary to ensure a completely automatic exchange between partners. This exchange model is inspired from several infrastructures proposed in the literature such as ebXML (ebXML, 2001), RosettaNet (RosettaNet, 2001a) OAGI (Randy, 2001), and so on. The model with its three layers is also called an integration model within the company processes. This model makes it possible to integrate processes remotely between several companies.

These processes can be industrial or logistic. Integration can require the installation of a workflow system between organizations (Trastour et al., 2003). This business model has as main objectives, the reduction of the coordination costs as well as the reduction of durations of exchange of goods and services.

The most categories of information (classes) identified by the model are summarized in the following:

1.  Information that allow a system to locate and discover automatically a partner, which provides the service required by the consumer (like a specific search engine for companies and services);
2.  Information about the supported business process, gathering different steps to be followed during collaboration. This is defined by several languages and protocols;
3.  Information describing products and services used in the exchange (products ontologies describe this category of information).

Figure 1 illustrates the architecture of the model with these three components.

This architecture allows exchange between two or several partners represented by the systems as A, B … Z, via interfaces between layers. These interfaces provide services making it possible to deliver the necessary information to the adjacent layer. The three levels represent the three parts of the system and can work conjointly to increase the automaticity of the B2B exchange model.

The partner must give some technical solutions describing various measurements taken and standards chosen to adapt the company local system to support a communication with others partners. This requires on one hand, the extension of the internal information system by tools belonging to these various levels and, in addition, the integration of these tools at the local level, allowing each company to have a uniform global system in accordance with the suggested B2B model (Aklouf & Drias, 2007).

As stated previously, to carry out exchanges between companies using this model, it is necessary to develop the following points.

•   First, use the discovering layer (1) and have the possibility to locate in an automatic way,

*Figure 1. The layered infrastructure representing the exchange model*

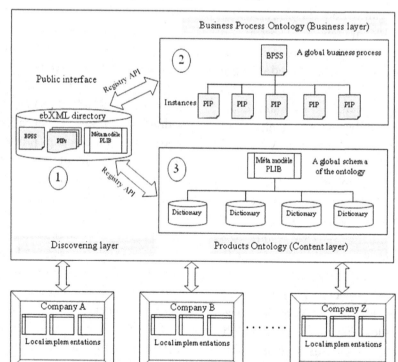

the company having the capability to answer the requests with the customer requirements whatever their nature might be;

- Then, once the localization of the partner is accomplished, a collaboration agreement is established by the layer business process (2). This layer provides all steps to be followed and executed during the exchange;

- Finally, the exchange can start with the use of a format of contents accepted by both actors (3). This supposes that a preliminary consensus on the nature and the representation of the product catalogs of data exchanged was established previously.

## Objectives of the Proposed Architecture

The objective of the suggested model is to set up an adaptive architecture which can be used as a horizontal or a vertical system. A vertical standard is a system which is specific to some kind of activities or some particular products. For instance, RosettaNet is a standard specific to semiconductors and electronic information commerce. A horizontal standard is a general system which defines exchange protocols and information formats without referencing any product or service. The standard ebXML is an example of a model which proposes generic and standardized services for the most industry branches and which can be adapted to particular fields and contexts. This model provides also a collaborative environment allowing industrial managers, the consortia and the developers of standards, to work conjointly or in collaboration in order to have an effective and a reliable exchange system in which the integration of the companies is done with lower cost.

The main objectives of this architecture are:

- The description of an infrastructure that proposes an intelligent module for discovering and localizing partners who propose services

and eBusiness catalogues: the most known standards are UDDI (Dogac, Cingil, Laleci, & Kabak, 2002) and the ebXML registry.

- The proposition of a business process ontology model based on the existing standards such as PIP of RosettaNet (RosettaNet, 2001c), ebXML BPSS (ebXML, 2005), BPMN (Business Process Management Notation), BPEL (Business Process Execution Language), and so on.

- And finally, the integration of the existing industrial catalogues of components describing objects or services from several industrial sectors. Among them we find, RNTD, RNBD of RosettaNet (RosettaNet, 2001b), PLIB (ISO 10303-11, 1994), and so on.

Our principal focus is on the definition of an open architecture allowing the integration of different technologies and knowledge coming from heterogeneous communities. This architecture requires the modeling of business processes adaptable to the needs and the requirements dictated by the specificity of these exchanges.

## Architecture Functionalities

This model presents a set of useful functionalities:

1.  The possibility of adding new functionalities to the system as a product catalogue model or as a separately developed dictionary;
2.  The possibility of managing applications and data locally or remotely;
3.  The factorization of a set of knowledge as standards and business rules useful for the various parts of the system;
4.  The possibility of modifying the topology of the model, following the adoption of new standards or the implementation of a new tool (ensure evolution of the system – scalability-);

5.  The flexibility of the model accepting the adhesion of new partners without modifying the architecture;

6.  the possibility offered by the loosely coupled aspect of the model, which offers the possibility to take into account competences and tools proposed by partners in order to be used by the defined architecture (Aklouf et al., 2003).

In the next section we describe separately and in more details each part of the system.

## Discovering Layer

The first task which must be realized by the exchange system consists in finding the partners with whom to collaborate. This part of the system must provide exactly the required service and the contact information about the supplier of services. To satisfy this requirement, a repository (directory) containing business documents, data, meta-data and necessary mechanisms to research and discover partners, must be developed. This module must be carried out with the collaboration of all partners involved on the development of a technical specification making it possible to publish and retrieve information, the companies' profiles and the provided services.

## Objectives of the Discovering Component

The initial goal of this module is to provide a shared and universal place where each company, whatever its size, its sphere of activity and its localization might be, could publish its services and find and localize in a dynamic way the required services. This vision is not yet materialized. There are, however, some concrete uses of standards such as UDDI and ebXML. Currently, it is about a limited use within a restricted and controlled framework: Intranets.

The fact of indexing the various services offered by the same organization is mainly important if this organization wishes that its services will be used and shared. The importance of having a central directory is to guarantee discovery of the services provided by organizations if they are published (it is like a specialized research engine for organizations profiles and services). It is exactly the same case for a Web page which will not be visited if it is not referred to in a search engine.

In other words, this component makes it possible to determine how company information and services must be organized in order to allow the community which divides this directory to have access. This directory or repository must provide a general schema and each company must publish its profile like its services according to this schema.

The repository must support the following principles bases:

*   The access to the directory and the suggested schema is free, without control and limit;
*   The access to the data directory is done by contextual research or through a hierarchical keys organization;
*   The management of the repository is ensured by one or more organizations;
*   The possibility of having broker space for receiving submissions before the publishing and validating the data is offered. This space makes it possible to correct and modify information with some errors.

## Directory Functionalities

The directory must provide to the various companies a set of functions and methods to ensure the following functionalities:

1.  Exchange messages and business documents;
2.  Manage business relationships between companies;

3. Communicate data in a standard format;
4. Define and save the business process;
5. Retrieve the ontology model defining the contents;
6. Download and install tools for managing the various existing ontologies.

## Business Process Ontology Layer

Once the exchange partner is located, it is necessary to agree on the various steps of the exchange scenario from the business process. A business process represents an ordered set of interactions. Each interaction represents an atomic exchange of messages between partners (Tellmann & Meadche, 2003). The emergence of business process modeling standards makes it possible to create a rationalization of the analysis methods of the processes and the creation of a community of knowledge shared by all exchange actors.

The description of the business processes must be based on formalism and a clear method, which allow a real sharing of this knowledge by the various actors (business or computer science). This formalism must integrate a typology of process, a strategy of rigorous decomposition which allows a homogenization and an optimal visibility of all levels of responsibility. A set of basic rules and ways of making the tools, adapted to the contexts of the company—for example, tools like UML, XML (Peltz & Murray, 2004)—make it possible to answer effectively the customer's requirements involved in such exchange.

## Objectives of the BP Ontology Component

The role and all tasks of the company are represented by a set of processes. These processes are in close connection with the components of the information system. For this purpose, the integration of the various applications must be implemented correctly.

However, the objective is the piloting of the architecture of the exchange model by business processes. This part of the model is fundamental because it is the basis of autonomy and the agility given to the company in the evolution of its information system. The assembly and the dismantling of the business functions are made available to the users from the system without having to call upon the usual supervision of the technical managers of the information system.

The goal desired by including various tools and business process models in this layer is to provide a generic and a flexible architecture. The characteristic of this multilevel model is in the integrality and the homogeneity of the tools and methods which are provided to create the necessary business processes. These tools will be discussed in the case study section.

## Business Process Ontology Functionalities

The functionalities of business process ontology are described as follows:

- Formalize collaborations and the dialogues between partners based on rules defined by the process model used;
- Increase the effectiveness and the quality of the exchanges between partners;
- Ensure interoperability between the various processes which reference the various contents;
- Ensure the coordination based on the shared resources. This is related to the scheduling and the control of the shared resources (a resource is an informational entity handled by the business process);
- Manage the choreography of the business activities.

The goal of Web services is to achieve a universal interoperability between applications using the Web standards (Randy & Hall, 2001). This is why they are basically integrated in the description of business processes. Indeed, the automation and the management of business processes were historically a difficult challenge for the companies because of the inflexibility of their data-processing infrastructure. The Service Oriented Architecture (SOA) provides this flexibility. It gives to the processes the necessary abstraction level for both the definition and the execution of the process. The advent of SOA makes integration disappear as a distinct activity.

## Content Ontology

Once the partner is localized and the exchange process well established and defined, it remains to have a consensus on the data (catalogues of products) which will be exchanged. It should be also guaranteed that the information used by the various systems during exchange is interpreted without ambiguity.

The management of contents in general covers, in the data-processing field, the set of steps governing the life cycle of the documents available on the information system: from their creation and validation to the management of the publication rules. Contents indicate any information and knowledge of a company intended to be exchanged between several systems. More precisely, contents are all document, component, data which can be involved as a part of the useful information (Pierra, 2000).

## Objectives of the Content Ontology

The contents management in companies and organizations became a major requirement these last years. From the architecture point of view, a content management system intended to be used by several heterogeneous infrastructures, requires two sub-systems, the first is backend to the company, and the other is shared by all the actors. This last is called ontology in our case. Indeed, the essential objective of the integration of ontologies in the exchange model is to ensure a reliable and a consensual sharing and managing of data during exchanges. This is provided by ontologies since they allow a mature product characterization by ensuring a unique identification of the concepts and their attributes. This identification ensures a non-ambiguous concept referenced by various partner's applications. Thus, the model integrating ontologies will be characterized by the possibility of separating the contents from the container (process) allowing a separate development on each level in a flexible way.

## Content Ontology Functionalities

The layer which manages the contents specifies the structure and the semantics of the data as well as the refinement constraints and the composition of the properties such as cardinality. Two types of ontologies can be used:

1. The business oriented ontology has as a role the identification of the properties related to the company business and is independent from any product or component. This information is necessary to achieve the collaboration and the transactions between partners.
2. The product oriented ontology represents useful information (payload) defining the object of exchange or the products catalogues on which the transactions will occur. It is, in general, a set of classes, properties and values domains (instances of objects).

The utility of this ontological level in the exchange model is to provide a common knowledge sharing of the products used by the actors of exchange and to make sure that the interpretation of the data will be done in a correct and non-ambiguous way.

The idea to separate the business contents from the useful contents is not completely new. RosettaNet uses this principle by proposing two separated dictionaries, one representing the business ontology (RosettaNet Business Dictionary

RNBD) and the other representing the products ontology (RosettaNet Technical Dictionary RNTD) (RosettaNet, 2001b). Let us note that PLIB (Jasper & Uschold, 1999) can be used to define separately these two types of ontology either separately or in the same dictionary.

Once the three defined levels for the model and the functionalities and the objectives of each part are established, the integration of these different modules describes the global exchange model. The following sections describe the technical choices adopted and the proposals made for each level of the model.

## CASE STUDY

Our work proposes the implementation and the realization of a B2B platform based on the three layers described in the previous section. The next step is to give answers to the three previously outlined questions to design a practical solution implementing these different levels.

First of all, in the discovering layer of our system,

1.  An ebXML registry (ebXML, 2002b) is developed for this level, in the business process layer,
2.  A Web service, based on the PIP2A9 RosettaNet BP for product information queries, is implemented, and finally,
3.  The content layer uses a PLIB model (ISO 13584-42, 2003) with its various tools (PLIBEditor and PLIBBrowser) to search and to retrieve the product information content.

The following sections describe in more detail the several parts of the architecture.

## ebXML Registry

The ebXML registry is central to the ebXML architecture (Kappel & Kramler, 2003). The registry manages and maintains the shared information as objects in a repository. Repositories provide trading partners with the shared business semantics, such as BP models, core components, messages, trading partner agreements, schemas, and other objects that enable data interchange between companies. The ebXML registry is an interface for accessing and discovering shared business semantics. In this section, we explain the registry usages, the business semantic model, and the registry functionality including registry classification, registry client/server communications, searching for registry objects, and managing registry objects.

Our registry implementation is based on information in the primary ebXML registry reference documents, including the "ebXML Registry Service Specification (ebXML, 2002b)" and the "ebXML Registry Information Model (ebXML, 2002a)." In a marketplace populated by computer companies with proprietary hardware, operating systems, databases, and applications, ebXML gives business users and IT groups control over their lives. The ebXML registry is not bound to a database product or a single hardware vendor. It is designed to interoperate on all kinds of computers. An ebXML registry serves as the index and application gateway for a repository to the outside world. It contains the API that governs how parties interact with the repository. The registry can also be viewed as an API to the database of items that supports e-business with ebXML. Items in the repository are created, updated, or deleted through requests made to the registry.

Once this part of system is developed (Takheroubt & Boudjemai, 2004), the second task is to define a model to describe business process ontology in both conceptual and technical ways. Web services are a new paradigm which is used to describe technical business processes (Speck,

2002). In the next section we give a short overview about this technology and a comparison with ebXML BPSS and a RosettaNet PIP in order to provide a new model to be used by our proposed model.

## Web Service for the BP Ontology Layer

Web services are modular, self-describing applications that can be published and located anywhere on the Web or on any local network. The provider and the consumer of the XML Web service do not have to worry about the operating system, the language environment, or the component model used to create or to access the XML Web service, as they are based on ubiquitous and open Internet standards, such as XML, HTTP or SMTP. An initiative from Microsoft and IBM to describe the messages between clients and the Web server, WSDL (Web Service Description Language) (Brydon, Murray, Ramachandran, Singh, Streans, & Violleau, 2004), describes and defines Web services. It helps the user to set up a system using a service ranging from connection details to message specification.

A WSDL document defines services as a set of network endpoints (ports) that is associated with a specific binding. This binding maps a specific protocol to a port-type composed of one or more operations. In turn, these operations are composed of a set of abstract messages, representing the data. The pieces of data in a message are defined by types.

## RosettaNet Business Process

This section presents the mechanisms and the approach used to design the Web service using the BP from RosettaNet named PIP2A9. First, the PIP2A9 role and tasks are introduced, then some details about the matching between PIP2A9 and Web service are outlined.

RosettaNet aims to align the BP of supply chain partners. This goal is achieved by the creation of Partner Interface Processes or PIPs. Each PIP defines how two specific processes, running in two different partners' organizations, will be standardized and interfaced across the entire supply chain. PIP includes all business logic, message flow, and message contents to enable alignment of the two processes. RosettaNet defines more than one hundred PIPs. The purpose of each PIP is to provide a common business/data model and documents, enabling system developers to implement RosettaNet e-Business Interfaces.

The PIP studied in this article is the PIP2A9 (Query Technical Product Information) (RosettaNet, 2001c). The technical product information is the category of information that describes the behavioural, electrical, physical, and other characteristics of products. There are numerous classes of customers within the supply chain that need to be able to access product technical information. These include distributors, information providers (such as Web portal companies, other commercial information aggregators, and end-customer information system owners), engineering, design engineering, manufacturing, and test engineering.

As mentioned previously, our work proposes a definition of a B2B architecture followed by an implementation of this platform based on the three technologies shown in the above sections. The next step uses these standards conjointly to provide a secure, a reliable and an interoperable architecture. Each partner providing a service must affect a URL to its BP. This URL is stored in a registry (UDDI or ebXML registry). In our case an ebXML registry is developed for this purpose (Glushko, Tenenbaum, & Meltzer, 1999). The BP will be discovered and retrieved as a set or a unique Web service. The activities that may be undertaken during this step are:

1. The use of a RosettaNet BP (in our example, the PIP2A9 is a BP for product technical information query );
2. The integration of PIP2A9 in the ebXML BP model;
3. The development of a Web service based on the resulting BP.

## Integrating PIP2A9 in the ebXML BPSS Model.

The next task will be the integration of the resulting PIP2A9 in the ebXML BP. This task will be achieved without any error if the mapping between RosettaNet PIP and the corresponding part of the ebXML BP is given correctly. A PIP corresponds to a Binary collaboration or exactly to a business transaction in the BPSS specification. A business transaction in ebXML is defined by a business transaction activity with document flows exchange based in general on a request and a response documents. Therefore, each PIP in the RosettaNet model will be integrated in the BPSS model as a business transaction activity. Figure 2 defines an excerpt of a BPSS with a PIP example document.

Figure 3 shows how the integration is realized using ebXML and RosettaNet standards in the same process model. An ebXML Business Process is defined by a set of documents exchanged on collaborations. Collaborations represent PIPs, and the business documents define the contents. This model will be implemented using the Web Services technology (see Web service section) according to the transformation realized as shown the figure 3.

Figure 3 shows the description of the BP (part A) as a Web Service via WSDL document (part B). A PIP represents a document exchange as a request/response messages. Each communication is described by a document which defines content for both request and response.

## PLIB Ontology in the Content Layer

The third and the last level of our architecture is the content layer. As shown previously, this layer defines data and products information for which the use of PLIB ontology model is proposed. PLIB, the Parts Library standardisation initiative, was launched at the ISO level in 1990. Its goal is to develop a computer-interpretable representation

*Figure 2. An integrated ebXML and PIP business process*

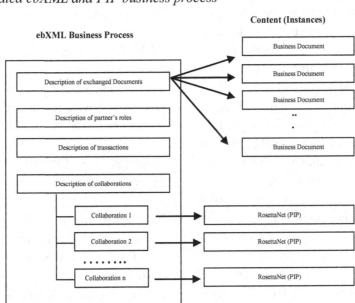

*Figure 3. PIP transformation on WSDL document*

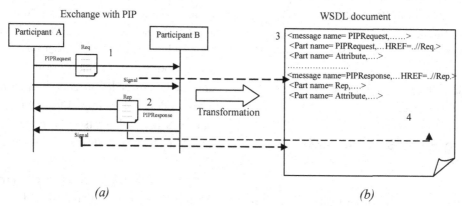

*(a)* *(b)*

of parts library data to enable a full digital information exchange between component suppliers and users. A PLIB data dictionary (ISO 10330-22, 1997; Shenck & Wilson, 1994) is based on the object oriented concepts (Coad & Yourdon, 1992): components are gathered in parts families that are represented by classes. This set of classes is organised in a simple hierarchy of classes on which factorisation/inheritance applies. Such classes are then, precisely described textually, with technical drawings.

Finally, each class is associated with a set of technical properties, also precisely described (domain of values, possible measurement unit…). A basic idea of the definition of a PLIB dictionary is that properties and classes shall be defined simultaneously: applicable properties allow defining precisely a parts family, and conversely, a parts family determines the meaning of the property in its particular context.

The modelling formalism used in PLIB is the EXPRESS language (ISO 10330-11, 1994; ISO 10330-22, 1997). The ontology model of PLIB is formally defined and a number of tools have been developed to create, validate, manage or exchange ontologies. They are available on the PLIB server (http://www.plib.ensma.fr) at LISI/ENSMA. The basis of all these tools is a representation of ontology in a processable exchange format. It can be exchanged in various automatically generated formats: XML document (SimPLIB DTD), associ-

ated possibly with XSL page (SimPLIBVIEWER), EXPRESS physical file or DHTML document (PLIBBrowser). Finally PLIBEditor makes possible to create and publish ontology (Shenck, & Wilson, 1994; Westarp et al., 1999).

PLIBEditor is a tool which allows users to define and to represent graphically and simultaneously a defined ontology and its instances. It is an application containing two parts on its user interface, the left part (frame) allows the definition of classes, properties and relations between them, and the right part defines the ontology population (instances). In another way, PLIBEditor defines in the same application, data and metadata of ontology. PLIBBrowser has the same role as PLIBEditor but it has a Web oriented presentation.

## PLIB Characteristics

This section presents the three main characteristics that motivate the use of the PLIB ontology/dictionary model in our infrastructure.

### Separation of Definitions and Identifications

Business partners or software involved in a B2B transaction must have some common understanding of the various pieces of information they use during an exchange. Therefore, descriptions and definitions of each piece of exchanged information must be shared between the parties involved in the exchange. Otherwise, they cannot understand each other. PLIB ontologies allow partners to share and use the same concepts without transferring their description each time an exchange is performed. In order to allow this, PLIB separates objects and/or concepts identification from their description. One can imagine what description that is local to each partner may be, because it was exchanged earlier. Then, identifications need to be exchanged.

## Universal Identification

One important characteristic of PLIB consists in providing a unique global identifier named BSU (Basic Semantic Unit) for each concept (class, property, etc.) of the ontology (Pierra, 2000). The BSU gives a unique worldwide identification for each concept, class, and property, defined in the ontology. As a result, referencing these concepts during exchange is unambiguous and easy. It is not necessary to get the whole concept or object; its BSU is enough to reference it.

## Orthogonality

Orthogonality results from universal identification. Indeed, this concept leads to a total independence between the two upper level layers. One may use any confusion of any business protocol (PIPs from RosettaNet or ebXML BP) for the BP ontology layer, together with any PLIB ontology (IEC 61360-4 for electronics components, ISO 13584-511 for fasteners, or ISO 13399 for cutting tools) for the products ontology layer. Thus, each business process of the Business Process layer can use any dictionary of the product ontology layer in its payload (McGuinness, 1999).

## TECHNICAL INFORMATION

Based on the WSDL (Peltz & Murray, 2004) document, several Web services will be designed using the Jbuilder development environment with the Enterprise version and Axis Box Tool for managing all Web services (Heather, 2001). Axis uses WSDL2Java tool which generates a set of skeleton classes and interfaces. The latter is used as containers for the developed Java code of our specific Web service.

Once the classes are increased with a PIP2A9 specific codes (Brydon et al., 2004), a set of Java Server Pages (JSPs) are developed to test the service. The general schema of the developed platform is shown in figure 4.

Since we use in our platform, the new database model (OBDB) cited above, and in order to manage data, a new query language is required. The same team at LISI laboratory is currently developing a new query language. It is named Ontology Query Language (OntoQL) (Jean, Pierra, Ait-Ameur, 2005) and a preliminary version runs on several OBDB implementations. Among these applications of OntoQL, we find the usage we propose in our platform. Moreover, in our architecture, when the customer tries to select products, he must create a query to retrieve the required product. This query is received and transmitted by our Web service. The Web service we developed supports this kind of query. To simplify the query creation for the consumer, PLIBEditor has been extended in order to support a user friendly querying user interface. This extension allows a user to interactively create the request.

For more details and comprehension, the scenario on the client side is described as follows. An interface creates the skeleton of the service implemented using the J2EE platform. It represents a set of classes implementing the interface of the Web service functions. This interface is responsible of displaying the results in a specific format according to the specific desire of the customer. In our case, PLIBEditor makes it possible

*Figure 4. The developed platform*

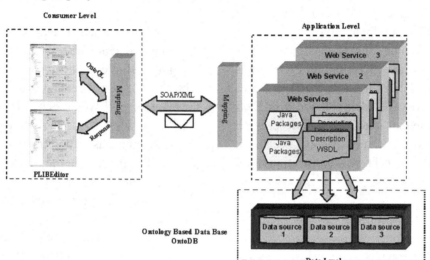

to either create the OntoQL query or display the results when returned from the server side. Notice that the returned content is specific to the OBDB model: a set of files representing the products in a PLIB defined format (EXPRESS format) (Schenck & Wilson, 1994). For other formats, the customer either creates a specific interface or uses its own proprietary existing applications for data visualization (Hunter & Grawford, 2002).

## CONCLUSION

We conclude that many organisations are increasingly searching for mechanisms and methods to achieve exchange of product catalogs and services with minimal cost and without modifying their local systems. Several architectures and standards try to accomplish this task both in horizontal and vertical situations. E-commerce consortia like ebXML and RosettaNet are developing standards and initiatives in order to allow interchange of business information among information systems. Ontologies aim at providing a shared computer-

sensible representation of domain knowledge, allowing exchange of semantic information across heterogeneous systems.

The article shows that in most exchange architectures, two categories of ontologies are used: ontologies of products and services and ontologies of business processes. Involving these two kinds of ontologies simultaneously in a business transaction enables a secure, automatic, and reliable B2B exchange.

Based on these two kinds of ontologies and on the standards mentioned above, a new architecture is proposed. The use of ontology to describe content provides a uniform representation of data in a common and shared format. Moreover, we have shown how B2B architecture can be abstracted and represented by an adaptive infrastructure based mainly on three layers. These three parts define the major concepts required for exchange between companies. Furthermore, the article has shown the need for having a common shared ontology for Business Process used between partners. We have developed a Web service platform as kernel for BP which was integrated to the proposed architecture in order to allow independence and scalability.

Our case study presents the possibility to integrate in the same architecture several parts of several standards simultaneously. For example, we have used ebXML and RosettaNet to design the BP ontology, PLIB dictionary to describe the content ontology and in the last part, the ebXML registry as a directory to localize and retrieve services and data of partners. For the future, we suggest developing a new collaboration model (Khelifa, Aklouf, & Drias, 2008), to be added to the architecture based on the Grid Services technology and also studying the possibility to integrate other ontology formalisms like OWL-S and DAML-S to our platform.

# REFERENCES

Aklouf Y. & Drias, H. (2007). Business process and Web services for a B2B exchange platform. *International Review on Computers and Software (I.RE.CO.S)*. Prize Worthy Prize.

Aklouf, Y., Pierra, G., Ait Ameur, Y., & Drias, H. (2003). PLIB ontology for B2B electronic commerce. *10th ISPE International Conference on concurrent engineering: Research and Applications*. Carlton Madeira Hotel, Madeira Island – Portugal, July 26 – 30.

Aklouf, Y., Pierra, G., Ait Ameur, Y., & Drias, H. (2005). PLIB ontology: A mature solution for products characterization in B2B electronic commerce. Special Issue: E-Business Standards. *International Journal of IT Standards and Standardization Research, 3*(2). IRMA& IGP publishing.

BIC. (2001). XML convergence workgroup: High-Level Conceptual Model for B2B Integration, *Business Internet Consortium, Version: 1.0*, October 5.

Brydon, S., Murray, G., Ramachandran, V., Singh, I., Streans, B., & Violleau, T. (2004). Designing Web services with the J2EE™ 1.4 Platform: JAX-RPC, SOAP, and XML Technologies'. *Sun Microsystems*, January

Coad, P. & Yourdon, E. (1992). *Object-oriented analysis.* , Englewood Cliffs, N.J.: Prentice Hall.

Dogac, A., Cingil, I., Laleci, G. B., & Kabak, I., (2002). Improving the functionality of UDDI registries through Web service semantics. *Proceedings of 3rd VLDB Workshop on Technologies E-Services (TES-02)*, Hong Kong, China, August.

ebXML Registry Information Model Schema (2002). Retrieved from http://www.ebxml.org/specs/ebRIM.pdf

ebXML Registry Services Specification Version 2.1 (2002). Retrieved from http://www.ebxml.org/specs/ebRS.pdf

ebXML. (2001). ebXML technical architecture specification. May 11. Retrieved from http://www.ebxml.org

ebXML. (2005). Business process team. Business Process Specification Schema v2.0 February.

Gartner Group. (2000). OAGI: Fostering standards evolution or revolution?. *A Gartner Advisory Research Note, December 14.*

Glushko, R. J. Tenenbaum, J. M., & Meltzer, B. (1999). An XML framework for agent-based e-commerce. *Communications of the ACM, 42*(3).

Heather, K. (2001). *Web Service Conceptual Architecture 1.0*, May 2001, IBM Software Group.

Hunter, J. & Grawford, W. (2002). Servlet java guide du programmeur, Edition O'REILLY.

ISO 10303-11. (1994). Industrial automation systems: and integration — Product data representation and exchange – Part 11: Description Methods: The EXPRESS language reference manual.

ISO 10303-22. (1997). Industrial automation systems and integration. – *Product data representation and exchange– Part 22: Implementation methods: Standard Data Access Interface.*

ISO 13584-42. (2003). Industrial automation systems and integration. Parts library– Methodology for structuring Parts Families, ISO, Geneva.

Jasper, R. & Uschold, M. (1999). A framework for understanding and classifying ontology applications. In B. Gaines, R. Cremer, & M. Musen (Eds.) *Proceedings 12th Int. Workshop on Knowledge Acquisition, Modeling, and Management KAW'99 (16-21 October 1999, Banff, Alberta, Canada),* volume I, pages 4–9–1— 4–9–20, Calgary. University of Calgary, SRDG Publications.

Jean S., Pierra G., Ait-Ameur Y. (2005). OntoQL: An exploitation language for OBDBs VLDB PhD Workshop, 29 Août 2005.

Kappel, G. & Kramler, G. (2003). *Comparing WSDL-based and ebXML based approaches for B2B protocol specification.* Martin Bernauer, Business Informatics Group. Vienna University of Technology, Austria.

Khelifa, L., Aklouf, Y., & Drias, H. (2008). Business process collaboration using Web services resource framework. To appear in *Proceedings of International Conference on Global Business Innovation and Development (GBID),* Rio de Janeiro, Brazil, January 16-19.

McGuinness, D. L. (1999). Ontologies for electronic commerce. *Proceedings of the AAAI '99 Artificial Intelligence for Electronic Commerce Workshop,* Orlando, Florida, July.

Peat, B. & Webber, D. (1997). XML/EDI - The E-business framework, August 1997,

Peltz, C. & Murray, J. (2004). Using XML schemas effectively in WSDL design. *Proceedings of the Software Development Conference and Expo,* March.

Pierra, G. (2000). Représentation et échange de données techniques, *Mec. Ind., 1,* 397-400.

Pierra G., Dehainsala H., Ait-Ameur Y., & Bellatreche L. (2005). Base de Données a Base Ontologique: Principes et mise en oeuvre. Appeared in *Ingénierie des Systèmes d'Information (ISI).*

Randy, E. H. (2001). W3C Web service position paper from Intel. *W3C Workshop, April 12.*

RosettaNet. (2001). RosettaNet architecture conceptual model, July.

RosettaNet. (2001). RosettaNet Implementation Framework: Core Specification *Version: Validated 02.00.00,* July 13.

RosettaNet. (2001). Specification: PIP Specification Cluster 2: Product Information, Segment A: Preparation for Distribution, PIP2A9: Query Technical Product Information, *Validated 01.01.01,* November 1.

Schenck, D. & Wilson, P. (1994). *Information modelling the EXPRESS way.* Oxford University Press.

Spek, A.W.A. (2002). Designing Web services in a business context. Master Thesis, University of Van Tilburg. Center of Applied Research, September.

Takheroubt, M., & Boudjemai, R. (2004). Etude et Mise en œuvre du registre ebXML dans une plate de commerce B2B. Master Thesis. USTHB Algeria.

Tellmann, R., & Meadche, A. (2003). Analysis of B2B standard and systems. *SWWS, Semantic Web Enabled Web Services.*

Trastour, D., Preist, C., & Colemann, D.(2003). Using semantic Web technology to enhance current business-to-business integration approaches. *Proceeding of the Seventh IEEE International Entreprise Distributed Object Computing Conference,* (EDOC'03).

Westarp, F. V., Weitzel, T., Buxmann, P., & König, W.(1999). The status quo and the future of EDI - Results of an empirical study. In *Proceedings of the European Conference on Information Systems (ECIS'99).*

## ENDNOTE

[1]   Ontology defines a shared conceptualization. In the case of e-business, it provides a conceptualization of the e-business concepts on which

business partners (i.e., companies, traders, vendors) have to agree to understand each other. By specializing and instantiating concepts and relations of the ontology for a particular case, a specific business process may be derived in a precise and structured way.

*This work was previously published in International Journal of Enterprise Information Systems, Vol. 4, Issue 4, edited by A. Gunasekaran, pp. 15-33, copyright 2008 by IGI Publishing (an imprint of IGI Global).*

# Compilation of References

Adkins, M., Kruse, J., Damianos, L. E., Brooks, J. A., Younger, R., Rasmussen, E., et al. (2001). Experience using collaborative technology with the United Nations and multinational militaries: Rim of the Pacific 2000 Strong Angel Exercise in humanitarian assistance. *Proceedings of the Hawaii International Conference on System Sciences, USA, 34*(1), 1066.

Adkins, M., Kruse, J., McKenna, T., Cuyugan, A., Nunamaker, J. F., Miller, S., et al. (2000). Experiences developing a virtual environment to support disaster relief with the United States Navy's Commander Third Fleet. *Proceedings of the Hawaii International Conference on System Sciences, USA, 33*(1), 1034.

Adriaans, P., & Zantige, D. (2002). *Adatbányászat.* Budapest, Hungary: Panem.

Ahmed, A. M. (2002). Virtual integrated performance measurement. *International Journal of Quality and Reliability, 19*(4), 414–441. doi:10.1108/02656710210421580

Ahuja, M. K., & Carley, K. M. (1999). Network structure in virtual organizations. *Organization Science, 10*(6), 741-757. doi:10.1287/orsc.10.6.741

Aklouf Y. & Drias, H. (2007). Business process and Web services for a B2B exchange platform. *International Review on Computers and Software* (I.RE.CO.S). Prize Worthy Prize.

Aklouf, Y., Pierra, G., Ait Ameur, Y., & Drias, H. (2003). PLIB ontology for B2B electronic commerce. *10th ISPE International Conference on concurrent engineering: Research and Applications.* Carlton Madeira Hotel, Madeira Island – Portugal, July 26 – 30.

Aklouf, Y., Pierra, G., Ait Ameur, Y., & Drias, H. (2005). PLIB ontology: A mature solution for products characterization in B2B electronic commerce. Special Issue: E-Business Standards. *International Journal of IT Standards and Standardization Research, 3*(2). IRMA & IGP publishing.

Aktas, M. S. (n.d.). Fault tolerant high performance information service-FTHPIS-hybrid WS-context service Web site. Retrieved from http://www.opengrids.org/wscontext

Aktas, M. S., Fox, G. C., Pierce, M. E. (2008). Distributed high performance grid information service. Submitted to *Journal of Systems and Software.*

Allen, J. H. (2001). *The CERT guide to system and network security practices.* Boston: Addison-Wesley.

Altay, N., & Green, W. G. (2006). OR/MS research in disaster operations management. *European Journal of Operational Research, 175,* 475–493. doi:10.1016/j.ejor.2005.05.016

Amburgey, T., Kelly, D., & Barnett, W. P. (1993). Resetting the clock: The dynamics of organization change and failure. *Administrative Science Quarterly, 38,* 51–73. doi:10.2307/2393254

Anzovin, S. (1993). *The green PC: Making choices that make a difference.* Windcrest/McGraw-Hill.

Arena, R. (2003). Relations interentreprises et communautés médiatées. *Revue d'Economie Politique,* Marchés en ligne et communautés d'agents, M. Gensollen (Ed.).

Argyris, C. (1982). *Reasoning learning and action: Individual and organizational.* Jossey Bass.

Argyris, C. (1991). Teaching smart people how to learn. *Harvard Business Review.*

Arora, H., Raghu, T. S., & Vinze, A. (2007, January). Optimizing regional aid during public health emergencies: An autonomic resource allocation approach. *40th Hawaii International Conference on System Sciences (HICSS)*, HI.

Arora, H., Raghu, T. S., & Vinze, A. (Manuscript submitted for publication). Optimizing antiviral allocation policy through regional aid during an Influenza pandemic. *Journal of Decision Sciences Special Issue on Decision Making in the Health-Sector Supply Chain.*

Arora, H., Raghu, T. S., Vinze, A., & Brittenham, P. (2006). Collaborative self-configuration and learning in autonomic computing systems: Applications to supply chain. *Poster, 3rd IEEE International Conference on Autonomic Computing (ICAC)*, Dublin, Ireland.

Bacharach, S., & Aiken, M. (1977). Communication in administrative bureaucracies. *Academy of Management Journal, 18*, 365-377.

Ballard, C., Herreman, D., Bell, D. S. R., Kim, E., & Valencic, A. (1998). *Data modeling techniques for data warehousing.* IBM Corporation, International Technical Support Organization Study. Retrieved on August 21, 2008, from http://www.redbooks.ibm.com/redbooks/pdfs/sg242238.pdf

Barbaroša, N. (2004). Platni sustav u Hrvatskoj: institucionalni, tehnički i pravni aspekt, HNB.

Baron, J. N., Burton, D. M., & Hannan, M. T. (1996). *The road taken: Origins and evolution of employment.*

Baron, R. S., & Roper, G. (1976). Reaffirmation of social comparison views of choice shifts: Averaging and extremity effects in autokinetic situation. *Journal of Personality and Social Psychology, 33*, 521–530. doi:10.1037/0022-3514.33.5.521

Behrmann, T., & Benz, T. (2005). Service-oriented-architecture-ERP. In T. Benz (Ed.), Forschungsbericht

2005 Interdisziplinäres Institut für intelligente Geschäftsprozesse.

Bellwood, T., Clement, L., & von Riegen, C. (2003). *UDDI version 3.0.1: UDDI spec technical committee specification.* Retrieved from http://uddi.org/pubs/uddi-v3.0.1-20031014.htm

Benbasat, I., & Lim, L. H. (1993). The effects of group, task, context, and technology variables on the usefulness of group support sSystems. *Small Group Research, 24*(4), 430–462. doi:10.1177/1046496493244002

Bentley, C. (2003). *Prince 2: A practical handbook.* Oxford: Butterworth-Heinemann.

Berends, H., Vanhaverbeke, W., & Kirschbaum, R. (2007). Knowledge management challenges in new business development: Case study observations. *Journal of Engineering and Technology Management, 24*, 314–328. doi:10.1016/j.jengtecman.2007.09.006

Berman, F., Fox, G., & Hey, T. (2003). Grid computing. *Making the global infrastrucure a reality.* Wiley.

Bernus, P., Nemes, L., & Schmidt, G. (2003). *Handbook on enterprise architecture.* Berlin: Springer-Verlag.

Berry, M. J. A. (2002). *Mastering data mining MS with data mining set.* New York: John Wiley.

Berry, M. J. A., & Linoff, G. (1997). *Data mining techniques: For marketing, sales, and customer support.* New York: John Wiley.

BIC. (2001). XML convergence workgroup: High-Level Conceptual Model for B2B Integration, *Business Internet Consortium, Version: 1.0, October 5.*

Blau, P., & Scott, W. (1962). *Formal organizations.* Chandler Publishing.

Bocij, P., Chaffey, D., Greasley, A., & Hickie, S. (2006). *Business information systems.* Harlow, UK: Prentice Hall Financial Times.

Boehm, B. W. (1988). A spiral model of software development and enhancement. [Los Alamitos, CA: IEEE Computer Society Press.]. *Computer IEEE, 21*(5), 61–72.

Booth, W. C., Williams, J. M., & Colomb, G. G. (2003). *The craft of research*. University of Chicago.

Bordens, K. S. (2005). *Research design methods*, 6ᵗʰ edition. Bruch & Abbot, TMH.

Boss, G., Malladi, P., Quan, D., Legregni, L., & Hall, H. (2007). *Cloud computing*. Retrieved from download. boulder.ibm.com/.../hipods/Cloud_computing_wp_final_8Oct.pdf

Bots, P. W. G., & Lootsma, F. A. (2000). Decision support in the public sector. *Journal of Multi-Criteria Decision Analysis*, *9*(1-3), 1–6. doi:10.1002/1099-1360(200001/05)9:1/3<1::AID-MCDA262>3.0.CO;2-D

Brehmer, B. (1992). Dynamic decision making: Human control of complex systems. *Acta Psychologica*, *81*(3), 211–241. doi:10.1016/0001-6918(92)90019-A

Briggs, R. O., Adkins, M., Mittleman, D. D., Kruse, J., Miller, S., & Nunamaker, J. F. Jr. (1999). A technology transition model derived from field investigation of GSS use aboard the U.S.S. Coronado. *Journal of Management Information Systems*, *15*(3), 151–196.

Brown, R. (1965). *Social psychology*. New York: Free Press.

Bry, F., Nagel, W., & Schroeder, M. (2004). Grid computing. *Informatik Spektrum*, *27*(6), 542-545.

Brydon, S., Murray, G., Ramachandran, V., Singh, I., Streans, B., & Violleau, T. (2004). Designing Web services with the J2EE™ 1.4 Platform: JAX-RPC, SOAP, and XML Technologies'. *Sun Microsystems*, January

Brynjolfson, E., & Hitt, L. M. (1993). Is information systems spending productive? New evidence and new results. In *Proceedings of the International Conference on Information Systems*, Orlando, FL (pp. 47-64).

Bulut, H., Pallickara, S., & Fox, G. (2004, June 16-18). Implementing a NTP-based time service within a distributed brokering system. In *ACM International Conference on the Principles and Practice of Programming in Java*, Las Vegas, NV.

Bunting, B., Chapman, M., Hurley, O., Little, M., Mischinkinky, J., Newcomer, E., et al. (2003). *Web services context (WS-context) version 1.0*. Retrieved from http://www.arjuna.com/library/specs/ws_caf_1-0/WS-CTX.pdf

Burbeck, S., (2000). *The Tao of e-business services*. IBM Corporation. Retrieved January 12, 2008, from http://www.ibm.com/software/developer/library/ws-tao/index.html

Burnstein, E. (1982). Persuasion as argument processing. In M. Braandstatter, J. H. Davis & G. Stocker-Kreichgauer (Eds.), *Group decision processes* (pp. 103-122). London: Academic Press.

Butner, K., Geuder, D., & Hittner, J. (2008). *Mastering carbon management-balancing trade-offs to optimize supply chain efficiencies*. IBM Institute for Business Value.

Callioni, G., de Montgros, X., Slagmulder, R., Van Wassenhove, L. N., & Wright, L. (2005). Inventory-driven costs. *Harvard Business Review*, *83*(3), 135–141.

Card, S. K., Mackinlay, J. D., & Shneiderman, B. (1999). *Readings in information visualization: Using vision to think*. San Francisco: Morgan Kaufmann.

Carriero, N., & Gelernter, D. (1989). Linda in context. *Communications of the ACM*, *32*(4), 444–458. doi:10.1145/63334.63337

Choi, S. W., Her, J. S., & Kim, S. D. (2007). Modeling QoS attributes and metrics for evaluating services in SOA considering consumers' perspective as the first class requirement. In the *2ⁿᵈ IEEE Asia-Pacific Services Computing Conference* (pp. 398-405). Seoul, Korea: IEEE Computer Society.

Christopher, M. (2000). The agile supply chain: Competing in volatile markets. *Industrial Marketing Management*, *29*(1), 37–44. doi:10.1016/S0019-8501(99)00110-8

Christopher, M., & Towill, D. R. (2000). Supply chain migration from lean and functional to agile and customized. *International Journal of Supply Chain Management*,

*5*(4), 206–213. doi:10.1108/13598540010347334

Christopher, M., & Towill, D. R. (2001). An integrated model for the design of agile supply chains. *International Journal of Physical Distribution and Logistics Management*, *31*(4), 235–246. doi:10.1108/09600030110394914

CIMOSA. (1993). *CIMOSA—open system architecture for CIM. ESPRIT consortium AMICE.* Berlin: Springer-Verlag.

Clegg, S. (1989). *Frameworks of power.* London: Sage.

Coad, P. & Yourdon, E. (1992). *Object-oriented analysis.* , Englewood Cliffs, N.J.: Prentice Hall.

Codd, E. F., Codd, S. B., & Salley, C. T. (1993). *Providing OLAP (online analytical processing) to user-analysts: An IT mandate.* Codd & Date, Inc. Retrieved on August 21, 2008, from http://www.fpm.com/refer/codd.html

Cohendet, P., & Diani, M. (2003). L'organisation comme une communauté de communautés: Croyances collectives et culture d'entreprise. *Revue d'Economie Politique.*

Comfort, L. K. (2007). Crisis management in hindsight: Cognition, communication, coordination, and control. *Public Administration Review*, *67*(s1), 189–197.

Committee on Payment and Settlement Systems., (2006, January). *General guidance for national payment system development,*. CPSS Publications No. 70,. Basel: Bank for International Settlements,. Basel, January 2006

ComputerWire Staff. (2008). *IBM opens four cloud computing centers.* Retrieved from rshttp://uk.news.yahoo.com/cwire/20080929/ttc-ibm-opens-four-cloud-computing-cente-78e70a2.html

Copelli, M., Zorzenon dos Santos, R. M., & Sa Martin, J. S. (2001). Emergence of hierarchy on a network of complementary agents. *arXiv:cond-mat/0110350v1*

COSO. (2004, September). *Enterprise risk management integrated framework.* Retrieved in January 2008, from www.coso.org7publications.htm

Coulsin-Thomas, C. (1996). Business process reengineering: Myth and reality. London: Kogna Page.

Courtney, N. (1996). BPR sources and uses. In C. Coulsin-Thomas (Ed.), Business *process engineering: Myth and reality* (pp. 226-250). London: Kogna Page.

Cover, R. (2004). *Web standards for business process modelling, collaboration, and choreography.* Retrieved January 12, 2008, from http://xml.coverpages.org/bpm.html

Cowan, R., Jonard, N., & Zimmermann, J. B. (2003). Complementarités cognitives et production de connaissances nouvelles. *Revue d'Economie Industrielle* N° 103.

Ćurković, P. (2004). *Platni promet: pojmovi, vrste namirenja, rizici, standardi, inicijative*, HNB, str. 7, 18. Definicija autentikacije, http://insideid.webopedia.com/TERM/A/authentication.html

Daft, R. L., & Lengel, R. H. (1986). Organizational information requirements, media richness, and structural design. *Management Science*, *32*(5), 554–571. doi:10.1287/mnsc.32.5.554

DAMA. (2008). *DAMA-DMBOK: Functional framework*, version. 3. Retrieved on August 16, 2008, from http://www.dama.org/files/public/DMBOK/DI_DAMA_DMBOK_en_v3.pdf

Davenport, T. H. (1993). *Process innovation: Reengineering work through information technology.* Boston: Harvard Business School Press.

Davenport, T., & Prusak, L. (2000). *Working knowledge.* Boston, MA: Harvard Business School Press.

Davis, C. H., & Sun, E. (2006). Business development capabilities in information technology SMEs in a regional economy: An exploratory study. *The Journal of Technology Transfer*, *31*, 145–161. doi:10.1007/s10961-005-5027-1

Dayal, I., & Thomas, J. M. (1968). Role analysis technique, operation KPE: Developing a new organization. *The Journal of Applied Behavioral Science*, *4*(4), 473–506. doi:10.1177/002188636800400405

Definicija smart kartice, http://insideid.webopedia.com/TERM/S/smart_card.html

Dennis, A. R., George, J. F., Jessup, L. M., Nunamaker, J. F., & Vogel, D. R. (1988). Information technology to support electronic meetings. *MIS Quarterly, 12*(4), 591–624. doi:10.2307/249135

Dennis, A. R., Haley, B. J., & Vandenberg, R. J. (1996). A meta-analysis of effectiveness, efficiency, and participant satisfaction in group support systems research. In J. I. DeGross, S. Jarvenpaa, & A. Srinivasan (Ed.), *Proceedings of the Seventeenth International Conference on Information Systems,* Cleveland, OH (pp. 278-289).

DeSanctis, G., & Gallupe, R. B. (1987). A foundation for the study of group decision support systems. *Management Science, 33*(5), 589–609. doi:10.1287/mnsc.33.5.589

Dialani, V. (2002). *UDDI-M version 1.0 API specification.* Southampton, UK: University of Southampton.

Dicle, Ü. (1974). *Bir yönetim aracı olarak örgütsel haberleşme.* Ankara: Milli Prodüktivite Merkezi.

Dogac, A., Cingil, I., Laleci, G. B., & Kabak, I., (2002). Improving the functionality of UDDI registries through Web service semantics. *Proceedings of 3rd VLDB Workshop on Technologies E-Services (TES-02),* Hong Kong, China, August.

Dostal, W., Jeckle, M., Melzer, I., & Zengler, B. (2005). *Service-orientierte architekturen mit Web services* [Service oriented architectures with web services]. Spektrum Akademischer Verlag.

Dove, R. (1999). Knowledge management, response ability, and the agile enterprise. *Journal of Knowledge Management, 3*(1), 18–35. doi:10.1108/13673279910259367

Dresner, H. (2008). *Howard Dresner predicts the future of business intelligence.* Retrieved on September 10, 2008 from http://searchdatamanagement.techtarget.com/generic/0,295582,sid91_gci1308688,00.html

Duplessie, S., Marrone, N., & Kenniston, S. (2003). The new buzzwords: Information lifecycle management. Retrieved on February 18, 2008, from http://www.computerworld.com/action/article.do?command=viewArticleBasic&articleId=79885&pageNumber=2

ebXML Registry Information Model Schema (2002). Re-

trieved from http://www.ebxml.org/specs/ebRIM.pdf

ebXML Registry Services Specification Version 2.1 (2002). Retrieved from http://www.ebxml.org/specs/ebRS.pdf

ebXML. (2001). ebXML technical architecture specification. May 11. Retrieved from http://www.ebxml.org

ebXML. (2005). Business process team. Business Process Specification Schema v2.0 February.

Eckerson, W. (2003). Four ways to build a data warehouse. What works. *Best Practices in Business Intelligence and Data Warehousing*, 15. Chatsworth, CA: Data Warehousing Institute.

Edelstein, H. A. (1999). *Introduction to data mining and knowledge discovery* (3rd edition). Potomac, MD: Two Crows Corp.

Edwards, W. (1962). Dynamic decision theory and probabilistic information processing. *Human Factors, 4*, 59–73.

El-Shinnawy, M., & Vinze, A. S. (1998). Polarization and persuasive argumentation: A study of decision making in group settings. *MIS Quarterly, 22*(2), 165–198. doi:10.2307/249394

EU. (1995). *Directive 95/46/EC of the European Parliament and the council on the protection of individuals with regard to the processing of personal data and on the free movement of such data.* Retrieved on September 2, 2008, from http://ec.europa.eu/justice_home/fsj/privacy/docs/95-46-ce/dir1995-46_part1_en.pdf

Federal Emergency Management Administration. (2004, July 23). *Hurricane Pam concludes.* Press release. Retrieved on September 1, 2008, from http://www.fema.gov/news/newsrelease.fema

Federal Emergency Management Administration. (2005, August 29). *First responders urged not to respond to hurricane impact areas unless dispatched by state, local authorities.* Press release. Retrieved on September 1, 2008, from http://www.fema.gov/news/newsrelease.fema

Feitzinger, E., & Hau, L. L. (1997). Mass customization at Hewlett-Packard: The power of postponement. *Harvard Business Review, 75*(1), 116–121.

Fernández-González, J. (2008). Business intelligence governance, closing the IT/business gap. *The European Journal for the Informatics Professional, IX*(1). Retrieved on September 25, 2008, from http://www.upgrade-cepis. org/issues/2008/1/upgrade-vol-IX-1.pdf

Florescu, D., Levy, A., & Mendelzon, A. (1998). Database techniques for the World Wide Web: A survey. *SIGMOD Record, 27*(3), 59–74. doi:10.1145/290593.290605

Friedrich, C. (Ed.). (1958). *Authority.* Cambridge, MA: Harvard University Press.

Galdos. *Galdos Inc.* Retrieved from http://www.galdosinc.com

Gartner Group. (2000). OAGI: Fostering standards evolution or revolution?. *A Gartner Advisory Research Note, December 14.*

Gartner Hype Cycle. (2008). Retrieved from http://www.techcrunch.com/wp-content/uploads/2008/08/gartner-hype-cycle1.jpg

Gartner Inc. (2006). *Defining, cultivating, and measuring enterprise agility.* Retrieved on September 15, 2008, from http://www.gartner.com/resources/139700/139734/defining_cultivating_and_mea_139734.pdf

Gartner. (2005). *Business drivers and issues in enterprise information management.* Retrieved on September 2, 2008, from http://www.avanade.com/_uploaded/pdf/avanadearticle4124441.pdf

Garwin, D. A. (1993). Building a learning organization. *Harvard Management Review,* 88-91.

George, J. F., Easton, G. K., Nunamaker, J. F., & Northcraft, G. B. (1990). A study of collaborative group work with and without computer-based support. *Information Systems Research, 1*(4), 394–415. doi:10.1287/isre.1.4.394

Glushko, R. J. Tenenbaum, J. M., & Meltzer, B. (1999). An XML framework for agent-based e-commerce. *Communications of the ACM, 42*(3).

Goff, M. K. (2004). *Network distributed computing: Fitscapes and fallacies.* Santa Clara, CA: Prentice Hall.

Goldsby, T. J., Griffis, S. E., & Roath, A. S. (2006). Modeling lean, agile, and leagile supply chain strategies. *Journal of Business Logistics, 22*(1), 57–80.

Gonzalez, C. (2005). Decision support for real-time, dynamic decision-making tasks. *Organizational Behavior and Human Decision Processes, 96,* 142–154. doi:10.1016/j.obhdp.2004.11.002

Goodman, J. H. (2005). Data protection and disaster recovery of local and remote file servers. *Computer Technology Review, 25.* Retrieved on June 5, 2008, from http://findarticles.com/p/ articles/mi_m0BRZ/is_5_25/ai_n15786523/print?tag=artBody;col1

Green Computing Staff. (2008). Retrieved from http://www.greenercomputing.com/news/2008/09/24/hp-posts-supply-chain-emissions-data-urges-it-cos-do-more

*Greener, leaner IT lowers costs, boosts efficiency.* Retrieved from http://www-304.ibm.com/jct03004c/businesscenter/smb/us/en/newsletterarticle/gcl_xmlid/131487?&ca=smbGreen031108&tactic=html&me=W&met=inli&re=smbNewsArticle1

GRIMOIRES. (n.d.). UDDI compliant Web service registry with metadata annotation extension. Retrieved from http://sourceforge.net/projects/grimoires

Gronau, N., Lämmer, A., & Andresen, K. (2006). Entwicklung wandlungsfähiger auftragsabwicklungssysteme [Development of adaptable enterprise systems]. In N. Gronau, A. Lämmer (Eds.), *Wandlungsfähige ERP-Systeme* (37-56). Gito Verlag.

Gronau, N., Lämmer, A., & Müller, C. (2006). Selbstorganisierte dienstleistungsnetzwerke im maschinen- und anlagenbau [Self organized service networks at engineering]. *Industrie-Management, 2,* 9-12.

Gross, D. A. (2005, September 23). What FEMA could learn from Wal-Mart-less than you think. *Slate.* Retrieved from http://www.slate.com/id/2126832

Groznik, A., Kovačič, A., & Spremić, M. (2003). Do IT investments have a real business value? *Applied Informatics, 4*, 180–189.

Gruman, G., & Knorr, E. (2008). *What cloud computing really means.* Retrieved from http://www.infoworld.com/article/08/04/07/15FE-cloud-computing-reality_1.html

Gulick, L., & Urwick, L. (Eds.). (1937). *Papers on the science of administration.* New York, NY: Institute of Public Administration.

Gupta, V. (2004). *Transformative organizations: A global perspective.* Response Books.

Gutierrez, N. (2006). *White paper: Business intelligence (BI) governance.* Retrieved on September 23, 2008, from http://www.infosys.com/industries/retail-distribution/white-papers/bigovernance.pdf

H.R. No. 109-396. (2006). A failure of initiative, final report of the select bipartisan committee to investigate the preparation for and response to Hurricane Katrina.

Habermas, J. (1967). Zur Logik der sozialwissenschaften. *Philosophische Rundschau, 14*, 149–176.

Habermas, J. (1971). *Hermeneutik und ideologiekritik.* Frankfurt: Suhrkamp.

Habermas, J. (1972). *Knowledge and human interest* (J. J. Shapiro, Trans.). London: Heinemann. (Original work published 1968).

Habermas, J. (1972). *Towards a rational society* (J. J. Shapiro, Trans.). London: Heinemann. (Original work published 1971).

Habermas, J. (1974). *Theory and practice* (J. Viertel, Trans.). London: Heinemann. (Original work published 1963).

Habermas, J. (1982). A reply to my critics. In J. B. Thompson & D. Held (Eds), *Habermas: Critical debates* (pp. 219-283). London: The Macmillan Press.

Habermas, J. (1984). *The theory of communicative action (volume 1): Reason and the rationalization of society* (T. McCarthy, Trans.). Oxford: Polity Press. (Original work published 1981).

Habermas, J. (1987). *The theory of communicative action (volume 2): The critique of functionalist reason* (T. McCarthy, Trans.). Oxford: Polity Press. (Original work published 1981).

Habermas, J. (1988). *On the logic of the social sciences* (S. W. Nicholson & J. A. Stark, Trans.). Cambridge, MA: The MIT Press. (Original work published 1970).

Habermas, J. (1995). *Moral consciousness and communicative action.* (C. Lenhardt & S. W. Nicholsen, Trans.). Cambridge, MA: The MIT Press. (Original work published 1983).

Hachman, M. (2008). *Dell shifting all laptops to LED backlights.* Retrieved from Extremetech.com

Hahn, D., Shangraw, R. F., Keith, M., & Coursey, D. (2007). Does visualization affect public perceptions of complex policy decisions: An experimental study. *Proceedings of the Hawaii International Conference on System Sciences, USA, 40*, 96.

Halevy, A. Y. (2001). Answering queries using views: A survey. *The VLDB Journal, 10*(4), 270–294. doi:10.1007/s007780100054

Hall, D., & McMullen, S. H. (2004). *Mathematical techniques in multisensor data fusion.* Norwood, USA: Artech House.

Hammer, M., & Champy, J. (1993). *Reengineering the corporation: A manifesto for business revolution.* New York: Harper Collins.

Hammer, M., & Stanton, S. A. (1995). *The reengineering revolution handbook.* London: Harper Collins.

Han, J., & Kamber, M. (2004). *Adatbányászat-Koncepciók és technikák (Data mining. Concepts and techniques.).* Budapest, Hungary: Panem.

Harris, A. (2004). Reaping the rewards of agile thinking. *Power Engineering, 18*(6), 24–27. doi:10.1049/pe:20040605

Hart, M., & Jesse, S. (2004). *Oracle database 10g high availability with RAC, flashback, and data guard (Osborne ORACLE Press Series)*. Emeryville: McGraw-Hill Osborne Media.

Hawkins, S., Yen, D. C., Chou, D. C. (2000). Awareness and challenges of Internet security

Healy, M. (2005). Enterprise data at risk: The 5 danger signs of data integration disaster (White paper). Pittsburgh, PA: Innovative Systems. Retrieved on August 22, 2008, from http://www.dmreview.com/white_papers/2230223-1.html

Hearn, G., & Rooney, D. (Eds.). (2008). *KNOWLEDGE policy: Challenges for the 21st century*. Cheltenham. UK & Northampton, MA: Edward Elgar.

Heath, C., & Gonzalez, R. (1995). Interaction with others increases decision confidence but not decision quality: Evidence against information collection views of interactive decision making. *Organizational Behavior and Human Decision Processes, 61*(3), 305–326. doi:10.1006/obhd.1995.1024

Heather, K. (2001). *Web Service Conceptual Architecture 1.0*, May 2001, IBM Software Group.

Helfert, M. (2007). Teaching information quality skills in a business informatics programme. *Proceedings of the MIT Information Quality Industry Symposium, Cambridge, Massachusetts*, USA (pp. 908-912). Retrieved on December 24, 2008, from http://mitiq.mit.edu/IQIS/2007/iq_sym_07/Sessions/Session %204C/Session%20 4C%20-%20Teaching%20Information%20Quality%20 Skills%20in%20a%20Business%20Information%20 Program%20-%20Markus %20Helfert.pdf

Helfert, M., & Duncan, H. (2005). *Business informatics and information systems–some indications of differences study programmes*. Retrieved on December 24, 2008, from http://www.computing.dcu.ie/~mhelfert/Research/publication/2005/HelfertDuncan_UKAIS2005.pdf

Helfert, M., & Duncan, H. (2006). Evaluating information systems and business informatics curriculum. *International Conference on Computer Systems and Technologies-CompSysTech'07*. Retrieved on November 24, 2008, from http://ecet.ecs.ru.acad.bg/cst07/Docs/cp/sIV/IV.4.pdf

Hewitt, C. (2008). ORGs for scalable, robust, privacy-friendly client cloud computing. *IEEE Internet Computing, 12*(5), 96–99. doi:10.1109/MIC.2008.107

Hickson, D., Hinings, C., Lee, C., Schneck, R., & Pennings, J. (1971). A strategic contingency theory of intraorganizational power. *Administrative Science Quarterly, 16*, 216-229.

Hinsz, V. B., & Davis, J. H. (1984). Persuasive arguments theory, group polarization, and choice shifts. *Journal of Personality and Social Psychology, 10*(2), 260–268. doi:10.1177/0146167284102012

Hirt, A. (2007). *Pro SQL server 2005 high availability*. New York: Apress.

Hoffman, W. (2004). Dell gets domestic. *Traffic World* (online edition). Retrieved on March 15, 2007, from www.trafficworld.com/news/log/12904a.asp

Hofmann, O. (2003). Web-services in serviceorientierten IT-Architekturkonzepten [Web services in service oriented concepts of IT architecture]. In H.-P. Fröschle (Ed.), *Web-services*. Praxis der Wirtschaftinformatik, HMD 234, dpunkt Verlag, Wiesbaden 2003, S.27-33.

Horling, B., Benyo, B., & Lesser, V. (2001) *Using self-diagnosis to adapt organizational structures*. Computer Science Technical Report TR-99-64, University of Massachusetts.

Hough, G. (2008). *Future trends in dana lifecycle management*. Retrieved on September 3, 2008, from http://www.continuitycentral.com/feature0314.htm

Hrvatska narodna banka. (1997). Sažetak godišnjeg izvješća za 1996. godinu.

Hrvatska narodna banka. (2002). *Odluka o Hrvatskom sustavu velikih plaćanja i o namiri na računima banaka u Hrvatskoj narodnoj banci*, Retrieved from http://www.nn.hr/clanci/sluzbeno/2002/0359.htmhttp://www.nn.hr/clanci/sluzbeno/2002/0359.htm

Hu, J. (2006, June). Balance of product greening cost and

benefit proceedings of service operations and logistics, and informatics. *SOLI '06, IEEE International Conference* (pp. 1146-1150).

Hugos, M. (2006). *Essentials of supply chain management*, 2ⁿᵈ edition (p. 40). Wiley.

Huguenard, B. R., & Ballou, D. J. (2006). Dispatcher: A theory-based design for study of real-time dynamic decision-making. *Proceedings of the 2006 Southern Association for Information Systems Conference* (pp. 117-122).

Hunter, J. & Grawford, W. (2002). Servlet java guide du programmeur, Edition O'REILLY.

Hunton, J. E., Bryant, S. M., & Bagranoff, N. A. (2004). *Core concepts of information technology auditing.* John Wiley &Sons Inc., SAD.

IBM. (2006). *Panic slowly. Integrated disaster response and built-in business continuity.* Retrieved on January 14, 2007, from http://www-935.ibm.com/services/us/bcrs/pdf/ wp_integrated-disaster-response.pdf

IBM. (2007). *The IBM data governance council maturity model: Building a roadmap for effective data governance.* Retrieved on August 22, 2008, from ftp://ftp.software.ibm.com/software/tivoli/whitepapers/LO11960-USEN-00_10.12.pdf

IBM. (2008). *Data recovery and high availability guide and reference–DB2 version 9.5 for Linux, UNIX, and Windows.* Retrieved on May 12, 2008, from http://www-01.ibm.com/ support/docview.wss?rs=71&uid=swg27009727

IBM. (2008). RPO/RTO defined. Retrieved on September 15, 2008, from http://www.ibmsystemsmag.com/mainframe/julyaugust07/ittoday/16497p1.aspx

Ice, J. W. (2007, Winter). Strategic intent: A key to business strategy development and culture change. *Organization Development Journal, 25*(4), 169–175.

IDS. (2008). *IDS white paper: The diverse and exploding digital universe.* Framingham: IDC.

Inmon, W. H. (2002). *Building the data warehouse* (3ʳᵈ edition). New York: Wiley.

International Journal of Bank Marketing. *Volume: 21* Issue: (1); 2003. Research Paper.

ISACA. (2007). *Top business/technology issues survey results.* Retrieved on September 26, 2008 from http://www.isaca.org/Content/ContentGroups/Research1/Deliverables/ISACA_Research_Pubs/Top_Bus-Tech_Survey_Results_1Aug08_Research.pdf

ISACA. (2008). *CISA review manual 2008.* IL: ISACA.

Isenberg, D. J. (1986). Group polarization: A critical review and meta-analysis. *Journal of Personality and Social Psychology, 50*(6), 1141–1151. doi:10.1037/0022-3514.50.6.1141

ISO 10303-11. (1994). Industrial automation systems: and integration — Product data representation and exchange – *Part 11: Description Methods: The EXPRESS language reference manual.*

ISO 10303-22. (1997). Industrial automation systems and integration. – *Product data representation and exchange– Part 22: Implementation methods: Standard Data Access Interface.*

ISO 13584-42. (2003). Industrial automation systems and integration. Parts library– Methodology for structuring Parts Families, ISO, Geneva.

Issing, F. (2003). Die softwarestrategie für web-services und unternehmensinfrastrukturen der firma Sun Microsystems [Software strategy for web services and enterprise infrastructures of Sun Microsystems]. In H.-P. Fröschle (Ed.), *Web-Services* (pp. 17-26). Praxis der Wirtschaftinformatik, HMD 234, dpunkt Verlag.

ITGI & PricewaterhouseCoopers. (2006). *IT governance global status report.* Rolling Meadows, IL: IT Governance Institute, SAD.

ITGI. (2003). *Board briefing on IT governance*, 2nd ed. Rolling Meadows, IL: IT Governance Institute, SAD.

ITGI. (2007). *IT control objectives for Basel II–the importance of governance and risk management for compliance*. Rolling Meadows, IL: IT Governance Institute, SAD.

ITGI. OGC, & itSMF. (2005). *Aligning COBIT, ITIL, and ISO 17799 for business benefit*. Retrieved on September 18, 2008, from http://www.isaca.org/ContentManagement/ContentDisplay.cfm?ContentID=32757

ITPI. (2006). IT process institute: Reframing IT audit and control resources decisions. Retrieved in April 2008, from www.itpi.org

James, T. (Ed.). (2001). *An INFORMATION policy handbook for Southern Africa: A knowledge base for decision-makers*. IDRC. Retrieved on December 24, 2008, from http://www.idrc.ca/ev.php?URL_ID=11439&URL_DO=DO_TOPIC

Jarvenpaa, S. L., & Leidner, D. (1999, Winter). Communication and trust in global virtual teams. *Organization Science*.

Jasen, V. A. A., & de Ross, A. M. (2000). The role of space in reducing predator-prey cycles. In U. Dieckmann, R. Law & J. A. J. Metz (Eds.), *The geometry of ecological interactions: Simplifying spatial complexity* (pp. 183-201). Cambridge University Press.

Jasper, R. & Uschold, M. (1999). A framework for understanding and classifying ontology applications. In B. Gaines, R. Cremer, & M. Musen (Eds.) *Proceedings 12th Int. Workshop on Knowledge Acquisition, Modeling, and Management KAW'99 (16-21 October 1999, Banff, Alberta, Canada)*, volume I, pages 4–9–1— 4–9–20, Calgary. University of Calgary, SRDG Publications.

Jean S., Pierra G., Ait-Ameur Y. (2005). OntoQL: An exploitation language for OBDBs VLDB PhD Workshop, 29 Août 2005.

Johnson, O. E. G., Abrams, R. K., Destresse, J.-M., Lybek, T., Roberts, N. M., & Swinburne, M. (1998). *Payment systems, monetary policy, and the role of the central bank*. Washington, D.C.: International Monetary Found, Washington D.C.

Jonker, C., & Treur, J. (2003). A temporal-inter-activist perspective on the dynamics of mental states. *Cognitive*

*Systems Research Journal, 4*, 137-155.

Josuttis, N. M. (2007). *SOA in practice*. Sebastopol, CA: O'Reilly.

Joyce, E. (2006). Q&A with Neal Creighton, CEO, GeoTrust. Retrieved from, http://www.insideid.com/credentialing/article.php/3589686http://www.insideid.com/credentialing/article.php/3589686

Juran, J. M., & Godfrey, A. B. (1999). *Juran's quality handbook*. McGraw-Hill.

Jurković, P., et al. (1995). *Poslovni rječnik*, Masmedia, Zagreb.

Kalakota, R., & Robinson, M. (2002). Praxishandbuch des e-business [Practice e-business]. *Book of practice financial times*. Prentice Hall, 317ff.

Kalton, G. (1983). *Introduction to survey sampling*, London: SAGE Publications, London.

Kantardzic, M. (2002). *Data mining: Concepts, models, methods, and algorithms*. USA: Wiley-IEEE Press.

Kappel, G. & Kramler, G. (2003). *Comparing WSDL-based and ebXML based approaches for B2B protocol specification*. Martin Bernauer, Business Informatics Group. Vienna University of Technology, Austria.

Kephart, J. O., & Chess, D. M. (2003). The vision of autonomic computing. *IEEE Computer, 36*(1), 41–50.

Kephart, J. O., & Walsh, W. E. (2004). An artificial intelligence perspective on autonomic computing policies. *Fifth IEEE International Workshop on Policies for Distributed Systems and Networks* (pp. 3-12).

Khelifa, L., Aklouf, Y., & Drias, H. (2008). Business process collaboration using Web services resource framework. To appear in *Proceedings of International Conference on Global Business Innovation and Development (GBID)*, Rio de Janeiro, Brazil, January 16-19.

Khiewnavawongsa, S. (2007). *Green power to the supply chain*. Retrieved from http://www.tech.purdue.edu/it/GreenSupplyChainManagement.cfm

Kimball, R., & Ross, M. (2002). *The data warehouse*

*toolkit second edition–the complete guide to dimensional modeling*. New York: Wiley Computer Publishing.

Kind, S., & Knyphausen-Aufseß, D. Z. (2007, April). What is "business development?"–the case of biotechnology. *The Schmalenbach Business Review, 59*, 176–199.

Koch, R. (1997). *The 80/20 principle: The secret of achieving more with less*. London: Nicholas Brealey.

Koop, H. J., Jäckel, K. K., & van Offern, A. L. (2001). Erfolgsfaktor content management—Vom Web-content bis zum knowledge management [Success factor enterprise content management—from web-content to knowledge management]. Vieweg:Verlag.

Krafzig, D., Banke, K., & Dirk, S. (2005). *Enterprise SOA: Service-oriented architecture best practices*. Upper Saddle River, NJ: Prentice Hall.

Kreps, G. L. (1989). *Organizational communication: Theory and practice,* 2nd edition. New York: Longman.

Kuropka, D., Bog, A., & Weske, M. (2006). Semantic enterprise services platform: Motivation, potential, functionality and application scenarios. In *Proceedings of the 10th IEEE International EDOC Enterprise Computing Conference* (pp. 253-261). Hong Kong.

Küster, M. W. (2003). Web-services—Versprechen und realität [Web services—promises and reality]. In H.-P. Fröschle (Ed.), *Web-services* (pp. 5-15). Praxis der Wirtschaftinformatik, HMD 234, dpunkt Verlag.

Kutsch, O. (2005). *Enterprise-content-management bei finanzdienstleistern—Integration in strategien, prozesse und systeme* [Enterprise content management at financial service provider—Integration at strategies, processes and systems]. Deutscher Universitäts: Verlag.

Lakshmanan, L. V., Sadri, F., & Subramanian, S. N. (2001). SchemaSQL: An extension to SQL for multidatabase interoperability. *ACM Transactions on Database Systems, 26*(4), 476–519. doi:10.1145/503099.503102

Lamm, H., & Myers, D. G. (1978). Group-induced polarization of attitudes and behavior. In L. Berkowitz (Ed.), *Advances in experimental social psychology* (pp.

145-195). New York: Academic Press.

Lang, B., & Colgate, M. (2003). Relationship quality, on-line banking, and the information technology gap. *International Journal of Bank Marketing; Volume: 21* Issue: (1).; 2003 Research paper.

Langseth, J. (2004). *Real-time data warehousing: Challenges and solutions*. Retrieved on August 29, 2008, from http://DSSResources.com/papers/features/langseth/langseth02082004.html

Lansley, P., Sadler, P., & Webb, T. (1975). *Organization structure, management style and company performance*. London: Omega.

Larson, D., & Matney, D. (2008). The four components of BI governance. Retrieved on September 17, 2008, from http://www.bibestpractices.com/view/4681

Lassar, W. M., & Dandapani, K. (2003). Media perceptions and their impact on Web site quality.

Latif-Shabgahi, G., Bass, J. M., & Bennett, S. (1999). Integrating selected fault masking and self-diagnosis mechanisms. In *Proceedings of the 7th Euromicro Workshop on Parallel and Distributed Processing*m, *PDP'99 IEEE Computer Society* (pp. 97-104).

Leedy, P. D., & Ormrod, J. E. (2004). *Practical research: Planning and design*. PHI.

Leonard, B. (2008). *Framing BI governance*. Retrieved on September 16, 2008, from http://www.bi-bestpractices.com/view/4686

Lerch, F. J., & Harter, D. E. (2001). Cognitive support for real-time dynamic decision making. *Information Systems Research, 12*(1), 63–82. doi:10.1287/isre.12.1.63.9717

Leung, A., & Rhodes, G. (2003). Best practices for implementing data lifecycle management solutions–tape/disk/optical storage. *Computer Technology Review, 5*. Retrieved on September 19, 2007, from http://findarticles.com/p/articles/mi_m0BRZ/is_7_23/ai_108112613/pg_4

Leymann, F. (2003). Choreography: Geschäftsprozesses

mit web services [Choreography: Business processes with web services]. *OBJECTspektrum, 6*, 52-59.

Leymann, F., & Roller, D. (2000). *Production workflow—Concepts and techniques*. Prentice Hall International.

Li, C., & Chen, G. (2004). Phase synchronization in small-world networks of chaotic oscillators. *Physica A, 341*, 73–79. doi:10.1016/j.physa.2004.04.112

Linden, R. (1984). *Seamless government: A practical guide to reengineering in public sector.*

Lu, J. J. (2006). *A data model for data integration.* (ENTCS 150, pp. 3–19). Retrieved on August 16, 2008, from http://www.sciencedirect.com

Lübke, D., Lüecke, T., Schneider, K., & Gómez, J. M. (2006). Using event-driven process chains of model-driven development of business applications. In F. Lehner, H. Nösekabel, & P. Kleinschmidt (Eds.), *Multikonferenz wirtschaftsinformatik 2006* (pp. 265-279). GITO-Verlag.

Luhn, H. P. (1958). A business intelligence system. *IBM Journal.* Retrieved on August 19, 2008, from http://www.research.ibm.com/journal/rd/024/ibmrd0204H.pdf

Lyons, P. (1999). *Assessment techniques to enhance organization learning.* Opinion papers.

MacAulay, A. (2000). *KM strategy.* 31.9.2000. Retrieved on June 12, 2001, from http://kmonline.netfirms.com/Terms/km strategy.htm

Manzano, M. (1996). Extensions of first order logic. Cambridge, UK: Cambridge University Press.

Marcus, E., & Stern, H. (2003). *Blueprints for high availability*. Indianapolis, IN: Wiley Publishing, Inc.

Martha, J., & Subbakrishna, J. S. (2002, September/October). Targeting a just-in-case supply chain for the inevitable next disaster. *Supply Chain Management Review* (pp. 18-23).

Martinet, B., & Marti, Y. M. (1996). *Diagnostic grid for business intelligence risks. Protecting information in business intelligence, the eyes and ears of the business.*

Paris: Editions d'Organisation.

Martz, W. B. Jr, & Cata, T. (2007). Business informatics as a research discipline. *International Journal of Teaching and Case Studies, 1*(1/2), 84–96. doi:10.1504/IJTCS.2007.014211

McGuinness, D. L. (1999). Ontologies for electronic commerce. *Proceedings of the AAAI '99 Artificial Intelligence for Electronic Commerce Workshop*, Orlando, Florida, July.

Mendonca, D. (2007). Decision support for improvisation in response to extreme events: Learning from the response to the 2001 World Trade Center attack. *Decision Support Systems, 43*, 952–967. doi:10.1016/j.dss.2005.05.025

Mendonca, D., Beroggi, G. E. G., van Gent, D., & Wallace, W. A. (2006). Designing gaming simulations for the assessment of group decision support systems in emergency response. *Safety Science, 44*, 523–535. doi:10.1016/j.ssci.2005.12.006

Meyerson, D., Weick, K., & Kramer, R. (1996). Swift trust and temporary groups. In *Trust in organizations: Frontiers of theory and research.* Thousands Oaks: Sage Publications.

Microsoft Website. (2008). Retrieved from http://www.microsoft.com/virtualization/casestudy-kentuckydoe.mspx

Microsoft. (2008). *SQL server 2008 books online.* Retrieved on August 28, 2008, from http://technet.microsoft.com/en-us/library/ms190202.aspx

Millhollon, M. (2005). Blanco says feds pledged buses. *Baton Rouge Advocate*, September, 20.

Mindtel. (2005). Observations on the response to Hurricane Katrina an unclassified draft. Retrieved September 2, 2008, from http://projects.mindtel.com/2007/0508.ops-memes/

Mintzberg, H. (1979). *The structuring of organizations.* Englewood Cliffs. NJ: Prentice Hall.

Moore, F. G. (2006). Storage virtualization for IT flexibility. Retrieved on May 15, 2008, from http://www.sun.

com/storage/virtualization/StgVirtWP.pdf

Motro, A., & Anokhin, P. (2006). Fusionplex: Resolution of data inconsistencies in the integration of heterogeneous information sources. [from http://www.sciencedirect.com]. *Information Fusion, 7,* 176–196. Retrieved on August 16, 2008. doi:10.1016/j.inffus.2004.10.001

Moynihan, D. P. (2007). From forest fires to Hurricane Katrina: Case studies of incident command systems. *Robert M. LaFollette School of Public Affairs, Networks and Partnerships Series, IBM Center for the Business of Government.* University of Wisconsin at Madison.

Müller, D. (2003). *Was ist enterprise-content-management?* [What is enterprise content management?] Retrieved January 14, 2008, from http://www.zdnet.de/itmanager/strategie/0,39023331,2138476,00.htm

Muller, P. (2003). *On reputation, leadership, and communities of practice.*

Mullins, C. S. (2002). *Database administration–the complete guide to practices and procedures.* Indianapolis, IN: Addison-Wesley.

MyGrid. (n.d.). UK e-science project. Retrieved from http://www.mygrid.org.uk

Naylor, J. B., Mohamed, M. N., & Danny, B. (1999). Leagility: Integrating the lean and agile manufacturing paradigms in the total supply chain. *International Journal of Production Economics, 62*(1-2), 107–118. doi:10.1016/S0925-5273(98)00223-0

Newcomer, E., & Lomow, G. (2005). *Understanding SOA with Web services.* Upper Saddle River, NJ: Pearson Education.

Nolan, R., & McFarlan, F. W. (2005, October). Information technology and board of directors. *Harvard Business Review.*

Nonaka, I., Toyama, R., & Konno, N. (2000). SECI, Ba, and leadership: A unified model of dynamic knowledge creation. *Long Range Planning, 33,* 5–34. doi:10.1016/S0024-6301(99)00115-6

Noronha, C. (2008). *19-square-mile ice sheet breaks loose in Canada.* Retrieved from http://sg.news.yahoo.com/ap/20080904/twl-arctic-ice-shelf-1be00ca.html

Nunamaker, J. F., Biggs, R. O., Middleman, D. D., Vogel, D., & Balthazard. (1996). Lessons from a dozen years of group support systems research: A discussion of lab and field findings. *Journal of Management Information Systems, 13*(3), 163–207.

Nunamaker, J. F., Dennis, A. R., Valacich, J. S., Vogel, D., & George, J. F. (1991). Electronic meeting systems to support group work. *Communications of the ACM, 34*(7), 40–61. doi:10.1145/105783.105793

O'Sullivan, D. (2002). Framework for managing business development in the networked organisation. *Computers in Industry, 47,* 77–88. doi:10.1016/S0166-3615(01)00135-X

OECD. (2004). *OECD principles of corporate governance.* Paris: OECD. Retrieved on June 21, 2008, from http://www.oecd.org/dataoecd/32/18/31557724.pdf

OGC (Great Britain Office of Government Commerce). (2002). *Managing successful projects with Prince2: Reference manual.* London: The Stationery Office.

OGF Grid Interoperation Now Community Group (GIN-CG). (n.d.). Retrieved from https://forge.gridforum.org/projects/gin

Ohara, D. (2007). *Green computing-build a green data centre by green computing.* Retrieved from http://www.osisoft.com/Resources/Articles/Green+Computing+-+Build+a+Green+Datacenter.htm

Ohno, T. (1988). *The Toyota production system: Beyond large-scale production.* Portland, OR: Productivity Press.

OMG. (n.d.). *The OMG and service-oriented architecture.* Retrieved on September 10, 2008, from http://www.omg.org/attachments/pdf/OMG-and-the-SOA.pdf

Open_GIS_Consortium_Inc. (2003). *OWS1.2 UDDI experiment. OpenGIS interoperability program report OGC 03-028.* Retrieved from http://www.opengeospatial.org/docs/03-028.pdf

Oracle. (2007). *Oracle database high availability overview 11g release 1 (11.1).* Retrieved on June 15, 2008, from http://www.oracle.com/technology/documentation/database.html

Oracle. (2008). *Oracle database 11g high availability–overview.* Retrieved on August 12, 2008, from http://www.oracle.com/technology/deploy/availability/htdocs/HA_Overview.htm

Oracle. (2008). *Oracle® database high availability overview 11g release 1 (11.1).* Retrieved on September 8, 2008, from http://download.oracle.com/docs/cd/B28359_01/server.111/b28281/overview.htm#i1006492

Otey, M., & Otey, D. (2005). *Choosing a database for high availability: An analysis of SQL server and oracle.* Redmond: Microsoft Corporation.

Oud, E. J. (2005). The value to IT of using international standards. [ISACA.]. *Information Systems Control Journal, 3,* 35–39.

Özdemirci, F. (1996). *Kurum ve kuruluşlarda belge üretiminin denetlenmesi ve belge yönetimi.* İstanbul: Türk Kütüphaneciler Derneği. İstanbul Şubesi.20.

Ozsu, T. P. V. (1999). *Principles of distributed database systems,* 2nd edition. Prentice Hall.

Pallickara, S., & Fox, G. (2003). NaradaBrokering: A distributed middleware framework and architecture for enabling durable peer-to-peer grids. In *Proceedings of ACM/IFIP/USENIX International Middleware Conference Middleware-2003,* Rio Janeiro, Brazil.

Pallickara, S., & Fox, G. (2003). NaradaBrokering: A middleware framework and architecture for enabling durable peer-to-peer grids. (LNCS). Springer-Verlag.

Panian, Ž. (2002). *Izazovi elektroničkog poslovanja,* Narodne novine d.d., Zagreb, str. 236, 417.

Panian, Ž. (2005). *Englesko-hrvatski informatički enciklopedijski rječnik,* Europapress holding d.o.o., Zagreb.

Pantelli, N., & Chiasson, M. (Eds.). (2008). *Exploring virtuality within and beyond organizations.* Palgrave Macmillan.

Papazoglou, M. P. (2008). *Web services: Principles and technology.* Harlow/England: Pearson Education Limited.

Pareek, U. (2002). *Training instruments in HRD & OD,* 2nd edition. TMH.

Parsons, T. (1947). The institutionalization of authority. In: M. Weber, *The theory of social and economic organization.* New York, NY: Oxford University Press.

Patterson, D. A. (2002). *A simple way to estimate the cost of downtime.* Retrieved on June 22, 2007, from http://roc.cs.berkeley.edu/papers/Cost_Downtime_LISA.pdf

Pavković, A. (2004). *Instrumenti vrednovanja uspješnosti poslovnih banaka,* Zbornik radova Ekonomskog fakulteta u Zagrebu, 2(1), str. 179-191.

Peabody, R. (1964). *Organizational authority: Superior-subordinate relationships in three public service organizations.* New York, NY: Atherton Press.

Peat, B. & Webber, D. (1997). XML/EDI - The E-business framework, August 1997,

Pelillo, M., Siddiqi, K., & Zucker, S. (2001, November). Matching hierarchical structures using association graphs. *IEEE Transactions on Patterns Analysis and Machine Intelligence, 21*(11).

Peltz, C. & Murray, J. (2004). Using XML schemas effectively in WSDL design. *Proceedings of the Software Development Conference and Expo,* March.

Pemmaraju, S., & Skiena, S. (2003). *Computational discrete mathematics.* Cambridge University Press.

Peppard, J., & Ward, J. (2004). Beyond strategic information systems: Towards an IS capability. *The Journal of Strategic Information Systems, 13,* 167–194. doi:10.1016/j.jsis.2004.02.002

Peterson, R. R. (2003). Information strategies and tactics for information technology governance. In W. Van Grembergen (Ed.), *Strategies for information technology governance.* Hershey, PA: Idea Group Publishing.

Petrocelli, T. (2005). *Data protection and information lifecycle management.* Upper Saddle River, NJ: Prentice

Hall.

Pierra G., Dehainsala H., Ait-Ameur Y., & Bellatreche L. (2005). Base de Données a Base Ontologique: Principes et mise en oeuvre. Appeared in *Ingénierie des Systèmes d'Information (ISI)*.

Pierra, G. (2000). Représentation et échange de données techniques, *Mec. Ind., 1,* 397-400.

Pikkarainen, T., Pikkarainen, K., Karjaluoto, H., & Pahnila, S. (2004). Consumer acceptance of online banking: aAn extension of the technology acceptance model. *Internet Research; Volume: 14* Issue: (3). 2004 Research paper.

Pinsonneault, A., & Kraemer, K. L. (1989). The impact of technological support on groups: An assessment of empirical research. *Decision Support Systems, 5,* 197–216. doi:10.1016/0167-9236(89)90007-9

Plambeck, E. L. (2007). *The greening of Wal-Mart's supply chain*. Retrieved from http://www.scmr.com/article/CA6457969.html

PMI (Project Management Institute). (2003). *A guide to the project management body of knowledge* (3rd edition). Project Management Institute. Retrieved from http://hu.wikipedia.org/wiki/Speci%C3%A1lis:K%C3%B6nyvforr%C3%A1sok/193069945X

Poelker, C. (2008). Shifting the emphasis: Disaster recovery as a service. *Disaster Recovery Journal, 21.* Retrieved on September 20, 2008, from http://www.drj.com/index.php?option = com _content&task=view&id =2237&Itemid=429

Pollard, D. (2005, September). CEPA and Pan Pearl River Delta economic integration: A comparative business development perspective. *Global Economic Review, 34*(3), 309–320. doi:10.1080/12265080500292617

Popova, V., & Sharpanskykh, A. (2007). Process-oriented organization modeling and analysis. In: J. Augusto, J. Barjis, U. Ultes-Nitsche (Eds.), *Proceedings of the 5th International Workshop on Modelling, Simulation, Verification and Validation of Enterprise Information Systems (MSVVEIS 2007)*(pp. 114-126). INSTICC Press.

Popova, V., & Sharpanskykh, A. (2007). Modelling organizational performance indicators. In: F. Barros, et al. (Eds.), *Proceedings of the International Modeling and Simulation Multi-conference IMSM'07* (pp. 165-170). SCS Press.

Popova, V., & Sharpanskykh, A. (2007). A formal framework for modeling and analysis of organizations. In: J. Ralyte, S. Brinkkemper, B. Henderson-Sellers (Eds.), *Proceedings of the Situational Method Engineering Conference, ME'07* (pp. 343-359). Berlin: Springer-Verlag.

Power, D. J. (2007). *A brief history of decision support systems*, version 4.0. Retrieved on August 19, 2008, from http://dssresources.com/history/dsshistory.html

Press Assoc. (2008). *Nature's budget has run out.* Retrieved from http://uk.news.yahoo.com/press-sass/20080923/tuk-nature-s-budget-has-run-out-6323e80.html

Pujol, F. A., Mora, H., Sánchez, J. L., & Jimeno, A. (2008). A client/server implementation of an encryption system for fingerprint user authentication. *Kybernetes;, Volume: 37* Issue: (8).; 2008

Radner, R. (2000). Costly and bounded rationality in individual and team decision-making. *Industrial and Corporate Change, 9*(4), 623–658. doi:10.1093/icc/9.4.623

Raghu, T. S., & Vinze, A. (2004, September). Collaborative self-configuration and learning in autonomic computing systems. IBM Proposal.

Rahm, E., & Bernstein, P. A. (2001). A survey of approaches to automatic schema matching. *The VLDB Journal, 10*(4), 334–350. doi:10.1007/s007780100057

Rains, S. A. (2005). Leveling the organizational playing field—virtually: A meta-analysis of experimental research assessing the impact of group support system use on member influence behaviors. *Communication Research, 32*(2), 193–234. doi:10.1177/0093650204273763

Randy, E. H. (2001). W3C Web service position paper from Intel. *W3C Workshop, April 12.*

Rayport, J. F., & Sviokla, J. J. (1995). Exploiting the

virtual value chain. *Harvard Business Review.*

Retzer, S., Fisher, J., & Lamp, J. (2003, November 26-28). Information systems and business informatics: An Australian German comparison. *14th Australian Conference on Information Systems*, Perth, Western Australia.

Rice, J. B., & Caniato, F. (2003, September/October). Building a secure and resilient supply network. *Supply Chain Management Review*, 22–30.

Roithmayr, F., & Kainz, G. A. (1994, April). An emprical-evidence and hypothesis about dissetations in business informatics. *Wirtschaftsinformatik, 36*(2), 174–184.

Rosenberg, J. M. (1983). *Dictionary of business management,* 2nd edition. New York: John-Wiley & Sons.

RosettaNet. (2001). RosettaNet architecture conceptual model, July.

RosettaNet. (2001). RosettaNet Implementation Framework: Core Specification *Version: Validated 02.00.00,* July 13.

RosettaNet. (2001). Specification: PIP Specification Cluster 2: Product Information, Segment A: Preparation for Distribution, PIP2A9: Query Technical Product Information, *Validated 01.01.01,* November 1.

Rowlands, I. (1996). *Understanding information policy.* London: Bowker-Saur.

Ruma, S. (1974). *A diagnostic model for organizational change, social change* (pp. 3-5).

Rusjan, B. (2005, May). Usefulness of the EFQM excellence model: Theoretical explanation of some conceptual and methodological issue. *Total Quality Management and Business Excellence, 16*(3), 363–380. doi:10.1080/14783360500053972

Sakaguchi, H. (2003). *Self-organization and hierarchical structures in nonlocally coupled replicator models. arXiv: nlin.*AO/0305003 v1.

Šarić, J. (2001). *Upravljanje sigurnošću informacija,* magistraski rad, Sveučilište u Zagrebu, Ekonomski fakultet, Zagreb, str. 124.

SAS. (1998). *Rapid warehousing methodology.* A SAS White Paper. Retrieved in August 2008, from http://www.sas.com

SAS. (2008). *SAS history.* Retrieved on August 19, 2008, from http://www.sas.com/presscenter/bgndr_history.html#2008

Scheckenbach, R. (1997). *Semantische geschäftsprozessintegration* [Semantic integration of business processes]. Deutscher Universitäts:Verlag.

Scheer, A.-W., & Nuettgens. M. (2000). ARIS architecture and reference models for business process management. In: W. van der Aalst, et al. (Eds.), LNCS 1806, Berlin, 366-389

Schenck, D. & Wilson, P. (1994). *Information modelling the EXPRESS way.* Oxford University Press.

Schmidt, K. (2006). *High availability and disaster recovery: Concepts, design, implementation.* Berlin/Heidelberg, Germany: Springer.

Schneier, B. (1996). *Applied cryptography,* New York: John Wiley & Sons, New York, 1996.

Schönherr, M. (2005). Enterprise applikation integration (EAI) und middleware, grundlagen, architekturen und auswahlkriterien [Enterprise application integration (EAI) and middleware, fundamentals, architectures and criteria of choice]. *ERP Management, 1,* 25-29.

Scofield, M. (1998). Issues of data ownership. *DM Review Magazine.* Retrieved on August 29, 2008, from http://www.dmreview.com/issues/19981101/296-1.html

Scott, W. (2001). *Institutions and organizations.* Thousand Oaks, CA: Sage Publications.

Search Data Center. (2007). *What is green computing?* Retrieved from http://searchdatacenter.techtarget.com/sDefinition/0,sid80_gci1246959,00.html

SearchStorage. (2004). *Information lifecycle management.* Retrieved on May 10, 2008, from http://searchstorage.techtarget.com/sDefinition/0,sid5_gci963635,00.html#

Seinge, P. (1991). An interview with Peter Seinge:

Learning organizations made plain. Training and Development.

Senge, P. (n.d.). *The fifth discipline: The art and practice of learning organizations*. Doubleday/Currency.

Sengupta, K., & Abdel-Hamid, T. K. (1993). Alternative conceptions of feedback in dynamic decision environments: An experimental investigation. *Management Science, 39*(4), 411–428. doi:10.1287/mnsc.39.4.411

ShaikhAli. A., Rana, O., Al-Ali, R., & Walker, D. (2003). UDDIe: An extended registry for Web services. In *Proceedings of the Service Oriented Computing: Models, Architectures, and Applications,* Orlando, FL. SAINT-2003 IEEE Computer Society Press.

Shajahan, S. (2005). *Research methods for management,* 3rd edition. Jaico Publishing House.

Shapovalov, A. V., & Evdokimov, E. V. (1998). *The geometry of the Fisher selection dynamics. arXiv:physics/*9805006 v1.

Sharpanskykh, A., & Treur, J. (2006) Verifying inter-level relations within multi-agent systems. *Proceedings of the 17th European Conference on AI, ECAI'06* (pp. 290-294). IOS Press.

Shen, H., Zhao, J., & Huang, W. W. (2008). Mission-critical group decision-making: Solving the problem of decision preference change in group decision-making using Markov chain model. *Journal of Global Information Management, 16*(2), 35–57.

Shim, J. P., Warkentin, M., Courtney, J. F., Power, D. J., Sharda, R., & Carlsson, C. (2002). Past, present, and future of decision support technology. *Decision Support Systems, 33*(2), 111–126. doi:10.1016/S0167-9236(01)00139-7

Sia, C. L., Tan, B. C. Y., & Wei, K. K. (2002). Group polarization and computer-mediated communication: Effects of communication cues, social presence, and anonymity. *Information Systems Research, 13*(1), 70–90. doi:10.1287/isre.13.1.70.92

Simon, H. (1957). *Administrative behavior* (2nd ed.). New York, NY: Macmillan Co.

Simon, H. (1960). *The new science of management decision*. New York: Harper and Row.

Simpson, W. (1994). *Guide to green computing*. Retrieved from http://wings.buffalo.edu/ubgreen/content/programs/energyconservation/guide_computing.html#sec04

Snedaker, S. (2007). *Business continuity and disaster recovery planning for IT professionals*. Burlington: Syngress Publishing, Inc.

Sneed, H. M. (2006). Reengineering von legacy programmen für die wiederverwendung als web services [Reengineering of legacy software for reuse as web services]. In *Proceedings zum Workshop Software-Reengineering und Services der Multikonferenz Wirtschaftsinformatik.*

Spek, A.W.A. (2002). Designing Web services in a business context. Master Thesis, University of Van Tilburg. Center of Applied Research, September.

Sprague, R. H. (1980). A framework for the development of decision support systems. *MIS Quarterly, 4*(4), 1–26. doi:10.2307/248957

Spremić, M., & Strugar, I. (2002). Strategic information system planning in Croatia: Organizational and managerial challenges. *International Journal of Accounting Information Systems, 3*(3), 183–200. doi:10.1016/S1467-0895(02)00033-7

Spremić, M., Žmirak, Z., & Kraljević, K. (2008). Evolving IT governance model–research study on Croatian large companies. *WSEAS Transactions on Business and Economics, 5*(5), 244–253.

Sprott, D., & Wilkes, L. (2004). *Understanding service-oriented architecture*. CBDI Forum. Retrieved on October 10, 2008, from http://www.msarchitecturejournal.com/pdf/Understanding_Service-Oriented_Architecture.pdf

Srivastara, S. K. (2007). Green supply-chain management: A state-of-the-art literature review. *International Journal of Management Reviews, 9*(1), 53–80. doi:10.1111/j.1468-2370.2007.00202.x

Stahlknecht, P., & Hasenkamp, U. (2002). Einführung in die wirtschaftsinformatik [Introduction to business computing] (10th ed). Springer Verlag.

Steinmueller, E. (2002). Virtual communities and the new economy. In Mansell (Ed.), *Inside the communication revolution*. OUP.

Stonebraker, P. W., & Liao, J. (2006). Supply chain integration: Exploring product and environmental coningencies. *Supply Chain Management, 11*(1), 34–43. doi:10.1108/13598540610642457

Straus, & McGrath. (1994). Does the medium matter? The interaction of task type and technology on group performance and member reaction. *Journal of Applied Psychology, 79*(1), 87-97.

Sun_Microsystems. (1999). JavaSpaces specification revision 1.0. Retrieved from http://www.sun.com/jini/specs/js.ps

Sushil. (1997). Flexible systems management: An evolving paradigm. *Systems Research and Behavioural Science, 14*(4), 259-275.

Sycline. *Sycline Inc.* Retrieved from http://www.synclineinc.com

Symons, C. (2005). *IT governance framework: Structures, processes, and framework*. Forrester Research, Inc.

Takheroubt, M., & Boudjemai, R. (2004). Etude et Mise en œuvre du registre ebXML dans une plate de commerce B2B. Master Thesis. USTHB Algeria.

Tam, K. Y. (1998). The impact of information technology investments on firm performance and evaluation: Evidence form newly industrialized economies. *Information Systems Research, 9*(1), 85–98. doi:10.1287/isre.9.1.85

Tchang, K. (2008). Implementing a disaster recovery strategy that's not an IT disaster. *Disaster Recovery Journal, 21*. Retrieved on September 20, 2008, from http://www.drj.com/ index.php?option=com_content&task=view&id=2236&Itemid=419&ed=47

Techweb. (2008, September 24). *Dell to move to greener notebook displays*. Techweb.

Tellmann, R., & Meadche, A. (2003). Analysis of B2B standard and systems. *SWWS, Semantic Web Enabled Web Services.*

Thatcher, A., & De La Cour, A. (2003). Small group decision-making in face-to-face and computer-mediated environments: The role of personality. *Behaviour & Information Technology, 22*(3), 203–218. doi:10.1080/0144929031000117071

Toigo, J. W. (2003). *Disaster recovery planning: Preparing for the unthinkable* (3rd edition). USA: Prentice-Hall.

Trastour, D., Preist, C., & Colemann, D.(2003). Using semantic Web technology to enhance current business-to-business integration approaches. *Proceeding of the Seventh IEEE International Entreprise Distributed Object Computing Conference*, (EDOC'03).

Trede, F. V. (2006). *A critical practice model for physiotherapy*. Unpublished doctoral dissetation, School of Physiotherapy, Faculty of Health Sciences, The University of Sydney, Australia. Retrieved on October 6, 2008, from http://ses.library.usyd.edu.au/bitstream/2123/1430/2/02whole.pdf

Turban, E., Aronson, J. E., & Tin-Peng, L. (2005). *Decision support systems and intelligent systems* (7th edition). Upper Saddle River, NJ: Pearson Prentice-Hall.

Udomleartprasert, P. (2004). Roadmap to green supply chain electronics: Design for manufacturing implementation and management. *Asian Green Electronics, International IEEE Conference* (pp. 169-173).

Ullman, J. D. (1997). Information integration using local views. In F. N. Afrati & P. Kolaitis (Eds.), *Proc. of the 6th Int. Conf. On Database Theory* (ICDT'97). (LNCS 1186, pp. 19-40). Delphi.

Valacich, J. S., Dennis, A. R., & Nunamaker, J. F. (1991). Electronic meeting support: The groupsystems concept. *International Journal of Man-Machine Studies, 34*(2), 261–282. doi:10.1016/0020-7373(91)90044-8

Valduriez, P., & Pacitti, E. (2004). Data management in large-scale P2P systems. *Int. Conf. on High Performance Computing for Computational Science (VecPar2004).* ( []. Springer.]. *LNCS, 3402,* 109–122.

Van Grembergen, W., & De Haes, S. (2005). Measuring and improving IT governance through the balanced scorecard. *Information System Control Journal, 2.*

Van Grembergen, W., De Haes, S., & Guldentops, E. (2003). Structures, processes, and relational mechanisms for IT governance. In W. Van Grembergen (Ed.), *Strategies for information technology governance.* Hershey, PA: Idea Group Publishing.

Vanderperren, W., Suvée, D., Verheecke, B., Cibrán, M. A., & Jonckers, V. (2005). Adaptive programming in JAsCo. In *Proceedings of the 4th International Conference on Aspect-Oriented Software Development.* ACM Press.

Vaughan, D. (1997). The trickle down effect: Policy decisions, risky work, and the challenge tragedy. *California Management Review, 39*(2), 80–102.

Velte, T., Velte, A., & Elsenpeter, R. C. (2008). *Green IT: Reduce your information system's environmental impact while adding to the bottom line.* McGraw-Hill.

Verma, K., Sivashanmugam, K., Sheth, A., Patil, A., Oundhakar, S., & Miller, J. (n.d.). METEOR–S WSDI: A scalable P2P infrastructure of registries for semantic publication and discovery of Web services. *Journal of Information Technology and Management.*

Vinokur, A., & Burnstein, E. (1978). Novel argumentation and attitude change: The case of polarization following group discussion. *European Journal of Social Psychology, 8,* 335–348. doi:10.1002/ejsp.2420080306

Vintar, T. (2006). *Ove godine Fina očekuje 12000 korisnika e-kartice,* Lider, God. 2, broj 17, str. 54-55. y. *Information Management & Computer Security;, Volume: 8* Issue: (3); 2000.

VisualLiteracy. (2008). Visual literacy: An e-learning tutorial on visualization for communication, engineering, and business. Retrieved on September 3, 2008, from http://www.visual-literacy.org/

Von Roessing, R. (2002). *Auditing business continuity: Global best practices.* USA: Rothstein Associates.

W3C. (2008). Platform for privacy preferences (P3P) project. Retrieved on September 2, 2008, from www.w3.org/P3P/

Wallace, M., & Webber, L. (2004). *The disaster recovery handbook: A step-by-step plan to ensure business continuity and protect vital operations, facilities, and assets.* New York: AMACOM.

Weber, M. (1958). From Max Weber: Essays in sociology. In: H. Gerth, & C. Mills (Eds.). New York, NY: Oxford University Press.

Weigts, W., Widdershoven, G., Kok, G., & Tomlow, P. (1993). Patients' information seeking actions and physicians' responses in gynaecological consultations. *Qualitative Health Research, 3,* 398-429. (Cited in Wilson 1997).

Weill, P., & Ross, J. W. (2004): IT Governance: How Top Performers Manage IT Decision Rights for Superior Results, Harvard Business School Press, 2004.

Weir, R., Peng, T., & Kerridge, J. (2002). *Best practice for implementing a data warehouse: A review for strategic alignment.* Retrieved on August 19, 2008, from, http://ftp.informatik.rwth-aachen.de/Publications/CEUR-WS/Vol-77/05_Weir.pdf

Westarp, F. V., Weitzel, T., Buxmann, P., & König, W. (1999). The status quo and the future of EDI - Results of an empirical study. In *Proceedings of the European Conference on Information Systems (ECIS'99).*

What is a Carbon Footprint? Retrieved from http://www.carbonfootprint.com/carbonfootprint.html

What is Green Computing? Retrieved from http://www.tech-faq.com/green-computing.shtml Wikipedia-Data Center. (2008). *Data center.* Retrieved from http://en.wikipedia.org/wiki/Data_center

White, S. R., Hanson, J. E., Whalley, I., Chess, D. M., & Kephart, J. O. (2004). An architectural approach to autonomic computing. *IEEE Proceedings of the International Conference On Autonomic Computing.*

Wikipedia-Carbon Footprint. (2008). Retrieved from http://en.wikipedia.org/wiki/Carbon_footprint

Wikipedia-Telecommuting. (2008). *Telecommuting.* Retrieved from http://en.wikipedia.org/wiki/Telecommuting

Wikipedia-Virtualization. (2008). Retrieved from http://en.wikipedia.org/wiki/Virtualization

Wilson, T. D. (1997). Information behaviour: An interdisciplinary perspective. *Information Processing & Management, 33*(4), 551–572. doi:10.1016/S0306-4573(97)00028-9

Womack, J. P., & Jones, D. T. (1996). *Lean thinking.* New York: Simon & Schuster.

Womack, J. P., Jones, D. T., & Roos, D. (1990). *The machine that changed the world.* New York: Rawson Associates.

Woods, D. D., Patterson, E. S., & Roth, E. M. (2002). Can we ever escape from data overload? A cognitive systems diagnosis. *Cognition Technology and Work, 4,* 22–36. doi:10.1007/s101110200002

Worthen, B. (2005). How Wal-Mart beat feds to New Orleans. *CIO Magazine.* Retrieved on November 1, 2005, from http://www.cio.com/archive/110105/tl_katrina.html?CID=13532

Xu, L., & Embley, D. W. (2004). Combining the best of global-as-view and local-as-view for data integration. *Information Systems Technology and Its Applications, 3rd International Conference ISTA'2004* (pp. 123-136). Retrieved on September 2, 2008, from www.deg.byu.edu/papers/PODS.integration.pdf

Yasuhi, U. (2004). Electronics industry in Asia: The changing supply chain and its effects. In E. Giovannetti, M. Kagami & M. Tsuji (Eds.), *The Internet revolution.* Cambridge University Press.

Zanikolas, S., & Sakellariou, R. (2005). A taxonomy of grid monitoring systems. *Future Generation Computer Systems, 21*(1), 163–188. doi:10.1016/j.future.2004.07.002

Zawada, B., & Schwartz, J. (2003). Business continuity management standards-a side-by-side comparison. *Information Systems Control Journal, 2.* Retrieved on August 21, 2008, from http://www.isaca.org/Template.cfm?Section=Home&Template=/ContentManagement/ContentDisplay.cfm&ContentID=15903

Žgela, M. (2000). *Some Ppublic kKey Ccryptography Iissues in Ee-business,* Međunarodni simpozij IIS, Varaždin.

Žgela, M. (2004). Trendovi – platni sustavi i Internet, pametne kartice i beskontaktna plaćanja, HNB, str. 16.

Zhu, Z., Scheuermann, L., & Babineaux, B. J. (2004). Information network technology in the banking industry. *Industrial Management & Data Systems; Volume: 104* Issue: (5).; 2004 Research paper.

Ziegler, P., & Dittrich, K. (2004). Three decades of data integration-all problems solved? In *WCC,* 3-12.

Zöller, B. (2005). Vom archiv zum enterprise content management [From archive to enterprise content Management]. *ERP Management, 4,* 38-40.

Zuber, J. A., Crott, H. W., & Werner, J. (1992). Choice shift and group polarization: An analysis of the status of arguments and social decision schemes. *Journal of Personality and Social Psychology, 62,* 50–61. doi:10.1037/0022-3514.62.1.50

# About the Contributors

**Nijaz Bajgoric** is a Professor of Business Computing and Information Technology Management at the School of Economics and Business, University of Sarajevo, Bosnia and Herzegovina. He has a PhD from the University of Sarajevo. He teaches and conducts research in information technology, business computing, information technology management and operating systems. He has published papers in the following peer-reviewed journals: International Journal of Enterprise Information Systems, Kybernetes, Information Management and Computer Security, Information Systems Management, Industrial Management and Data Systems, International Journal of Production Research, European Journal of Operational Research, International Journal of Agile Management Systems, Journal of Concurrent Engineering, International Journal of Agile Manufacturing and has authored and co-authored chapters in the edited books published by: Elsevier Science, Kluwer Academic Publishers, CRC Press, and Auerbach Publications. His current areas of research include continuous computing technologies, business continuity, enterprise information systems, and information technology management.

\* \* \*

**Dr. Mehmet Aktas** received his PhD in Computer Science from Indiana University in 2007. During his graduate studies, he worked as a researcher in Community Grids Laboratory of Indiana University in various research projects for six years. During this time period, Dr. Aktas has also worked for a number of prestigious research institutions ranging from NASA Jet Propulsion Laboratory to Los Alamos National Laboratory in various projects. Before joining the Indiana University, Dr. Aktas attended Syracuse University where he received an MS Degree in Computer Science and taught undergraduate-level computer science courses. He is currently working as a senior researcher in Information Technologies Institute of TUBITAK-Marmara Research Center. He is also a part-time faculty member in Computer Engineering Department of Marmara University, where he teaches graduate-level computer science courses. His research interests span into systems, data and Web science.

**Hina Arora** is a doctoral candidate in the Department of Information Systems at the W. P. Carey School of Business at Arizona State University. She has degrees in Physics and Electrical Engineering and eight years of Industry experience. Prior to joining ASU, she worked in the capacity of a Software Engineer at IBM, Endicott, and as a Research Scientist at the Center for Excellence in Document Analysis and recognition, Buffalo. Hina's research focuses on modeling information supply chains and associated demand surge issues in the healthcare context. She is also interested in research involving security and self-management of information systems. Her work has been published in leading international journals and conference proceedings.

**Dr. Mirjana Pejić Bach** is Associate Professor of Informatics at Economics & Business, University of Zagreb, Croatia. She received her ScD, MSc and BSc degrees from the Faculty of Business and Economics, University of Zagreb. She completed the Guided Study Program in System Dynamics at Sloan School of Management, MIT, USA. Author of numerous internationally reviewed articles in journals including System Dynamics Review, Acta Turistica, Zagreb Business Review, Journal of Information and Organizational Sciences, Sex Roles, Cross-Cultural Research.

**Serdal Bayram,** PhD Candidate, received a BSc degree in Computer Engineering from Marmara University, Turkey in 2004. In 2007, he was awarded an MSc degree in Computer Engineering from Marmara University. Since 2007, he has been studying for PhD program in Engineering Management department at the same university. Since 2003, he has been working in CIO (Corporate Information Office) for Siemens in Istanbul, Turkey. Firstly, he started to be a Software Engineer in Web applications and then he continued to work as Project Manager in several internal enterprise applications. Now, his position in Siemens is Solution Consultant.

**Jessica Block** is a senior research associate with the Global Institute of Sustainability at Arizona State University. Her research focuses on how cities adapt to natural hazards such as flooding and drought. She also does research on sciences policy and natural resource sustainability for urban regions. She received her BS in geology from UCLA and her MS in Geological sciences from ASU as an associate with the Integrative Graduate Education and Research Training Program (IGERT) in Urban Ecology. Professionally, she was a researcher in the urbanized Pacific Northwest and was a research scientist for ASU's Decision Theater working to connect science and policymaking by designing water resource models with regional stakeholders. She also has experience in groundwater resource consulting and in watershed restoration in California.

**Ridwan Kuswoyo, Bong,** graduated with a Master of Computing in Infocomm Security degree by Coursework from the NUS School of Computing in Jan 2008. He completed his undergraduate degree in Computer Science from the Faculty of Computer Studies in Indonesia. His previous research experience includes working on Neptune Orient Lines (NOL) project grant. His current research interests are in the field of multi-criteria time-depending routing and scheduling problem, supply chain modeling and simulations, supply chain technological framework development using SCML, supply chain optimization, information technology infrastructure and architecture, and information technology security. He is actively involved in industry as well as academic research.

**Dr. Sumita Dave** is presently Associate Professor & Head of the department of Business management in Shri Shankarachaya College of Engineering and Technology. She has 12 yrs. of teaching experience. She has been previously associated as teaching faculty on FMS, Dr. Harisingh Gour University, Sagar (M.P.), FOMS, College of materials management, Jabalpur and Centre of management studies, Jabalpur. She is engaged in research guidance for M.Phil and PhD. Her areas of interest include Change Management, Human Behaviour in Organizations and International business. She has about 40 papers published in both national and international journals and conference proceedings.

**Ms. Martina Draganic** is Information Security Specialist at Zagrebacka bank, Zagreb, Croatia. She received her MSc degree from "Finance and banking", Faculty of Economics and Business, University of Zagreb and BSc degree at Department of Mathematics, Faculty of Science, University of Zagreb, Croatia. She completed numerous Information Tehnology courses.

**Miti Garg** graduated with M.Sc. (Management) by Research from the NUS Business School in 2006. She completed her undergraduate degree in architecture from the School of Planning and Architecture, N. Delhi, India. Her industry research experience includes working with the Retail and Leisure Advisory team for Jones Lang LaSalle Ltd., Delhi, India. Her current research interests are in the field of global supply chain management, supply chain optimization and integration of multimodal transport networks. She is actively involved in industry as well as academic research and her work has been accepted for several Tier 1 conferences including AOM, AIB and INFORMS and IMECS.

**Mark Goh** is a former Colombo Plan Scholar, Dr. Goh holds a Ph.D. from the University of Adelaide. In the National University of Singapore, he holds the appointments of Director (Industry Research) at the Logistics Institute-Asia Pacific, a joint venture with Georgia Tech, USA , Principal Researcher at the Centre for Transportation Research, and was a Program Director of the Penn-State NUS Logistics Management Program. His current research interests focus on supply chain strategy, performance measurement, buyer-seller relationships and reverse logistics. With more than 130 technical papers in internationally refereed journals and conferences, some of his recent academic articles on supply chain management have appeared in the Journal of Purchasing and Materials Management, Industrial Marketing Management, European Journal of Purchasing and Supply Chain Management, IIE Transactions, Naval Research Logistics, Physical Distribution and Logistics Management, Production and Operations Management, EJOR, Supply Chain Management Journal, Industrial Organisations, and Logistics Information Management.

**Sumeet Gupta** received PhD (Information systems) as well as MBA from National University of Singapore. He has worked as a research fellow with the Logistics Institute – Asia Pacific, Singapore, where he worked on consultancy projects with SAP A.G., DFS Gallerias, ASEAN secretariat, and EDB Singapore. He has published several papers in top tier International journals (Decision Support Systems, International Journal of e-Commerce, European Journal of Operations Research, Information Resources Management Journal and Omega) and Conferences (International Conference of Information Systems, AMCIS, ECIS, AOM and POMS. He has also published many book chapters for leading International books. He is also a reviewer for decision support systems and International conference on information systems (ICIS). Currently, he is working on an AICTE (India) sponsored project on RFID aided supply chain design for Indian retail and manufacturing firms.

**Deirdre Hahn** is the Associate Director for the Decision Theater at Arizona State University – an innovative state of the art collaboration facility. Deidre is an affiliated faculty in the Department of Information Systems, W.P. Carey School f Business. Dr. Hahn is a member of a multi-disciplinary team of professionals within ASU's Global Institute of sustainability. She specializes in public policy projects that examine advanced collaboration technologies and their influence on decision making for complex policy issues. Her research background includes: education policy, emergency planning, and regional urban initiatives. For the past two years, Deirdre has been focused on project collaborations in the Middle East and Asia. She regularly lectures at ASU in policy informatics and MBA courses. Dr. Han holds a Ph.D. in Education Psychology, an MA in Counseling Psychology from Arizona State University.

**Mr. Bozidar Jakovic** is Assistant of Informatics at Economics & Business, University of Zagreb, Croatia. He received his MSc and BSc degrees from the Faculty of Business and Economics, University of Zagreb. Author of numerous internationally reviewed articles in journals including WSEAS TRANSACTIONS on SYSTEMS, Acta Turistica, WSEAS Transactions on Information Science & Applications.

**Mark Keith** is a doctoral student in the Department of Information Systems in the W. P. Carey School of Business at Arizona State University. His research focuses include coordination of IT projects, business process management, social networks, service-oriented software, development, and IT security. He holds a BS in Business Management with an emphasis in Information Systems and a Master of Information Systems Management from Brigham Young University. His research has appeared in the International Journal of Human-Computer Studies and INFORMS Decision Analysis as well as leading information systems conference proceedings.

**Melih Kirlidog** holds a BSc in Civil Engineering from Middle East Technical University, Turkey, an MBA in MIS, and a PhD from University of Wollongong, Australia. He has worked as an ICT analyst and consultant for over twenty years in Turkey and Australia. His current research interests include intercultural ICT development and implementation, ICT in developing countries, Decision Support Systems, and community informatics. Since November 2002 he works as a full time academic in Department of Computer Engineering at Marmara University, Turkey.

**Andrea Kő, PhD:** Associate Professor at the Corvinus University of Budapest, Hungary. She has MSc in Mathematics and Physics from Eötvös Lóránd University of Budapest, Hungary (1988), a University Doctoral degree in Computer Science (1992) from Corvinus University of Budapest, Hungary and a PhD degree in Management and Business Administration (2005) from Corvinus University of Budapest, Hungary. She participated in several international and national research projects In the areas of: identity management and IT audit; semantic technologies; knowledge management; e-government. She has published more than 50 papers in international scientific journals and conferences. Her research interests include business intelligence, intelligent systems, knowledge management, semantic technologies and IT audit.

**Maya Kumar** is the Manager of THINK Executive and a Research Engineer at the Logistics Institute – Asia Pacific in Singapore. She obtained her MBA from City University of Hong Kong and has international experience managing and researching globally distributed work and virtual teams. She also has case writing experience with the Asia Case Research Centre and has worked on a number of industry consultancy projects in Asia and North America. In addition to her MBA, Ms. Kumar has completed her M.S. degree from Tufts University, USA and her B.Sc. degree from University of Waterloo, Canada.

**Stephane Ngo Mai** is Professor of economics , Dean of the Faculty of law, political, economic and management sciences of University of Nice Sophia Antipolis. His research is mainly devoted to the study of self-organizing processes in economics and management. The economics of internet is in line with this interest. Stephane Ngo Mai is Professor of economics , Dean of the Faculty of law, political, economic and management sciences of University of Nice Sophia Antipolis. His research is mainly devoted to the study of self-organizing processes in economics and management. The economics of internet is in line with this interest.

**Brano Markić** is full time professor at the University of Mostar, Department of business informatics. He earned M.Sc. in business informatics from the Faculty of Economics University of Sarajevo (Bosnia and Herzegovina) and Ph.D. in informatics from the Faculty of Organization and Informatics – University of Zagreb (Croatia). His research interests include computer applications in business, especially business expert and knowledge-based systems and their integration into business information system. He is also highly interested in formal theories of uncertainty, particularly in fuzzy set theory, fuzzy logic, data mining, *knowledge discovery in databases, data warehouse, business intelligence and different* aspects of the philosophy of science, particularly of the state and future impact of artificial intelligence to business systems.

**T. S. Raghu** (Dr. Santanam) is a faculty member in the W. P. Carey School of Business at Arizona State University. His current research focuses on Security and Information Supply Chains, especially in the public health domain. His past research has contributed to Business Process Change, Collaborative Decision-making and Electronic Commerce. Dr. Santanam has worked with a number of organizations on information Systems and Business Process related changes. He recently worked with the Arizona Department of Health Services (ADHS) and the Maricopa County Department of Public Health (MCDPH) in analyzing process and systems gaps in rolling out a surveillance system, MEDSIS, for the state of Arizona. Dr. Santanam is co-guest editing a special issue of the Journal Decision Support Systems on "Cyberinfrastructure for Homeland Security: Advances in Information Sharing, Data Mining, and Collaboration Systems." He is also guest editing a special issue of the International Journal of Human Computer Studies on ""Information Security in the Knowledge Economy." He is one of the editors of a Handbook being published by Elsevier entitled, "Handbooks in Information Systems: National Security."

**Alain Raybaut** is senior researcher Centre National de la Recherche Scientifique (CNRS) and University of Nice Sophia Antipolis. His research is mainly dedicated to complex economic dynamics. In this field he has published several contributions devoted to endogenous business cycles, electronic markets and organization dynamics.

**Müjgan ŞAN** works at the Management Information Center of The State Planning Organization in Turkey as system analyst for knowledge and information management. She worked as a librarian and a documentalist for international meetings between 1982-1994. Her dissertation is entitled as "The Knowledge/Information Management in Development Planning and The Knowledge/Information Policy Model for the State Planning Organization" at the Department of Information Management of the Hacettepe University. She has taken some responsibilities such as a member of the Internet High Council in the Department of the Transportation in Turkey between 1998-2008, and a member of "Ad Hoc Committee for Knowledge Economy" preparing for "8. Five-Year Development Plan in Turkey", 1999 – 2000.

**Mrs. Monica Shrivastava** is currently working as a Reader in the Department of Business Management in Shri Shankaracharya College of Engineering and Technology. She has 7 yrs. of teaching experience and is currently pursuing doctoral research in the area of Change Management in IT Enabled Organizations. She has been previously associated as teaching faculty in Aptech Computer Education, Bhilai. Her areas of interest include Change Management, Human Behaviour in Organizations, Enterprise

Resource Planning, Operating systems and Database Management. She has about 17 papers published in both national and international journals and conference proceedings.

**Robert de Souza** is the Executive Director of The Logistics Institute – Asia Pacific. Prior to joining TLI – Asia Pacific, Dr de Souza was Executive Vice President for V3 Systems in the Asia Pacific. His extensive tenure in the industry also includes serving as the Corporate Senior Vice President and Global Chief Knowledge Officer at Viewlocity Inc. In November 1998, Dr. de Souza co-founded SC21 Pte, Ltd., a Singapore-based supply chain software firm and served as its Vice Chairman and CEO up to its acquisition by Viewlocity Inc. As an educator and researcher, Dr de Souza is an Adjunct Professor at the School of Industrial and Systems Engineering at Georgia Institute of Technology in the USA and a Senior Fellow at the Department of Industrial and Systems Engineering at the National University of Singapore.

**Mario Spremić, Ph.D., CGEIT** is an Associate Professor at the Faculty of Economics & Business, University of Zagreb, Croatia. He received a B.Sc. in Mathematical Sciences, M.Sc. in IT Management and Ph.D. in IT Governance from the University of Zagreb. He had published 8 books and more than 150 papers in scientific journals, books and conference proceedings mainly in area of e-business, web site evaluation and audit, IT governance, IT risk management, IS strategy and IS control and audit. He is also visiting professor at various postgraduate studies in Croatia and neighboring countries and very often a key speaker at various experts meetings and conferences. He is program director and co-founder of the 'CIO Academy', a regional executive development program in the field of IT Governance and Business / IT Alignment. Also, he is an academic director of Bachelor Degree in Business study at the Faculty of Economics & Business. Mario has been included in Who's Who in Science and Engineering, 2006-2008 and Who's Who in World 2008 listings. He is an ISACA and IIA member and holds ISACA's CGEIT international certificate (Certificate in Governing of Enterprise IT). Mario is reviewer and a program committee member at wide range of international conferences (ICETE, IADIS, WSEAS, etc., full list available at www.efzg.hr/mspremic). Mario has also been acting as a consultant for a number of companies preferably in areas of IS strategy, IT governance and risk compliance, business process change and IS control and IS audit with the experience in implementing various IT projects and conducting wide range of information system audit projects. As a qualified information system auditor and consultant he has been participating in a number of regulatory-based IS audits and advisory projects and besides scientific, gain in-depth expert knowledge of commonly used standards such as CobiT, ISO 27001, Basel II, SoX, ITIL, etc. Previously he had been working as system analyst, project manager and CIO deputy.

**Balan Sundarakani,** is a Research Fellow at The Logistics Institute – Asia Pacific since Sep 2006. He worked as a Lecturer in National Institute of Technology, Trichirappalli and Hindustan University, Chennai, India for two years before joining as a research fellow at TLI. He earned his B.Eng (Distinction) in Mechanical Engineering in 2000 from M.S University, Tirunelveli and M.Eng (Distinction) in Industrial Engineering in 2002 from National Institute of Technology, Trichy and PhD in Mechanical and Industrial Engineering in 2006 from Indian Institute of Technology, Roorkee, India. He has published 40 research papers in referred International Journals, National Journals and Conference Proceedings. At TLIAP he has worked for research projects with EDB, IBM, DHL and Mindef Singapore.

**Dražena Tomić** is Professor of Database Systems and Accounting information Systems at the Faculty of Economics and of Database Systems at the Faculty of Mechanical Engineering and Computing at University of Mostar. She earned M.Sc. in organizational and computer science from Faculty of Organizational Science at University of Belgrade (Serbia) and Ph.D. in economics from Faculty of Economics at University of Mostar (Bosnia and Herzegovina). Her research interests include databases, data warehouse, business information systems and software application in business. She is co-founder of a software company in Mostar and has almost two decades of experience in developing and implementing business information systems.

**Mladen Varga** obtained B. Sc. in Electronics, M. Sc. and Ph. D. in Computer Science from the Faculty of Electrical Engineering and Computing at the University of Zagreb. He has extensive experience of working in industry on corporate information systems while he was at the University Computing Centre in Zagreb. Currently he is a professor in Data Management and Information Systems at the Department of Informatics at the Faculty of Economics & Business, University of Zagreb. His research interests include data management, data bases, data warehouses, data modeling, information systems and software engineering. He published over 80 papers and several books.

**Özalp Vayvay**, Ph.D., is working of Industrial Engineering Department at Marmara University. He is currently the Chairman of the Engineering Management Department at Marmara University. His current research interests include new product design, technology management, business process engineering, total quality management, operations management, supply chain management. Dr. Vayvay has been involved in R&D projects and education programs for an over the past 10 years.

**Ajay Vinze** is the Davis Distinguished Professor of Business in the W.P. Carey School of Business at Arizona State University. Dr. Vinze's Research focuses on technology enablement for emergency preparedness and response, information supply chain, collaborative computing and security/privacy issues for e-health. His publications have appeared in most leading MIS journals and various IEEE Transactions. Dr. Vinze regularly interfaces with organizations in the US – Government IT Agency, Arizona Department of Health Services, Avnet, CHW, Cisco Systems, IBM, Intel and Sun Microsystems, and Internationally in Argentina , Australia, Bosnia, and Herzegovina, Czech Republic, India, Mexico, New Zealand, Peru, Philippines, Russia, Saudi Arabia, Slovakia and Trinidad and Tobago. He is also a Fulbright Senior Specialist (2008-2013). Before joining the academic environment, he was an IT consultant based out of Manila, Philippines.

# Index

RosettaNet 278, 279, 281, 284, 285, 286, 287, 289, 290, 291, 292

**S**

service, attributes of 93, 94
service-oriented architecture (SOA) 58, 59, 91, 92, 93, 94, 95, 96, 98, 99, 100, 101, 102, 103, 104, 107, 108, 265, 266, 267, 272, 273
SOA, advantages of 94, 95
social comparison theory 47
Social Informatics Profile (SOC) 198, 200
standby database 136, 137, 138, 139
supply chain demand surges 205, 206, 208, 209, 212, 213, 215
supply chain supply disruptions 205, 206, 208, 215
supply chain vulnerabilities 205, 206
swift trust 231, 233, 234, 236, 237, 239, 240, 242, 248, 250

**T**

telecommuting 225, 226, 227, 230
teleworking 225, 226, 227
Toyota Production System 176, 186, 306
traditional supply chains 207

**U**

universal description, discovery and integration (UDDI) specification 295, 59, 60, 61, 298, 62, 299, 63, 69, 306, 74, 75, 76

**V**

virtual communities 232, 233, 234, 248, 250
virtual communities, self-organizing 231
virtualization 142, 146, 148, 218, 220, 224, 225, 226, 227, 228, 229
virtual organizations 233, 234, 251

**W**

Wal-Mart emergency operations center 206, 216, 217
Weber, Max 252, 253, 256, 264
Web services (WS) 294, 59, 296, 61, 62, 64, 65, 66, 68, 69, 71, 74, 75, 76, 265, 266, 268, 270, 271, 274, 275, 276
WS-context specification 59, 61, 62, 64, 65, 66, 68, 69, 70, 71, 74, 76

**X**

XML API 63, 64, 65, 66, 67, 68, 69, 70, 74
XML stylesheet language (XSL) 74